To JenFeng

CONTENTS AT A GLANCE

About the Author xvii

About the Technical Reviewers xviii

About the Cover Image Designer xix

Acknowledgments xx

Introduction xxi

PART ONE **INTRODUCING THE ARCHITECTURE** 1

Chapter 1 **OOP in Component Design** 3

Chapter 2 **Core Classes and Component Design** 33

Chapter 3 **Exploring the UI Components** 59

Chapter 4 **Building Component-based Applications** 91

PART TWO **EXPLOITING THE ARCHITECTURE** 129

Chapter 5 **Architecture-based Development** 131

Chapter 6 **XML for Defining User Interfaces** 149

Chapter 7 **Extending the Application Framework** 171

Chapter 8 **Making Your XML Life Easier** 201

Chapter 9 **The Customization Process** 219

PART THREE **CUSTOMIZING THE COMPONENTS** **251**

Chapter 10 **The Accordion Component** 253

Chapter 11 **The Button Component** 275

Chapter 12 **The CheckBox and RadioButton Components** 295

Chapter 13 **The List, ComboBox, and DataGrid Components** 309

Chapter 14 **The DateChooser and DateField Components** 349

Chapter 15 **The Loader, ScrollPane, and ProgressBar
Components** 371

Chapter 16 **The Menu and MenuBar Components** 395

Chapter 17 **The NumericStepper Component** 427

Chapter 18 **The TextArea, TextInput, and Label Components** . . . 439

Chapter 19 **The Tree Component** 459

Chapter 20 **The Window and Alert Components** 483

Chapter 21 **Handling the Scrollbars** 507

PART FOUR **APPENDIXES** **521**

Appendix A **Locating the Source Code of the Component
Architecture** 523

Appendix B **Transitions and Easing Classes** 529

Index 535

CONTENTS

About the Author . . . . **xvii**

About the Technical Reviewers . . . . **xviii**

About the Cover Image Designer . . . . **xix**

Acknowledgments . . . . **xx**

Introduction . . . . **xxi**

PART ONE **INTRODUCING THE ARCHITECTURE** **1**

Chapter 1 **OOP in Component Design** **3**

A very short history of the architecture 4
Creating Flash components 4
An apparently useless component 5
Creating the Vogon component 5
Adding a method 7
Variables, properties, and metadata tags 8
Implementing a property explicitly 9
Implementing a property implicitly 11
Properties in the authoring environment 12
Inheritance 14
A little help from Darwin 15
Appreciating the benefits of inheritance 17
ActionScript limit on multiple inheritance 19
Events 20
What is an event in component terms? 21
Implementing a custom event 21
Triggering a custom event 21
Listening to a custom event 23
Building the example 23
Polymorphism 26
And God took a rib from a Vogon 26
A method's signature 29
Appreciating the benefits of polymorphism 30
Summary 31

Chapter 2 **Core Classes and Component Design** **33**

The legacy of the UIObject class 36
   Creating a component instance dynamically 37
      Overriding the symbolName property 38
      Overriding the symbolOwner property 38
      Overriding the className property 38
      The createClassObject method 39
      Our components join the architecture 40
   Inside the process of building a component instance 44
   Step 1: Initialization 44
   Step 2: Creating the children 45
   Step 3: Drawing the component instance 45
Refining our sample components 46
The component framework 51
   The UIComponent class 51
      Accessibility/Keyboard use 51
      Other features of the UIComponent 52
   The View class 53
   The ScrollView class 54
   An ActionScript template for new components 54
Summary 57

Chapter 3 **Exploring the UI Components** **59**

The Reusability Card 60
   Frequency (of use) 61
   Complexity 62
   Stability 62
   Maturity 63
   Popularity 64
Multitier applications 64
UI components provided with Flash 65
   Button components 65
      Button component 66
      CheckBox component 66
      RadioButton component 67
   Text components 67
      Label component 68
      TextInput component 68
      TextArea component 69

Cell-structured components 69
List component 70
ComboBox component 70
DataGrid component 71
Tree component 72
Container components 72
ScrollPane component 73
Loader component 74
Window component 74
Accordion component 75
Peculiar components 76
Alert component 76
DateChooser component 77
DateField component 78
Menu component 78
MenuBar component 79
NumericStepper component 80
ProgressBar component 80
UIScrollBar component 81
Using the UI components 82
A first example of interaction 82
Typical structure of a component 85
The actions layer 87
The assets layer 87
The bounding box layer 88
Summary 88

Chapter 4 **Building Component-based Applications** **91**

Screens 92
Building an application using screens 93
Content hierarchy in nested screens 95
Reviewing the purpose of slides and forms 96
Forms visibility 98
Conclusion: should you use slides or forms? 99
Screen hierarchies with external subtrees 99
The complete path to an external screen 101
Creating a slide presentation dynamically 102
Building the example 103
Importing the Slide class 108
Creating the screen hierarchy dynamically 108
Adding navigation in the master screen 109
Implementing the buttons-based navigation 110
Using Loader components in the child screens 111
Introducing the transitions 111
Importing the transition classes 112
Screen events and transition sequencing 113
Working with forms 114

Manager classes 114
Managing depth 115
MovieClip methods for handling depth 115
A more flexible way of stacking objects 116
Testing the DepthManager behavior 118
Managing the keyboard focus 120
Defining a focus schema 121
Setting a default button 123
Tab order in a browser 123
Disabling the focus rect 124
Managing windows 124
A simple window-based system 124
Creating a window instance 126
Experimenting with modal windows 127
Summary 128

PART TWO EXPLOITING THE ARCHITECTURE 129

Chapter 5 Architecture-based Development 131

Exploiting the architecture 132
Key benefits of a component architecture 132
What is your job, really? 133
Raising the bar 134
Extend, expand, and alter 134
Extending the architecture 134
Expanding the architecture 136
Altering the architecture 137
From abstract ideas to a concrete example 137
What is an XML layout engine? 138
Benefits of an XML layout engine 138
Further benefits in the Flash context 140
XLEFF 140
XLEFF main features 144
Beyond generating user interfaces 144
XLEFF internal architecture 145
Summary 146

Chapter 6 XML for Defining User Interfaces 149

Basics of the XML data structure 150
The Color Names section 151
The Styles section 151
Class styles 152
Predefined styles 153
Nested styles 153
Custom styles 154
The Stage section 155

XLEFF sampler 158
How to use it 159
Playing with the sampler 161
Examining a more complex user interface 164
User interface patterns 165
A first look into the substructures 166
Using custom classes 167
Events to be handled 169
Summary 169

Chapter 7 **Extending the Application Framework** **171**

Defining an FLA template 172
Using scenes 173
The Preloader scene 174
The Dynamic Assets scene 176
The Main scene 178
Licensing issue 179
Including the standard components source code 179
Progressive update of the template 181
Analyzing the size report 181
Moving the symbols after the first frame 182
Moving the classes after the first frame 183
Defining a folder structure 183
The role of classpath 185
Facilitating event-driven programming 186
The Main class 187
A concrete example 188
Skeleton of the Main class 189
Handling the user interface events 190
Event handler naming convention 194
Managing content 194
Pushing the separation paradigm further 196
The role of CDATA 197
Summary 198

Chapter 8 **Making Your XML Life Easier** **201**

Parsing XML in ActionScript 202
Object models and trees 204
The typical job of an XML developer 207
Simplifying the parsing process 209
Parsing an XML document 210
Document root and other nodes 211
Identifying a node name 211
Identifying a node type 212
Accessing the attributes of a node 214
Browsing the structure of an XML document 215
A few notes on the use of XModel 217
Summary 217

Chapter 9 **The Customization Process** **219**

Working with styles 220
   Parameters controlled by styles 221
   The style lookup process 221
   Styles as properties of a component instance 222
   The styleName property 223
   Class-level styles 225
   Inheriting styles from a container 226
   Global styles 227
Analyzing skins 228
   What is a skin? 228
   Handcrafted skins 228
   Mixed skins 231
   Purely coded skins 234
Working with themes 236
   Changing skins and the mirage of code separation 236
   Changing skins at authoring time 237
   Changing skins programmatically 240
   Skins that reflect styles 243
   In search of a unified approach: subclassing 245
   An alternative to subclassing 249
Summary 249

PART THREE **CUSTOMIZING THE COMPONENTS** **251**

Chapter 10 **The Accordion Component** **253**

A minimal example 254
   Code-based version 255
   Codeless version 256
   XLEFF version 257
The component structure 257
   Segment header 258
   Segment content area 258
A richer example 259
   Codeless version 259
   Code-based version 261
Supported styles 262
   Common styles 263
   Specific styles 265
Skinnability 265
   The border 265
   The headers 266
Solved mysteries 268
   Inheriting styles 268
   Creating header styles on a per-instance basis 271
Reasons for subclassing 273

Chapter 11 **The Button Component** **275**

Minimal example of the Button component 276
   A richer example 277
Supported styles 279
   Common styles 280
   Specific styles 281
      Halo theme case 281
      Sample theme case 282
Skinnability 284
   Replacing the purely coded skin 285
   The 32 skins of a button 289
      Implementing a toggle button 289
      Emphasizing a button instance 289
      Iconic buttons 289
Solved mysteries 290
   A purely coded classic: the pill button 290
Reasons for subclassing a Button component 293

Chapter 12 **The CheckBox and RadioButton Components** **295**

Minimal example of the CheckBox and the RadioButton components 296
   XLEFF version 297
   Comparing the authoring parameters 297
Supported styles 298
   Common styles 298
   Specific styles 300
Skinnability 302
Solved mysteries 305
   Where to find the RadioButtonGroup instance 305
Reasons for subclassing the CheckBox and the RadioButton components 307

Chapter 13 **The List, ComboBox, and DataGrid Components** **309**

Minimal example including the List, ComboBox, and DataGrid components 310
   XLEFF version 313
Richer examples 314
   Itemization 315
   Custom labels 317
   Scrolling 320
   Sorting 323
   Selection management 327
   Making it editable 331
Supported styles 333
   Common styles 336
   DataGrid-specific styles 336
   List-specific styles 337
   ComboBox-specific styles 337

Skinnability 338
Solved mysteries 339
   Cell rendering 339
      Building a custom cell renderer 343
      DataGrid column headers 345
   The undefined item bug 346
Reasons for subclassing the List, ComboBox, and DataGrid components 347

Chapter 14 The DateChooser and DateField Components 349

Minimal example of the DataChooser and DataField components 350
   XLEFF version 351
A richer example 351
   Code version 353
   How to retrieve and set a date 353
   Ranges definition 355
   The scroll event 358
Supported styles 360
   Common styles 360
   Specific styles 360
Skinnability 363
   Skinning the arrow buttons 363
   Skinning the DateField icon 365
Solved mysteries 366
   Displaying the date in custom format 367
   A DateField bug 367
Reasons for subclassing the DataChooser and DataField components 369

Chapter 15 The Loader, ScrollPane, and ProgressBar Components 371

Minimal examples 372
   A minimal example of the Loader component 372
   A minimal example of the ScrollPane component 375
   A minimal example of the ProgressBar component 377
      The ProgressBar's animated behavior 377
      The indeterminate ProgressBar 379
   XLEFF versions 381
Combined examples 381
   The ProgressBar communication modes 382
   Codeless interaction 382
      ProgressBar and Loader interaction 382
      ProgressBar and ScrollPane interaction 384
   Mediated interaction 385
Supported styles 387
Skinnability 389
Solved mysteries 392
Reasons for subclassing 393

Chapter 16 **The Menu and MenuBar Components** **395**

Minimal examples 396
    Minimal example of the Menu component 396
    Minimal example of the MenuBar component 398
Richer examples 399
    Generating richer menus by coding 399
    Generating richer menus using XML 405
    XLEFF version 408
Supported styles 409
    Stylizing the MenuBar (and its Menu instances) 409
        Common styles 409
        Specific styles 410
        Exploring the styles 410
Skinnability 414
Solved mysteries 417
    Further customization of a MenuBar skin 417
    Creating persistent Menu instances 420
Reasons for subclassing the Menu and the MenuBar components 424

Chapter 17 **The NumericStepper Component** **427**

Minimal example of the NumericStepper component 428
    XLEFF version 429
    Retrieving the value 429
        Minor bug for Flash MX 2004 users 431
Styles supported by the NumericStepper component 431
Skinning the NumericStepper component 433
Solved mysteries 435
Reasons for subclassing the NumericStepper component 437

Chapter 18 **The TextArea, TextInput, and Label Components** **439**

Minimal example 440
    XLEFF version of the minimal example 442
    How the Label component resizes automatically 442
    The text field inside 445
Richer example of the TextInput and TextArea components 446
    Handling the input process 446
Supported styles 448
    Note on the skins 450
Solved mysteries 450
    Hiding the background 451
    Handling the combination linefeed/CR 453
Reasons for subclassing the Label, TextInput, and TextArea components 456

Chapter 19 **The Tree Component** **459**

Minimal example of the Tree component 460
   XLEFF version of the minimal example 464
Supported styles 465
   Color styles 466
   Text styles 466
   Animation styles 466
   Icon styles 467
   Other component-specific styles 467
   A note on skins 467
   Stylizing the minimal example 468
Solved mysteries 470
   Taking full control 471
   Implementing isBranch and other XML attributes 477
Reasons for subclassing the Tree component 480

Chapter 20 **The Window and Alert Components** **483**

Minimal example of the Window and Alert components 484
   Dynamically creating windows 487
   Dynamically creating alerts 489
Managing the content of a Window instance 490
Supported styles 495
Skinning the Window and Alert components 499
   Skin properties of the Window component 499
   Skin properties of the Alert component 500
   Adding skins to our previous stylized example 500
Reasons for subclassing the Window and Alert components 505

Chapter 21 **Handling the Scrollbars** **507**

Minimal example of the UIScrollBar component 508
Customizing the scrollbars inside a component 510
   Step 1: Building a stylized version of the DataGrid component . . . 510
   Step 2: Skinning the scrollbars 512
Conclusion 519

PART FOUR **APPENDIXES** **521**

Appendix A **Locating the Source Code of the Component Architecture** **523**

If you are a Windows user 524
If you are a Mac user 525
FLA source files 525
Link them 526

Appendix B **Transitions and Easing Classes** **529**

Parameters common to all of the transition types 530
    Easing classes 531
Transition-specific parameters 532
    The Blinds transition 532
    The Fly transition 532
    The Iris transition 532
    The PixelDissolve transition 532
    The Rotate transition 532
    The Squeeze transition 533
    The Wipe transition 533
Example of a transition parameters object 533

Index **535**

ABOUT THE AUTHOR

Antonio De Donatis, who graduated in Computer Science from Pisa University, has been designing and implementing object-oriented software since 1989, seems like a lifetime, when the first OOP developing tools appeared on the market. So far Antonio has managed, designed, and in several cases single-handedly implemented numerous projects for a variety of industries, ranging from media/communications to pharmaceuticals.

Antonio has worked for both large corporations and leading new media agencies, and currently trades under the name of Managed Source Limited, based in Surrey, England, where he has lived since 1998 after moving from Italy, his native country.

His commercial experience with Flash goes back to the fourth version of the software, released in 1999. In recent years, the object-oriented evolution of ActionScript has allowed him to reuse knowledge and techniques that he mastered when utilizing older programming languages such as C++ and Java.

Antonio is a specialist in the design of component-based architectures for the implementation of knowledge and content management systems and is now working on several projects, including the open source XML layout engine for Flash mentioned in this book, the latest version of which can be downloaded from www.xleff.org.

Antonio considers programming a form of art and also enjoys chess, painting, and photography.

ABOUT THE TECHNICAL REVIEWERS

Sas Jacobs is a web developer who loves working with Flash. She set up her business, Anything Is Possible, in 1994, working in the areas of web development, IT training, and technical writing. The business works with large and small clients building web applications with ASP.NET, Flash, XML, and databases. Sas has spoken at such conferences as Flash Forward, MXDU, and FlashKit on topics relating to XML and dynamic content in Flash. She is the author of the book *Foundation XML for Flash* (friends of ED, 2005) and contributed two chapters to *Object-Oriented ActionScript for Flash 8* (friends of ED, 2006).

After studying architecture for seven years, **Paul Barnes-Hoggett** changed his mind and decided to spend his time designing the "intergoogle." He spent time as a lead developer at boxnewmedia, where he built award-winning sites for clients such as Select Model Management. (In his own words, he admits, "It's a tough job looking at pictures of beautiful people all day, but someone has to do it.") He set up Eyefodder in 2003, which specializes in building rich Internet applications for the media industry, and has built solutions for clients including FHM, Adidas, Air Miles, and ITV. When not pushing pixels, Paul likes to eat, drink, and be merry. To get in contact with him, visit www.eyefodder.com.

ABOUT THE COVER IMAGE DESIGNER

Bruce Tang is a freelance web designer, visual programmer, and author from Hong Kong. His main creative interest is generating stunning visual effects using Flash or Processing.

Bruce has been an avid Flash user since Flash 4, when he began using Flash to create games, websites, and other multimedia content. After several years of ActionScripting, he found himself increasingly drawn toward visual programming and computational art. He likes to integrate math and physics into his work, simulating 3D and other real-life experiences onscreen. His first Flash book was published in October 2005. Bruce's folio, featuring Flash and Processing pieces, can be found at www.betaruce.com, and his blog at www.betaruce.com/blog.

The cover image uses a high-resolution Henon phase diagram generated by Bruce with Processing, which he feels is an ideal tool for such experiments. Henon is a strange attractor created by iterating through some equations to calculate the coordinates of millions of points. The points are then plotted with an assigned color.

$$x_{n+1} = x_n \cos(a) - (y_n - x_n^p) \sin(a)$$

$$y_{n+1} = x_n \sin(a) + (y_n - x_n^p) \cos(a)$$

ACKNOWLEDGMENTS

I would like to thank every member of the team involved in this project—Chris Mills for sharing the ambitious vision of this book since its inception; Julie Smith for her essential help in coordinating and controlling the disparate processes that have made this book possible; Sam Robbins, Sas Jacobs, and Paul Barnes-Hoggett for their constructive criticism that undoubtedly raised the quality of the content; my warmest thanks also go to Ami Knox, Laura Cheu, and Marilyn Smith for ensuring that my work was properly transferred in a professional format.

On a more personal note, I would like to thank my parents for their infinite love and support and my special friend Rowena Jay, talented photographer, for my portrait utilized in this book.

Finally, I cannot end this section without mentioning my sister Angela, otherwise she will not talk to me ever again.

INTRODUCTION

AdvancED ActionScript Components: Mastering the Flash Component Architecture is about exploiting the Flash Component Architecture to rapidly produce powerful Flash applications by reusing the many powerful components included in it, its underlying functionality, and the knowledge captured in its source code.

In the world of software development, the concept of reusability is frequently met with skepticism or even total disbelief. Here are the most common reasons:

- Components are released most frequently in a compiled format, meaning that their implementation cannot be modified or amended whenever needed.
- Without proper guidance, the time required to learn how to reuse functionality can become comparable with the time requested to implement it from scratch.
- Experienced developers tend to trust their own code more than code written by someone else.

The first point in the previous list does not apply to the Flash Component Architecture since its source code is available with the Flash authoring environment—a truly major benefit, because developers can both learn from it and tweak it if necessary.

I wrote this book to address the second point by providing a concrete guide to teach you how to reuse each component successfully, and in a fairly convenient amount of time.

Finally, experienced developers can trust this book since it provides information that can truly save a lot of their valuable time. Being a developer myself, I know how disappointing it can be to deal with incomplete information that leaves you with time-consuming problems to solve. That is why I took particular care in providing complete examples that go beyond using the components to also demonstrate how to fully customize them, and how to fix any bugs in their default implementation.

The structure

Component-based development can be very intimidating for the uninitiated. That's why the content has been organized into three parts:

Part One: Introducing the Architecture—A fast-paced exploration of how key object-oriented concepts are applied to the design and implementation of the Flash Component Architecture. The first four chapters show you how to build your own components based on the shared functionality made available by the component architecture and how to efficiently reuse those components within the framework of a component-based application.

Part Two: Exploiting the Architecture—Explains the most advanced programming techniques in this topic area, with the help of XML as the ideal language for describing the structure of a component-based user interface. By reading Chapters 5 to 9, you will gain the knowledge required to master the processes of utilizing and customizing any component in the architecture. This part also includes XLEFF, an XML layout engine for Flash, implemented by the author and released under an open source license. XLEFF allows dynamic generation of user interfaces from XML definitions.

Part Three: Customizing the Components—This part of the book is the largest and provides plenty of complete examples that show you how to use and customize each standard component in the architecture. Chapters 10 to 21 allow you to rapidly learn how to use and customize the components proficiently by grouping them according to their common purpose and highlighting their shared functionality.

Intended audience

The Flash Component Architecture is a vast topic, and this book has been designed to offer you a very efficient and effective path to learning it. However, in order to benefit from it, you should have a good understanding of ActionScript and be familiar with XML and the Flash authoring environment.

This book is also very valuable for developers who have worked with other OOP languages such as Java or C++ and are now considering the Flash technology for building rich Internet applications.

Version issues

Another major plus of this book is that its contents are compatible with both the Flash MX 2004 and Flash 8 authoring environments. What we call the Flash Component Architecture was originally named the Macromedia Component Architecture Version 2 when first introduced in Flash MX 2004. The same architecture, slightly improved by fixing a few bugs, has been included in the recently released Flash 8.

The techniques illustrated in this book are based on ActionScript 2, the language supported by both versions of the Flash authoring environment. All of the examples have been tested in both Flash MX 2004 and Flash 8, and any differences in operation on the two versions have been highlighted as they occur.

Layout conventions

To keep this book as clear and easy to follow as possible, the following text conventions are used throughout:

- Important words or concepts are normally highlighted on the first appearance in **bold type**.
- Code is presented in `fixed-width` font.
- New or changed code is normally presented in **`bold fixed-width font`**.
- Pseudo-code and variable input are written in *`italic fixed-width font`*.
- Menu commands are written in the form Menu ➤ Submenu ➤ Submenu.

Where I want to draw your attention to something, I've highlighted it like this:

> *Ahem, don't say I didn't warn you.*

Sometimes code won't fit on a single line in a book. Where this happens, I use an arrow like this: ➡.

```
This is a very, very long section of code that should be written all on ➡
the same line without a break.
```

The complete source code

This book includes numerous complete examples that can be downloaded from the web by visiting this book's page at `www.friendsofed.com`.

You can also visit the website `www.xleff.org` to obtain the latest version of XLEFF, the open source XML layout engine discussed in this book.

Part One

INTRODUCING THE ARCHITECTURE

Chapter 1

OOP IN COMPONENT DESIGN

Wax on, wax off.
Mr. Kesuke Miyagi

Most modern software technologies descend from the **object-oriented programming (OOP)** methodology, and the Flash Component Architecture is no exception. The goal of this chapter is to expose how the OOP paradigm influences the design and development of components and component-based applications.

In the following pages, we will implement a component that will act as a vehicle for introducing and demonstrating every OOP concept at work.

> *The completed source code introduced in this chapter can be found in the package* `src01.zip`, *downloadable from this book's page at* www.friendsofed.com.

A very short history of the architecture

This book is based upon build 2.0.2.126 of the component architecture that is loosely defined as "version 2." This build of the component architecture was released with Flash 8.

If you are working with a different version of the architecture, you may find that some information has changed.

As it has been implemented, the design of the architecture makes an extensive use of object-oriented programming techniques and concepts, and the source code of the second version of the component architecture is a full rewrite of the first version, so unfortunately the two versions are incompatible. Such a high level of incompatibility between the two versions is due to the fact that some very essential OOP features were introduced at a later stage with the release of ActionScript 2 that were not available when the architecture was first implemented.

The design and implementation of the first version was rather sloppy because the developers of the component architecture had to work around the absence of fundamental mechanisms such as the class construct.

The appearance of crucial OOP constructs in ActionScript 2 required sacrificing backward compatibility in order to achieve a much neater design and drop various clumsy aspects of the previous version.

The good news is that this technological tsunami is unlikely to happen again, and any incompatibility introduced by future versions of ActionScript will have a very minor impact on the architecture, compared to the paradigm shift between its first two versions.

Creating Flash components

The high relevance of the class construct in the component architecture will become clear once you take into account that creating a Flash component is essentially a two-step process:

- Create a movie clip symbol in the authoring environment.
- Associate the symbol with an ActionScript class that implements the component behavior and/or its look and feel.

Once the association between the symbol and the class is completed, the Library panel in the authoring environment will show that the symbol's type is changed from "movie clip" to "component." Furthermore, a new icon shown alongside the symbol's name in the Library panel will emphasize such a change of status.

Component instances can be created by dragging the component symbol from the Library panel onto the stage as you would have done with the more basic kind of symbols (such as movie clips, buttons, or graphics).

Component instances can also be created dynamically by coding, as you will see in the next chapter.

In addition to providing properties and methods, as expected by such an object-oriented mechanism, an ActionScript class can also include metadata tags that are a facility to control the features (usually the properties) of a component instance via the Flash authoring environment.

So, without further ado, let us look at an example: in the upcoming section we will create a very simple and apparently useless component to start exploring Flash component design in more concrete terms. The component will be expressly designed to be purposeless to avoid distracting your attention from what the component does: this is the stage when you must learn what a component is.

An apparently useless component

Different components serve different purposes, and the design of a component is usually optimized on the specific functionality provided.

We are going to create a component that will be useful by being useless. By not being optimized for a specific purpose, our component will serve as a test vehicle for any concept that will be introduced from now on. Furthermore, its isolated and abstract features will help you focus on the deep conceptual basis behind OOP and component design.

Our component will grow gradually from a very minimal version up to a complete example including all of the essential features that are available to a component belonging to the component architecture.

Creating the Vogon component

Apply the following steps in order to create your first minimal component called Vogon:

1. Create a new Flash document and save it as vogon1.fla; we will enumerate some Flash documents progressively to keep track of our component's versions. Define the document dimensions as 800×600 pixels.

2. Create a shape of approximately 100×100 pixels. The shape is supposed to be ugly, so don't waste your time in improving its appearance. Aesthetic issues are not relevant in the first part of this book.

3. Remove the border from the shape, if any, and define its fill color as #00FF00 (green).

4. Convert the shape into a symbol. Be sure that the selected symbol behavior is movie clip, and define the name of the symbol as Vogon Component.

Once the previous procedure has been completed, the Library panel should display a movie clip symbol named Vogon Component.

As mentioned earlier, to create a component, we need to associate a symbol with an ActionScript class.

We have created the symbol, so let us create the ActionScript class.

5. While still in the Flash authoring environment, create an ActionScript file and save it as Vogon.as; note that class filenames are case sensitive, so always pay attention to the name of the file and the name of the ActionScript class: they must be identical (file extension excluded).

6. Insert the following code into the ActionScript file and save it:

```
class Vogon {

    public function Vogon() {
        trace("creating an instance of the Vogon Component");
    }

}
```

The first incarnation of the Vogon class is very minimal and includes the class constructor only. A **class constructor** is a special function sharing the same name as the class.

The Flash engine invokes constructors automatically each time a new component instance is created. A constructor plays the important role of initializing the newly created component instance. It is a good practice to include the constructor in the implementation of a class even when its body is empty: its presence does not affect performance, and it is an important reminder of where to write initializing code, whenever needed.

Let us now complete the component creation process by associating the Vogon Component symbol with the Vogon class.

Probably because of some legacy issue, associating a class with a symbol to create a component requires two very similar actions:

- Define the name of the associated ActionScript class in the Linkage Properties dialog box of the movie clip.

- Define the name of the associated ActionScript class again as Vogon in the Component Definition dialog box of the movie clip.

Go back to the vogon.fla document where the component's symbol is. The following steps detail what you must do to complete the creation of your first Flash component:

7. Right-click the Vogon Component symbol in the Library window and select the Linkage... command.

8. Check the Export for ActionScript option.

9. Fill the AS 2.0 Class field with the name of our component class: Vogon.

10. Click the OK button to confirm the settings.

11. Once again, right-click the Vogon Component symbol in the Library window, but this time select the Component Definition... command.

12. Fill the AS 2.0 Class field with the name of our component class: Vogon.

13. Click the OK button to confirm the settings.

As you can see, the two procedures are almost identical, but only after completing the second one can you see that both the icon of the Vogon Component symbol and its description in the Library window have changed to show that the symbol has indeed become a component (as shown in Figure 1-1).

The document's library contains the component symbol, but to actually see the component at work, we must create at least one of its instances on the stage:

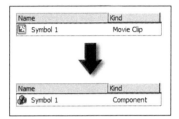

Figure 1-1. Our Vogon has become a component.

14. Drag the Vogon Component symbol from the Library panel onto the stage to create one instance of the component. Set the component position precisely by defining x = 200.0 and y = 200.0 in the Properties panel.

You can now test the Flash movie and the first version of the Vogon component.

Testing the movie within the Flash authoring environment will affect two windows:

- The SWF window will show a green shape, which is the same as the one you defined for your component.

- The constructor of the Vogon class is executed once automatically to initialize the only component instance in the movie. As a result, the Output panel will open to show the following text:

```
creating an instance of the Vogon Component
```

Our first example shows us that the component mechanism provides a neat separation between code and visual representation. Not only is the ActionScript code included in a separated file, but also no ActionScript code is required inside the Flash document to execute the code in the component's class.

Adding a method

Methods is an object-oriented term that refers to functions implementing the actions that an object can take. In the case of the Vogon component, we imagine the component instances to be "creatures" that love to read poems, and therefore we are going to provide the Vogon class with a readPoem method.

1. Copy both files from the previous example (vogon1.fla and Vogon.as) into a new folder.

2. Rename vogon1.fla as vogon2.fla as a reminder that we are working with a new version of the previous example.

3. Open the Vogon.as file and replace the existing code with the following:

```
class Vogon {

    public function Vogon() {
        readPoem();
    }

    public function readPoem():Void {
        trace("You do not really want to hear this..");
    }

}
```

Testing the new example in the Flash authoring environment will produce the following outcome:

- The SWF window will show the same green shape as the component instance present on the stage from the previous example.

- The constructor of the Vogon class is executed once automatically to initialize the only component instance in the movie. In this case, the constructor invokes the readPoem method, which in turn prints some text in the Output panel, as displayed in Figure 1-2.

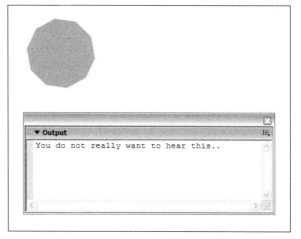

Figure 1-2. The Vogon component

What is the sense of this?

We are fleshing out a component step by step, introducing all of its typical features one by one. As the component grows larger, you will see more significant techniques at work, and thanks to this approach, you will be able to apply them to your own components or, per the scope of this book, you will be able to recognize them when they are applied to components of the component architecture.

Variables, properties, and metadata tags

Properties are used to store information about an object or even a class.

In our example, we will implement a myColor property to be able to assign different colors to the objects created using the Vogon class.

Component properties can be implemented in an ActionScript class in two different ways:

- **Explicitly, by using a variable definition**: This is the simpler option. It requires far less programming (one line of code), although it is not recommended by object-oriented purists.
- **Implicitly, by using get/set methods**: This option is considered the best practice of the two because it encapsulates the data and filters the access to it using two separate functions for read/write access. Considering that you have to implement two functions for each property, this option is certainly more demanding in programming terms. On the other hand, those two functions are the best place to store any code that should process a property's value before reading/writing it.

We are going to add a myColor property to our component, the purpose of which is to enable the user to change the color of a Vogon component instance. We will implement the myColor property both explicitly and implicitly so that you can compare the differences between the two options.

Implementing a property explicitly

In the following example, we are going to add an explicit property to the Vogon component that allows us to define its color.

1. Copy both files from the previous example (vogon2.fla and Vogon.as) into a new folder.
2. Rename vogon2.fla as vogon3.fla to remind you that we are working with a new version of our component.
3. Drag the Vogon Component symbol from the Library panel onto the stage to create a second instance of the component. Set the component position precisely by defining x = 400.0 and y = 200.0 in the Info panel.
4. Select the first component instance and name it blueVogon using the Properties panel.
5. Select the second component instance and name it redVogon using the Properties panel.
6. Select the first (and only) frame on stage and add the following ActionScript code in the Actions panel (Window ➤ Actions):

   ```
   #include "test.as"
   ```

7. Open the Vogon.as file and replace the existing ActionScript code with the following:

   ```
   class Vogon {

       public var myColor:Number;

       public function Vogon() {}

       public function applyNewColor():Void {
           var objColor:Color = new Color(this);
           objColor.setRGB(myColor);
       }

   }
   ```

9

8. Create a new ActionScript file and save it as `test.as`.

9. Copy the following code into the new ActionScript file:

```
blueVogon.myColor = 0x0000ff;
blueVogon.applyNewColor();
redVogon.myColor = 0xff0000;
redVogon.applyNewColor();
```

The new Vogon class implements the `myColor` property via a public variable of the Number type:

```
public var myColor:Number;
```

However, to assign a color value to this variable is not sufficient to change the color of a component instance; that's why we have to provide a method:

```
public function applyNewColor():Void {
```

This method must be called after assigning a new value to the `myColor` property to set the RGB color of the component instance accordingly. And that is what is done by our test code twice.

You can now test the movie in the authoring environment. There will not be any text printed in the Output window this time, and the only outcome will be the following:

■ The SWF window will show two identical shapes, one for each component instance on the stage, that have a different color (one shape is blue, the other red).

We implement the color attribute of our Vogon component for a very specific reason: ActionScript does not allow you to change the color of a movie clip in one step.

As shown in the implementation of the cumbersome `applyNewColor` method, you first need to access the color object of the movie clip associated with the instance:

```
var objColor:Color = new Color(this);
```

And then you can change it by using the numeric value stored in the `myColor` variable:

```
objColor.setRGB(myColor);
```

It would be nice if we could change the color of a component instance in a single step, avoiding the need to call the `applyNewColor` method each time, like in the following test code:

```
blueVogon.myColor = 0x0000ff;
redVogon.myColor = 0xff0000;
```

The previous code cannot work if the `myColor` property is implemented explicitly. Could it work if the property is implemented implicitly? Let us find out.

Implementing a property implicitly

To implement the myColor property implicitly, follow these steps:

1. Copy the files from the previous example (vogon3.fla, Vogon.as, and test.as) in a new folder.

2. Rename vogon3.fla as vogon4.fla to remind you that we are working with a new version of our component.

3. Open the Vogon.as file and replace the existing code with the following:

```
class Vogon {

    public function Vogon() {}

    public function get myColor():Number {
        var objColor:Color = new Color(this);
        return objColor.getRGB();
    }

    public function set myColor(aColor:Number):Void {
        var objColor:Color = new Color(this);
        objColor.setRGB(aColor);
    }

}
```

4. Open the test.as file and replace the existing code with the following:

```
blueVogon.myColor = 0x0000ff;
redVogon.myColor = 0xff0000;
```

That's all. You can test the movie and verify that the outcome is exactly the same as in the previous example where the myColor property was implemented explicitly: the SWF window still shows the two shapes that differ in color only (one is blue, the other red).

So we made it. Thanks to the implicit implementation of the myColor property, we can now set the color of a component instance in a single statement, as shown in the new version of the testing code. Let us examine how it works.

Properties are implemented explicitly via the use of two special kinds of methods:

- The get method retrieves the current value of a property.
- The set method stores a new value in a property.

The get and set methods have the same name of the property being implemented. Their declarations differ because of the presence of the get/set keywords and in the parameters since the get method returns the property's value, while the set method expects a value to be assigned to the property.

The get method returns a number and has no input parameters:

```
public function get myColor():Number {
```

The set method expects an input parameter of type Number and doesn't return any value:

```
public function set myColor(aColor:Number):Void {
```

The get/set methods usually store and retrieve the value of a property in a private variable of the class, but that is not always the case. In fact, in the case of the myColor property, the value is stored in and retrieved from the RGB color of the movie clip associated with the component instance, as can be seen in the implementation of the get/set methods of myColor in this example.

It is an OOP best practice to implement properties implicitly via get/set methods because

- They offer much finer control when accessing the property.
- They separate the implementation of the property (how it is stored and retrieved) from its access inside applications that use instances of a class, therefore eliminating inconvenient dependencies.

While the benefits of this approach remain theoretical in some cases, they soon become evident whenever some action is required when accessing the property, as in the case of the myColor property that we have implemented for our component.

Properties in the authoring environment

Although the use of the Flash authoring environment is beyond the scope of this book, you should be aware of certain coding features that have been expressly introduced to enhance the productivity of the authoring environment.

In particular, it is possible to use metadata tags to expose the properties of a component instance at design time, therefore empowering both designers and developers who create component instances statically by dropping them on the Flash document stage.

There can be a design-time alternative to defining the myColor property of our component as we did in these lines:

```
blueVogon.myColor = 0x0000ff;
redVogon.myColor = 0xff0000;
```

In fact, it is possible to make the myColor property accessible in a couple of panels in the authoring environment:

- In the Parameters tab of Properties panel, and
- In the Parameters section of the Component Inspector panel

Let us modify the previous example to implement this:

1. Copy the files from the previous example (vogon4.fla, Vogon.as, and test.as) in a new folder.
2. Rename vogon4.fla as vogon5.fla to remind you that we are working with a new version of our component.

3. Open the Vogon.as file and update the existing code by adding the metadata tag line just before the declaration of the myColor set method, as shown in the following code:

```
class Vogon {

    public function Vogon() {}

    public function get myColor():Number {
        var objColor:Color = new Color(this);
        return objColor.getRGB();
    }

      [Inspectable(name="My Color", type="Color",
                   defaultValue="#00FF00")]
    public function set myColor(aColor:Number):Void {
        var objColor:Color = new Color(this);
        objColor.setRGB(aColor);
    }

}
```

Compile and test the movie once to force the authoring environment to re-read the definition of the Vogon class that has now been extended with the metadata tag associated with the myColor property and add it to the Properties panel:

```
[Inspectable(name="My Color", type="Color", defaultValue="#00FF00")]
```

The syntax of the Inspectable metadata tag is rather intuitive; it defines three parameters:

- name: This parameter provides the name of the property as it will be shown in the panels of the authoring environment.

- type: This parameter specifies how the property should be handled by the panels in the authoring interface. We know that the myColor property implemented in the Vogon class is of type Number, but we also know that it represents the numeric value of a color. By telling the authoring environment that the property type is Color, we will exploit a mechanism provided by the authoring environment that allows us to set the numeric value by picking a color in a pop-up palette.

- defaultValue: This parameter allows us to specify a default value for the property. We know that the default color of our component is green because that is the color we chose for the component's shape when we created it.

We can verify that the presence of this metadata tag in the definition of the Vogon class has indeed influenced the authoring environment.

1. Close the SWF window in the authoring environment, if still open.

2. Select the blueVogon component instance on the stage.

3. Look in the Parameters tab of the Properties panel (or in the Parameters section of the Component Inspector panel).

13

4. You will find that there is a row dedicated to the My Color parameter, corresponding to the myColor property.

5. By double-clicking the swatch of the My Color parameter, you will access a color palette. Select the blue color in it (#0000FF). The swatch color will change from green (the default color) to blue.

6. Select the redVogon component instance on the stage and repeat the previous process to set its My Color parameter to the color red (#FF0000).

7. Open the test.as file and replace the existing code with the following:

```
trace("the color of the component instances has now been set
        at design time");
```

After testing the movie again, a message in the Output window will say the following:

```
the color of the component instances has now been set at design time
```

That message highlights that the blueVogon instance will be displayed in blue and the redVogon instance in red.

Note that we have applied the Inspectable metadata tag to the implicit implementation of the myColor component by postponing its inclusion until the declaration of the property's set method.

It is also possible to apply the Inspectable metadata tag to properties that have been implemented explicitly by postponing its inclusion until the variable declaration.

If you wish to modify our explicit option example, all you have to do is insert the metadata tag just before the myColor variable declaration like so:

```
[Inspectable(name="My Color", type="Color", defaultValue="#00FF00")]
public var myColor:Number;
```

Inheritance

Inheritance is one feature of OOP that has made it one of the most powerful programming approaches in existence—it refers to the ability of a class to inherit the features of another class.

The class providing such features is frequently called the **base class**, while the class inheriting them is usually defined as the **subclass**.

```
"base class" -> "subclass"
```

In ActionScript, inheritance is implemented via the extends keyword.

A little help from Darwin

In the following very short example, the extends keyword informs ActionScript that the class Man inherits from the class Animal:

```
class Man extends Animal {

    public function Man() {}

}
```

Therefore, in our example, Animal is the base class, while Man is its subclass; you could say, quite scientifically, *"(the class) Man derives from (the class) Animal."*

Let us define the class Animal as follows:

```
class Animal {

    public var species:String;

    public function Animal() {}

    public function breathe():Void{}

}
```

A direct consequence of such a definition is that any object created using the class Man will have a variable species and a method breathe because the class Man inherits those features from the class Animal.

Also, the Animal constructor will be called before the Man constructor, whenever creating an object of the class Man.

Given that the constructor is a special function having the same name as the class, it is a good practice to include it in the class definition even if it is initially empty. An empty constructor does not impact the performance, and it reminds us where to include any initialization code that we may need in the future.

Inheritance introduces a new rule about what type of objects can be legally assigned to variables of a certain type: we can assign an object to a variable only if their classes are the same or the object's class inherits from the variable's class.

```
var a:Animal = new Man(); // legal
var m:Man = new Animal(); // illegal !!!
```

Executing the second line of this example in the authoring environment would generate the following error at compilation time:

```
Line 2:
Type mismatch in assignment statement:
found Animal where Man is required.
```

which sounds almost like a joke!

Let us build an example to check inheritance at work in ActionScript.

1. Create a new Flash document and save it as manimal.fla in a new folder.

2. Select the first (and only) frame on stage and add the following ActionScript code to the Actions panel:

```
#include "test.as"
```

3. Create three ActionScript files and save them in the same folder with the names Animal.as, Man.as, and test.as. Remember that ActionScript filenames are case sensitive; therefore, you must pay attention and define their names accurately.

4. Copy the following code into the Animal.as file and save it:

```
class Animal {

    public var Species:String;

    public function Animal() {
        trace("creating an animal");
    }

    public function breathe():Void{
        trace("I breathe");
    }

}
```

5. Copy the following code into the Man.as file and save it:

```
class Man extends Animal {

    public function Man() {
        trace("creating a man");
    }

}
```

6. Copy the following code into the test.as file and save it:

```
var m:Man = new Man();
m.breathe();
```

If you now test the Flash movie, you will notice that the following lines will be displayed in the Output window:

```
creating an animal
creating a man
I breathe
```

The output produced by the code in the test.as file proves a few facts:

- The creation of an instance of the Man class triggers the execution of the constructor of the Animal class first; the constructor of the Man class runs just after that.
- The last line ("I breathe") demonstrates that an instance of the Man class inherits the breathe method from the Animal class: such a method was not defined in the Man class!

Appreciating the benefits of inheritance

Although intuitive, the previous example was possibly too abstract to let you truly appreciate the benefits of the inheritance mechanism, so let us apply inheritance to our Vogon component and see if we can come out with something more useful.

In the last version of the component, we introduced the myColor property, which allows the user to define the color of the component both programmatically and at design time in the Flash authoring environment.

The goal of the next version of the component is to separate this feature (the color) from the Vogon class and encapsulate it in another class, Colorable. The Vogon class will then inherit the myColor property and its behavior from the Colorable class.

1. Copy the files vogon5.fla, Vogon.as, and test.as from last version of our component into a new folder.
2. Rename vogon5.fla as vogon6.fla to remind you that we are working with a new version of the component.
3. Create a new ActionScript file and save it as Colorable.as.
4. Add the following code to the new ActionScript file and save it:

```
class Colorable {

   public function Colorable() {}

   public function get myColor():Number {
      var objColor:Color = new Color(this);
      return objColor.getRGB();
   }

   [Inspectable(name="My Color", type="Color",
                defaultValue="#00FF00")]
   public function set myColor(aColor:Number):Void {
      var objColor:Color = new Color(this);
      objColor.setRGB(aColor);
   }

}
```

5. Open the Vogon.as file and replace the existing code with the following:

```
class Vogon extends Colorable {

    private var pBuffer:String;

    public function Vogon() {}

    public function readPoem():Void {
        trace(myPoem);
    }

    public function get myPoem():String {
        return pBuffer;
    }

    public function set myPoem(aPoem:String):Void {
        pBuffer = aPoem;
    }

}
```

You will notice a number of changes in the Vogon class:

- The implementation of the myColor property disappeared from the code of the class.
- The Vogon class is now a subclass of Colorable, suggesting that it will inherit the myColor property from its base class.
- A new method (readPoem) and the implicit implementation of a new property (myPoem) were added for later use.
- As you can see, the implementation of the myColor property disappeared from the definition of the Vogon class.

Let us now change the code in the test.as file to test the new property and the new method.

6. Open the test.as file and replace the existing code with the following:

```
redVogon.myPoem =
        "...Groop, I implore thee, my foonting turlingdromes...";
redVogon.readPoem();
```

After saving the new versions of Vogon.as and test.as, you are ready to test the movie.

The only difference with the outcome of the previous example is the new message in the Output window:

```
...Groop, I implore thee, my foonting turlingdromes...
```

The SWF window still shows the blueVogon and redVogon instances with their expected colors, as we set them at design time in the previous example.

In fact, if you check the Parameters tab of the Properties panel for both component instances, you will find that the My Color property is still there, and it is defined as blue for the blueVogon and red for the second instance of the stage.

However, quite a bit has happened behind the scenes. The myColor property is no longer implemented in the Vogon class. Its implementation is provided via inheritance by a new class, Colorable, created for this specific purpose.

So, why we did modify our component to introduce the Colorable class, and what are the benefits of inheritance?

Well, let us consider the case of implementing another new component. We will start with an almost empty class with only the constructor in it:

```
class MySecondComponent {

    public function MySecondComponent() {}

}
```

Now, what if you wish to add a color property that behaves exactly like the one we implemented for the Vogon component?

Without inheritance, you should first evaluate what the implementation of this property could be in the context of the new component and, ultimately, reimplement its get/set methods.

However, using inheritance is going to cost you very little; indeed, all it requires is the addition of just two words to your code:

```
class MySecondComponent extends Colorable {

    public function MySecondComponent() {}

}
```

Almost magically, extends Colorable is all you need to add the myColor property to your new component to make its instances "colorable"!

Apart from any hype associated with OOP, it should be evident by now what benefits inheritance can produce when used properly: a neater design, a more robust implementation, and a higher level of reusability.

ActionScript limit on multiple inheritance

Now that you have seen how powerful the inheritance mechanism can be, you are probably considering implementing any essential functionality you can think of into different classes to be able to create new components in a snap by inheriting from a selection of those classes. That is what architecture designers do, and their job is easier when new classes can inherit from more than one class at the

19

same time. The concept of inheriting from more than one class at the same time is called **multiple inheritance**, and it would be nice if ActionScript had implemented it using something like the following syntax:

```
class Vogon extends Colorable,MovieClip {
// NOTE: this is NOT valid ActionScript code
```

Unfortunately, the current version of ActionScript does not support multiple inheritance. When designing OOP applications or components for Flash, we must keep in mind that an ActionScript class can inherit directly (extends) from one class only.

However, there is a way to get around this.

In the case of the Vogon class, we wish it to inherit from both the Colorable and MovieClip classes in order to add the features of both classes to the Vogon class. This is possible by implementing a **chain of inheritance**—defining the Vogon class as a subclass of Colorable class, which in turn is defined as a subclass of the MovieClip class.

In order to implement our first chain of inheritance, we need to modify only one line in the Colorable class to define it as a subclass of the MovieClip class:

```
class Colorable extends MovieClip {
```

After this change, all the Vogon objects will have both the features defined in the Colorable class and those defined in the MovieClip class by simply inheriting from the Colorable class through the implemented chain of inheritance:

```
Vogon -> Colorable -> MovieClip
```

So, what's the difference between multiple inheritance and a chain of inheritance?

In the first case, the Colorable class would not need to inherit from the MovieClip class and would remain a smaller, neatly defined, class.

Some designs are better implemented by organizing the features in classes that are well separated via multiple inheritance. Other designs are better implemented by adding features incrementally as in a chain of inheritance.

At the time of writing, ActionScript provides the second option only.

Events

In addition to defining the properties and methods of its instances, an ActionScript class may also implement further functionality to allow its objects to communicate among each other and with objects that are instances of other classes.

In OOP, interobject communication is based on events.

What is an event in component terms?

Events play such a major role in modern software development that a new definition was forged to refer to programs that are based on events: **event-driven applications**.

Flash applications have always been event-driven, which is why Flash applications can handle components so well. Components, in fact, communicate among each other by triggering events or reacting to them.

But what is an event in component terms?

An **event** is the abstraction of a specific action, such as the user clicking a component instance. When the user clicks the instance of a component, implementing the click event, the component instance acts as a source object. A **source object** creates an event object and dispatches it to all the other objects that are waiting for it.

The objects waiting for an event to happen are called **listeners**, and they usually react to an event by executing some code.

These concepts will become clearer after we have built up a concrete example.

Implementing a custom event

Continuing with the practical approach we have followed so far, we are going to implement a custom event for our Vogon component.

To make a significant example, we need at the very least two component instances, one that can act as the event source, and another that can act as the listener.

In our last example, we had a couple of instances (blueVogon and redVogon) on stage; therefore, we can continue from where we left off and write some code that will allow the redVogon instance to create and dispatch an event and some other code that will permit to the blueVogon instance to receive the event and do something about it.

But what custom event could we possibly implement? The myPoem property that we added lately can be useful to arrange a scenario. Let us assume that an instance of the Vogon class triggers an onNewPoem event every time that the myPoem property is assigned a new value.

Another instance of the same component could then be interested in listening to such an event and react accordingly.

Let us implement the first part of the example.

Triggering a custom event

The Flash engine and the classes provided with it trigger many system events.

Events created by the programmer for a specific purpose, such as the onNewPoem defined in our scenario, are usually referred as **custom events** to underline the fact that they are user-defined.

Unlike properties and methods, events are not included in the syntax of the class construct, so we rely on different ways of implementing events.

The technique introduced in this section is the most appropriate in the case of component-based applications, since it utilizes a mix-in class included in the architecture for the specific purpose of implementing events: the UIEventDispatcher class.

This class implements a communication protocol among objects and therefore is able to dispatch the event created by a source object to all of its listeners.

Our Vogon class will use the UIEventDispatcher class to be able to trigger its own custom event and, at the same time, to be able to listen to it, as we will see in the next step.

We will add the definition of three initially empty functions to our Vogon class:

```
public function dispatchEvent(eventObject:Object) {}
public function addEventListener(event:String, listener:Object) {}
public function removeEventListener(event:String, listener:Object) {}
```

Such functions are part of the communication protocol implemented by the UIEventDispatcher class. In fact, by including the line

```
mx.events.UIEventDispatcher.initialize(this);
```

in the constructor of the Vogon class, we will ask the UIEventDispatcher class to provide the implementation of those three methods.

The dispatchEvent method allows triggering of a custom event. Only one parameter is expected by this method: the event object.

Event objects are implemented as instances of the built-in Object class, which is a dynamic class. If an object is based on a dynamic class, you are able to add properties to it at runtime, a feature that can be very handy when implementing event objects.

An event object must have at least two properties:

- target: A reference to the object that triggered the event
- type: A string value containing the name of the custom event

In the Vogon class, we will implement the event object and dispatch it in the following way:

```
var eventObject:Object = {target:this, type:'onNewPoem'};
eventObject.poem = pBuffer;
dispatchEvent(eventObject);
```

As you can see, we initially create the event object with the two mandatory properties (type and target) and then we add another property that stores information associated with the specific event (the value of the myPoem property, which is stored in the pBuffer variable).

The name chosen for our custom event is onNewPoem, a choice that will make our code more readable when implementing the listening part of the interaction in the next section.

Listening to a custom event

When a source object triggers a custom event via the dispatchEvent method, the method implementation provided by the UIEventDispatcher class dispatches the event object to all of its listeners.

But how can a component instance become a listener?

A component instance must register itself using the addEventListener method in order to become the listener of a custom event. The listener role can also be dropped, as the component instance can stop listening to an event by invoking removeEventListener.

In addition to registering itself as a listener of a specific event, a component instance must also have a method that has the same name of that custom event.

Therefore, in order to enable instances of the Vogon class to react to the onNewPoem method, we must implement a method in the Vogon class with the same name: onNewPoem.

That is the reason for choosing such a name for our custom event. Ultimately, the onNewPoem method will be invoked whenever the value of the myPoem property changes and, therefore, "on (the creation of a) new poem."

Methods like onNewPoem are implemented for the specific purpose of reacting to a custom event, and because of this are also known as **event handlers**.

Our event handler will be implemented by the following code:

```
public function onNewPoem(eventObject:Object):Void {
    trace("I am " + this._name);
    trace("and I just received a new poem from " +
            eventObject.target._name);
    trace('"' + eventObject.poem + '"');
}
```

In reaction to receiving the event, the Vogon component instance will print some useful information in the output window. More specifically:

- The first trace will show the name of the object listening to the event (the listener).
- The second trace will show the name of the object that triggered the event (the source object).
- The third trace will display the value of the myPoem property of the source object (the new poem).

Building the example

The following example demonstrates the implementation of a custom event:

1. Copy the files vogon6.fla, Vogon.as, Colorable.as, and test.as from last version of our component into a new folder.
2. Rename vogon6.fla as vogon7.fla to remind you that we are working with a new version of the component.

3. If you have not done so already while working on the previous example, modify the Colorable class to inherit from the MovieClip class. We will need it to access the name of the movie clip associated with the component instance. The MovieClip class encapsulates all the features that are available to a Flash movie clip and makes them available to other classes.

```
class Colorable extends MovieClip {
```

4. Open Vogon.as to implement the new version of the Vogon class. Replace the existing code the with the following:

```
import mx.events.UIEventDispatcher;

class Vogon extends Colorable {

    private var pBuffer:String;

    public function Vogon() {
        UIEventDispatcher.initialize(this);
    }

    public function dispatchEvent(eventObject:Object) {}
     public function addEventListener(event:String,
                                        listener:Object){}
     public function removeEventListener(event:String,
                                          listener:Object) {}

    public function readPoem():Void {
        trace(myPoem);
    }

    public function get myPoem():String {
        return pBuffer;
    }

    public function set myPoem(aPoem:String):Void {
        pBuffer = aPoem;
        var eventObject:Object = {target:this, type:'onNewPoem'};
        eventObject.poetry = pBuffer;
        dispatchEvent(eventObject);
    }

    public function onNewPoem(eventObject:Object):Void {
        trace("I am " + this._name);
        trace("and I just received a new poem from " +
                    eventObject.target._name);
        trace('"' + eventObject.poetry + '"');
    }

}
```

5. Open the `test.as` file and replace the existing code with the following:

```
redVogon.addEventListener("onNewPoem", blueVogon);
blueVogon.addEventListener("onNewPoem", redVogon);
redVogon.myPoem =
        "...Groop, I implore thee, my foonting turlingdromes...";
```

Even if very simple, the testing code has been defined to prove almost any aspect related to the event dispatching mechanism as it is implemented by the UIEventDispatcher class:

- The first line registers the blueVogon instance as a listener of the onNewPoem event when triggered by the redVogon instance.

- The second line registers the redVogon instance as a listener of the onNewPoem event when triggered by the blueVogon instance.

- In the third line, the redVogon instance acts as the source object of the onNewPoem event because its myPoem property is assigned a new value. Our custom event is triggered by the set method of myPoem as a result of this statement.

In response to the source object (redVogon) triggering the event, the UIEventDispatcher class will execute the onNewPoem method in the scope of the listener (blueVogon).

As a result of the execution of such method, the following lines will be displayed in the Output window when you test the movie in the authoring environment:

```
I am blueVogon
and I just received a new poem from redVogon
"...Groop, I implore thee, my foonting turlingdromes..."
```

Note that the line

```
blueVogon.addEventListener("onNewPoem", redVogon);
```

does not influence the outcome of the test because the myPoem property of the blueVogon does not change, and, therefore, blueVogon never acts as source object in our example.

The line has been added to demonstrate that when an event (onNewPoem) is triggered, the UIEventDispatcher delivers it only to the objects that have registered themselves as listeners of the specific source object.

Basically, when the myPoem property of redVogon is assigned a new value, redVogon does not receive the event object because it is listening to blueVogon but not listening to itself!

The redVogon instance could have been listening to itself if we had added the following line before assigning a new value to the myPoem property:

```
redVogon.addEventListener("onNewPoem", redVogon);
```

Add this line to the test yourself, and see how the outcome changes.

Polymorphism

Polymorphism is a term associated with another fundamental OOP concept.

The word comes from the Greek, and its original meaning is "having multiple forms."

Polymorphism can work in a number of subtle ways depending on how it is implemented in the programming language of choice; in the most general case, polymorphism refers to the ability of a programming language to connect a method call with a method implementation depending on the runtime class of the object invoking the method.

Let us create an example of polymorphism at work within the scope of component design.

And God took a rib from a Vogon

At least two classes are needed to build an example of polymorphism.

Because of this, we are going to create a second component. This will not be a lengthy task, because we are going to derive the class of the new component from the Vogon class. We are going to create a Vogoness for the Vogon to socialize with.

The following example is also an opportunity to see how inheritance allows us to further specialize existing components by creating new ones based on existing ones.

1. Copy the files `vogon7.fla`, `Vogon.as`, `Colorable.as`, and `test.as` from last version of our component into a new folder.

2. Rename `vogon7.fla` as `vogon8.fla` to remind you that we are working with a new version of the component.

3. Duplicate the Vogon component by right/CTRL-clicking it in the Library panel and choosing the Duplicate option from the pop-up menu.

4. Define the new name of the component (as requested in the Duplicate Symbol dialog box) as Vogoness and click the Advanced button to reveal additional options.

5. Check the Export for ActionScript option and in the AS 2.0 Class text field add Vogoness, the name of the class that we are going to create.

6. Let us complete the association between the new component and its class by right/CTRL-clicking the Vogoness component in the Library panel and selecting the Component Definition… option. Once again, in the AS 2.0 Class text box add Vogoness.

7. We are now going to modify the shape of the Vogoness component to be able to distinguish its instances from those of the Vogon component. Right/CTRL-click the Vogoness component in the Library panel and select the Edit option. Alter the shape, but do not change the color.

8. After editing the component shape, go back to the main stage of the document and create an instance of the Vogoness component by dragging its symbol from the Library panel to the stage.

9. Select the newly created instance on the stage and define its instance name as greenVogoness. Move the greenVogoness to the location (x = 300.0, y = 350.0) by using the Info panel. Since the Flash document was a copy of the one created in the previous example, we should now have three instances on the stage that are named blueVogon, redVogon, and greenVogoness, respectively.

10. You can now pass to the implementation of the Vogoness class by creating a new ActionScript file and saving it with the name Vogoness.as after copying the following code into it:

```
class Vogoness extends Vogon {

    private var txtPoetry:TextField;

    public function Vogoness() {}

    public function readPoem():Void {
        createTextField("txtPoetry", getNextHighestDepth(), 0,
                                100, 250, 100);
        txtPoetry.multiline = true;
        txtPoetry.wordWrap = true;
        txtPoetry.text = this.myPoem;
        var tf:TextFormat = new TextFormat();
        tf.align = "right";
        txtPoetry.setTextFormat(tf);
    }

}
```

The Vogoness class is a subclass of the Vogon class. The new class overrides the readPoem method by providing a different implementation for it.

The readPoem implementation in the Vogon class is much simpler and shows the content of the myPoem property in the Output window. The new implementation, in the Vogoness class, creates a TextField instance in the component's movie clip showing the content of the myPoem property.

We are now ready to change the test.as file and write the code that will show us how polymorphism can work in a Flash application.

11. Open the test.as file and replace the existing code with the following:

```
greenVogoness.myPoem = "Uglier things than my husband have been
➡ spotted, but not by reliable witnesses.";
redVogon.myPoem = "The best way to get a drink out of blueVogon is
➡ to stick your finger down his throat.";
blueVogon.myPoem = "redVogon is not above corruption in
➡ the same way that the sea is not above the clouds.";

var objects = Array(greenVogoness, redVogon, blueVogon);

var o:Object;
for (var i:Number=0; i<objects.length; i++) {
    o = objects[i];
    o.readPoem();
}
```

The first three statements of this code define a different "poem" for each of the three objects that we have on stage. Remember that two of those objects are instances of the Vogon component, blueVogon and redVogon, while the third one, greenVogoness, is an instance of the Vogoness component.

The fourth statement creates an array that contains the three objects.

The following lines iterate through the newly created array to invoke the readPoem method of each object for a total of three calls, since there are three objects in the array.

If you now test the Flash movie, you will notice that the Output window shows the two poems associated with the blueVogon and redVogon objects:

```
The best way to get a drink out of blueVogon is to stick your finger
down his throat.

redVogon is not above corruption in the same way that the sea is not
above the clouds.
```

On the other hand, the third "poem," associated with the greenVogoness object, appears in the Flash movie itself, underneath its shape, as shown in Figure 1-3.

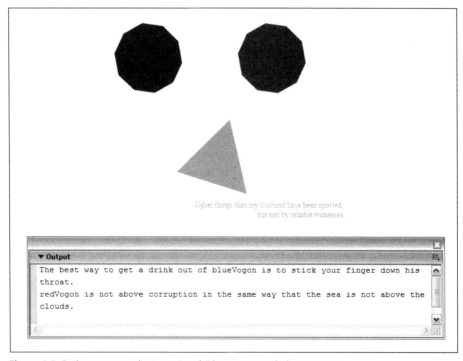

Figure 1-3. Each component instance "reads" its own poem in its own way.

To understand what has happened, you need to realize that the Object class plays a vital part in this example.

The Object class is at the root of the ActionScript class hierarchy; every other class in ActionScript belongs to an inheritance chain that has the Object class at its root.

Basically, every ActionScript class is a subclass of the Object class; you do not need to use the extends statement to explicitly declare it.

As a result of this, the Vogon and Vogoness classes inherit from the Object class as well.

It is then legal to assign both Vogon and Vogoness objects to a variable of the class Object, as we do in our example in the following line:

```
o = objects[i];
```

Actually, the whole example would have worked without the o variable by directly accessing the method, as in

```
objects[i].readPoem()
```

The example was made a couple of lines longer to explicitly illustrate the key role played by the Object class. In fact, ActionScript implicitly considers objects[i] as an instance of the Object class at compilation time. It is only at runtime that objects[i] will be an instance of the Vogoness class or of the Vogon class, depending on the value of i.

The "magic" of polymorphism is that the Flash engine checks the actual class of an object at runtime and calls the method's implementation provided by that class.

In our example, what really happens is this:

```
i=0 => objects[i] is a Vogoness => Vogoness implementation of readPoem
i=1 => objects[i] is a Vogon => Vogon implementation of readPoem
i=2 => objects[i] is a Vogon => Vogon implementation of readPoem
```

Like most subtle OOP concepts, polymorphism initially seems like a way of complicating things unnecessarily. It is only with experience that we start appreciating its power and benefits and, consequently, how to use it properly.

A method's signature

In order to work, polymorphism requires that the method implementations that will be invoked share the same "signature."

The signature of a method can be found in the function declaration of the method and includes

- The method's name
- The method's number of parameters
- The types of each of the method's parameters
- The type of the value returned by the method

The readPoem had a short signature, which was the same for both the Vogon and the Vogoness classes:

```
public function readPoem():Void {
```

A longer signature may have included two parameters, the first of type String and the second of type Number, and return a value of type Object. So, for example, if the Vogon class would have defined a readPoem method with a signature as follows:

```
public function readPoem2(param1:String, param2:Number):Object {
```

then in order to implement polymorphism, the signature of the readPoem method implemented in the Vogoness class should have been something like

```
public function readPoem(p1:String, p2:Number):Object {
```

This is the same signature because the names of the parameters are not influential, but the following two signatures are different:

```
public function readPoem(p1:String):Object {
public function readPoem(p1:Number, p2:String):Object {
```

The first is different because of the number of parameters (one instead of two); the second, because of the order of the parameters' types (Number and then String instead of String and then Number).

Appreciating the benefits of polymorphism

Polymorphism makes our applications highly scalable. **Scalability** is the quality of software to gracefully manage an increased number of objects or even objects of newly created types.

A concrete example of scalability can be found in some of the code presented earlier. Compare the case of invoking the readPoem method sequentially by using the object instance names:

```
// sequential approach
greenVogoness.readPoem();
blueVogon.readPoem();
redVogon.readPoem();
```

to the code required by the iterative approach:

```
// iterative approach
var o:Object;
for (var i:Number=0; i<objects.length; i++) {
    o = objects[i];
    o.readPoem();
}
```

The iterative approach may well look overly complicated if we are dealing with three objects, but imagine if you had to modify your application to handle a hundred objects.

The sequential approach would require one hundred lines of code, while the iterative approach would require not only the same number of lines, but would also work without requiring any modification! In fact, the code of the iterative approach would also work with a thousand objects or more without undergoing any change!

Also, the iterative approach can even manage objects of any newly created class as long as the invoked methods have the same signature!

That's why a method's signature is sometimes referred as a "contract" established when designing and implementing an application.

By respecting such a contract, the objects of new classes created at a later stage will be processed by the existing application seamlessly.

Summary

In this chapter, you have learned

- What a Flash component is
- How the most essential principles of OOP influence the design and implementation of components
- How to create Flash components
- How to integrate a component in the authoring environment

The next step is to examine the core classes of the component architecture and learn how to use them to create Flash components that belong to this architecture.

Chapter 2

CORE CLASSES AND COMPONENT DESIGN

A design is perfect when there is nothing left to take away.

Zen proverb

In the previous chapter, you created a couple of components (Vogon and Vogoness) using all of the basic object-oriented features that a Flash component can have.

You also discovered the convenience of encapsulating functionality into a specific class (Colorable) to make it reusable by different components.

It is now time for you to gain an understanding of what the component architecture is, how it works, and the value that it can bring to your applications.

The component architecture is much more than a collection of components. In addition to providing a powerful set of components, the component architecture features patterns that capture proven, effective software design.

The main purpose of the architecture is to define general system rules that can be applied to every component, thereby producing more robust applications and speeding development. Furthermore, you will find in the architecture numerous reusable assets that can be used in conjunction with the components.

However, the best assets of an architecture are abstract, and you must become familiar with them in order to exploit their benefits. The assets of the component architecture can be roughly classified into three categories:

1. The components
2. The component framework
3. The application framework

While components themselves represent a concrete, visible asset, the other two categories define abstract functionality that plays a very important role in the development of a component-based application.

As suggested by its name, a **component framework** is not a complete component, but only a skeleton that captures all the basic features that a component should have. Among those features are also communication mechanisms that define how components interact among each other.

All of the components provided within the Flash component architecture are based upon the same component framework. By learning to recognize the component framework when you come across it, you will be able to learn to use different components much faster because they will likely have functionality in common with components you already know.

Like the component framework, the **application framework** is an incomplete application embedded with established design patterns and plenty of basic behaviors.

When developing a complete application, you just specialize some of those behaviors to fulfill your requirements while reusing the rest of them as they are!

The component architecture takes advantage of the inheritance mechanism to implement its component framework, as depicted in Figure 2-1. Basically, the architecture defines a few classes that progressively capture all the functionality of the component framework.

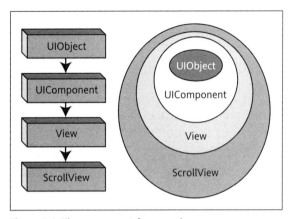

Figure 2-1. The component framework

Figure 2-1 emphasizes three aspects:

1. **The hierarchical relationship**: The ScrollView class extends the View class, which in turn extends the UIComponent class, which in turn extends the UIObject class.

2. **The functional containment relationship**: The ScrollView class contains the functionality of all the other classes, and so on.

3. **The complexity relationship**: The ScrollView class is the "bigger" class in terms of functionality, and so on.

Not every component inherits from the ScrollView class, as you see in Figure 2-2.

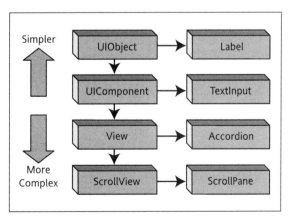

Figure 2-2. Inheritance examples

Figure 2-2 shows four components, each inheriting from a different class of the component framework. The Label component, for example, does not inherit from the ScrollView component because it doesn't need to scroll its contents.

Note that the fact that UIObject is a much simpler class than the ScrollView class doesn't necessarily imply that components based upon the UIObject class are simpler than components based upon the ScrollView class, even if that is most likely to be the case.

Later on in the book, you will find out that the component framework includes other classes in addition to those already listed here (UIObject, UIComponent, View, and ScrollView). In this chapter, however, we focus on these four classes because they are the most essential ones. They can be quite appropriately referred to as "core classes" since they have been included in a package with that name (core).

The UIObject class is the root of the component architecture. The information about each core class included in the rest of this chapter will help you to do the following:

- Make the right choice about which core class to pick as the base class whenever you create a component from scratch.
- Understand the influence of the core classes on the components already included in the architecture.

We will now proceed to examining the functionality implemented by each of the core classes starting from the simplest and most essential one, which is the root of the component architecture: UIObject.

> *The completed source code introduced in this chapter can be found in the package* src02.zip, *downloadable from this book's page on* www.friendsofed.com.

The legacy of the UIObject class

You may find it useful to look at the source code of the UIObject class while reading this section. (See Appendix A to find the source code of the component architecture on your computer.)

The UIObject class is implemented as a subclass of MovieClip. In fact, the first line of its class declaration is

```
class mx.core.UIObject extends MovieClip {
```

mx.core.UIObject is the fully qualified name of the UIObject class and, as such, includes its package information. In the case of the UIObject class, the package information indicates that the class file can be found in the core folder, which is a subfolder of the mx folder. Fully qualified names are frequently used in the component architecture in order to reduce the chances of name collisions and to group the classes by functional similarity.

After reading the previous chapter, you should not be too surprised to find out that the base class of the UIObject class is MovieClip. We already saw that the MovieClip class is an ActionScript built-in class that encapsulates all of the attributes and functions of a movie clip. A component instance is essentially a movie clip associated with an ActionScript class; by defining the UIObject class as a subclass of the MovieClip class, the architecture propagates the MovieClip features to all of its components.

The UIObject class implements one of the most important features of the component framework: the functionality to create component instances dynamically.

Creating a component instance dynamically

In the examples of the previous chapter, we statically included component instances in the Flash document by dragging the component's symbol from the library to the stage.

In many cases, it can be convenient to create component instances via ActionScript. Using ActionScript to create component instances dynamically allows us to determine the number of instances to be created at runtime in response to user input or as a result of the information provided by other sources such as databases.

Another advantage of creating component instances dynamically is that such components can be removed after they have completed their function, allowing us to optimize both the performance and the memory requested by the Flash application.

Such components will not be visible on the Flash document's stage because they do not exist until the movie runs. When creating components dynamically, the component definition must include a **linkage identifier** that can be referred to at runtime to create instances of that specific component.

If you right-click the example components in the Library panel and choose the Linkage... option, you will find that these components already have a linkage identifier that is the same as the symbol's name: Vogon Component and Vogoness Component, respectively. The authoring environment automatically defines the linkage identifier as the symbol name when creating a new component. However, you are free to change it and use whatever naming convention you like when developing your own components.

If you are indeed creating a new component, you must override some properties defined by the UIObject class to enable functionality, such as making it dynamically creatable.

You may be thinking, Wait a second. Why should I do something? Didn't the UIObject class implement such functionality already?

The definition I gave earlier of what a component framework is provides the answer to this question. Ultimately, a component framework is an incomplete component that you can complete in two different ways:

1. Adding further functionality to it in the form of new properties and/or new methods
2. Modifying the behavior predefined by the framework by overriding some properties or methods (i.e., by providing a new implementation of those properties or methods)

The next sections will show you which features of the UIObject class you must override when creating a new component, thus explaining the role of each feature in the component framework.

Overriding the symbolName property

The UIObject class defines a symbolName property (implemented as a static variable) that is used during the process of creating component instances dynamically.

This property must store the String value of the linkage identifier as we defined it earlier.

The UIObject class defines this property as

```
static var symbolName:String = "UIObject";
```

The component framework will not be able to create instances of our components unless we override this property with the proper linkage identifiers, which is why the Vogon class must override this property as follows:

```
static var symbolName:String = "Vogon Component";
```

Similarly, the Vogoness class will override this property by providing its own linkage identifier, as in

```
static var symbolName:String = "Vogoness Component";
```

Overriding the symbolOwner property

The UIObject class defines a second static property that affects the process of creating component instances dynamically: symbolOwner.

This property stores an Object value that is the fully qualified name of component's class. In the case of our two components, the fully qualified names of both classes coincide with their short names because we did not implement any package information.

The UIObject class defines this property as

```
static var symbolOwner:Object = UIObject;
```

Once again, the component framework will not be able to create instances of our components unless we override this property with the proper class definitions, which is why the Vogon class must override this property as follows:

```
static var symbolOwner:Object = Vogon;
```

Similarly, the Vogoness class will override this property by providing its own linkage identifier, as in

```
static var symbolOwner:Object = Vogoness;
```

Overriding the className property

Before looking at how to create components dynamically, we must pay attention to a third property, introduced by the UIObject class, which should be redefined when creating new component's class. The name of this third property is className.

This property does not influence the dynamic creation process; however, it is a best practice to assign it a proper value to make the new component class ready to be used by the component architecture.

Much later in the book, you will find out that this property plays a key role in the style functionality implemented by the architecture.

The className property stores a String value that uniquely identifies the component class. Usually such a value is the name of the component's class itself.

The UIObject class defines this property without assigning any value to it:

```
var className:String;
```

Our two components will define the className property, assigning to it the following values respectively:

```
var className:String = "Vogon";
```

and

```
var className:String = "Vogoness";
```

Now that you have learned about the three properties that must be overridden when creating a new component class, we can move on and examine the method provided by the UIObject class that allows us to create component instances dynamically.

The createClassObject method

The createClassObject is a method defined in the UIObject class to allow the dynamic creation of components that belong to the component architecture.

```
newComponentInstance =
➥ anExistingUIObject.createClassObject(
➥ className, instanceName, depth, initObject);
```

The method expects four parameters:

1. className: An object indicating the class of the component instance being created

2. instanceName: A string indicating the name of the component instance being created

3. depth: A number indicating at what depth the component instance must be created

4. initObject: An object providing values to initialize some of the properties of the component instance being created

The method returns a reference to the newly created component instance.

The createClassObject method uses both the symbolName and symbolOwner properties of the component being created; therefore such properties must be properly overridden in the component's class, otherwise the method will fail and the component instance will not be created.

In order to create instances of the Vogon and Vogoness components dynamically, we are going to extend their classes by integrating them with the component architecture.

Our components join the architecture

The components created earlier, although Flash components, do not belong to the component architecture since they do not inherit from the UIObject class and, therefore, they do not support nor benefit from the component framework.

The following example will show you the basic steps for integrating Flash components in the component architecture:

1. Copy the files vogon8.fla, Vogon.as, Vogoness.as, Colorable.as, and test.as from the last version of our components into a new folder.

2. Rename vogon8.fla as vogon9.fla to keep track of the new version of our main Flash document.

The createClassObject method comes with the apparent contradiction that you need a static instance of a component in order to create a dynamic one. In fact, we need only one static instance of a UIObject-based component on stage to be able to create any number of component instances dynamically.

By making this single static instance act as a container of the dynamic instances being created, we will also enjoy the benefits of good practice: encapsulating our newly created components into a container object. Let us create such a container component in a very quick and simple way:

3. While in the vogon9.fla document, create a new empty symbol (Insert ➤ New Symbol) of the movie clip kind.

4. Define the new symbol name as VContainer and its AS 2.0 class as mx.core.UIObject. Remember that the AS2.0 field must be defined in both the Linkage... and Component Definition... dialog boxes in order to associate the symbol with the class and create a component.

We pulled quite a stunt in the last step. Instead of creating a new class for our new component, we used the UIObject class straight away, avoiding creating a new class for our container just to access the createClassObject.

5. Close the edit window of the VContainer symbol, if open, by selecting the main stage of the document.

6. Drag the VContainer symbol from the Library panel onto the stage and define the instance name of the newly created instance as container. Also, position this instance at the x:200.0, y:200.0 location by using the Info panel.

7. Apart from the newly created instance, there are already three other instances on the stage, created in the previous examples (blueVogon, redVogon, and greenVogoness). Delete all of them: the purpose of this example is to create them dynamically via ActionScript.

We have prepared the stage for creating as many dynamic instances as we wish by using a static instance of the VContainer class named as container.

Our intent is to reproduce the functionality of the last example in the previous chapter without having any Vogon or Vogoness component instances on stage—we will create them dynamically instead.

You have learned previously in this chapter that our component classes must inherit from one of the core classes of the architecture and override certain properties in order to be able to use the functionality provided by the architecture, so let us modify the Vogon and Vogoness classes to integrate both of our components in the architecture.

The chain of inheritance that we defined before will make our work even easier. The following hierarchy shows the inheritance relationships among the classes at the moment:

```
MovieClip -> Colorable -> Vogon -> Vogoness
```

Making the Colorable class a subclass of the UIObject class will do most of the porting! Note also that the UIObject class is a subclass of the MovieClip class, therefore the new hierarchy will be fully compatible with the previous implementation that used some features of the MovieClip class. The new hierarchy will be

```
MovieClip -> UIObject -> Colorable -> Vogon -> Vogoness
```

8. Open the Colorable.as class file and replace its code with the following:

```
import mx.core.UIObject;

class Colorable extends UIObject {

    public function Colorable() {}

    public function get myColor():Number {
        var objColor:Color = new Color(this);
        return objColor.getRGB();
    }

    [Inspectable(name="My Color", type="Color",
➥ defaultValue="#00FF00")]
    public function set myColor(aColor:Number):Void {
        var objColor:Color = new Color(this);
        objColor.setRGB(aColor);
    }

}
```

We are almost there. We just need to override the UIObject properties previously introduced in both the Vogon and Vogoness classes:

9. Open the Vogoness.as file and implement the three properties symbolName, symbolOwner, and className, as shown in the following:

```
class Vogoness extends Vogon {

    private var txtPoetry:TextField;

    static var symbolName:String = "Vogoness Component";
    static var symbolOwner:Object = Vogoness;
```

```
    var className:String = "Vogoness";

    public function Vogoness() {}

    public function readPoem():Void {
        createTextField("txtPoetry", getNextHighestDepth(),
➡ 0, 100, 250, 100);
        txtPoetry.multiline = true;
        txtPoetry.wordWrap = true;
        txtPoetry.text = this.myPoem;
        var tf:TextFormat = new TextFormat();
        tf.align = "right";
        txtPoetry.setTextFormat(tf);
    }

}
```

The `className` property is not required by the `createClassObject` method, but we are implementing it for the sake of completeness.

10. Similarly to the previous step, you must now implement the three properties for the Vogon class by adding the following code to the `Vogon.as` file:

```
static var symbolName:String = "Vogon Component";
static var symbolOwner:Object = Vogon;
var className:String = "Vogon";
```

The values assigned to such variables have been redefined to specify the Vogon component.

We did it! We implemented the minimal requirements needed to port both of our components into the component architecture, and we can now start creating their instances dynamically.

11. Open the `test.as` file and add the following three lines at the very top of the file, while the rest of the file remains unchanged:

```
var blueVogon = container.createClassObject(Vogon,
➡ "blueVogon", 1, {_x:0, _y:0, myColor:0x0000ff});
var redVogon = container.createClassObject(Vogon,
➡ "redVogon", 2, {_x:150, _y:0, myColor:0xff0000});
var greenVogoness = container.createClassObject(Vogoness,
➡ "greenVogoness", 3, {_x:300, _y:0});
```

That's all we need to create our components dynamically. Now all that remains is to test our new code. When testing the movie of this example, you should not notice any difference with the outcome of the previous example (see Figure 2-3).

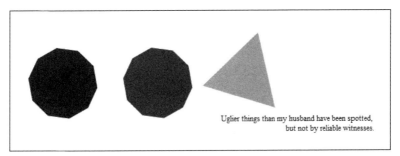

Uglier things than my husband have been spotted,
but not by reliable witnesses.

Figure 2-3. Instances are created dynamically now.

- There will still be three shapes in the SWF window. As in the previous example, two of them are instances of the Vogon component, while the third one is an instance of the Vogoness component.
- Inheritance and polymorphism will still be working as demonstrated by the presence of the poems (two in the Output window, a third one in the SWF window, just underneath the instance of the Vogoness component).

But this time the three component instances are not present on the stage of the Flash document. Instead, they have been created dynamically using ActionScript, but they are still perfectly compatible with any static counterparts created at design time.

It is also worth noting that the myColor property, implemented by our Colorable class, is now set at runtime by including its value in the initialization object passed to the createClassObject method.

As well as for myColor, we can define programmatically the position of the component instances at creation time by setting the _x and _y properties inherited from the MovieClip class. And, by using the same initialization object, we could define additional properties of the instances. This greatly empowers the developer and requires very little coding effort thanks to the many layers of logic already implemented by the component architecture.

As shown by this latest example, your knowledge of the architecture must not be limited to the methods and properties that are available, but must also include the features of the architecture that you should override to adapt their behavior to the requirements of the application, or component, that you are developing.

The features that you can override to exploit the architecture's functionality are not only properties, as in the case we already saw, but also methods.

To override a method means that you provide your own implementation of the function associated with it. It is time to learn why you may need to do so.

Inside the process of building a component instance

Essentially, every method in the component architecture falls into one of three kinds:

1. A concrete method implementing a fundamental feature of the architecture that, most probably, you will never need to override (like `createClassObject`, which allows you to create component instances dynamically).

2. A concrete method that provides a basic implementation of a certain functionality that you may wish to override to adapt it to your requirements (like the `size` method that we are going to examine in a short while).

3. A placeholder method with an empty implementation that is invoked by some algorithm that exploits polymorphism. You usually end up overriding this kind of method on a per-need basis in order to influence some functionality provided by the component framework, as in the case of the init method that we are going to examine next.

Whether to override a method or not is a matter of judgment and always depends on the requirements that you have at hand.

This book will help you by providing the knowledge of what methods you may need to override, starting with those involved during the process of building a new component instance.

The `UIObject` class defines the process of building a component instance. For the sake of simplicity, such a process can be summarized in three fundamental steps:

1. Initialize the component specific attributes.

2. Create the component's children.

3. Draw the component instance.

While this sequence is the same for every component, components must provide an implementation of each step whenever it is necessary.

By examining each step in greater detail, we will find certain methods that we may need to override when implementing a new component or modifying the behavior of an existing one to fulfill our requirements.

Step 1: Initialization

The first step in the process of building a new component instance executes the init method.

The following example shows the basic template for implementing such a method:

```
function init():Void {
➥ super.init();
         // whatever...
}
```

The example indicates that the implementation of the init method is usually divided into two parts:

1. Invocation of the base class method to initialize the inherited features

2. Further code to initialize component-specific features

It is a good practice, when creating a new component, to implement the init method, even when there are no component-specific features to be initialized.

We can now move our attention to the second step of the process of building a component instance: creating its children.

Step 2: Creating the children

The process of dynamic creation can work in a cascade when a component is made of subcomponents: in this case, in fact, each subcomponent must be created dynamically as well. Complex components are made of various subcomponents that, in turn, can be components as well. The term "children" generally indicates subcomponents that are components and subcomponents that are just movie clips created dynamically via the linkage identifier associated with their symbols.

Simple components usually don't have any subcomponents. However, if a component does have subcomponents, they should be created dynamically by overriding the createChildren method:

```
function createChildren(Void):Void {
        // create the component's children here
}
```

The framework of the component architecture invokes the createdChildren method after the init method, therefore creating the children whenever needed.

After initializing a component instance and creating its children (if any), only one more step remains before the process of building a component instance is complete: drawing the instance.

Step 3: Drawing the component instance

Quite naturally, the UIObject class assigns the responsibility of drawing a component instance to the following method:

```
function draw(Void):Void {
}
```

The UIObject class does not provide a default implementation for this method and, therefore, it is up to the component developer to provide one whenever needed.

The UIObject class provides a default implementation of the size method that is invoked when the size of a component instance is changed via setSize. However, the default implementation of the size method simply resizes the movie clip of the component instance by changing its width and height:

```
function size(Void):Void {
        width = __width;
        _height = __height;
}
```

If you are implementing a new component that has a particular layout including various subobjects, you may well like to take control over the following:

- How the layout is defined initially, by implementing the `draw` method
- How the layout will look after resizing, by implementing the `size` method

Note that this information is quite relevant even if you are not developing new components but just interested in using existing ones. In fact, each of the components provided with the component architecture implements its own `draw` method, and most of them override the `size` method as well.

When examining how those methods are implemented by the existing components, you should also be aware of another important aspect of the drawing process: **invalidation**. Invalidation suggests that the `draw` method should never be invoked directly when a component view must be refreshed. Instead of calling the `draw` method, the framework code, and your own code, should call the `invalidate` method.

The `invalidate` method annotates that the component view is no longer updated (valid) and, therefore, it must be refreshed.

As you may know, the Flash rendering system updates a movie only once per frame. Because of that, multiple calls to the `draw` method within the same frame would be ineffective. Furthermore, a large number of such calls may well affect the performance severely, causing flickering or even delays.

By using the invalidation approach, the architecture is able to redraw the invalidated component instances only once per frame, optimizing the performance and avoiding redundant calls!

Refining our sample components

Earlier in this chapter we ported both of our components (Vogon and Vogoness) into the component architecture by defining the `Colorable` class as a subclass of `UIObject`. This move created the following inheritance chain:

        UIObject -> Colorable -> Vogon -> Vogoness

Inheritance has ensured that both of our components now belong to the architecture and share the features made available by the component framework.

You have now learned a lot about working with components and should understand that inheritance alone is not a measure of how well a component is integrated within the architecture. By refining the implementation of our components to raise their level of integration within the architecture, we will see how applying the previous guidelines produces more robust code that is easier to maintain.

We will do this like so:

1. Copy the files `vogon9.fla`, `Vogon.as`, `Vogoness.as`, `Colorable.as`, and `test.as` from the last version of our components into a new folder.
2. Rename `vogon9.fla` as `vogon10.fla` to keep track of the new version of our main Flash document.

We are not going to change the behavior of our components. In fact, we want to keep the same behavior while raising the integration level of both components by applying what you have just learned. This objective will involve changes to the existing implementations of the Vogon and Vogoness classes.

3. Open the Vogon.as file and replace the existing code with the following:

```
import mx.events.UIEventDispatcher;

class Vogon extends Colorable {

    private var pBuffer:String;

    static var symbolName:String = "Vogon Component";
    static var symbolOwner:Object = Vogon;
    var className:String = "Vogon";

    function Vogon() {
        UIEventDispatcher.initialize(this);
    }

    public function dispatchEvent(eventObject:Object) {};
    public function addEventListener(event:String,
➡ listener:Object) {};
    public function removeEventListener(event:String,
➡ listener:Object) {};

    function init(Void):Void{
        super.init();
        pBuffer = "<No poem defined>";
    }

    function draw(Void):Void {
        trace(myPoem);
    }

    public function get myPoem():String {
        return pBuffer;
    }

    public function set myPoem(aPoem:String):Void {
        pBuffer = aPoem;
        var eventObject:Object = {target:this, type:'onNewPoem'};
        eventObject.poetry = pBuffer;
        dispatchEvent(eventObject);
    }
```

```
    public function onNewPoem(eventObject:Object):Void {
        trace("I am " + this. _name);
        trace("and I just received a new poem from " +
➥ eventObject.target. _name);
        trace('"' + eventObject.poetry + '"');
    }
}
```

4. Open the Vogoness.as file and replace the existing code with the following:

```
class Vogoness extends Vogon {

    private var txtPoetry:TextField;

    static var symbolName:String = "Vogoness Component";
    static var symbolOwner:Object = Vogoness;
    var className:String = "Vogoness";

    public function Vogoness() {}

    function init(Void):Void{
        super.init();
    }

    function createChildren(Void):Void {
        createTextField("txtPoetry", getNextHighestDepth(),
➥ 0, 100, 250, 100);
        txtPoetry.multiline = true;
        txtPoetry.wordWrap = true;
        var tf:TextFormat = new TextFormat();
        tf.align = "right";
        txtPoetry.setTextFormat(tf);
    }

    function draw(Void):Void {
        txtPoetry.text = this.myPoem;
    }

}
```

5. Open the test.as file and remove all the lines after the definition of the myPoem properties. The final code should look like this:

```
var blueVogon = container.createClassObject(Vogon,
➥ "blueVogon", 1, {_x:0, _y:0, myColor:0x0000ff});
var redVogon = container.createClassObject(Vogon,
➥ "redVogon", 2, {_x:150, _y:0, myColor:0xff0000});
var greenVogoness = container.createClassObject(Vogoness,
➥ "greenVogoness", 3, {_x:300, _y:0});
```

```
greenVogoness.myPoem = "Uglier things than my husband have been
spotted, but not by reliable witnesses.";
redVogon.myPoem = "The best way to get a drink out
➡ of blueVogon is to stick your finger down his throat.";
blueVogon.myPoem = "redVogon is not above corruption in the same way
➡ that the sea is not above the clouds.";
```

If you save the three modified ActionScript files and test the movie, you will notice no differences from the previous behavior, regardless of the fact that we have stripped away a lot of code from the `test.as` file.

You may find it quite surprising that the poems are still displayed in the Output window and in the movie itself as they were before, since the code removed from the `test.as` file was invoking the readPoem methods.

The explanation, of course, is in the code that we added to our component classes. Both the Vogon and Vogoness classes do not provide a readPoem method anymore. To display a poem was an intended visual behavior of the corresponding components and, therefore, that behavior has been encapsulated into their draw methods:

```
// the Vogon way of reading a poem
function draw(Void):Void {
        trace(myPoem);
}
```

```
// the Vogoness way of reading a poem
function draw(Void):Void {
        txtPoetry.text = this.myPoem;
}
```

In our case, the integration step of implementing a draw method shows quite clearly what a time-saver the component framework can be.

In fact, the draw method is invoked by the framework itself because each component instance is invalidated when created. That is the reason why we do not need those lines of code in the `test.as` file anymore (nor the readPoem method for that matter). Basically, it would be correct to say that the old readPoem methods have been replaced by the new draw methods.

You may have also noticed that the draw method of the Vogoness class contains far less code than its old readPoem method:

```
// the Vogoness readPoem method as it was
public function readPoem():Void {
        createTextField("txtPoetry", getNextHighestDepth(),
➡ 0, 100, 250, 100);
        txtPoetry.multiline = true;
        txtPoetry.wordWrap = true;
        txtPoetry.text = this.myPoem;
        var tf:TextFormat = new TextFormat();
        tf.align = "right";
```

A component that you want to benefit from the focus management features should override a couple of event handlers and a drawing function:

```
function onSetFocus(oldFocus:Object):Void {
        super.onSetFocus(oldFocus);
        // your component's specific code goes here
}

function onKillFocus(newFocus:Object):Void {
        super.onKillFocus(newFocus);
        // your component's specific code goes here
}

function drawFocus(isFocused:Boolean):Void {
        // your component's specific code goes here
}
```

The two event handlers onSetFocus and onKillFocus are invoked whenever a component instance gets or loses the focus, respectively. Both functions expect a single object parameter that is a reference to the component instance that lost the focus (oldFocus) or is going to get it (newFocus).

The drawFocus function is invoked whenever a component instance receives or loses the focus, and it is responsible for visually representing the component's state. This function should be aware of styles and themes, as you will further discover later on in this book.

Keyboard management and accessibility are the main reasons why UIComponent is so frequently chosen as the base class of new components: almost every GUI component requires such functionalities.

Other features of the UIComponent

The UIComponent also provides another couple of features:

1. The ability to enable/disable a component instance
2. Independence from the UIObject resizing implementation

The first feature is implemented by the setEnabled method:

```
// to enable a component instance
aComponentInstance.setEnabled(true);

// to disable a component instance
aComponentInstance.setEnabled(false);
```

The overriding of the size method with a function that does nothing may look weird at first, but the point is that the size method defined in the UIObject resizes a component instance by modifying its scale factor. As a result of this, every subobject within the component will be resized accordingly. This may not be the proper thing to do in a variety of cases, for example, if the size of certain subobjects must remain constant even when the component instance is resized.

By overriding the size method with an empty function, the UIComponent class reassigns the responsibility of implementing the size method to its subclasses.

In the end, when your component's class inherits from UIComponent, you must remember to override the size method to resize your component instances in accordance with their intended behavior.

The View class

The View class captures some visual aspects of a component that were not considered yet by its base classes (UIObject and UIComponent).

A component's class should be based on the View class if it has at least one of the following two features:

1. A well-defined border, which surrounds the layout of the component instances and usually emphasizes the visual status of a component instance when it gets or loses the keyboard focus

2. A children-based layout, in which the children are movie clips created to host instances of symbols, subcomponents, or externally loaded content

Basically, if your component does not have a border and its layout does not include any child object, then you should not consider the View class, instead picking either the UIObject or UIComponent class as the base class.

If your component has a border that plays an active role in the component's behavior, then you should definitely consider inheriting the related skinning and stylizing logic implemented by the View class. In fact, the View class implements the component's border as part of component architecture, enabling the definition of skins and styles for the border itself.

Simply inheriting from the View class is all the programming that is required to provide your component with a border that is fully integrated in the component framework. Of course, you will have to define your border's skins and styles in a theme or individually using techniques that are common to all the components—which will be explained in Chapter 9.

Apart from implementing the component's border logic, the View class is really helpful when dealing with components that have child objects in their layout.

By now, you should get used to how the architecture provides a fair number of features: it defines the way things must be done and it implements the most generic aspects of it. It is up to the component developer to provide the implementation of those features that are component specific. The View class is no different from the other base classes, and it expects the component developer to provide the implementation of the doLayout method:

```
function doLayout(Void):Void {
    // your component's specific code goes here
        hasBeenLayedOut = true;
}
```

Your doLayout implementation is supposed to define the position, size, and every other aspect of your component's children. Note that when doLayout is eventually called, the component's children will already exist, having been created by your implementation of the createChildren method that we discussed earlier in this chapter.

When implementing the createChildren method, you can use the createChild method provided by the View class instead of the createClassObject method:

```
function createChild(className, instanceName:String,
➥ initProps:Object):MovieClip {
```

The createChild method is a slightly more powerful way of creating subobjects dynamically than the createClassObject method because it allows you to load an external resource as a child via the className parameter. In addition to accepting the same values as in the createClassObject, the className parameter of the createChild method can also be assigned a local path or an URL.

In some cases, you may need to initialize the state of your component before the execution of the doLayout method. The best way to perform such initialization is by overriding the default implementation of the initLayout method, provided by the View class, as in the following example:

```
function initLayout():Void {
    // your component's specific code goes here
        super.initLayout();
}
```

The ScrollView class

The ScrollView class adds another layer of logic on top of the View class that turns out to be particularly useful whenever a component's content must be scrolled.

Components based upon ScrollView are the most complex ones not only because they include all of the four levels of logic implemented in the component framework (UIObject, UIComponent, View, and ScrollView) but also because the last functionality added, scrolling, is by far the most complicated.

To analyze the implementation of the scrolling mechanism goes beyond the scope of this book and would steal precious time that we could devote to our main objective of learning how to customize existing components. The architecture provides three components (ScrollPane, TextArea, and Window) that cover any scrolling requirement you may need to implement; therefore, we don't need to go into details of how it is actually implemented.

Of course, such components do have scrollbars that you may wish to customize both in appearance, with skins and styles, or in the way they scroll (for example, the rate of scroll). See Chapter 21 for a detailed description of the techniques required to customize this aspect of any component that supports scrolling.

An ActionScript template for new components

Even though the main focus of this book is on using and customizing the components that are already built in the architecture, developers of component-based applications could not achieve a high level of proficiency without being aware of how components are created.

The first two chapters of this book have been dedicated to introducing the most essential concepts of component design in the scope of the component architecture.

Before moving on, we will define a sort of template, or skeleton, that can be reused to add a new component to the architecture or, quite simply, to remind us of the key points of the component framework that we discussed so far.

Create a ComponentSkeleton.as file and add the following code into it:

```
import mx.events.UIEventDispatcher;
// add one of the following depending on the base class you choose:
// import mx.core.UIObject
// import mx.core.UIComponent
// import mx.core.View
// import mx.core.ScrollView

// 1. redefine both the class name and the filename accordingly
// 2. change inheritance to extend from UIComponent
//    or View or ScrollView, as appropriate for the new component
class ComponentSkeleton extends UIObject {

    // Redefine assigning the linkage identifier
    // of the actual component
    static var symbolName:String = "Component Skeleton";
    // Redefine assigning the fully qualified class name
    // of the component
    static var symbolOwner:Object = ComponentSkeleton;
    // Redefine assigning the name of the actual component
    var className:String = "Component Skeleton";

    // CONSTRUCTOR - Rename it accordingly
    function ComponentSkeleton() {
        mx.events.UIEventDispatcher.initialize(this);
    }

    // Required if you need to implement custom events
    // triggered by your component
    public function dispatchEvent(eventObject:Object) {};
    public function addEventListener(event:String, listener:Object) {};
    public function removeEventListener(event:String,
  ➥ listener:Object){};

    // get-set functions of a generic property to modify and reuse
    public function get genericProperty():Number {
        // retrieve the property value here
        // and return it
        return 1;
    }
    [Inspectable(name="Generic Property", type="Number",
  ➥ defaultValue="0")]
    public function set genericProperty(aValue:Number):Void {
        // store the property value here
    }
```

```
function init(Void):Void{
    super.init();
    // add your component instance initialization code here
}

function createChildren(Void):Void {
    // add the code to create your component children here
}


function draw(Void):Void {
    // add your component's drawing code here
}

// ***
// if you inherit from UIObject you can remove the following
// ***

function onSetFocus(oldFocus:Object):Void {
    super.onSetFocus(oldFocus);
    // add the code to be executed when the component
    // receive the focus
}

function onKillFocus(newFocus:Object):Void {
    super.onKillFocus(newFocus);
    // add the code to be executed when the component
    // loses the focus
}

function drawFocus(isFocused:Boolean):Void {
    // add the code to draw the current status of the component
}

function size():Void {
    // add the code to handle resizing without scaling
}

// ***
// if you inherit from UIComponent you can remove the following
// ***

function initLayout():Void {
    // add initialization code to be executed before doLayout()
    super.initLayout();
}
```

```
        function doLayout(Void):Void {
            // draw the component layout, including its children
            hasBeenLayedOut = true;
        }

    }
```

The component skeleton has been thoroughly commented, so you can follow along with the code easily and delete what isn't needed for any particular instance of component creation. The process for using the skeleton is outlined here:

1. Rename the file with the actual class name of your component.

2. Remove the comment from the import related to the base class chosen for your component.

3. Redefine the class name and its related variables accordingly.

4. Rename the constructor accordingly.

5. Reuse and customize the genericProperty for each new property needed (most likely you will also need to add variables to store/retrieve the properties' values).

6. Add the initialization code to the init method, if needed.

7. Add the children creation code, if any, to the createChildren method.

8. Implement the draw method, if necessary.

9. If your class inherits from UIObject, you can strip away everything else after the draw method. Otherwise, implement the methods inherited from the UIComponent class accordingly.

10. If your class inherits from UIComponent, you can strip away everything else after the size method. Otherwise, implement the methods inherited from the View class accordingly.

The Vogon and Vogoness components we created in Chapter 1 show perfect examples of how to use the component skeleton.

Summary

In this chapter, you have completed your knowledge of creating a Flash component by learning how to integrate it with the framework provided by the component architecture.

You should have started to appreciate how much time you can save by inheriting features that are already implemented or, at least, already well defined in the framework. Those features are made available by a number of core components that can be used as base classes whenever creating a new component.

The next chapter will introduce the components that are included in the architecture, grouping them into functional categories.

Chapter 3

EXPLORING THE UI COMPONENTS

*Future Perfect: A term which has been abandoned
since it was discovered not to be.*

Douglas Adams

*If the only tool you have is a hammer,
you treat everything like a nail.*

Abraham Maslow

Component frameworks usually encompass thousands of lines of code, numerous classes grouped in packages (or subsystems), various patterns, and many concepts. The Flash Component Architecture is no exception, and its size is the main obstacle in learning how to use it proficiently in a reasonable amount of time.

But the sheer magnitude of a component framework is not the only complication that developers have to face when attempting to reuse its code. Any software can be expected to have a certain number of bugs, and large developments such as component architectures are often plagued with a high number of quirks.

The component architecture again is no exception, but it is still a powerful tool for developing web applications, even if it is far from being perfect. Knowing its limits without having to discover them at the expense of lengthy trials is a definite advantage, and that's (in part) what this book is here to help you with!

In the last chapter, I briefly touched upon the component framework defined by the architecture and then integrated some sample components into it. Now we are going to examine the rich collection of components provided with the built-in component architecture, based on that same component framework; this chapter will also group the components by functional similarity, and you will begin to learn how to use them.

I will also introduce you to the concept of Reusability Cards, an abstract mechanism that represents a simple way of capturing the strengths and weaknesses of each feature in the component framework. By looking at the Reusability Card of a component (or a class) of the framework, you can quickly grasp how reusable that feature is, allowing you to plan how to use it most effectively.

> *The completed source code introduced in this chapter can be found in the package* src03.zip, *downloadable from this book's page at* www.friendsofed.com.

The Reusability Card

Although both activities are frequently compared metaphorically, playing with software components is not exactly the same thing as playing with Lego blocks.

- Lego blocks and component instances share a couple of significant similarities: both of them are designed with a limited number of "connecting points" (the connecting point of a component being its properties, methods, and events).
- In both cases, their instances are put together to build a more complex object: an application in the case of components.

However, to assemble component instances is rarely as simple as fitting together Lego blocks. The Lego blocks, in fact, have perfect interfaces that merge into each other seamlessly with no internal behavior. Ideally, software components would be as reliable as Lego blocks but, unfortunately, their essence is far more complex and less stable; due to its much simpler nature, a Lego block is far more reusable than a software component.

The goal of the Reusability Card is to capture a number of aspects that immediately communicate to the developer how reusable a component is.

In order to become an effective tool, the Reusability Card includes criteria common to all software components that clearly address what makes them reusable or not. As you can see in the example shown in Figure 3-1, the main criteria are as follows:

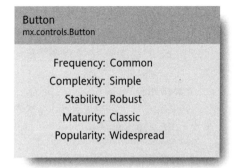

Button
mx.controls.Button

Frequency: Common
Complexity: Simple
Stability: Robust
Maturity: Classic
Popularity: Widespread

- Frequency (of use)
- Complexity
- Stability
- Maturity
- Popularity

Figure 3-1. The Button component, implemented by the class mx.controls.Button

The following sections explain the meaning of each of these criteria and the values that they can have in the approach described in this book.

Frequency (of use)

Frequency of use is the most intuitive among the criteria listed in the Reusability Card, and it is the place to start for developers who are deciding what to learn first.

It is a quantitative criterion that indicates how frequently a certain feature appears in applications based on the component architecture. Frequency is graded at three different levels:

- **Essential**: Indicates a feature that is arguably used by every component-based application
- **Common**: Indicates a feature that is used by the majority of the applications based on the component architecture
- **Rare**: Indicates a feature that is occasionally used by a component-based application

The main reason for the presence of this criterion is that, by looking at it, developers can better distribute their time when learning the component framework; it makes sense to start with the features that are essential first and then to move on to the less common ones, leaving the study of the rare ones to the end or when they are actually needed.

For example, in the Reusability Card associated with the mx.controls.Button class and the related Button component, you will find that frequency is defined as follows:

```
Frequency: Common
```

In fact, buttons are arguably not an essential feature (you can build a component-based application without using them), but they are frequently found in applications and, therefore, a grade of Rare for their frequency would have made no sense.

Complexity

Complexity of usage is a quantitative criterion that provides an estimate of how much additional code, or work, must be produced by developers employing a certain feature of the component architecture.

Complexity is graded with three different levels:

- **Plug and Play**: Indicates a component that does not require any coding. Most likely, it is sufficient to drop an instance of the component on stage to add the component services and functionalities to the application being developed. Unfortunately, this is a rare case.
- **Simple**: Indicates a component that requires a minimal amount of coding. This is the most common case and usually implies the definition of a few basic properties at runtime and/or the implementation of an event handler.
- **Heavy**: Indicates a component or class that can require more than a few lines of code due to the particular nature of its features. This is mainly the case with components participating in a complex interaction model and/or requiring some complex initialization.

This criterion gives developers an idea of the programming effort required when using a certain component or class available in the framework.

For example, in the Reusability Card associated with the `mx.controls.Button` class and the related Button component, you will find that complexity is defined as follows:

```
Complexity: Simple
```

There isn't much extra code needed when adding buttons to an application. However, developers must provide an event handler that will execute a specific action in response to the user clicking the button.

Stability

Stability is a qualitative criterion indicating the tendency of a particular feature to be error prone. Software programs are error free in our dreams only. Errors are so common that they have given rise to a specific programming mechanism (error handling) supported by many object-oriented languages, including ActionScript.

However, some programs are more stable than others: they generate errors less frequently and most of the time behave as expected.

Per the other criteria, we assess stability using three grades:

- **Defective**: Indicates that the component does not work and cannot be used for its intended purpose. In this case, developers are left with the choice of waiting for the next version of the framework or replacing the defective component with their own implementation.
- **Quirky**: Indicates a component that works, but in some cases its behavior can generate errors or differ from what is expected. The main difference from the defective case is given by the presence of a workaround that allows using the component proficiently.
- **Robust**: Indicates a component that behaves as expected most of the time, generating errors in exceptional cases only. The term "robust" was preferred to the idealistic "bug free" because software cannot really be 100 percent free of errors.

Stability is the most important criterion, and developers should regard it highly enough to completely avoid using defective features and use the quirky ones only when strictly necessary. Luckily, the component architecture is pretty stable even if there are quite a few quirky features; developers will be able to handle the quirky cases with patches and workarounds found throughout this book.

For example, in the Reusability Card associated with the `mx.controls.Button` class and the related Button component, you will find that stability is defined as follows:

    Stability: Robust

As you will see later in the book in Chapter 11, the implementation of this component is almost flawless.

Maturity

Maturity is another quantitative criterion and, although it may be confused with the previous one, maturity is not the same thing as stability. Maturity refers to the "age" of a certain feature within the component framework; the fact that a certain feature is old indicates that it was already implemented in previous versions of the architecture.

A mature feature is usually stable, but not necessarily so, if, for instance, new bugs have been introduced in its latest version. Also, a brand-new feature may have gone through a lot of testing before its release and, therefore, be stable since its first appearance. However, most of the time software that has had many versions released is better than "younger" software because its features have had more time to evolve and stabilize.

Following the same approach chosen for the other criteria, we rate maturity in three grades:

- **Novelty**: A feature is considered a novelty if it appears in the component architecture for the first time, indicating that it was not present in the previous version of the component framework.

- **Pre-existing**: A pre-existing feature refers to functionality already present in the previous version of the component architecture.

- **Classic**: When associated with a feature, the grade Classic indicates not only that the feature existed in the previous version of the component architecture, but also that it was one of its cornerstones.

Maturity is a significant criterion that offers a quick glimpse into the history of a particular feature in the component framework while hinting at its chances to survive in future versions of the architecture. For example, in the Reusability Card associated with the `mx.controls.Button` class and the related Button component, you will find that maturity is defined as follows:

    Maturity: Classic

It's not really possible to imagine a component-based architecture for user interfaces without including a Button component, is it?

Popularity

Popularity is qualitative criterion measuring the diffusion of a certain feature across different component architectures.

Although this book focuses solely on the component architecture, developers are probably aware of the existence of many other object-oriented programming languages (Java, C++, etc.) and of various component frameworks developed on top of those technologies.

This criterion differentiates among three different degrees of popularity:

- **Innovation**: Due to the evolutionary nature of complex system such as component architectures, very rarely is a feature innovative. However, in our approach, we will mark a feature as an Innovation if such functionality is uncommon in component frameworks.

- **Specific**: There is a subtle difference between the use of Specific and Innovation to define the popularity of a certain feature. As in the previous case, Specific indicates that a particular functionality is uncommon but with a difference: the reason for being rare is due to the specific object model more than to an innovative approach. For example, the movie clip entity is a cornerstone of the Flash object model, but such an object is not found in other object models because it is specific to this technology.

- **Widespread**: This attribute refers to features that are common among component frameworks and that can be found in almost any component architecture. A widespread function is basically a sort of "wheel" reinvented in the scope of a specific architecture, be it ActionScript, Java, C++, etc.

For example, in the Reusability Card associated with the `mx.controls.Button` class and the related Button component, you will find that popularity is defined as follows:

```
Popularity: Widespread
```

Even the inexperienced developer will recognize that buttons are a widespread feature among different component frameworks: they are present in almost any Windows, Mac, or Linux GUI-driven application, regardless of the technology used to develop them.

Multitier applications

Modern applications are based on a multitier model that assigns to each tier a well-defined role.

At its simplest, the multitiered model is made of three different tiers:

- The **user interface tier**, dedicated to the interaction between the users and the software application.

- The **business logic tier**, implementing the business rules and any other business-related logic defining the software application.

- The **data tier**, providing a means for storing information used by the application, usually in a database.

The component architecture has been designed to specifically address one of these tiers—the user interface tier. In fact, the class at the root of the whole architecture, UIObject, owes its name to the definition of **U**ser **I**nterface object.

Although ActionScript can also be used to contribute to the implementation of the business logic and data tiers, in this book we will focus primarily on the user interface tier, since it captures the truest nature of the component architecture: designing and implementing rich user interfaces.

UI components provided with Flash

The component architecture provides a large set of components that can be used for designing and implementing very effective user interfaces as Flash movies. Such user interfaces may represent the front end of powerful web applications that can be accessed utilizing a browser such as Firefox or Microsoft Internet Explorer.

The following categories are defined in a broad functional sense to provide a means for grouping components that are related to each other by shared functionality and/or a common purpose:

- **Button**: Button components are characterized by a simple user interaction that is limited to the click of a button over the component's area.
- **Text**: Text components share the characteristic of managing text content, allowing the user to edit or just display it.
- **Cell structured**: The most complex UI components are characterized by the presence of a cell structure. Such structures can significantly differ—for example, lists, grids, and even tree-like structures all fall under this category. However, what they all have in common is that they are built by replicating a similar conceptual unit: the cell.
- **Container**: Container components provide an area that can be populated by developers with some kind of content. Such content can be loaded externally and/or include child components.
- **Peculiar**: This is basically a miscellaneous category for components that don't fit comfortably in another category.

The following sections introduce the UI components available in the component architecture, grouped by their functional category and "rated" with a Reusability Card. Thanks to short and intuitive descriptions, you should be able to quickly grasp the purpose of each component and refer to the third part of this book for a detailed description of how to use and customize each of them.

Button components

The architecture's component set includes three different kinds of buttons:

- Button
- CheckBox
- RadioButton

Button component

The Button component, the Reusability Card for which was shown at the beginning of the chapter in Figure 3-1, provides the most classic user interface element: a button that can be clicked by the user to trigger a certain action.

Figure 3-2 shows an instance of the Button component.

Figure 3-2. Button example

The use and customization of this component are detailed in Chapter 11.

CheckBox component

The CheckBox component (shown in Figure 3-3) provides a button that changes its checked/unchecked state when clicked. This type of button is typically utilized to implement the selection of a yes/no option.

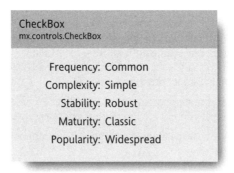

Figure 3-3. The CheckBox component, implemented by the class mx.controls.CheckBox

Figure 3-4 shows a couple of instances of the CheckBox component.

Figure 3-4. CheckBox example

The use and customization of this component are detailed in Chapter 12.

RadioButton component

The RadioButton component (shown in Figure 3-5) is a button that, when clicked, always changes its state to selected while unselecting any other RadioButton instances belonging to its same group.

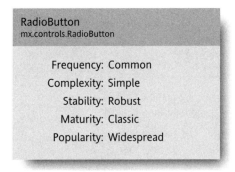

Figure 3-5. The RadioButton component, implemented by the class mx.controls.RadioButton

You can see an example of the RadioButton in Figure 3-6. Because of its nature, a RadioButton is never used in isolation: two or more RadioButton instances are usually grouped to implement a mutually exclusive choice. The CheckBox component is better suited for a single choice such as yes/no.

Figure 3-6. RadioButton example

The use and customization of this component are detailed in Chapter 12.

Text components

The architecture provides three different components that can satisfy almost any development need that may arise when handling text content:

- Label
- TextInput
- TextArea

Label component

The Label component (shown in Figure 3-7) is the simplest among all the UI components. It can handle single-line or multiline text content that cannot be altered by the user interaction. However, the text content of a label can be defined at runtime programmatically or, of course, at design time. You can see an example of the Label component in Figure 3-8.

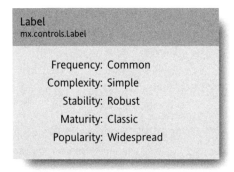

Figure 3-7. The Label component, implemented by the class mx.controls.Label

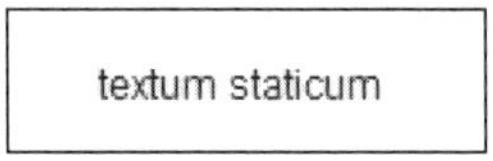

textum staticum

Figure 3-8. Label example

The use and customization of this component are detailed in Chapter 18.

TextInput component

The TextInput component (shown in Figure 3-9) implements a text field that can be added to user interfaces for retrieving a single line of text content. Unlike the other two components in the Text category, the TextInput component does not support the HTML format for the text content. Figure 3-10 shows you an example of the TextInput component.

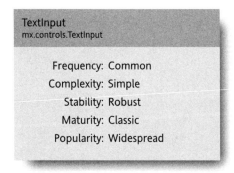

Figure 3-9. The TextInput component, implemented by the class mx.controls.TextInput

Editable line of text

Figure 3-10. TextInput example

The use and customization of this component are detailed in Chapter 18.

TextArea component

The TextArea component (shown in Figure 3-11) implements a text field that can be added to user interfaces for retrieving multiline text content. For an example of the TextArea component, see Figure 3-12.

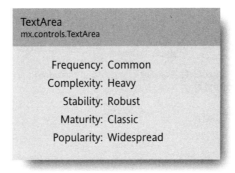

TextArea
mx.controls.TextArea

Frequency: Common
Complexity: Heavy
Stability: Robust
Maturity: Classic
Popularity: Widespread

Figure 3-11. The TextArea component, implemented by the class mx.controls.TextArea

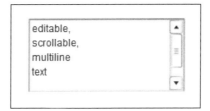

editable,
scrollable,
multiline
text

Figure 3-12. TextArea example

The use and customization of this component are detailed in Chapter 18.

Cell-structured components

The architecture provides four different components that can be used to arrange content in a cell-based structure:

- List
- ComboBox
- DataGrid
- Tree

List component

The List component (shown in Figure 3-13) is the simplest among the cell-structured components, and it provides a visual interface to a list of objects that, by default, are text objects. You can see an example of the List component in Figure 3-14.

Figure 3-13. The List component, implemented by the class mx.controls.List

Figure 3-14. List example

The use and customization of this component are detailed in Chapter 13.

ComboBox component

The ComboBox component (shown in Figure 3-15) combines a List object with a TextInput object to enhance the behavior of the List component by adding a single editable text field and implementing the list as a drop-down list, displayed only after clicking in the input area and hidden after selecting an item in the list or after clicking the input area again. You can see an example of the ComboBox element in Figure 3-16.

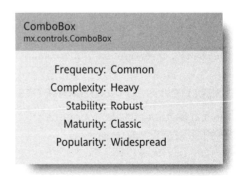

Figure 3-15. The ComboBox component, implemented by the class mx.controls.ComboBox

Figure 3-16. ComboBox example

The use and customization of this component are detailed in Chapter 13.

DataGrid component

The DataGrid component (shown in Figure 3-17) is arguably the most complex among the cell-structured components. As the name suggests, the DataGrid component arranges its objects, which by default are text objects, in a grid defined by rows and columns.

This component usually implements tables and, as with any other cell-structured component, it implements the scrolling of its contents. You can see an example in Figure 3-18.

Figure 3-17. The DataGrid component, implemented by the class mx.controls.DataGrid

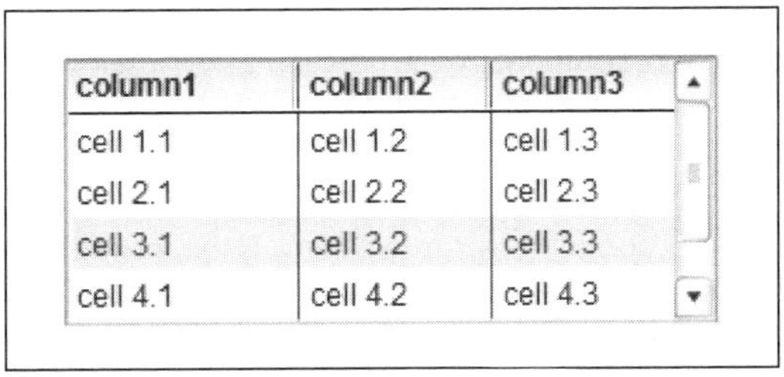

column1	column2	column3	
cell 1.1	cell 1.2	cell 1.3	
cell 2.1	cell 2.2	cell 2.3	
cell 3.1	cell 3.2	cell 3.3	
cell 4.1	cell 4.2	cell 4.3	

Figure 3-18. DataGrid example

The use and customization of this component are detailed in Chapter 13.

Tree component

The Tree component (shown in Figure 3-19) challenges the DataGrid component for the top spot among the most complex UI components. The Tree component implements a tree-like structure where cells are nested in branches. This component enables you to implement hierarchical and interactive content. You can see an example of the Tree component in Figure 3-20.

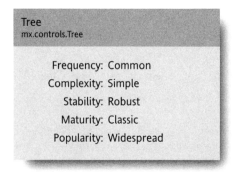

Figure 3-19. The Tree component implemented by the class mx.controls.Tree

Figure 3-20. Tree example

The use and customization of this component are detailed in Chapter 19.

Container components

Container components are not "complete" on their own. They are meant to act as hosts for various types of content that may also include other component instances. Containers define a controlled area where such content will be displayed.

The architecture provides four different container components:

- ScrollPane
- Loader
- Window
- Accordion

ScrollPane component

The ScrollPane component (shown in Figure 3-21) can display scrollable content that can be internal to the Flash document or loaded from an external source. Internal content must be encapsulated in a movie clip that has a linkage identifier, while external content can be a JPG image or another Flash movie (SWF). External content can reside locally or on the Internet. You can see an example of the ScrollPane component in Figure 3-22.

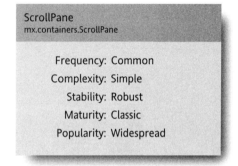

ScrollPane
mx.containers.ScrollPane

Frequency: Common
Complexity: Simple
Stability: Robust
Maturity: Classic
Popularity: Widespread

Figure 3-21. The ScrollPane component, implemented by the class mx.containers.ScrollPane

Figure 3-22. ScrollPane example

The use and customization of this component are detailed in Chapter 15.

Loader component

The Loader component (shown in Figure 3-23) can display external content stored as a JPEG file or a Flash movie (SWF). Unlike the ScrollPane component, such content is not scrollable, but it is scaled to fit into the component's size or, alternatively, it is the container's area to be resized in order to accommodate the original size of the content. You can see an example of the Loader component in Figure 3-24.

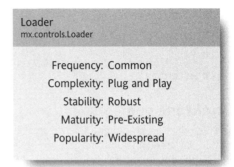

Loader
mx.controls.Loader

Frequency: Common
Complexity: Plug and Play
Stability: Robust
Maturity: Pre-Existing
Popularity: Widespread

Figure 3-23. The Loader component, implemented by the class mx.controls.Loader

Figure 3-24. Loader example

The use and customization of this component are detailed in Chapter 15.

Window component

The Window component (shown in Figure 3-25) can display internal and external content in the same formats displayed by the ScrollPane component. Unlike the ScrollPane component, the Window component does not implement any scrolling functionality.

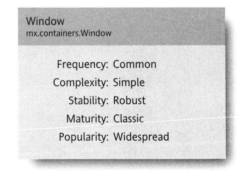

Window
mx.containers.Window

Frequency: Common
Complexity: Simple
Stability: Robust
Maturity: Classic
Popularity: Widespread

Figure 3-25. The Window component, implemented by the class mx.containers.Window

Window instances can be dragged by the user and moved around on the stage; the instances are usually created dynamically with the help of the PopUpManager (see Chapter 4 for further details). Figure 3-26 shows an example of the Window component.

The use and customization of this component are detailed in Chapter 20.

Accordion component

The Accordion component (shown in Figure 3-27) is arguably the most complex of the containers. Unlike the other components in the same category, the Accordion component can manage more than one content area at the same time.

Figure 3-26.
Window example

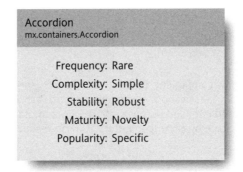

Figure 3-27. The Accordion component, implemented by the class mx.containers.Accordion

The Accordion component shows one area at a time while providing headers that the user can click to display the other areas. The number of areas, as well as the labels of their headers, can be defined both at design time and at runtime.

The Accordion's areas can display internal content only, although its areas may well contain an instance of the ScrollPane component, which will be able to load external content eventually.

Following an official recommendation, each content area should host an object that inherits from the View class or, at least, from the UIObject class. However, the current version of the Accordion works pretty well even with symbols that have a linkage identifier, with the sole exception of the tabbing order, which requires at least a View class to be supported (see Figure 3-28).

The use and customization of this component are detailed in Chapter 10.

Figure 3-28.
Accordion example

Peculiar components

In the last category, Peculiar, I include all the components that, because of their particular features, do not fit well in any of the previous categories.

These remaining components are as follows:

- Alert
- DateChooser
- DateField
- Menu
- MenuBar
- NumericStepper
- ProgressBar
- UIScrollBar

Alert component

Although it extends the Window component, the Alert component (shown in Figure 3-29) is not considered a true container in our classification. This component, in fact, is a simplified and specialized version of a Window: its sole and intended purpose is to display a message to the user and, optionally, allow him or her to make a choice by clicking a button. You can see an example of the Alert component in Figure 3-30.

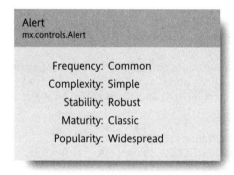

Figure 3-29. The Alert component, implemented by the class mx.controls.Alert

Figure 3-30. Alert example

The use and customization of this component are detailed in Chapter 20.

DateChooser component

The DateChooser component (shown in Figure 3-31) implements an interactive calendar that the user can navigate to select a date. You can see an example of this component in Figure 3-32.

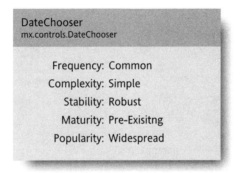

Figure 3-31. The DateChooser component, implemented by the class mx.controls.DateChooser

Figure 3-32. DateChooser example

The use and customization of this component are detailed in Chapter 14.

DateField component

Similar to how the ComboBox merges a TextInput object and a List object, the DateField component (shown in Figure 3-33) merges a TextInput object and a DateChooser object, displaying the text field only by default. The calendar object is displayed when the user clicks the drop-down icon on the right side of the text field, and it disappears when the user selects a date or clicks over the text field. You can see an example of the DateField component in Figure 3-34.

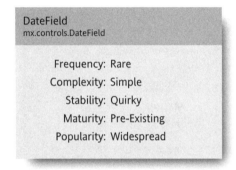

Figure 3-33. The DateField component, implemented by the class mx.controls.DateField

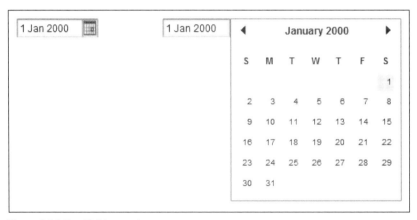

Figure 3-34. DateField example

The use and customization of this component are detailed in Chapter 14.

Menu component

The Menu component (shown in Figure 3-35) is usually created dynamically by code in response to an event such as, for example, the user clicking over a certain area. This component imitates the pop-up menus seen in modern operating systems, and its actual nature would be more accurately described by a name of PopUpMenu, rather than its generic Menu name. You can see an example of the Menu component in Figure 3-36.

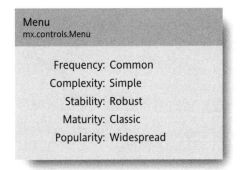

Figure 3-35. The Menu component, implemented by the class mx.controls.Menu

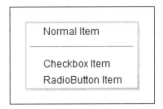

Figure 3-36. Menu example

The use and customization of this component are detailed in Chapter 16.

MenuBar component

The MenuBar component (shown in Figure 3-37) imitates the traditional menu bar present in almost any modern software application. This component usually creates pop-up menus dynamically when the user clicks over one of the options available in the horizontal bar. You can see an example of this component in Figure 3-38.

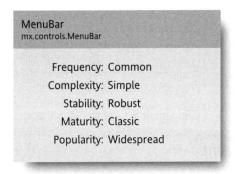

Figure 3-37. The MenuBar component, implemented by the class mx.controls.MenuBar

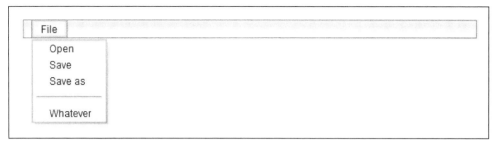

Figure 3-38. MenuBar example

The use and customization of this component are detailed in Chapter 16.

NumericStepper component

The NumericStepper component (shown in Figure 3-39) is an input field specialized in retrieving a numeric value chosen from a predefined series of numbers. You can see an example of the NumericStepper component in Figure 3-40.

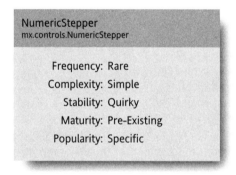

Figure 3-39. The NumericStepper component, implemented by the class mx.controls.NumericStepper

Figure 3-40. NumericStepper example

The use and customization of this component are detailed in Chapter 17.

ProgressBar component

The ProgressBar component (shown in Figure 3-41) is used to graphically represent the progress of loading external content. This component usually operates in conjunction with a container capable of loading external content such as the ScrollPane or the Loader components. You can see an example of the ProgressBar component in Figure 3-42.

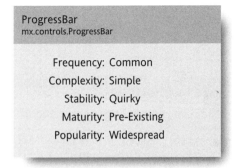

Figure 3-41. The ProgressBar component, implemented by the class mx.controls.ProgressBar

Figure 3-42. ProgressBar example

The use and customization of this component are detailed in Chapter 15.

UIScrollBar component

The UIScrollBar component (shown in Figure 3-43) is a scrollbar that can be added to text fields. This component is almost useless, since the TextArea component already provides a fully functional and scrollable Text component. Most likely, this component will disappear in future versions of the architecture to be replaced by a scrollbar not limited to text fields only. You can see an example of the UIScrollBar component in Figure 3-44.

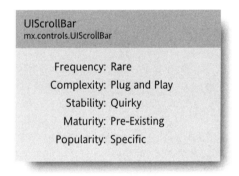

Figure 3-43. The UIScrollBar component, implemented by the class mx.controls.UIScrollBar

Figure 3-44. UIScrollBar example

The use and customization of this component are detailed in Chapter 21.

Using the UI components

As explained in the previous chapter, we have two radically different ways of creating component instances:

- **Statically**: By dragging a component to the stage and defining the property of its instance via the panels in the authoring environment
- **Dynamically**: By coding both the component's creation and the definition of its properties

Although the static approach may appear simpler, it is more limited: ActionScript cannot remove static instances from the stage. Furthermore, some components must be created dynamically to work as expected. On the other hand, creating components at design time is easier because of the visual feedback about the actual size and position of the component instance. However, guide layers can help developers to obtain the best of both worlds.

Any layer can be made a guide layer by right-clicking its name and choosing the Guide option. Component instances added to a guide layer appear in the authoring environment but are not included in the movie when published.

By using a guide layer, developers can design a component-based layout visually, check the values of attributes such as size and position in the various panels available in the authoring environment, and reuse those values in the ActionScript code creating the component instances at runtime.

A first example of interaction

In the following example, we dynamically create three component instances and implement some user interaction. To keep the example pretty small, we are going to use three of the simplest components in the architecture: Button, Alert, and Label.

1. Create a new Flash document and save it as example01.fla.

2. We are going to create a simple container component inheriting from the UIObject class like we did in the previous chapter. Create an empty component named UIContainer and define its class as mx.core.UIObject in both the Linkage and Component Definition dialog boxes.

3. Drag the UIContainer component from the document library to the stage and define its instance name as container; move the instance into the top-left corner of the stage {x:0, y:0}.

4. Add the following code to the first (and only) frame of the main timeline:

```
#include "example01.as"
```

5. Create an ActionScript file and save it as example01.as.

6. Add the following code to the ActionScript file and save it:

```
import mx.controls.*;

var initObject:Object = { _x:250, _y:100, _width:300, _height:50};
```

```
function click(eventObject:Object) {
    Alert.show("Click OK or cancel to close this Alert",
        "Example", Alert.OK | Alert.CANCEL, this, responseHandler);
}

function responseHandler(eventObject:Object) {
    container.destroyObject("myButton");
    var myLabel:Label = container.createClassObject(Label,
        "myLabel", container.getNextHighestDepth(), initObject);
    switch (eventObject.detail) {
        case Alert.OK:
            myLabel.text = "you clicked the OK button";
            break;
        case Alert.CANCEL:
            myLabel.text = "you clicked the CANCEL button";
            break;
        default:
            myLabel.text = "this message should never appear";
    }
}

var myButton:Button = container.createClassObject(Button,
        "myButton", container.getNextHighestDepth(), initObject);
myButton.label = "Create an Alert instance";
myButton.addEventListener("click", this);
```

Important note: if you now open the document's library, you will find that it is empty—but the library must contain the Alert, Button, and Label symbols, otherwise ActionScript will not be able to create them dynamically. The quickest way of adding these symbols to the document's library is to create a component instance on the stage for each of them and then delete it.

7. Drag the Alert component from the Components panel to the stage to create on Alert instance, and then select the newly created instance and delete it.

8. Repeat the previous step twice (create an instance and then delete it) for the Button and Label components as well.

9. Save the files created for this example.

When testing the movie, you will initially see only one button on the stage labeled Create an Alert instance. The button is created dynamically by the following command:

```
var myButton:Button = container.createClassObject(Button,
        "myButton", container.getNextHighestDepth(), initObject);
```

After defining the label of the newly created button instance, we register the _root object as a listener of the button instance's click event:

```
myButton.addEventListener("click", this);
```

A click function is implemented in the _root scope as the event handler of the click event. This function is invoked when the user clicks over the button's instance:

```
function click(eventObject:Object) {
    Alert.show("Click OK or cancel to close this Alert",
        "Example", Alert.OK | Alert.CANCEL, this, responseHandler);
}
```

Executing the click event handler will create an Alert instance. Once the Alert instance appears on the stage, you can move it around by dragging its title bar. An Alert, in fact, inherits its behavior from the Window component.

However, if you try to click over the Create an Alert instance button instance again, you will discover that it is not responsive; the Alert instance has been created as a modal Window, stopping any interaction with other components present on the stage until it is removed. This is done by clicking one of its buttons. Responding to the user action, the component framework will destroy the Alert instance and invoke the callback that was specified in the call to the Alert.show method.

In our example, we specify a callback named responseHandler. The callback's first action is to destroy the myButton instance, demonstrating that we can remove component instances selectively, assuming that they have been created dynamically:

```
container.destroyObject("myButton");
```

The next command creates a Label instance in the same place where the myButton instance once was, reusing the initObject definition to define its size and position:

```
var myLabel:Label = container.createClassObject(Label,
        "myLabel", container.getNextHighestDepth(), initObject);
```

After myLabel has been created, the switch statement examines the detail property of the eventObject, dispatched by the application framework when the Alert instance was destroyed, to determine which Alert button was clicked by the user and define the Label's content accordingly.

```
switch (eventObject.detail) {
    case Alert.OK:
        myLabel.text = "you clicked the OK button";
        break;
    case Alert.CANCEL:
        myLabel.text = "you clicked the CANCEL button";
        break;
    default:
        myLabel.text = "this message should never appear";
}
```

Typical structure of a component

There is no mandatory rule for defining the structure of a movie clip that implements a component belonging to the component architecture. However, an analysis of the file StandardComponents.fla reveals that there is a common approach in defining the structure of a component's main timeline.

The StandardComponents.fla file contains the source of every UI component of the component architecture. The file is already stored in your hard disk if you have installed the authoring environment (see Appendix A for instructions on how to find it). Once opened, the file shows an empty stage. If you open the document library, however, you will discover that it already includes many symbols; those symbols were required to implement the UI components available in the component architecture.

Note that the StandardComponents.fla file is supposed to be a library and, as such, it should be opened using the File ➤ Import ➤ Open External Library command instead of the more common File ➤ Open command.

Let's make a quick test to fully capture the importance of this library.

1. Close the StandardComponents.fla file whether you opened it as a document or as an external library.

2. Create a new Flash document.

3. Add an instance of the Button component to the document, dragging it from the Components panel to the stage.

4. Right/CTRL-click the Button instance on the stage. You will notice that the Edit command is disabled.

Conclusion: developers cannot edit UI component instances created by dragging them from the Components panel because they are compiled. Their source is not available. This is further demonstrated when you open the new document's library. There is only one symbol waiting in there: Button. The Kind field of this symbol in the document's Library does not say Component, as you may have expected, but Compiled Clip. Developers cannot edit compiled clips nor see how they have been implemented.

Let's continue with our test.

5. Create another new Flash document.

6. Open the StandardComponents.fla file as an external library (File ➤ Import ➤ Open External Library).

7. The StandardComponents.fla Library panel contains a folder named Flash UI Components 2 where you can find the source of all the UI components. Look at the Kind field of the Button symbol, which is there: it says Component, not Compiled Clip.

8. Drag the Button symbol from the StandardComponents.fla library panel onto the stage of the newly created document.

9. You may be slightly confused by seeing an empty box instead of a button—it is a noncompiled button instance. Test the movie to verify that it works exactly as a compiled version.

10. Open the document library and take note of an important difference from the previous case. The Library contains much more than a single Button symbol. It contains three folders (Base Classes, Component Assets, and Themes) and various other symbols. All those symbols are required by the Button implementation and represent its physical structure!

11. If you now right-click the Button instance on the stage or the Button symbol in the document's library, you will find that the Edit command is enabled. By selecting the Edit command, you will be able to see the structure of the timeline of a Button component and examine its implementation.

Now that you have explored the implementation of the Button component, you can also inspect the implementation of any other UI component in the component architecture.

If you do, you will notice that there is a certain common approach in defining the layers of a component's movie clip. In all the components, in fact, you will find one or more of the following layers:

- actions
- bounding Box
- assets

In some cases, you may find two of those layers merged into one; you may also find components where such layers have been not renamed or have been defined slightly differently. Such inconsistency may well be confusing; however, the three layers listed here identify a specific approach that is omnipresent in the architecture, an approach that will be explained by examining the purpose of each of those layers.

Figure 3-45 shows the structure of the symbol implementing the Button component that follows the typical approach described in this section.

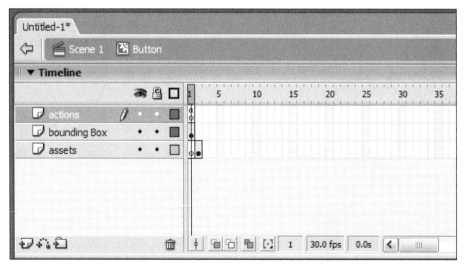

Figure 3-45. Component structure example

The actions layer

ActionScript can be added to any layer of the timeline. It is good practice to have a topmost layer named actions, dedicated to the code present in the timeline—all the code in the timeline should be placed in the actions layer, and it should also be kept empty of any graphical assets.

The use of a layer such as this promotes a neat separation of the code and the content in the timeline, resulting in a clearer Flash document, which is easier to maintain.

In the case of a component's symbol main timeline, the actions layer contains one frame only; the code attached to its first and only frame should be

```
stop();
```

The reason behind this code will be clear once we look at what is included in the assets layer.

The assets layer

The purpose of the assets layer (shown in Figure 3-46) is to ensure that every asset required by the component is packaged with the component and, therefore, available in any context where the component will be utilized.

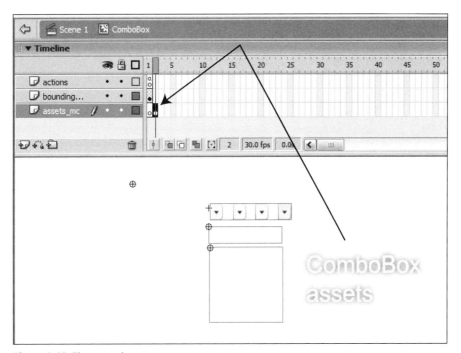

Figure 3-46. The assets layer

However, the packaging of such assets should not influence the component's performance at runtime. To achieve this goal, the assets layer is built with two keyframes instead of a single frame.

The first keyframe is always empty, while the second keyframe contains all the assets required by the component: base classes, subcomponents, skins, etc.

Thanks to the stop action present in the first frame of the actions layer, the playhead never reaches the second keyframe and, therefore, the assets never appear on the stage. Conclusion: their presence in the component package does not influence the overall performance of the Flash application.

The bounding box layer

The bounding box layer contains a single frame hosting an instance of the BoundingBox movie clip. The name of the instance is usually boundingBox_mc.

The bounding box is particularly useful in the case of components that create all of their assets at run-time: its purpose is to avoid having instances of empty components at design time; therefore, the bounding box plays an essential role in allowing resizing and live preview at design time. However, although useful at design time, the bounding box will disrupt the visual representation of the component instances and even their behavior at runtime, so it must be removed somehow at runtime.

Since, as we already know, a movie clip created statically cannot be removed from the stage via ActionScript, developers have had to overcome this limitation by using the following code:

```
boundingBox_mc._visible = false;
boundingBox_mc._width = boundingBox_mc._height = 0;
```

The result is that the bounding box disappears at runtime but is still on the stage. Of course, there is no need for a bounding box when there are static assets that can define a component's bounding, since those assets can be used for the same purpose as the bounding box.

Summary

After reading this chapter, you will be aware of which components have been included in the Flash Component Architecture and what functionality they provide.

You have also found a tool (the Reusability Card) that will tell you at a glance how reusable a component actually is.

You may well consult this chapter again when deciding what components to use in your next project.

In the next chapter, we are going to examine the many options offered by the architecture to efficiently integrate different component instances into a robust component-based application.

Chapter 4

BUILDING COMPONENT-BASED APPLICATIONS

Divide et impera (Latin for divide and rule)

Macchiavelli

In previous chapters, we examined the component framework, a skeleton of functionality shared by each component in the architecture that can be used as a starting point when developing a new component. Our focus now moves to building applications that are based on components.

At this point, you may be wondering whether there is something else in the architecture, apart from the components and the component framework, to help you design applications.

The answer is yes: the component architecture offers more than a collection of components. It provides additional functionality that is implemented outside and around the components in order to further speed up your work when developing a component-based application.

The application-oriented features provided by the architecture can be grouped into two major categories:

- **Application frameworks**: Similarly to a component framework, an application framework is a skeleton to be fleshed in. In this case, however, we are dealing with the skeleton of a whole application instead of the skeleton of a single component.
- **Managers**: Managers are classes that encapsulate specific application-oriented functionality, such as handling the keyboard focus or managing the life cycle of windows.

In the component architecture, you can find two different application frameworks that are characterized by the classes implementing their core objects: the Slide class and the Form class.

Both classes are based on the same concept: the screen, which is encapsulated in the homonymous class Screen, which acts as base class for both Slide and Form.

> *The completed source code introduced in this chapter can be found in the package* src04.zip, *downloadable from this book's page on* www.friendsofed.com.

Screens

Being an ActionScript developer, you will certainly be familiar with the Flash timeline, and you may have found it rather unfriendly when developing an application.

The revolutionary model captured by the timeline, with its layers and frames, has been present since the very first version of Flash, and it is an integral part of Flash's success.

The timeline was originally designed to implement "movies." This has never been a mystery, since the most important Flash objects are still called **movie clips** and even the final product, the SWF file, has always been defined as a **Flash movie**.

However, Flash has come a long way since its beginnings; it is now a powerful object-oriented application platform, even endowed with its own component architecture.

Flash creators, realizing that its timeline had been designed for a purpose other than implementing software applications, added two new types of document in the MX 2004 version of the authoring environment, as you see in Figure 4-1.

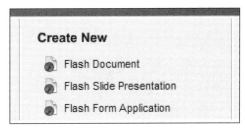

Figure 4-1. Flash document types

When creating a new document, you now have the following choices in addition to the "traditional" Flash Document option:

- Flash Slide Presentation
- Flash Form Application

Both of the new document types are based on the same concept: the screen.

In some of the examples introduced previously in this book, we have already explored the convenience of having a high-level container hosting components generated dynamically. The creators of the component architecture arrived to a similar conclusion when including the Screen class in the architecture: designing, implementing, and even maintaining applications can be much easier if components and other content (graphics, text, etc.) are grouped into a hierarchical structure of high-level containers (or screens).

Building an application using screens

The screen concept is introduced in the component architecture via the Screen class. This class is not used directly to create objects; its purpose is to encapsulate functionality that is common to both of its largely used subclasses: the Slide class and the Form class.

Figure 4-2 illustrates the main inheritance relationships among the screen classes.

Both the Form and Slide classes are derived from the Screen class, which in turn is a subclass of the Loader class. The Loader class is the same class used to implement the Loader component, which is a container, as you saw in the previous chapter.

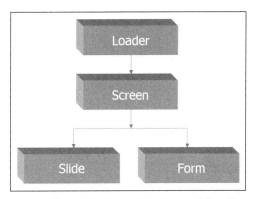

Figure 4-2. Screen inheritance relationships

Screens, whether they are slides or forms, define the user interface of a Flash application hierarchically via a containment relationship very similarly to nested movie clips. In fact, at runtime, a screen is essentially a movie clip most likely containing other, nested, movie clips.

Being a high-level container derived from the Loader class, a screen can hold various type of content such as

- Text or graphics.
- Components.
- External SWF movies or JPG images.
- Other screens (namely child screens). You can create screens statically in the authoring environment inside documents based on either the Slide Presentation or the Form Application document types.

After creating a Slide Presentation (or a Form Application) document, the authoring environment presents a workspace that is quite different from that of a traditional Flash document:

- The timeline seems to be missing (although it is just hidden).
- A new window, referred to as Screens by its associated menu item under the Window menu, appears on the left side of the stage.

The purpose of the Screens window is to outline the current screen hierarchy of the document, while providing a pane that can be used to add new screens, rearrange the screen hierarchy, and select the screen you wish to work on.

The initial configuration of the Screens window always includes two screens:

- **The master screen**: This is the root of the hierarchy: the screen containing any other screen. Such screen has a default name of presentation in the case of a Slide Presentation document and application in the case of a Form Application document.
- **A child screen**: One child screen to start building your application from. Such a screen has a default name of slide1 in the case of a Slide Presentation document and form1 in the case of a Form Application document.

Figure 4-3 compares the differences in the naming conventions used in the screen hierarchy of a Slide Presentation and the screen hierarchy of a Form Application.

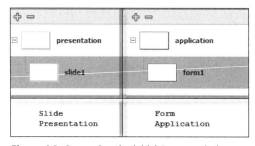

Figure 4-3. Comparing the initial Screens windows

A screen hierarchy is a tree-like structure representing containment relationships: each node is a screen that can contain other screens. The master screen, root of the structure, is the only screen that has no parent screen, and it contains all other content present in the document.

Learn to recognize the relationships among nodes in the screen hierarchy with the help of the following role names:

- **Master screen**: The root of the structure and the only screen that has no parent screen
- **Child screen**: A screen that is contained in another screen
- **Children**: The collection of screens that are directly contained in a screen
- **Descendants**: All of the screens that are nested into a screen
- **Parent screen**: The screen containing a screen
- **Ancestors**: All the screens above a nested screen from its parent up to the master screen
- **Leaf**: A screen that has no child screens
- **Siblings**: Two or more screens that share the same parent screen

Content hierarchy in nested screens

Note that a screen hierarchy is also a content hierarchy: the content of a child screen is usually placed over the content of its parent screen and, consequently, over the content of all of its ancestors. Note that the content of the ancestors could still be visible if not overlapped by the child's content.

This is particularly important when you define the content of the master screen, because its content can be visible on the stage every time that another screen is displayed.

Figure 4-4 is an example based on a Form Application document that clearly shows how the contents of nested screens are related to each other. The Screens window of the example shows that the master screen (called application by default) has a child (screen2) that in turn has its own child (screen3). Each of the three screens has some text content ("Master Screen Content", "Screen2 Content", and "Screen 3 Content", respectively).

When screen3 is visible on the stage, you can also see the contents of the other two screens, since screen3 is contained in screen2, which in turn is contained in the master screen, application.

However, the content of a child screen can overlap the content of its ancestors, since it is usually placed on top of their content as displayed in Figure 4-4.

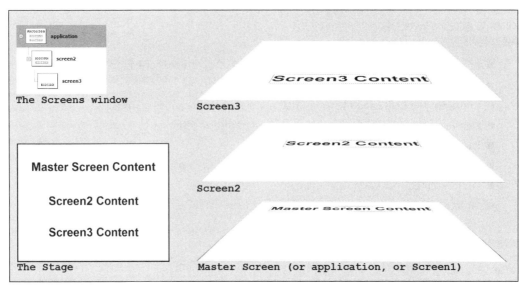

Figure 4-4. Content hierarchy in nested screens

All the concepts that you have learned so far apply to both forms and slides, since both of their classes are derived from the Screen class.

As was mentioned earlier, the Slide class and the Form class identify two slightly different application frameworks by extending the Screen class.

Let's examine the main differences between the two application frameworks and, ultimately, what their purpose is.

Reviewing the purpose of slides and forms

At its simplest, the main difference between a document based on forms and a document based on slides lies in how the user navigates among the different screens defined in the respective documents.

While the Slide class implements a navigation loosely inspired by the sequential nature of a slideshow, the Form class does not implement any navigation model, and, when building an application based on forms, it will be your responsibility to implement one by using ActionScript.

Beware that the absence of a predefined navigation for forms and the names chosen by in the Flash authoring environment for the two screen-based document types (Slide Presentation, Form Application) can be very deceiving and lead to a couple of *WRONG* conclusions:

- The Slide Presentation document type should only be used when creating slideshows. The Form Application document type is a mandatory choice when developing applications.
- Slides are simpler than forms.

Although the names of the two document types were chosen to suggest their purpose in an intuitive way, they can be deceiving when it comes to understanding the actual nature of the application models encapsulated in the slides and the forms, respectively.

When using slides, you are working with a stateful application framework. Contrarily, forms embody a stateless application framework. In other words, slides maintain a state of the application, while forms don't (unless you add that capability with your code).

The state of the sapplication is maintained by the Slide class via a number of methods that implement the navigation among screens (slides). Those methods are

- gotoFirstSlide: Navigates to the first slide among the descendants of a slide
- gotoLastSlide: Navigates to the last slide among the descendants of a slide
- gotoNextSlide: Navigates to the next slide in the hierarchy
- gotoPreviousSlide: Navigates to the previous slide in the hierarchy
- gotoSlide: Navigates to the specified slide

It is evident by the functionality provided in these methods that, in the case of slides, the screen hierarchy is not only a containment relationship, but also an ordered one.

There is an order among the child screens of a screen. There is a first child, a last child, and, even more importantly, a current child! That current child represents the current state of the application.

Furthermore, slides navigation is based on the concepts of incoming/outgoing slides: the current slide becomes the outgoing slide and, as such, is going to be hidden, while the incoming slide becomes the new current slide and is revealed just after.

This incoming/outgoing mechanism has an even deeper impact when the screen hierarchy is nested several levels deep. If the incoming and outgoing slides have different ancestors, then all the different ancestors of the outgoing slide will be hidden as well, while all the different ancestors of the incoming slide will be made visible just after.

This rather complex behavior is built into the Slide class. Considering that forms do not implement any navigation, you can start to understand why the second conclusion mentioned earlier is actually wrong: the Slide class is indeed more complex than the Form class.

The greater complexity of slides is also indicated by the number and nature of a slide's parameters that you can set in the authoring environment (5) compared with the parameters of a form (3).

When selecting a slide in the authoring environment, you can set the following parameters:

- autoKeyNav: Enables/disables the built-in keyboard handler that allows navigating to the next and previous slides by using the arrow keys.
- contentPath: Defines the slide's content, which can be internal if it is a linkage identifier, or external if it is an absolute or relative URL to a SWF or JPG file.
- autoLoad: Determines whether the content specified in the contentPath parameter will be loaded automatically or only when the load method is explicitly invoked.

- overlayChildren: Indicates whether the children slides remain visible or not when navigating from one child to another; this parameter is false by default, that is, children are hidden and revealed while being navigated.

- playHidden: Determines whether the slide, considered as a movie clip, continues to play or not once it is hidden; this parameter is true by default, meaning that the slide continues to play unless otherwise specified.

As mentioned previously, selecting a form in the authoring environment will allow you to define three parameters only:

- contentPath: Same functionality as in the slide case.

- autoLoad: Same functionality as in the slide case.

- visible: Determines whether the form is visible when its parent is visible; this parameter is true by default, meaning that all of the forms are visible by default.

Forms visibility

While slides are revealed or hidden via a rather sophisticated mechanism that is built into the Slide class, which can be influenced by the related methods and parameters, forms are displayed or hidden by directly setting their visible property via the homonymous parameter in the authoring environment or via ActionScript at runtime.

The visible property implemented in the Form class emphasizes the difference between the form-based application framework and the one based on slides, since all forms are visible by default as shown in Figure 4-5.

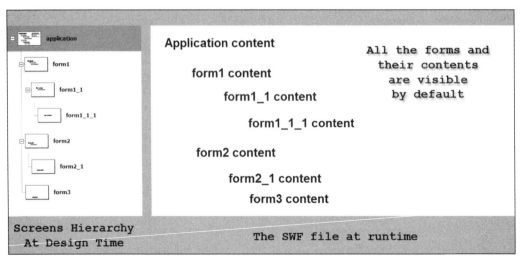

Figure 4-5. Forms visibility example

If you create a random form-based hierarchy like the one shown in Figure 4-5 and fill each form with some content, you will notice that unless you explicitly set the visible property of some form to false, all the forms and their contents will be visible at the same time when the movie is tested.

Conclusion: should you use slides or forms?

If you can get used to how the slide navigation works, then you may well be willing to reuse that functionality when building your applications.

Alternatively, if you prefer to implement a fully customized navigation setup, then forms provide the option of an application framework without any built-in navigation.

In the end, slides are more intelligent than forms, and you may decide to reuse their functionality, maybe even mixing up slides and forms.

Note that when using slides, you are not forced to have a strictly sequential navigation: you can disable the default keyboard navigation by setting autoKeyNav to `false` and using the gotoSlide method to jump to a specific slide.

Because of their flexibility, slides are probably a better high-level container than forms, although forms are still useful in all the cases where any predefined navigation would be useless.

Before implementing a complete example, let's consider another very interesting functionality available to screen-based applications: a screen hierarchy can be extended with external subtrees.

Screen hierarchies with external subtrees

A screen-based application can be divided into several subsystems that can be developed separately and merged together in a central document.

This possibility is enabled by the fact that you can load external SWF files into a screen, and by the capabilities of the screen classes handle the screen hierarchies of such external files.

Let's create a template that you may use as starting point when designing an application made of different subsystems, each implemented in a different document. The template that we will create represents the main system that will coordinate the interaction among the different subsystems.

1. Launch the Flash authoring environment and create a new Slide Presentation. We will be using slides as the screen of choice for our template to have the chance to use the navigation built into the Slide class whenever needed. However, you can also create a similar template starting from a Form Application document, if you like.

2. Save the newly create document as a template by choosing the menu command File ➤ Save As Template.

3. Fill in the Save as Template dialog box, shown in Figure 4-6, that has appeared after you executed the last command.

   Give the new template the name Large Application while associating it with a newly defined category named Slide-based apps. Then provide a short description to act as a reminder of the scope of this template: Starting point for a slide-based application that integrates sub-systems implemented externally.

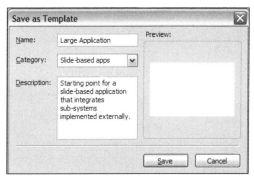

Figure 4-6.
Creating a new document template

So far, our new template looks exactly like a document created via the Slide Presentation document type. Let's change that:

4. Change the master screen name from presentation to mainMenu. This change of name is far from being just a cosmetic issue. It reminds us that the content in the master screen is available when every other screen is displayed and, as such, is the ideal place to implement the application main menu, if any. Such a menu will allow the user to navigate from one subsystem to another.

5. Select the mainMenu screen, and in the parameters pane set autoKeyNav as false. We are disabling the built-in keyboard handling that allows navigating slides using the arrow keys. Most likely the main menu will be implemented by navigating to a specific slide via the gotoSlide method.

6. Select the slide1 screen and rename it as appState1. Once again, the definition of a proper name is very important. In this case, appState1 indicates that this screen is dedicated to the first (initial) state of the application. Remember that slides are capable of maintaining an application state, as we saw earlier in this chapter.

7. After selecting the appState1 screen, fill the contentPath with the value subsystem1.swf. Once again, the names used are very indicative. We are suggesting that the first state of the application is the one hosting the first subsystem. This subsystem is implemented externally in an SWF file simply called subsystem1.swf.

8. Since our "large application" is likely to have more than one subsystem, create another two slides at the same level as appState1 and rename them appState2 and appState3 to indicate that they are dedicated to the second and third state in the application.

9. After creating the appState2 and appState3 screens, define their contentPath as subsystem2.swf and subsystem3.swf respectively. The second state of the application (appState2) will host the second subsystem that is implemented in the subsystem2.swf file. Similarly, the third state of the application will host the third subsystem that is implemented in an external SWF as well.

10. Save the file again to store all of the changes made to the template. Now you really have a good starting point when it comes to developing large applications based on external subsystems.

The final screen hierarchy of our newly created template should be the same as that shown in Figure 4-7.

This new template is highly reusable, since we used abstract concepts such as "application state" and "subsystems." Because of such abstractions, we can use this template as starting point for a wide range of different applications.

For instance, you could place a MenuBar component in the mainMenu slide to navigate among the application states. Alternatively, you could use a set of Button components or even a single ComboBox component for the same purpose.

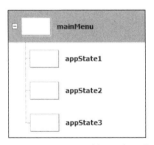

Figure 4-7. Screen hierarchy of the Large Application template

Each application state hosts what we called a **subsystem** of the application. Such a subsystem is an external SWF file that contains its own screen hierarchy.

In concrete terms, the initial application state (appState1) could possibly host the login subsystem, controlling the user access to the rest of the application. The second application state (appState2) could host some kind of query subsystem used to retrieve some information that is eventually displayed in the third application state (appState3) hosting some sort of reporting subsystem.

This template would allow you to implement the three subsystems (login, query, reporting) in separate screen-based documents and then coordinate their functionality with the help of the mainMenu. The possibilities are endless, since each subsystem can be defined separately and, quite possibly, implemented by different developers or even teams.

Furthermore, a very modular approach like the one shown in this template would grant further benefits, such as

- Facilitating application maintenance by keeping its functionality neatly separated
- Allowing for greater flexibility and extensibility since subsystems can be added or removed very easily

The core idea in this approach is the screen concept (slide or form) and its related application framework. In fact, such a framework allows also for cross-subsystem communication that basically means referring a screen included in a subsystem from the context of another subsystem.

The complete path to an external screen

When implementing a subsystem using our new template, you may need to navigate (or refer) to a screen present in another subsystem.

Because we are using slides, we can easily achieve this using an ActionScript statement similar to this one:

```
this.gotoSlide(absolutePathToTheSlide);
```

where absolutePathToTheSlide is a placeholder for what will be the actual path in the runtime context of your application. Let's make a concrete example showing such a path.

Let's assume that the subsystem1.swf file loaded in appState1 of the application contains the very simple screen hierarchy shown in Figure 4-8.

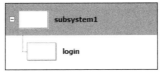

Figure 4-8. Screen hierarchy example of a subsystem

101

At runtime, the screen hierarchy of your application will change to include the screen hierarchy of subsystem1.swf, which will be appended underneath the appState1 node as shown in Figure 4-9.

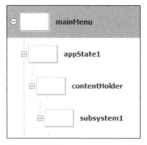

Figure 4-9. Runtime screen hierarchy of the application after loading subsystem1.swf

Note the presence of an unexpected node named contentHolder between the appState1 node and the root of the subsystem1 screen hierarchy. This node is always present and automatically created by the application framework once the external content has been loaded.

Once you know how the screen hierarchy changes at runtime, you can refer to the login slide from within another subsystem.

The complete path to the login slide in our example, in fact, is quite simply, if not shortly

    _root.mainMenu.appState1.contentHolder.subsystem1.login

You can use such a path from within the context of a slide in another subsystem, as in the following example:

    this.gotoSlide(_root.mainMenu.appState1.contentHolder.subsystem1.login)

We have seen enough about the screen concept and its concrete implementations (slides and forms) to create our first highly dynamic screen-based application.

In the next section, you will learn about additional concrete aspects related to screens, plus a technique for creating them dynamically within a classic Flash document.

Creating a slide presentation dynamically

You certainly have realized by now that the component architecture is based on a large collection of classes, some of them (the screens) implemented to provide an application framework that can be used as a starting point when developing a component-based application.

Even more, you learned that the two screen-based document types (Slide Presentation and Form Application) are nothing more than very simple document templates, and that you can build your own screen-based templates using either slides or forms.

Being a developer, you will have started wondering whether you could use the Slide and Form classes in a traditional Flash document. Developers know that the infrastructure of the authoring environment is useful for producing simple prototypes visually, but it can be limiting in the case of implementing real-life requirements.

In order to overcome the limits of the authoring environment, you must be able to take full control over the application that you are developing by creating its objects dynamically and programmatically defining their appearance and behavior via ActionScript.

Therefore, it is important to be able to create screens dynamically and even extend their class if and when needed.

The next example shows you how to create a complete slideshow dynamically, using the Slide class in the context of a typical Flash document without having a single object on the stage at design time.

The example will also be your first screen-based application created the developer's way: by controlling each of its aspects via ActionScript code.

Building the example

1. Start by creating a Flash document and saving it as dynamic_slideshow.fla. Note that we are going to use screens (slides) in a typical Flash document: you will not be able to open the Screens panel to examine the screen hierarchy, because the menu option to open it is disabled in the case of Flash documents. However, even if present, the Screens panel would be empty, since we are going to create all the screens we need at runtime. This example just demonstrates that it is possible to do so and control every aspect of the screens programmatically.

2. Change the document dimensions by opening the Document Properties dialog box. Set the new dimensions as 640×480 pixels. The size of the document stage is important, since it will need to be the same as the three external JPG files that we will load dynamically when running the slideshow. You can find these three files (image1.jpg, image2.jpg, and image3.jpg) in the source code. However, you can replace any of these JPG files with your own graphics as long as your files will have the same names (image1.jpg, image2.jpg, and image3.jpg) and size (640×480) as the ones used by the example.

3. Select the first and only frame on the first layer of the document and add the following ActionScript line to it:

```
#include "slideshow.as"
```

4. Create an ActionScript file and save it as slideshow.as; this file will contain all the code that generates the slideshow dynamically.

5. We are going to use a few of components in this example and create them dynamically. Since we need those components to be present in the document library, we reapply the same trick we saw in an earlier example by dragging them onto the stage and then deleting them (that is enough to have them included in the document's library and, eventually, in the SWF file). In the ActionScript code of this example, we will create a Button and a Loader component. Therefore, drag a Button and then a Loader component on the stage and, just after, delete both of them.

6. In order to use the Slide class in a Flash document and create slides dynamically, we must find it in the library. Since there is no Slide component, we are quickly going to create one. Select Insert ➤ New Symbol and create a new movie clip symbol named Slide. Go back to the main scene (Scene1), since we will leave the Slide symbol empty.

103

7. Select the newly created Slide symbol in the document library and specify that is implemented using the ActionScript class mx.screens.Slide both in the Linkage Properties and the Component Definition dialog boxes. As a result of both settings, the document library should display that the Slide symbol is now a component.

8. The previous steps completed the creation of the Flash document, but its stage is empty. Its library contains three components (Button, Loader, and the one we created and named Slide). The first frame includes an external ActionScript file named slideshow.as; it is this code that will create the whole slideshow application dynamically!

Copy the following code into the slideshow.as file. After copying the code and saving the ActionScript file, you can test your movie.

```
import mx.screens.Slide;
import mx.transitions.*;
import mx.transitions.easing.*;
import mx.controls.Button;
import mx.controls.Loader;

// initialization objects
var initMasterSlide = {
    _x:0, _y:0,
    autoKeyNav: "true",
    overlayChildren: false,
    playHidden: true,
    tabChildren: true,
    tabEnabled: false,
    focusEnabled: true
};

var initChild = {
    _x:0, _y:0,
    autoKeyNav: "inherit",
    overlayChildren: false,
    playHidden: true,
    tabChildren: true,
    tabEnabled: false,
    focusEnabled: true
};

var initFade = {
    type:Fade,
    duration:2,
    easing:None.easeNone,
    param1:empty,
    param2:empty
};
```

```
var initPixelDissolve = {
    type:PixelDissolve,
    duration:2,
    easing:None.easeNone,
    xSections:32,
    ySections:24
};

var initBlinds = {
    type:Blinds,
    duration:2,
    easing:None.easeNone,
    numStrips:24,
    dimension:1
};

// handle button navigation - keyboard works too without any
➥ handler to be implemented
function click(eventObject) {
    switch (eventObject.target) {
    case sldMainNavigation.btnPrev:
        sldMainNavigation.currentSlide.gotoPreviousSlide();
        break;
    case sldMainNavigation.btnNext:
        sldMainNavigation.currentSlide.gotoNextSlide();
        break;
    }
}

function reveal(eventObject) {
    switch (eventObject.target) {
        case sld01:
            if (!eventObject.target._isSlide ||
➥ (eventObject.target._isSlide &&
➥ eventObject.target.currentSlide)) {
                initFade.direction = 0;
                TransitionManager.start(eventObject.target, initFade);
                }
                break;
        case sld02:
            if (!eventObject.target._isSlide ||
➥ (eventObject.target._isSlide &&
➥ eventObject.target.currentSlide)) {
                initPixelDissolve.direction = 0;
                TransitionManager.start(eventObject.target,
➥ initPixelDissolve);
                }
```

```
                    break;
                case sld03:
                    if (!eventObject.target._isSlide ||
➥   (eventObject.target._isSlide &&
➥   eventObject.target.currentSlide)) {
                        initBlinds.direction = 0;
                        TransitionManager.start(eventObject.target, initBlinds);
                    }
                    break;
            }
        }

        function hide(eventObject) {
            switch (eventObject.target) {
                case sld01:
                    if (!eventObject.target._isSlide ||
➥   (eventObject.target._isSlide &&
➥   eventObject.target.currentSlide)) {
                        initFade.direction = 1;
                        TransitionManager.start(eventObject.target, initFade);
                    }
                    break;
                case sld02:
                    if (!eventObject.target._isSlide ||
➥   (eventObject.target._isSlide &&
➥   eventObject.target.currentSlide)) {
                        initPixelDissolve.direction = 1;
                        TransitionManager.start(eventObject.target,
➥   initPixelDissolve);
                    }
                    break;
                case sld03:
                    if (!eventObject.target._isSlide ||
➥   (eventObject.target._isSlide &&
➥   eventObject.target.currentSlide)) {
                        initBlinds.direction = 1;
                        TransitionManager.start(eventObject.target, initBlinds);
                    }
                    break;
            }
        }

        // create rootSlide
        var sldMainNavigation = this.createClassObject(Slide,
➥   "sldMainNavigation", this.getNextHighestDepth(),
➥   initMasterSlide);
```

```
// create child slides
var sld01 = sldMainNavigation.createChild(Slide, "sld01",
➥ initChild);
var sld02 = sldMainNavigation.createChild(Slide, "sld02",
➥ initChild);
var sld03 = sldMainNavigation.createChild(Slide, "sld03",
➥ initChild);

// create rootSlide content
sldMainNavigation.createClassObject(Button, "btnPrev",
➥ sldMainNavigation.getNextHighestDepth(),
➥ {_x:10, _y:10, label:'Prev'});
sldMainNavigation.createClassObject(Button, "btnNext",
➥ sldMainNavigation.getNextHighestDepth(),
➥ {_x:120, _y:10, label:'Next'});

// add listeners to rootSlide buttons
sldMainNavigation.btnPrev.addEventListener("click", this);
sldMainNavigation.btnNext.addEventListener("click", this);

// create child slides content
sld01.createClassObject(Loader, "myLoader",
➥   sld01.getNextHighestDepth(),
➥   {_x:0, _y:0, _width:640, _height:480,
➥   contentPath: "image1.jpg"});
sld02.createClassObject(Loader, "myLoader",
➥ sld02.getNextHighestDepth(),
➥ {_x:0, _y:0, _width:640, _height:480,
➥ contentPath: "image2.jpg"});
sld03.createClassObject(Loader, "myLoader",
➥ sld03.getNextHighestDepth(),
➥ {_x:0, _y:0, _width:640, _height:480,
➥ contentPath: "image3.jpg"});

// add listeners to slides reveal/hide
sld01.addEventListener("hide", this);
sld01.addEventListener("reveal", this);
sld02.addEventListener("hide", this);
sld02.addEventListener("reveal", this);
sld03.addEventListener("hide", this);
sld03.addEventListener("reveal", this);

// go to the first slide
sldMainNavigation.gotoFirstSlide();
```

Let's now examine each relevant part of the slideshow.as code separately.

Importing the Slide class

The first line of the ActionScript file imports the Slide class so that we can use its short name (Slide) in the rest of the code:

```
import mx.screens.Slide;
```

Creating the screen hierarchy dynamically

Our example creates a screen hierarchy of four slides (master screen included). If this screen hierarchy could have been displayed in a Screens window, its outline would have been like that shown in Figure 4-10.

Figure 4-1. Screen hierarchy generated dynamically in the example

The master screen is created using the same createClassObject method that we used in the previous chapter:

```
var sldMainNavigation = this.createClassObject(Slide,
➡ "sldMainNavigation", this.getNextHighestDepth(), masterSlideInit);
```

while the three children are created using the createChild method, which is more appropriate in this case, since we are creating screens that do have a parent:

```
var sld01 = sldMainNavigation.createChild(Slide, "sld01",
➡ childSlideInit);
var sld02 = sldMainNavigation.createChild(Slide, "sld02",
➡ childSlideInit);
var sld03 = sldMainNavigation.createChild(Slide, "sld03",
➡ childSlideInit);
```

Note that, very similarly to the slides created in a Slide Presentation document, the master screen will contain, directly or indirectly, all the content of the slideshow.

When created dynamically, the master screen is initialized using the following object, which provides the initial values of some of its properties:

```
var initMasterSlide = {
    _x:0, _y:0,
    autoKeyNav: "true",
    overlayChildren: false,
```

```
        playHidden: true,
        tabChildren: true,
        tabEnabled: false,
        focusEnabled: true
    };
```

Similarly, the three child screens are also initialized using an object:

```
    var initChild = {
        _x:0, _y:0,
        autoKeyNav: "inherit",
        overlayChildren: false,
        playHidden: true,
        tabChildren: true,
        tabEnabled: false,
        focusEnabled: true
    };
```

Adding navigation in the master screen

The name of the master screen, sldMainNavigation, was chosen to emphasize that this screen will contain two buttons replicating the slideshow navigation. Although the Slide class has built-in functionality to allow users to navigating via the arrow keys, adding a couple of buttons to the interface and replicating the slideshow navigation is both an excuse to provide an example using components in the main screen and a design that may become essential in the case of slideshows installed on a system with a touch-screen but no keyboard.

The two buttons are created dynamically and added to the master screen *AFTER* adding the three child screens:

```
    sldMainNavigation.createClassObject(Button, "btnPrev",
    ➥ sldMainNavigation.getNextHighestDepth(),
    ➥ {_x:10, _y:10, label:'Prev'});
    sldMainNavigation.createClassObject(Button, "btnNext",
    ➥ sldMainNavigation.getNextHighestDepth(),
    ➥ {_x:120, _y:10, label:'Next'});
```

By adding the buttons after the three slides, we can modify the standard rule that a child's content appears on top of the father's content. Each child slide will load a JPG image that is as big as the whole stage.

If the same slideshow would have been created statically, the JPG images would have overlapped any content present in the parent screen (the master screen), making the two buttons invisible and, therefore, inaccessible.

Since we are creating the whole slideshow programmatically, we can modify that behavior, and we can make the master screen's content (the two buttons) appear on top of the children's content; thus the

JPG images that will be loaded at runtime will appear underneath the navigation buttons, as shown in Figure 4-11.

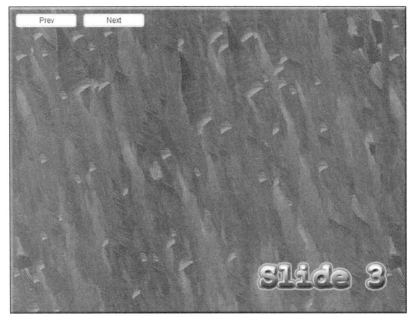

Figure 4-11. The navigation buttons added to the main screen

This simple, yet significant, case shows how coding can overcome the limitations introduced by the authoring environment.

Implementing the buttons-based navigation

Now that we have ensured that two buttons (Prev and Next) are always visible on top of the child screens, we need to handle the click event and react by navigating to the previous or next slide respectively.

The click event handlers are implemented at the _root level in two steps; first we register what object is listening to both click events:

```
sldMainNavigation.btnPrev.addEventListener("click", this);
sldMainNavigation.btnNext.addEventListener("click", this);
```

and then we provide an event handler that checks what button has been clicked and reacts accordingly:

```
function click(eventObject) {
    switch (eventObject.target) {
        case sldMainNavigation.btnPrev:
            sldMainNavigation.currentSlide.gotoPreviousSlide();
            break;
```

```
        case sldMainNavigation.btnNext:
            sldMainNavigation.currentSlide.gotoNextSlide();
            break;
    }
}
```

Using Loader components in the child screens

Apart from the two Button instances in the main screen, our example creates three additional components dynamically by adding a Loader component instance to each of the three child screens:

```
sld01.createClassObject(Loader, "myLoader",
➡ sld01.getNextHighestDepth(),
➡ {_x:0, _y:0, _width:640, _height:480,
➡ contentPath: "image1.jpg"});
sld02.createClassObject(Loader, "myLoader",
➡ sld02.getNextHighestDepth(),
➡ {_x:0, _y:0, _width:640, _height:480,
➡ contentPath: "image2.jpg"});
sld03.createClassObject(Loader, "myLoader",
➡ sld03.getNextHighestDepth(),
➡ {_x:0, _y:0, _width:640, _height:480,
➡ contentPath: "image3.jpg"});
```

You may well remember that the Slide class is a descendant of the Loader class, and, therefore, you may wonder why we added a Loader component instance to each slide instead of directly loading the JPG files via their contentPath property.

By adding a Loader component to the slides, we create a more flexible design that allows us to include external imagery (and components) inside a screen.

For instance, by following the approach demonstrated here, you could easily implement a screen containing several loaders, each of them fetching an image from a different external source.

Introducing the transitions

Since we are implementing a dynamic slideshow, it makes sense to use one of the fancier functionalities included in the component architecture: **transitions**.

Transitions are capable of animating a screen when it becomes visible or before it disappears from the stage.

The component architecture includes ten different transition effects, each of them encapsulated in its own class and customizable via effect-specific parameters and several, already implemented, easing methods. **Easing methods** control the speed of an animation, defining its accelerations and decelerations.

The combinations of transition effects, effect parameters, and easing methods are endless and worth experimenting with to achieve realistic animations of the content when it appears or disappears from stage.

For a full list of the available transitions, their parameters, and the easing methods, refer to Appendix B.

111

The example that we have built demonstrates how to apply transitions programmatically by using three of them: Fade, PixelDissolve, and Blinds. Note that the name of a transition is also the name of the ActionScript class that implements it. All the transition classes are derived from the common base class Transition.

Transitions are created and managed with the help of another class: the TransitionManager class.

As you may recall from previous discussions, the TransitionManager class is a manager class. Manager classes specialize in supporting an application-oriented functionality that, in the case of the TransitionManager, involves starting the transitions and stopping them whenever necessary. In the section "Manager Classes" later in this chapter, we will examine the other manager classes included in the component architecture.

Importing the transition classes

In order to avoid the very long names that would have made the source code lengthier and less readable, we import all the transitions and easing classes by adding the following lines at the beginning of the slideshow.as file:

```
import mx.transitions.*;
import mx.transitions.easing.*;
```

Since we import all the transition-related classes, you can reuse this example later on to quickly experiment with other transitions by using their short names. Just remember to create the proper initialization objects, since each transition class has its own specific parameters. In the current example, we use three different transition effects and, therefore, we define three different initialization objects:

```
var initFade = {
    type:Fade,
    duration:2,
    easing:None.easeNone,
    param1:empty,
    param2:empty
};

var initPixelDissolve = {
    type:PixelDissolve,
    duration:2,
    easing:None.easeNone,
    xSections:32,
    ySections:24
};

var initBlinds = {
    type:Blinds,
    duration:2,
    easing:None.easeNone,
    numStrips:24,
    dimension:1
};
```

Screen events and transition sequencing

It makes sense to animate a screen's content via a transition effect whenever it becomes visible and just before it becomes invisible.

Screens provide two events that can be used to synchronize the start of a transition effect:

- reveal: Broadcasts when the screen's state changes from invisible to visible
- hide: Broadcasts when the screen's state changes from visible to invisible

It is interesting to note that both events are originally implemented in the UIObject class and are therefore available to every component in the architecture.

In order to intercept the change of the visibility state of the children slides, the _root object is registered as a listener to both the events (hide and reveal) of each slide:

```
sld01.addEventListener("hide", this);
sld01.addEventListener("reveal", this);
sld02.addEventListener("hide", this);
sld02.addEventListener("reveal", this);
sld03.addEventListener("hide", this);
sld03.addEventListener("reveal", this);
```

Two event handlers are implemented to react to those events:

```
// reveal event handler
function reveal(eventObject) {
        .........................
}

// hide event handler
function hide(eventObject) {
        .........................
}
```

Note that the implementations of the two functions are identical with the sole exception of the definition of the direction parameter.

To make the example clear and visually consistent, we use the same transition effect in association with a specific slide and define the direction of the effect according to the initial state of the screen (invisible/visible):

- A Fade transition is associated with the first child screen (sld01), and starts when the slide becomes either visible (reveal event) or invisible (hide event). The direction parameter is set according to the specific event.
- A PixelDissolve transition is associated with the second child screen (sld02), and starts when the slide becomes either visible (reveal event) or invisible (hide event). The direction parameter is set according to the specific event.
- A Blinds transition is associated with the third child screen (sld03), and starts when the slide becomes either visible (reveal event) or invisible (hide event). The direction parameter is set according to the specific event.

113

The association slide/transition effect is created by starting the transition in response to the specific event (hide or reveal). Each transition is started by first defining the direction parameter and then passing the refined initialization object to the start method of the TransitionManager class as shown in the following lines:

```
initFade.direction = 0;
TransitionManager.start(eventObject.target, initFade);
```

The direction parameter is set to 0 or 1 depending on whether the slide is being revealed (fade in) or hidden (fade out). Apart from the direction parameter, all the other parameters in the initialization object (initFade) have the same values regardless of whether the screen is appearing or disappearing.

Run the example and navigate among the screens of the slideshow to fully grasp what is going on and what the TransitionManager contributes in controlling the concurrent execution of the various transition effects.

Working with forms

Forms are in many ways similar to slides because both of their classes are derived from the Screen class. However, we have already seen that forms are a more general-purpose kind of screen, since they do not include any default navigation.

Basically, the Form class adds very little to the base Screen class and, therefore, is a simpler class than the Slide class. In fact, the only feature of practical interest introduced by the Form class is the visible property that has been defined to facilitate the design of custom form-based navigations.

The final section of this chapter is dedicated to completing our exploration of the application-oriented features included in the component architecture by examining the manager classes.

Manager classes

Manager classes provide specific functionality that can be helpful when building a component-based application. Typically, an application contains only one instance of a specific manager that is instantiated by the architecture itself on an as-needed basis.

The component architecture includes six manager classes:

- DepthManager: Manages the depth of the components and movie clips in the application. The depth concept is the same as the one provided in the Flash model: an object's depth is a number indicating its position in an imaginary z-order. The z-order determines whether an object is in front or behind another object.

- FocusManager: Manages the keyboard focus and provides a means to specify the tab order of components. The tab order defines which component receives focus when the user presses the *TAB* key to navigate among the components in an application.

- PopUpManager: Manages the creation and destruction of overlapping windows that can be modal or nonmodal. When created, a modal window restricts the user interaction to its own area until it is removed from the stage.

- `StyleManager`: Manages the styles defined for each component and their inheritance, and is mostly used internally by the architecture. You would be interested in using this class manager only when creating new styles for a new component.

- `SystemManager`: Mostly used internally by the architecture, it implements a screen property that provides an almost redundant functionality to access the stage coordinates. At the time of writing, the implementation of this class is not very mature, and its use should be avoided because the existence of the Stage object, a built-in ActionScript object, provides similar information to the one you may extract from the screen property.

- `TransitionManager`: Manages the life cycle transitions that can also happen concurrently.

Not all the manager classes are important from a developer's perspective. The current `SystemManager` is of no interest, being mostly a mechanism used internally by the architecture, so we will not spend time looking at it. The `TransitionManager` becomes handy only when you intend to include transitions in your application by using similar techniques to the one that we have already examined in this chapter. The `StyleManager` is another manager class used mostly internally, and you will see some example of its rare use when learning to use styles, later on in the book.

So, there are really just three manager classes that are frequently used and contribute significantly to the structure of a component-based Flash application: `DepthManager`, `FocusManager`, and `PopUpManager`. Let's examine each of them in greater detail.

Managing depth

The depth of a movie clip or component is an attribute specifying its position in the z-order of a specific timeline.

The z-order indicates the arrangement of objects one over another. The depth of an object is just a number that refers to the z-order: an object with a certain depth will appear behind an object with a higher depth, and its content may be hidden if the outlines of the two objects overlap.

MovieClip methods for handling depth

The `MovieClip` class provides four methods that allow you to control the depth of an object programmatically. Since the `MovieClip` class is an ancestor of the `UIObject` class, these methods are available to every component in the architecture.

The four methods are as follows:

- `getDepth`: Returns the depth of a movie clip instance.

- `getInstanceAtDepth`: Returns the reference to a `MovieClip` instance located at the specified depth, if any; undefined is returned if there is no instance at that depth.

- `getNextHighestDepth`: Returns an integer that is associated with the next available depth that would place a newly created object on top of all the objects already existing in the same timeline. We used this method in the dynamic slideshow example to stack the objects created dynamically in the most intuitive way.

- `swapDepths`: Exchanges the depth of two objects so that the object that was on top moves behind the other one.

The four methods implemented by the MovieClip class are very useful, and you will certainly invoke some of them when handling the depth of a specific object.

With the DepthManager class, the component architecture goes a step further by providing a centralized point that allows you to stack objects with flexibility while keeping certain depths reserved for specially identified uses.

A more flexible way of stacking objects

The DepthManager allows you to achieve a better organization of your application's depths by splitting the z-order into two separate spaces:

- **The Relative Space**: In this space, you can freely define the depths of your objects in relative terms. Such terms can be expressed by using depth categories or referring to another, already existing, object. Note that, in both cases, the DepthManager can rearrange the depths of other objects, if necessary, to fulfill your request.
- **The Reserved Space**: This space is maintained by placing a specially created movie clip at the highest depth of the _root object and by creating the objects at reserved depths inside this special movie clip.

Most of the time, you will create or move objects in the Relative Space. The DepthManager methods for allocating objects in the Relative Space are

- createChildAtDepth: Creates an instance of a symbol in the library at the specified relative depth category
- createClassChildAtDept: Creates a component instance of the specific class at the specified relative depth category
- setDepthAbove: Places an object just above another object, moving any other object in the timeline if necessary
- setDepthBelow: Places an object just below another object, moving any other object in the timeline if necessary
- setDepthTo: Places an object in a relative depth category

DepthManager divides the Relative Space into three relative depth categories:

- **Bottom Layer**: This category contains depths that are below the other two categories in the Relative Space.
- **Top Layer**: This category contains depths that are on top of those in the Bottom Layer and below those in the Topmost Layer.
- **Topmost Layer**: This category contains depths that are on top of those in the other two categories in the Relative Space.

DepthManager defines four constants to allow you to obtain depths within a category in the relative space:

- kBottom: Specifies a depth within the Bottom Layer category.
- kTop: Specifies a depth within the Top Layer category.

- kTopmost: Specifies a depth within the Topmost Layer category.
- kNotopmost: Specifies a depth not within the Topmost Layer category. This constant is typically used to remove objects from the Topmost Layer category.

DepthManager also implements reserved depths to be used in special cases. Such depths are allocated in a special space, a Reserved Space, which is above any other object in the _root.

DepthManager provides two methods for creating objects at such depths:

- createClassObjectAtDepth: Creates a component instance of the specific class at the specified reserved depth
- createObjectAtDepth: Creates an instance of a symbol in the library at the specified reserved depth

At the time of writing, DepthManager includes two reserved depths in the Reserved Space, which are accessed via their respective constants:

- kCursor: This is the topmost of all depths and is usually reserved for a cursor-like object as suggested by the name of its constant.
- kTooltip: This is just below the previous reserved depth, and it is intended for use as tooltip-like content, as suggested by the name of its constant.

Figure 4-12 shows the depth relationships among the Relative Space (and its depth categories) and the Reserved Space (and its reserved depths).

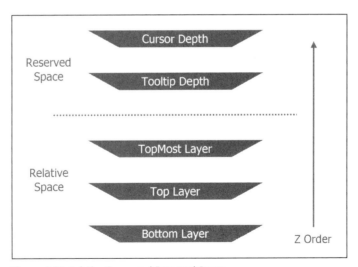

Figure 4-12. Relative Space and Reserved Space

The methods and constants implement by DepthManager may seem obscure at first. However, they can indeed help you in better organizing the depths of your application's objects, since it models them rationally in two different spaces (Relative and Reserved), plus it rearranges automatically all the object depths in the background to keep those models consistent with your specification.

Let's make a few simple tests so you can quickly grasp how to use DepthManager and let it organize the depths of the objects in an application.

Testing the DepthManager behavior

In the following examples, we will create instances of the Button component dynamically for test purposes only. Remember that, in order to create a component instance dynamically, such a component must be present in the library of the Flash document, and the quickest way of ensuring this is to drag the component onto the stage of the document once and then remove it.

The first test is very simple; you can create a new Flash document and just drop the following ActionScript in its first and only frame:

```
import mx.managers.DepthManager;
import mx.controls.Button;
trace("DepthManager.kTop = " + DepthManager.kTop);
button1 = createClassChildAtDepth(Button, DepthManager.kTop,
➡ {_x: 10, _y:10, label: "Button 1"});
trace("button1 depth = " + button1.getDepth());
button2 = createClassChildAtDepth(Button, DepthManager.kTop,
➡ {_x: 15, _y:15, label: "Button 2"});
trace("button2 depth = " + button2.getDepth());
```

The result of testing the movie in the environment is displayed in Figure 4-13.

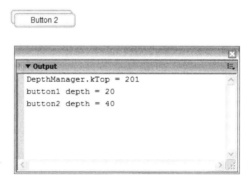

Figure 4-13. DepthManager, test 1

We create two Button instances dynamically using a DepthManager method (createClassChildAtDepth) and a constant (kTop) to place both of them in the Top Layer category. As a result of this, the second instance appears on top of the first one because new instances automatically appear on top if put in the same depth category.

In particular, DepthManager assigns a depth of 20 to button1 and a depth of 40 to button2. The gap of 20 positions is intentionally left by DepthManager to allow you to fit objects in between without having to necessarily rearrange other depths. Such gaps, therefore, increase the performance of the application transparently.

In the example, we also trace the value of the kTop constant to show that it is insignificant for the developer, since it does not have any relationship with the actual depth values of the objects. What you need to remember is the name of the constant (kTop) and the fact that it specifies placing the objects in the Top Layer, which is between the Bottom Layer and the Topmost Layer in the Relative Space of depths managed by the DepthManager.

Our second example is almost as simple as the first one. Once again, create an empty Flash document and drop the following code into its first and only frame:

```
import mx.managers.DepthManager;
import mx.controls.Button;

createClassObject(Button, "button1", 20,
➥ {_x: 10, _y:10, label:'Button 1'});
trace("button1 depth = " + button1.getDepth());
button2 = createClassChildAtDepth(Button,
➥ DepthManager.kTop, {_x: 15, _y:15, label: "Button 2"});
trace("button2 depth = " + button2.getDepth());
button3 = createClassChildAtDepth(Button,
➥ DepthManager.kTop, {_x: 20, _y:20, label: "Button 3"});
trace("button3 depth = " + button3.getDepth());
```

The result of testing the movie in the environment is displayed in Figure 4-14.

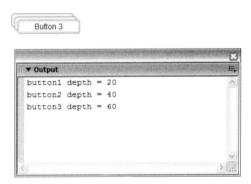

Figure 4-14. DepthManager, test 2

In this example, we create three Button instances. For the first, we do not use DepthManager, instead creating it by invoking the createClassObject method of the UIObject class and specifying an absolute depth of 20.

Why do we do this? We are trying to be naughty and create a problem for DepthManager. In the previous example, we discovered that DepthManager "likes" to place the first object created in the Top Layer at an absolute depth of 20.

What happens then if, like in our second example, an object already exists there?

The answer is shown in the output window. The DepthManager realizes this and, quite simply, adds a depth of 40 to button2 and 60 to button3, keeping faith in its previously examined incremental policy. This demonstrates that DepthManager is aware of depths and handles them quite consistently.

By now, you will have realized that you can use DepthManager to avoid having to deal with absolute depths!

Furthermore, the Relative/Reserved Spaces model implemented by DepthManager suggests a rational way of arranging your objects' depths when designing your application.

We can now move on and examine the next manager class.

Managing the keyboard focus

Some users may prefer to interact with your Flash applications by using the keyboard more than the mouse.

Because of this, the design of your applications should include the implementation of a logical tab order to allow your users to navigate through the various components using the *Tab* key.

The FocusManager is the manager class you should be using when defining the order in which component instances receive the keyboard focus when the user presses the *Tab* key.

Each component in the architecture is aware of the FocusManager and uses it transparently so that, most of the time, you don't have to write any code at all to manage the keyboard focus.

Note that there are a couple of issues that you may find annoying when testing the tab order of a Flash movie:

- The *Tab* key does not work when testing the movie in the authoring environment. You must run the compiled movie in the Flash player outside of the authoring environment or in a browser.
- When testing the movie in the Flash player or in a browser, you must ensure that the movie has the focus by clicking its area once before pressing the *Tab* key and testing the tab order.

If you launch one of the last two examples we built for the DepthManager in the Flash player and take the precaution of clicking the stage once to transfer the keyboard focus to the movie, you will realize that the FocusManager is indeed already handling the tab order; in fact, when you press the *Tab* key, a light green rectangle (the focus rect) surrounds the area of the first button and, if you keep pressing the *Tab* key, moves through all the Button instances on the stage.

By default, the FocusManager looks at the tabIndex property of the objects on stage to define the tab order, starting from the lowest tabIndex value up to the highest one and then cycling by going back to the lowest one. If the tabIndex property is not defined, the FocusManager looks at the depth of the object, which explains why the DepthManager examples had a tab order even if we didn't explicitly define one.

Defining a focus schema

In addition to tabIndex, the FocusManager utilizes two additional properties of an object (if it is either a movie clip or a component):

- tabChildren: Indicates whether the object has children that can receive the focus
- tabEnabled: Indicates whether the object itself can receive the focus

An object that can receive the focus is usually referred as a **tab target**. You define the tab targets of your application by setting their tabChildren/tabEnabled property accordingly.

You also define the navigation order of the tab targets (tab order) by assigning the proper values to the tabIndex property of each tab target.

In the end, a tab schema is implemented by properly defining up to three properties for each object in your application (tabEnabled, tabChildren, tabIndex).

The following code implements a simple focus schema:

```
container_mc.tabChildren=true;
container_mc.tabEnabled=false;

textInput1.tabIndex = 1;
textInput2.tabIndex = 2;
container_mc.textArea1.tabIndex = 3;
container_mc.textInput3.tabIndex = 4;

textInput1.text = "textInput1";
textInput2.text = "textInput2";
container_mc.textArea1.text = "textArea1";
container_mc.textInput3.text = "textInput3";

focusManager.setFocus(container_mc.textArea1);
```

To implement this example, you must have two TextInput instances on the _root (named textInput1 and textInput2, respectively) and another two component instances (a TextArea named textArea1 and another TextInput named textInput3) inside a movie clip named container_mc that is placed at _root level as well.

Remember to run this example inside the Flash player since the last line (setting the focus on the textArea1) would not be effective in the authoring environment. You can find a test01.html file in the source code associated with this section that you can use for this purpose. Note that, at the time of writing, Internet Explorer is the only browser to support the JavaScript focus function of the Flash player accessible, which is accessible via JavaScript as displayed in this code segment extracted from the test01.html file:

```
window.onload = function () {
    window.document.test01.focus();
}
```

In the case of other browsers, the user must click the Flash movie clip embedded in the HTML file in order to transfer the focus to the Flash player and then test the example.

The main points to take away from this example are the following:

- You can define a tab order programmatically that can include containers and their children. Such a tab order is supported transparently and intuitively by the FocusManager.
- Since there are components in the application, you can access a FocusManager instance named focusManager at the _root level. The example accesses it to invoke the setFocus method, initially giving the focus to the textArea1 instance inside container_ mc.

Figure 4-15 shows the output of the example run within the Flash player.

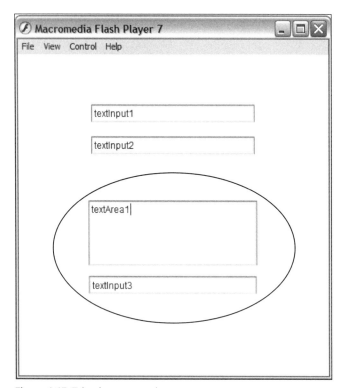

Figure 4-15. Tab schema example

At the time of writing, the implementation of the setFocus method presents a little quirk: it sets the focus to the specified object (textArea1 in our example) without making the focus rect appear around the object. The focus rect appears in this example only when you start pressing the *TAB* key to navigate around the components and test that the implementation of the focus schema follows the intended tab order.

Setting a default button

The FocusManager supports the definition of a default button. This button receives a click event whenever the user presses the *ENTER* key (or the *RETURN* key on a Mac).

You can specify a default button via the defaultPushButton property as in the following example:

```
focusManager.defaultPushButton = buttonInstance;
```

The FocusManager also provides a method for sending a click event to the default button program-matically: sendDefaultPushButtonEvent.

```
focusManager.sendDefaultPushButtonEvent();
```

When the previous line of code is executed, the default button receives a click event that is also propagated to any other listener of the default button click event, if any.

Tab order in a browser

You may experience a couple of unwanted behaviors when your Flash application is embedded inside an HTML page in your browser:

- The Flash movie usually does not receive the focus once the page is loaded. As a result, any call to the setFocus method may be ineffective.
- When navigating the component instances in the application by pressing the *TAB* key, the focus eventually moves outside of the Flash application to the HTML page and then to the browser.

Unfortunately, the FocusManager cannot handle such situations, since they fall beyond its scope. In fact, the only way you can address such misbehaviors is by modifying the code of the HTML page hosting the Flash movie.

In the first case, in order to pass the focus to the Flash movie, once that HTML page is loaded, you can resort to some JavaScript code as in the following example:

```
<script language="JavaScript">
<!--

window.onload = function () {
    window.document.test01.focus();
}

-->
</script>
```

where test01 is the value of the id/name attributes of the HTML tag embedding the Flash movie (either object or embed).

However, the JavaScript focus method does not work in some combinations of browser platform/Flash player. Eventually, the best way of setting the focus to the Flash movie still is to click once on its stage.

To restrict/allow the focus to move away from the Flash application when navigating with the *TAB* key, you can specify an additional attribute (SeamlessTabbing) in the HTML code, as in this example:

```
<param name="SeamlessTabbing" value="false"/>
```

This keeps the focus inside the Flash movie, since SeamlessTabbing was set to false.

Disabling the focus rect

A component instance knows how to draw a focus rect around its area to highlight that it has received the focus.

You can disable this behavior programmatically by setting a component instance drawFocus method to null, as in the following example:

```
componentInstance.drawFocus = null;
```

If the focus rect of a component instance looks unpleasant in the design of your application, the previous line prevents it from being drawn.

In the end, you can write an application without bothering about the functionality provided by the FocusManager. However, such functionality becomes essential when the requirements of your application include a specific focus schema.

Let's now examine the last manager class to be covered in this chapter, PopUpManager.

Managing windows

Nowadays many applications imitate the multiwindow environment typical of modern operating systems. If your intent is to design a similar kind of application, you will certainly find a big help in the functionality provided by the PopUpManager.

The PopUpManager is capable of creating and destroying overlapping windows that can be either modal or nonmodal and exposes its functionality via two public methods only:

- createPopUp: Creates a pop-up window dynamically.
- deletePopUp: Added by the PopUpManager to a window instance previously created by invoking the createPopUp method. Calling windowInstance.deletePopUp destroys the related window instance.

The createPopUp method of the PopUpManager offers a number of options that are worth a thorough examination. Following the usual concrete approach, we are going to explore its functionality via a complete example.

A simple window-based system

The following example will create a window-based application with very few lines of code, exploiting the functionality provided by the PopUpManager.

In order to create the example, you just need a new Flash document that includes the Window and the Button components in its library. By now, you should be well aware that the easiest way to fulfill such a requirement is to create an instance of each type of component on stage and then delete it.

The rest of the example relies on the following code to be placed on the first and only empty frame of the Flash document:

```
import mx.managers.PopUpManager;
import mx.containers.Window;
import mx.controls.Button;

var windowId:Number = 1;

function onCloseClicked(eventObject) {
    eventObject.target.deletePopUp();
}

function getWindowInitObject() {
    return { _x:50,
        _y:50,
        _width: 400,
        _height: 400,
        closeButton:true,
        title: "Window" + windowId++
    }
}

function click(eventObject) {
    var windowInstance = PopUpManager.createPopUp(this,
➥ Window, false, getWindowInitObject());
    var closeListener = new Object();
    closeListener.click = onCloseClicked;
    windowInstance.addEventListener("click", closeListener);
}

btnCreateWin = createClassObject(Button, "btnCreateWin", 1,
➥ { _x:10, _y:10, label:'Create Window'});
btnCreateWin.addEventListener("click", this);
```

It is almost incredible that such a tiny script can create a window-based system within a Flash movie. Of course, the code of this example could have been even shorter, but that would have affected its readability and would not have sufficiently highlighted the most essential aspects of creating the window-based system.

Before analyzing the code, you may find it convenient to test the movie and check out its behavior.

Once you run the movie, the stage will look almost empty. Only a single button labeled Create Window appears. Once you clicked it a few times, several window instances will have been created on the stage, although you may notice only the last one created, since they are stacked on top of each other.

You can move the window instances around by dragging their title bar in exactly the same way that you move the windows of your operating system. After dragging the windows around to discover how many of them you have actually created, your stage may well resemble the one shown in Figure 4-16.

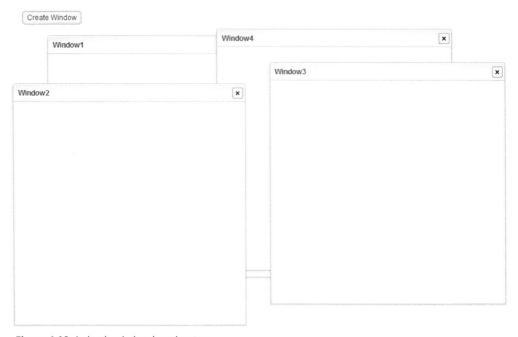

Figure 4-16. A simple window-based system

You will certainly have noticed the little x button at the top-right corner of each window instance. Its function is, again, as you'd expect. When you click it, the window instance is destroyed and, hence, disappears from the stage.

You are welcome to play around with this example, but, apart from creating and destroying window instances, there isn't much more to it.

Destroying and creating window instances is, indeed, the core of the functionality provided by the PopUpManager. Let's examine how it has been exploited by our example.

Creating a window instance

You have already learned how to create a Button instance dynamically and react to its click event; therefore, we can jump directly to examining how the reaction to clicking the Create Window button actually creates a window instance.

Window instances are created by the following line of code:

```
var windowInstance = PopUpManager.createPopUp(this, Window, false,
➥ getWindowInitObject());
```

This requests PopUpManager to create a window instance that is a child of the _root object (first parameter), is an instance of the Window class (second parameter), is a nonmodal window (third parameter), and should be initialized with properties included in the initialization object returned by the getWindowInitObject function (fourth parameter).

It may seem excessive to implement a function (getWindowInitObject) for creating an initialization object but, if you look at its code, you will discover that it manages a windowId variable that allows us to have a different name in the title of each window: quite handy for visually distinguishing window instances from each other.

The createPopUp method returns a reference to the created object that is stored in the windowInstance variable. This variable is used in the next lines of code to implement an object that is listening to the click event of the window's close button:

```
var closeListener = new Object();
closeListener.click = onCloseClicked;
windowInstance.addEventListener("click", closeListener);
```

You may be wondering why you have to implement the code for reacting to the user clicking the close button. Well, apart from the fact that it gives us a golden opportunity for invoking the deletePopUp method, it also gives us maximum flexibility as to how to handle such a user request. In fact, quite frequently you may request the user to confirm his or her choice, especially if it is a critical one.

The actual handler of this click event is implemented at _root level by the following function:

```
function onCloseClicked(eventObject) {
    eventObject.target.deletePopUp();
}
```

This small function does more than it may appear to at first sight. It actually knows that the deletePopUp is a method of a window instance, and that it was the PopUpManager that added such a method to the window instance. It also knows that the window instance associated to the specific event instance is stored in the target property of the eventObject passed as parameter to the event handler. By uniting all this information, the onCloseClicked function is able to close the proper window instance in a single line of code.

You may well refer back to this example again when you start building your first window-based application and experiment with its implementation. Before leaving this topic, however, there is an experiment that you may like to try immediately.

Experimenting with modal windows

A window that behaves like the ones in the previous examples, allowing you to interact with the objects on the stage that are outside of the window itself, is called **nonmodal** or **modeless**. For example, the fact that all the windows in the previous example were modeless allowed you to move from one window to the other and also interact with the Create Window button.

Modal windows, on the other hand, restrict user interaction to the content of the active window instance only. You can experience such behavior by changing a single line of code in the previous example. The change will impact the createPopUp method, and the new line will look as follows:

```
var windowInstance = PopUpManager.createPopUp(this, Window, true,
➥ getWindowInitObject());
```

What changed is the Boolean value passed as the third parameter. The value of true indicates that the window instance being created is modal.

If you run the example again, you will experience pretty different behavior. Once you have created the first window, you cannot access the Create Window button anymore. The button is still there, but you cannot click it until you destroy the existing window instance by clicking its close button. It is only after destroying the modal window instance that you can access the Create Window button again.

A modal window restricts the user interaction to the window instance itself. Every other component outside the window instance becomes inaccessible until the modal window instance is destroyed.

Summary

In this chapter, you have learned that the scope of the component architecture extends far beyond the set of components—it includes application frameworks and application-oriented functionality encapsulated in manager classes.

In particular, you have learned about the screen concept and how it can be conveniently used to model your applications around a screen-based hierarchy.

You have also encountered the really productive features provided by the manager classes, and you now know how and when to use them.

However, soon you will realize that this very rich set of functionality made of components and classes needs substantial experience to be used properly and conveniently.

This chapter ends the first part of the book, in which we focused on introducing the component architecture, its features, and how the most basic object-oriented programming techniques can be applied to such features.

The second part of the book will expose advanced techniques and tools that will allow you to exploit the full potential of the component architecture and be able to design and implement large-scale component-based applications in which any aspect of the architecture's standard components can be customized.

Part Two

EXPLOITING THE ARCHITECTURE

Chapter 5

ARCHITECTURE-BASED DEVELOPMENT

I not only think that we will tamper with Mother Nature,
I think Mother Nature wants us to.

Willard Gaylin

The previous chapter ended the introductory part, Part 1, of this book.

By reading Part 1, you have learned that the component architecture is a pretty large beast, made of many thousands of lines of code that implement components via established design patterns, provide frameworks for building new components and component-based applications, and implement various classes that encapsulate application-specific functionality.

Starting with this chapter, Part 2 of the book will show you not only how to avoid getting lost in that sea of options, but also how to leverage the existing application framework to bring it closer to the sort of applications that you want to create using the architecture.

Exploiting the architecture

The component architecture is very rich in functionality, but can it really be successfully exploited? In the early days of software development, function libraries were the ancestors of modern component architectures. To exploit function libraries, however, was a pretty straightforward process: your program either needed the functionality of the fooXYZ function or it didn't; and if it did, you just had to invoke the function fooXYZ and obtain its output.

In those days, computer displays were character-based, and program output was not much more complex than a single line of text.

Nowadays, computer displays not only have very high resolutions, but they also are gates to multi-window environments in which each window can contain all sorts of media, from high-quality graphics to movies. In addition to multimedia capability, modern GUIs also support a wide range of formats, data exchange via drag-and-drop, and much more.

Function libraries made of self-encapsulated functions could have never coped with this new virtual reality: object-oriented architectures have become the natural answer to the new scenario.

The immense high complexity of an application user interface imposes a new, more complex, programming paradigm.

It is true that object orientation simplifies the problem of developing a modern software application, but let's face it: reusing a component architecture is significantly more complex than using a library of functions.

The only reason to accept such an increase in complexity is because of the numerous benefits that we as developers can enjoy by choosing the object-oriented methodology and defining/reusing a component architecture. This is a good place in the chapter to examine in detail what those benefits are.

Key benefits of a component architecture

By using the component architecture, you expect to be able to develop better, more powerful applications at a fraction of the time required to fully develop them on your own.

The following criteria should be considered whenever evaluating whether to use the component architecture in your application or not:

- **Features**: How much would it cost for you to re-create all the components and the functionality included in the architecture?

- **Robustness**: How much would it cost for you to implement similar or even better design patterns than those encapsulated in the architecture?

- **Scalability**: How much would it cost for you to make your application as extensible as it can be made using the architecture?

- **Maintenance**: What's the cost of producing a well-separated design like the one included in the architecture to reduce the cost of testing and having an application resilient to changes when requests will come in?

If you can successfully exploit what the component architecture can offer, then any other option becomes insignificant. What you now need is to learn how you must work to make your applications enjoy those benefits by learning how to gain advantage by using the component architecture.

What is your job, really?

Not infrequently, marketing hype can turn away real developers even before they actually evaluate a product. *"Use the XYZ technology and you will develop your application in an instant"* is the kind of advertisement you will typically see, and that can instantly trigger a negative reaction.

Most experienced developers are well aware that there isn't such a thing as a silver bullet where application development is concerned.

In this book, you have already read that you may produce better applications in less time by using the component architecture. However, that is far from stating that it is a very quick process; it can still take a significant amount of time.

The combination Flash Player/component architecture has achieved a level of maturity to be worth being considered for serious, custom-made, large Internet applications. And nobody is going to develop one of those overnight, not even the fastest gun in town.

Regardless of its simplicity, the diagram in Figure 5-1 illustrates what is probably the most important objective of any software project based on the component architecture.

On the left side of the diagram, notice the component architecture with a reference to all of its components, classes, frameworks, and design patterns. On the right side is a complete application, like the ones that you will be creating. In between is a dotted line labeled "Functional Distance."

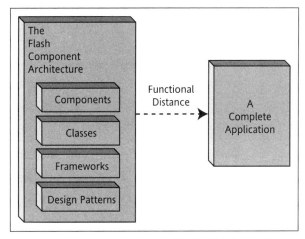

Figure 5-1. The Functional Distance

The Functional Distance is an abstract measure of the functionality required by your application that you will not find in the architecture, regardless of its many features; creating it is your job. The term "distance" has been chosen to indicate a length that you must cover in order to complete your project. Every time you develop an application based on the component architecture, you must cover that distance.

The whole of Part 2 of this book is dedicated to showing you how to cover that distance, and also how to make it conveniently shorter.

Raising the bar

Learning is a never-ending process, and a good developer, no matter how experienced, constantly discovers better practices.

A component architecture represents an ideal place to store any hard-won knowledge so that it doesn't get lost and can be reused in the future.

Let's examine what options you have to store your knowledge into the architecture.

Extend, expand, and alter

The logic of the component architecture is stored in the source code of a set of ActionScript classes that developers can find in the Flash authoring environment.

The availability of the source code of the architecture is usually a requisite of serious projects since it allows you to overcome the architecture's limitations, if any.

Apart from learning a lot by examining that source code, developers face three different possibilities when building applications that use such code:

- **Extend the architecture**: By adding new classes that are derived from classes already existing in the architecture and, as such, inheriting their functionality and purpose

- **Expand the architecture**: By adding new classes that are not derived directly from the existing ones although may use them

- **Alter the architecture**: By modifying the architecture's already existing classes to fix a bug or add/modify a global behavior

The three options have been listed in decreasing order of the frequency they are utilized. However, it is important that you keep in mind all of them when planning to use the architecture, since each option impacts the architecture in a very different way, and the choice of using one or the other can severely influence the fortunes of your project.

Let's examine what each option has to offer and how it affects your use of the architecture and, eventually, your work.

Extending the architecture

Extending the architecture involves creating a new class that inherits the functionality (and part of its own identity) from one of the classes already present in the architecture.

Figure 5-2 illustrates a few examples and, more importantly, the "direction" of your developments when you are extending the architecture.

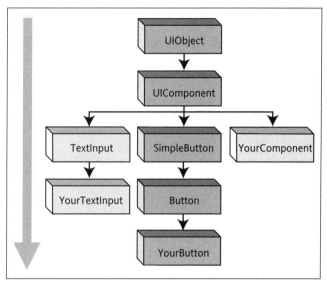

Figure 5-2. Direction of extension

This diagram includes only a fragment of the component architecture (UIObject, UIComponent, TextInput, SimpleButton, Button) and three different examples that extend it:

- YourTextInput: A dummy name for a class that you may create to further specialize the behavior of the TextInput component.
- YourButton: Similar to the previous example, this is another class that you may create to add new functionality to the Button component.
- YourComponent: A class that inherits from UIComponent and, as such, it is up to you to implement its specific functionality by creating a brand-new component.

By creating new components that are based on existing ones or simply on the existing component framework, your components can inherit a functional identity (as in the case of YourButton, which, apart from any additions, is still a button) or, at least, be compliant with the interfaces/behavior set by the architecture (as in the case of the brand-new component YourComponent).

When extending the architecture, you are making its class structure deeper, as illustrated by the direction line in Figure 5-2, which is vertical and points toward the bottom.

The main objectives of increasing the depth of the architecture are to customize existing components or to create new components that are architecturally compatible with the preexisting ones (since they inherit from a common base class if it is either UIObject or UIComponent).

The most frequent reason for customizing components is to have greater control over their appearance. You will learn more about this when we examine the techniques for modifying the look of a component via skins and styles later in the book.

135

Expanding the architecture

Expanding the architecture involves creating new classes that are not derived from classes in the architecture but that do utilize classes in the architecture.

Typically, but not necessarily, you discover the necessity of such classes when working on a particular problem domain. Some of those classes will be useful only in the domain that originates them; in other cases, you will expand the architecture with functionality that can be reused in almost any other context.

Figure 5-3 illustrates a case where further functionality was added in the direction of the problem domain. The ExoticOption class is utilized as a business object, the logic of which is added to the component architecture instead of being derived from it.

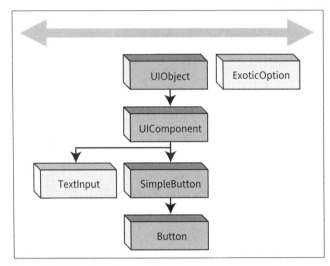

Figure 5-3. Direction of expansion

In finance, an exotic option is any nonstandard security.

In our example, ExoticOption stands for a context-specific class and, as such, is not derived from any of the classes already present in the architecture. ExoticOption is not a component of the user interface. However, the ExoticOption class is expanding over the architecture because it makes use of one or more of the classes in the architecture. For example, ExoticOption may use the Alert class when the user must make a yes/no decision. This is not the same thing as being derived from the architecture.

When expanding the architecture, you add classes that are figuratively at the same level of the root of the structure (UIObject), since they are not derived from any preexisting class in the architecture. As a result, the class structure of the architecture becomes wider, as illustrated by the direction line in the Figure 5-3, which is horizontal and points toward the left and right sides of the structure.

Note that the difference in the direction of development is not just a figurative issue. As we saw earlier, when extending the architecture, the new classes inherit some kind of functional identity (a new kind of button or a new kind of UI component). Conversely, expanding the architecture implies adding classes that introduce new functional identities in the architecture. Some of those functional identities may be related to the business logic of the domain of your application (ExoticOption if your client is in the financial industry, AminoAcids if instead your client belongs to the pharmaceutical sector), but others may be domain independent and, therefore more reusable, as in the concrete examples that we are going to examine later on when we expand and extend the architecture at the same time to implement an XML layout engine.

Altering the architecture

Altering the architecture does not involve the creation of new classes, but modifications to the ones already existing in the architecture. Figure 5-4 illustrates an example of this.

Figure 5-4 includes the same fragment of the component architecture utilized in Figures 5-2 and 5-3. But in this case, there are no new classes added, since the change happened within one or more of the existing classes.

While the class structure of the architecture remains the same, modifying the source code provided with the Flash authoring environment can still alter the architecture.

Altering the architecture usually requires an in-depth knowledge of its internals, and it is not recommended. However, you may find yourself in a couple of different situations where this is necessary or convenient. For example:

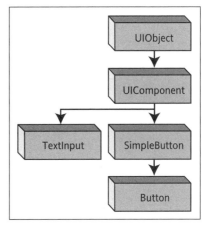

Figure 5-4. Alteration (no direction)

- When you need to fix a bug that is hindering your project. Since fixing a bug does not alter a class-intended behavior, such alteration is very convenient as long as the final result actually fixes the bug.

- If you also decide to implement a global requirement. For instance, if all of your components must be able to rotate in a 3D space, then you may well consider implementing such functionality via a rotate3D method and including the definition of this method in the UIComponent class so as to have it consistently available for every component in the architecture.

From abstract ideas to a concrete example

From what you're read so far, you are probably starting to appreciate that the contents of this chapter are rather abstract, and the concepts discussed are fairly high level.

Component architectures usually start from a big picture, made of several high-level concepts. The same is true for significant applications or additional layers of logic that are developed on top of a large architecture.

Building a functional application requires more than learning what functionality is available in the architecture and what programming techniques are required to use it. It also demands the ability to translate high-level ideas into a logic design that can be successfully implemented on top of the architecture.

In order to see the many abstract concepts introduced earlier at work, we need a concrete example capable of exploiting several, if not all, of the benefits that our component architecture can offer.

A classic application, such as an address book or a stock options manager, would leave much of the functionality offered by the component architecture untouched and, as such, would not play the role of a concrete example successfully.

Our ideal example should act as a logic layer developed on top of the component architecture, employing not only every component, but also any other class included in the architecture. That is what an XML layout engine must do in order to provide its own functionality, so we'll use it as an ideal example to put into practice the concepts we have discussed so far.

What is an XML layout engine?

In the context of this book, an **XML layout engine** represents an ideal tutorial since it can rationally connect the numerous concrete examples required to introduce every aspect involved in controlling the appearance and behavior of each UI component included in the architecture.

There's an added bonus here—in its own right, an XML layout engine is a logic layer that can help you a lot when it comes to building large-scale applications or even rapid prototyping.

An XML layout engine is a layer of logic that allows you to describe a complete user interface via a single text file. The text file contains the XML necessary to describe the user interface; we can then use that data to build it dynamically. Due to its nature, XML is particularly appropriate for describing complex user interfaces, the likes of which are usually implemented using components nested inside a hierarchy of containers.

An XML layout engine uses XML to achieve a neat separation between the implementation of a user interface and the application-specific code. Such separation largely facilitates both the development and maintenance of a component-based application.

XML layout engines are utilized in many software technologies these days. Operating systems, Internet browsers, and several major applications already have embedded XML layout engines, or announcements have been made of their availability in the next version.

Basically, several products have already successfully demonstrated that an XML layout engine can play a strategic role in the implementation of user interfaces for reasons that we are going to examine in the next section.

Benefits of an XML layout engine

Most of the benefits of an XML layout engine are due to its logical place within the structure of an application, as shown in Figure 5-5.

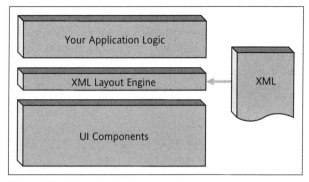

Figure 5-5. Placing the XML layout engine

Typically, an XML layout engine "sits" on top of a set of UI components and is capable of generating them dynamically following a layout specification provided via XML.

While providing such functionality, an XML layout engine neatly separates the application-specific logic from its user interface. Plenty of benefits derive directly from such separation:

- Having the user interface described via XML allows us to easily provide different user interfaces for the same application. Such freedom becomes tremendously cost effective in all the cases when your application must address different accessibility issues, localization (user interfaces for different languages/countries), different hardware platforms, even down to different branding and different user preferences. You can address all these cases plus many others by simply providing different XML files for each client scenario.

- The nested structure of the XML description of the user interface directly reflects the nested structure of its layout, making it much easier to work with complex user interfaces, which ultimately enables a much easier and faster development.

- The mix of user interface and application code can produce hybrid scripts that are difficult to maintain. An XML layout engine eliminates any scripting code usually required to create the user interface and in doing so avoids your code being cluttered.

- By defining the user interface of your application independently from its business logic, it allows you to modify the layout and appearance of your application without having to rebuild it.

- It enforces the implementation of the Model-View-Controller design pattern that is well known for greatly simplifying the process of implementing an application.

- The resulting application is much more flexible and resilient to changes. You can rewrite the whole UI without touching the business logic.

- It facilitates the coordination of activities that are interdependent and usually assigned to different roles in the case of large projects. Workflows involving developers, designers, and content producers can be defined in a more efficient way thanks to a neater degree of separation.

All these benefits are very important, plus the bigger your application, the more they become evident: the tight coupling of user interface code with application-specific logic is one of the major downfalls of software development projects.

In the end, an XML layout engine can dramatically reduce the time and effort that you put into developing component-based applications. The benefits listed apply to the most general concept and are already more than enough, if you are like me, for you to crave for an XML layout engine when creating user interfaces.

And as if that were not enough, the list of benefits becomes even longer specifically in the context of Flash.

Further benefits in the Flash context

The component architecture, ActionScript, the Flash player, and the SWF format represent the main technologies targeted by the specific XML layout engine that will be introduced in this book—it has been designed to improve productivity by

- Easing the writing of XML parsing code
- Easing the writing of event management code

Applications based on the engine will enjoy a high degree of flexibility because we will be

- Adding new XML tags that generate new components
- Updating the implementation of an existing XML tag to align it with the latest version of a component

Note that the last option can drastically reduce the cost of porting an application from one version of the component architecture into the next one: Since the engine generates the components dynamically, once it is updated, it will start generating the latest version of each component for each of your applications that use it.

Some work has also been done to further enforce the consistency of the look and feel of your applications by including style support in the XML syntax used to describe the layout of a user interface.

XLEFF

XLEFF (**X**ML **L**ayout **E**ngine **F**or **F**lash) is the official name of the XML layout engine introduced in this book.

XLEFF should not be compared to FLEX, since FLEX is a server-side technology based on a Java application server, while XLEFF is a client-side technology that does not require a particular technology on the server side. Basically, projects that benefit from the use of FLEX would not benefit from the use of XLEFF and vice versa. Scenarios where both the technologies could be considered are very unlikely because of their different natures.

XLEFF has been designed to be a thin layer of logic on top of the component architecture residing inside the SWF file, as you see in Figure 5-6.

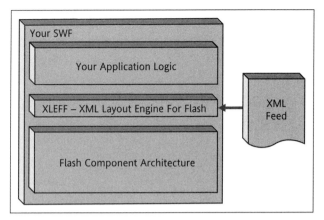

Figure 5-6. XLEFF

Apart from sharing substantial similarities with the diagram in Figure 5-5, Figure 5-6 shows that your application logic, XLEFF, and the functionality of the component architecture (components, etc.) will be packaged in a single SWF file that consumes an external XML feed as a specification to generate the user interface dynamically.

The XML vocabulary supported by XLEFF is very close to that of the architecture and, therefore, of immediate use once you know the architecture.

The following XML description would generate a form including two buttons:

```
<?xml version="1.0"?>
<XLEFF>
    <stage>
        <form>
            <name>MainForm</name>
            <xpos>0</xpos>
            <ypos>0</ypos>
            <button>
                <name>YesButton</name>
                <lbl>Yes</lbl>
                <xpos>270</xpos>
                <ypos>280</ypos>
                <width>160</width>
            </button>
            <button>
                <name>NoButton</name>
                <lbl>No</lbl>
                <xpos>470</xpos>
                <ypos>280</ypos>
                <width>160</width>
            </button>
        </form>
    </stage>
</XLEFF>
```

141

Figure 5-7 shows what this form would look like.

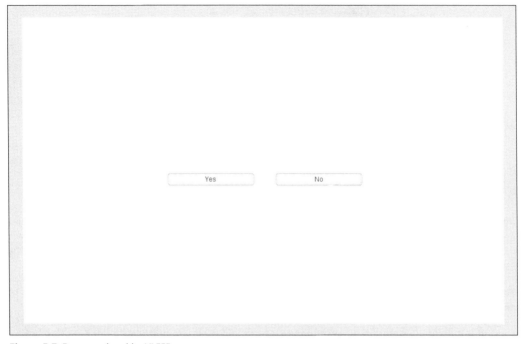

Figure 5-7. Form rendered by XLEFF

The previous XML description was purposely defined using the bare minimum attributes that you may need to specify to place a form on the stage and two button instances inside it. However, XLEFF supports many more features and is capable of handling via XML almost any functionality present in the component architecture.

Additionally, thanks to the combination of styles and skins, XLEFF provides an easy and consistent path for the definition of new component themes (including also a sample theme called XLEFFtheme).

By just slightly changing the previous XML description, it is possible to generate buttons belonging to the XLEFFtheme. The necessary XML would be modified as follows:

```
<?xml version="1.0"?>
<XLEFF>
    <stage>
        <form>
            <name>MainForm</name>
            <xpos>0</xpos>
            <ypos>0</ypos>
            <button cls="XLEFFtheme.subclassed.XleffButton">
                <name>YesButton</name>
                <styleName>XLEFFthemeNormalStyle</styleName>
                <lbl>Yes</lbl>
                <xpos>270</xpos>
```

```
                    <ypos>280</ypos>
                    <width>160</width>
                </button>
                <button cls="XLEFFtheme.subclassed.XleffButton">
                    <name>NoButton</name>
                    <styleName>XLEFFthemeNormalStyle</styleName>
                    <lbl>No</lbl>
                    <xpos>470</xpos>
                    <ypos>280</ypos>
                    <width>160</width>
                </button>
            </form>
        </stage>
    </XLEFF>
```

Note that the most significant changes are

- The introduction of a cls attribute specifying a different component class (XLEFFtheme. subclassed.XleffButton) instead of the default one (Button) to be used when generating button instances

- The introduction of an additional tag (styleName) specifying the set of styles to use when creating the button instances

The resulting user interface is displayed Figure 5-8.

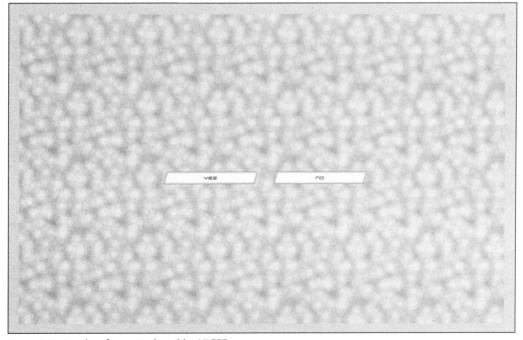

Figure 5-8. Another form rendered by XLEFF

This example was chosen because achieving such a skewed shape for the buttons requires more than just acting on styles and skins. Of course, you could obtain a skewed shape with a skin, but it would not work well with the focus rect (the rectangle highlighting a button when selected) since the default implementation of the focus rect is done via the drawing API, and such implementation assumes that buttons have a rectangular (not skewed) shape.

An instance of XLEFFtheme.subclassed.XleffButton handles styles, skins, and also the focus rect by using the drawing API as well. You will learn how to achieve this level of customization of buttons (and other components) in Part 3 of the book.

XLEFF main features

XLEFF targets the component architecture by supporting all of the standard UI components. In addition, it also supports styles at various levels:

- **Color names**: By declaring color names, you can easily reuse specific colors in different contexts.
- **Style sets**: You can also declare different sets of styles that can be applied at once by utilizing the name of a style set.
- **Global styles**: You define global styles that are used as defaults throughout the application.
- **Instance-specific styles**: You can assign specific styles to a single instance of a component.
- **Class-specific styles**: You can also assign styles to all the instances of a specific component class.

XLEFF can also handle custom classes and can be easily extended to match the new functionality introduced by those classes, if any.

XLEFF supports nesting of containers and components without limitations.

In addition to the functionality typical of an XML layout engine, XLEFF also improves dramatically on the application frameworks available when building applications based on the component architecture.

Beyond generating user interfaces

Applications developed using XLEFF tend to have their ActionScript code entirely contained inside classes.

In the case of the Flash authoring environment, this object-oriented best practice offers a further important advantage. Since classes must be implemented via external ActionScript files, the whole source code of the application will reside outside of the FLA file, making it extremely easier to maintain: you will not have to work hard to find the code cluttered around different frames in different layers of different movie clips—a task that haunted Flash developers until now!

In addition to that, XLEFF also provides an easier way of implementing event management. User interfaces are dead unless your application handles the events that they generate. XLEFF facilitates the writing of event handlers by raising the productivity of the development environment to a level that is comparable to rapid application tools such as Visual Basic or Delphi.

By associating event handlers to component instances in a consistent way, XLEFF further contributes to achieving a neat separation of the three major dimensions of an application: user interface, data model, and business logic.

XLEFF internal architecture

XLEFF was designed to be a very straightforward, thin layer over the architecture components. Because of that, you will be able to extend and customize it whenever you will need to add new components or align it to a new version of the component architecture.

The first rule to start with when designing a system is to keep it small and simple. Of course, it is not always possible to respect such a rule, but every successfully implemented system started from a simple core design, even the most complex ones.

At the time of writing, XLEFF is still very manageable since its internal architecture can be illustrated by the rather simple diagram shown in Figure 5-9.

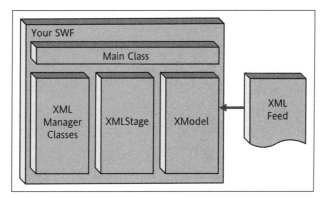

Figure 5-9. XLEFF internal architecture

This diagram zooms inside Figure 5-6 to focus on the XLEFF internals.

The major actors in the implementation of XLEFF are as follows:

- XModel: ActionScript already provides the functionality required for parsing an XML document and exposes it via the XML built-in class. XModel is a class that extends the XML class to facilitate the process of writing business logic code for applications that make an extensive use of XML, as described in Chapter 8.

- XMLStage: XMLStage is the actual core of XLEFF. XMLStage is capable of generating components dynamically whether they are standard or customized components. As you will find out, achieving such a goal requires much more than just invoking the createClassObject method.

- XML manager classes: Similarly to the manager classes in the component architecture, each of the XML manager classes provides some application-specific functionality.

- Main class: The Main class represents the entry point of your application. If you have ever used other programming languages, such as C, you may well know where the name of this class comes from.

It is very unlikely that you will need to extend or modify the XModel class, but you still need to understand what services it provides and why it has been created instead of using the XML class directly.

You will extend the XMLStage occasionally, when you want to generate new components via XLEFF or you want to align it to a new version of a component. Its internals, however, capture the rather complicated workflow of stylizing and skinning a component via bitmaps and/or the drawing API, so it does represent the concrete example you were looking for to learn what techniques to apply for achieving that.

Again, it is very unlikely that you will need to extend the XML manager classes. As in the case of the manager classes provided with the component architecture, it will be enough to know what services they provide and when to use them.

Every time you build an application, you will also provide your implementation of the Main class. The Main class captures the application framework defined by XLEFF and dramatically helps you in reducing the Functional Distance I was talking about at the beginning of this chapter.

The next chapters will delve deeper into XLEFF, and you are going to find out about a lot of advanced techniques during the process.

XLEFF news and updates can be found at www.xleff.org/.

Summary

In this chapter, the focus of the book moved from introducing the component architecture into using it in the scope of a project.

You then learned the key concepts to consider and the best practices to apply in order to successfully exploit the architecture in the context of commercial applications.

You also learned what an XML layout engine is and the many benefits it can provide. And you discovered that this book contains and exposes one of those engines and that, by learning how it has been implemented, you will also capture the knowledge required to customize the appearance and behavior of any GUI component in the architecture, a knowledge that you may also reuse separately in all sorts of projects.

Note that this is by far the most conceptual chapter in the book and, because of that, probably the most important one. You may well find it beneficial to read it again after having explored the concrete examples in the rest of the book, because every time you come back to this chapter, it will probably show you those same examples in a different, richer light.

Chapter 6

XML FOR DEFINING USER INTERFACES

Efficiency is intelligent laziness.

David Dunham

XML is a markup language well suited for describing information.

The component architecture already includes a couple of components (Menu and Tree) that use XML to describe the structure and contents of their instances.

XLEFF, the XML layout engine utilized in this book as part of our tutorial, pushes that approach even further by applying it not only to every other component, but also to colors, styles, and the stage itself.

By using the same vocabulary of the component architecture, XLEFF supports an XML data structure that very closely resembles the nature of component-based user interfaces implemented using Flash.

> *The source code and completed files that are introduced in this chapter can be found in the package* `src06.zip`, *downloadable from this book's page at* `www.friendsofed.com`.

Basics of the XML data structure

The XML data structure supported by XLEFF is a natural extension to the approach already hinted in the architecture and has been designed to be simple to learn and use.

The following template provides a high-level view of the data structure supported by XLEFF:

```
<?xml version="1.0"?>
<xleff>
    <!-- Color Names section -->
    <!-- Styles section -->
    <!-- Stage section -->
</xleff>
```

The three lines of comment in the previous template are placeholders for the three main sections of the XML data structure:

- The Color Names section allows you to define color names.

- The Styles section allows you to define styles.

- The Stage section describes the layout of the user interface that will be generated dynamically. The description of the user interface can include color names and styles defined in the previous two sections.

After examining the big picture of the XML data structure as further illustrated in Figure 6-1, we now turn to examine the contents of the three major sections in greater detail.

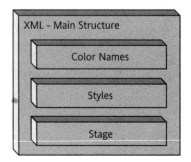

Figure 6-1. XML data structure, the big picture

The Color Names section

The section dedicated to color names is the first of the three major sections in the XML syntax supported by XLEFF (as mentioned, the remaining two sections are dedicated to the styles and the stage description).

Even if color naming is arguably the simplest among all the features supported by the component architecture, color names should not be overlooked, since they can be very helpful in designing user interfaces that are both flexible and consistent.

A single XML element is sufficient to declare a color name, and the Color Names section of the XML data structure can be used to quickly declare several color names as in the following example, in which three XML lines are sufficient to associate three names with their respective color values:

```
<color name="xleffThemeColor" rgb="0xDDDDFF" />
<color name="xleffTextColor" rgb="0x000099" />
<color name="xleffDisabledColor" rgb="0xDDDDDD" />
```

Color names provide at least four substantial advantages:

- A color name can be easier to remember than its numerical value.

- A color name can associate a color value with a particular scope (xleffTextColor clearly indicates the color of text in the user interface).

- Color names enforce the consistency of look and feel throughout the design of a user interface.

- Well-defined color names significantly increase the flexibility of a user interface, since they allow you to change color to several related objects at the same time by changing a single color value.

In the end, color names have been included in the main XML data structure of XLEFF because they are a native feature of the component architecture, they are easy to use, and they provide significant advantages while promoting the use of best practices.

The Styles section

Every section of the XML data structure describes some feature supported by the component architecture, and the Styles section is no exception.

The component architecture supports several kinds of styles; some styles have a "global effect" in the sense that they affect several component instances at the same time, while other styles have a limited "local effect" affecting a specific component instance only.

The Styles section of the XML data structure is dedicated to the styles that can influence more than a component instance at the same time.

All the styles in the XML data structure are described by applying the same XML syntax shown in the following example:

```
<style name="aStyleName">
    <property name="aPropertyName">
        <value type="valueType">aPropertyValue</value>
    </property>
    <!-- other properties -->
</style>
```

Such syntax emphasizes that a style is nothing more than a set of properties with a name (the style's name). The style defines a value for each of the properties it contains.

Each property has its own name and a type attribute specifying the ActionScript type of the property's value stored in the XML value element.

If no type attribute is defined, the property's value is assumed to be of type String.

You can influence the appearance of a component instance in several ways by applying a style to it. The following example defines a custom BlackAndWhite style that you can apply to any component instance to define the color of its text as black (0x000000) and the color of its background as white (0xffffff):

```
<style name="BlackAndWhite">
    <property name="color">
        <value type="Number">0x000000</value>
    </property>
    <property name="backgroundColor">
        <value type="Number">0xffffff</value>
    </property>
</style>
```

When assigning the BlackAndWhite style to a component instance, you are asking the component architecture to assign new values to the color (0x000000) and colorBackground (0xffffff) style properties of that component instance.

Note that some style properties may not make sense in the scope of some component classes: applying the style will have no effect in those cases. Each component in the architecture comes with a list of the style properties that are supported by its class. You can find the list of styles supported by a specific component in the chapters dedicated to each component in Part 3 of the book.

Although the XML syntax for defining a style is always the same, the name that you assign to a style can significantly change the way it works. The Styles section can include different kind of styles: class styles, predefined styles, nested styles, and custom styles. Let us examine how they differ from each other.

Class styles

Class styles are applied automatically by the architecture without your having to assign them to any component instance. That is because a class style applies to all the component instances of a specific component class.

Class styles can be easily recognized because their name is exactly the same (case included) as the class name of a component.

For example, let us rename the style we defined earlier from BlackAndWhite to Button, as in the following:

```
<style name="Button">
    <property name="color">
        <value type="Number">0x000000</value>
    </property>
    <property name="backgroundColor">
        <value type="Number">0xffffff</value>
    </property>
</style>
```

By assigning to it a new name that happens to be the name of a component class (Button), we have transformed our style into a class style.

As a result of this, the component architecture will apply that style automatically to all the Button instances in the user interface described later on in "The Stage Section."

Class styles are a powerful way for defining the standard appearance of instances belonging to a certain component class.

Once again, you obtain a lot from doing very little; in fact, you can influence the appearance of all the instances of a certain class by defining a single style.

Predefined styles

A style defined programmatically is a style that was first implemented in the architecture via ActionScript using the CSSStyleDeclaration class.

Such a style will have a name like windowStyles or dataGridStyles that has been defined by the architecture to influence some visual aspect of the Window and DataGrid components, respectively.

By using one of those predefined names in the XML definition of a style, you will be able to override any properties that may have been defined programmatically by those styles.

Once again, as in the case of class styles, the predefined style will be applied automatically to all the component instances in the user interface that already use such a style.

Predefined styles are not applied consistently in the component architecture, and you need to know about their existence if you want to use them for customizing the appearance of the few components that have them.

Nested styles

Nested styles are the most complicated kind of style that you may need to describe in the Styles section. The good news is that you can easily do this by nesting the same XML syntax that we have been using so far.

For example, the Alert class implements a few nested styles that you can easily redefine by using the syntax shown in the following:

```
<style name="Alert">
    <property name="color">
        <value type="Number">0xff0000</value>
    </property>
    <style name="titleStyleDeclaration">
        <property name="color">
            <value>0xfd765</value>
        </property>
    </style>
    <style name="buttonStyleDeclaration">
        <property name="color">
            <value>0x00fff0</value>
        </property>
    </style>
    <style name="messageStyleDeclaration">
        <property name="color">
            <value>0xa0a0a0</value>
        </property>
    </style>
</style>
```

The previous example shows that nested styles must be included within a class style. The class style in the example is defined by the name Alert and contains its own properties plus three substyles (titleStyleDeclaration, buttonStyleDeclaration, messageStyleDeclaration).

You may notice that in the previous example the color property is defined four times, which is why it is a good example for demonstrating the role of nested styles in complex components.

In the case of the Alert component, in fact, there may be cases when you want to define a different text color for different parts of the component such as the Alert contents, the Alert title, the Alert buttons, and the Alert message.

Without nested styles, you could have set the color property only once, and all those subparts of the component would have been forced to have the same color since you have no other option to specify different values for them.

Note that even in the case of nested styles, it is characteristic of the component architecture to apply the style automatically to all the related component instances once you have defined it in the Styles section.

Custom styles

Custom styles are the simplest and, almost certainly, the most useful among all the kinds of styles that you may use in the Styles section.

They differ substantially from the other three kinds of styles previously discussed, since they are not applied automatically by the component architecture.

Custom styles cannot be applied automatically because their names do not belong to any class, predefined, or even nested style.

Basically, the name of a custom style does not exist in the architecture until you define it. One of our earliest examples, the BlackAndWhite style, was a custom style:

```
<style name="BlackAndWhite">
    <property name="color">
        <value type="Number">0x000000</value>
    </property>
    <property name="backgroundColor">
        <value type="Number">0xffffff</value>
    </property>
</style>
```

Since there is no predefined relationship among a custom style and the component instances in the user interface that you are defining, you must expressly link a custom style to all the component instances that should be influenced by that style. This relationship is very easily established by assigning the value of the custom style name to a property that every component instance in the architecture has: styleName.

Concrete examples of the application of custom styles will be shown in the next section, which introduces the biggest and most important of the three sections in the XML data structure: the Stage section.

The Stage section

The goal of the XML data structure defined in this chapter is to describe the user interface of a component-based Flash application.

The first two sections of the XML data structure, dedicated to colors and styles, usually have a very flat structure, and it is only in the Stage section that we exploit the natural ability of XML to describe nested structures.

The Stage section can have arbitrary levels of nesting, since its substructure describes user interfaces that can have component instances arranged using an arbitrary number of containers.

Figure 6-2 shows an abstract example of a very simple nested structure that could be described in the Stage section with two containers at stage level: Container1, which contains one component instance (ComponentInstance1); and Container2, which contains two component instances (ComponentInstance2 and ComponentInstance3).

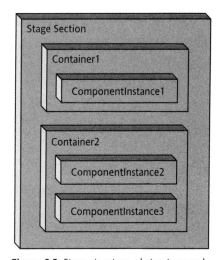

Figure 6-2. Stage structure, abstract example

155

The first-level container in the XML data structure supported by XLEFF must be a form element. All the XML elements supported by XLEFF reflect objects implemented by the component architecture, and the form element is no exception. The form element is based upon the Form class, which is the most general of the two concrete screen classes implemented by the component architecture.

The structure of the Stage section becomes deeper whenever forms include other forms or components that can act as containers (Accordion, ScrollPane, Loader, Window).

The following XML data has been stripped of the XML attributes of each element to highlight the bare structure of the stage section in our example:

```
<stage>
    <form>
        <label />
        <textinput />
        <label />
        <textinput />
        <label />
        <textarea />
        <button />
        <button />
    </form>
    <form >
        <label />
        <textarea />
    </form>
</stage>
```

The previous XML data describes a user interface made of two different forms, each of them containing a few component instances belonging to very common components such as Label, TextInput, TextArea, and Button.

Figure 6-3 illustrates how such an interface may look like once the forms and the component instances have been generated dynamically.

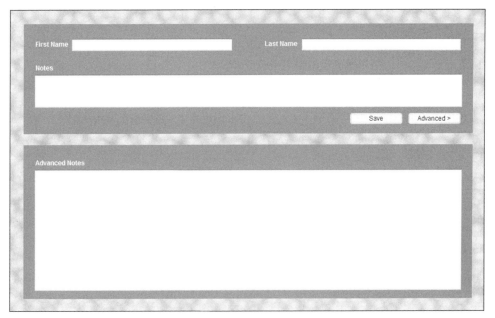

Figure 6-3. Dynamically generated user interface

Looking at the XML data presented earlier, you may not be able to immediately recognize which component instances correspond to what you see in Figure 6-3. The following XML data, complete with the attributes, may look less readable at first, but you will be able to quickly explore it once you get used to separating the interface structure (emphasized in the previous incomplete version of the same XML data) from the details specified by the attributes:

```
<stage>
    <form name="DefaultForm" x="25" y="25" width="840" height="200"
        transparentBackground="false" styleName="xleffForm">
        <label name="label1" x="20" y="27" autoSize="left"
            text="First Name" />
        <textinput name="FirstName" styleName="xleffNormal" x="89"
            y="27" width="300" height="22" />
        <label name="label2" x="447" y="27" autoSize="left"
            text="Last Name" />
        <textinput name="LastName" styleName="xleffNormal" x="517"
            y="27" width="300" height="22" />
        <label name="label3" x="20" y="70" autoSize="left"
            text="Notes" />
        <textarea name="Notes" styleName="xleffNormal" x="20"
            y="92" width="800" height="60" />
        <button name="SaveButton" styleName="xleffNormal" x="607"
            y="162" width="100" height="22" label="Save" />
        <button name="AdvancedButton" styleName="xleffNormal"
            x="717" y="162" width="100" height="22"
            label="Advanced >" />
```

157

```
            </form>
            <form name="AdvancedForm" x="25" y="245" width="840"
                  height="280" transparentBackground="false"
                  styleName="xleffForm">
                <label name="label3" x="20" y="23" autoSize="left"
                      text="Advanced Notes" />
                <textarea name="AdvancedNotes" styleName="xleffNormal"
                          x="20" y="45" width="800" height="220" />
            </form>
        </stage>
```

Note that almost every attribute that you will find in the stage structure reflects the homonymous property of a component class. Do not worry if at this point the name of some properties may sound less intuitive than others: we will examine the actual significance of each component's property in greater detail in Part 3 of the book. At the moment, we are focusing on the XML data structure and how its syntax is capable of describing almost any component-based user interface that you may need to implement.

Even without knowing all the details yet, you should still be able to recognize that the Button instance labeled Save in Figure 6-3 is generated by the following XML element:

```
        <button name="SaveButton" styleName="xleffNormal" x="607"
                y="162" width="100" height="22" label="Save" />
```

since it is the sole button element (of two) to have a label defined as "Save".

It should also be intuitive to you that the remaining attributes of that XML element define the other properties of the component instance such as its position, its size, its style, and the component instance name (SaveButton); the last is arguably the most important of all the attributes, as you will discover in Chapter 9 when learning how to connect the user interfaces generated dynamically via an XML description with actual applications.

XLEFF sampler

The **XLEFF sampler** is the simplest among the applications that can be developed using XLEFF; nevertheless, it is a useful tool for testing the XML data defining a particular user interface.

We are not going to examine the implementation of the sampler here, since our current focus is on the XML structure defined so far, and the sampler has been introduced at the sole scope of providing an immediate way of creating and testing concrete XML examples.

You are not expected to define complete user interfaces until you will have read the rest of the book, which contains all the information you need to define the XML for every component in the architecture, but you are encouraged to experiment with the XML examples provided here to fully grasp the most basic principles introduced by the XML layout engine mechanism.

How to use it

The XLEFF sampler is embedded in an HTML file (XLEFFsampler.html) that you can quickly modify to test your own XML data. The HTML file plays an important role since it defines a variable (xmlDefFileName) that is passed to the Flash player to tell the sampler which XML file should be used as a descriptor of the user interface to be generated dynamically.

If you open the HTML file (XLEFFsampler.html) in a text editor, you will notice that it defines the xmlDefFileName variable by using the FlashVars option of the Flash player by setting it in both the object and embed tags.

The HTML line related to the object tag looks like this:

```
<param name="FlashVars" value="xmlDefFileName=sample01.xml" />
```

while the embed tag includes the following attribute definition:

```
FlashVars="xmlDefFileName=sample01.xml"
```

In both cases, the xmlDefFileName variable will tell XLEFFsampler.swf to load the sample01.xml file. The sampler will then generate a component-based user interface dynamically based on the description contained in that XML file.

If you want to generate the user interface by using a different XML file, all you have to do is change both occurrences of the sample01.xml filename in the HTML file with the actual name of the file that you want to use and, of course, reload the HTML file in your browser.

The sample01.xml file is the completed version of the interface previously shown in Figure 6-3 and contains the following XML data:

```
<?xml version="1.0"?>
<xleff>
    <color name="xleffThemeColor" rgb="0xDDDDFF" />
    <color name="xleffTextColor" rgb="0x000099" />
    <style name="xleffNormal">
        <property name="themeColor">
            <value>xleffThemeColor</value>
        </property>
        <property name="color">
            <value>xleffTextColor</value>
        </property>
        <property name="fontFamily">
            <value>_sans</value>
        </property>
        <property name="fontSize">
            <value type="Number">12</value>
        </property>
    </style>
    <style name="xleffForm">
        <property name="backgroundColor">
            <value>0xa2a2c4</value>
```

159

```
                </property>
            </style>
            <style name="Label">
                <property name="color">
                    <value type="Number">0xFFFFFF</value>
                </property>
                <property name="fontFamily">
                    <value>_sans</value>
                </property>
                <property name="fontWeight">
                    <value>bold</value>
                </property>
                <property name="fontSize">
                    <value type="Number">12</value>
                </property
            </style>
            <stage>
                <form name="DefaultForm" x="25" y="25" width="840" height="200"
                     transparentBackground="false" styleName="xleffForm">
                    <label name="label1" x="20" y="27" autoSize="left"
                         text="First Name" />
                    <textinput name="FirstName" styleName="xleffNormal" x="89"
                             y="27" width="300" height="22" />
                    <label name="label2" x="447" y="27" autoSize="left"
                         text="Last Name" />
                    <textinput name="LastName" styleName="xleffNormal" x="517"
                             y="27" width="300" height="22" />
                    <label name="label3" x="20" y="70" autoSize="left"
                         text="Notes" />
                    <textarea name="Notes" styleName="xleffNormal" x="20"
                              y="92" width="800" height="60" />
                    <button name="SaveButton" styleName="xleffNormal" x="607"
                             y="162" width="100" height="22" label="Save" />
                    <button name="AdvancedButton" styleName="xleffNormal"
                             x="717" y="162" width="100" height="22"
                             label="Advanced >" />
                </form>
                <form name="AdvancedForm" x="25" y="245" width="840"
                    height="280" transparentBackground="false"
                    styleName="xleffForm">
                    <label name="label3" x="20" y="23" autoSize="left"
                         text="Advanced Notes" />
                    <textarea name="AdvancedNotes" styleName="xleffNormal"
                              x="20" y="45" width="800" height="220" />
                </form>
            </stage>
        </xleff>
```

The most important items to take note of in the complete XML example are as follows:

- The interface structure described in the Stage section is exactly the same as that which was emphasized in the very first incomplete example.

- Component instances of different classes frequently share the same attributes names (x, y, height, width, etc.). With very few exceptions, those names describe the same functionality (position, size, etc.) and match the properties defined by the component architecture.

- Occasionally, XLEFF extends the component architecture, implementing, for instance, a colorable background for forms that can also be transparent.

- The example defines two custom styles (xleffNormal and xleffForm) that are applied to component instances via their styleName attribute.

- The example defines a class style (Label) to influence the appearance of every instance of the Label component in the interface, without having to apply a custom style to each Label instance via the styleName attribute.

Playing with the sampler

A good approach to gaining confidence with the XML structure is to modify the sample01.xml file and reload the XLEFFsampler.html file in your browser, so as to have immediate feedback of the effects of your changes on the dynamically generated user interface.

The initial experiments should include minor changes such as modifying the attributes that influence the position or size of a component instance. After that, you can start adding new instances of the simplest component classes such as labels or buttons.

Eventually you will realize that a proficient way of creating an XML description of a component interface is to use the Flash authoring environment to draw a draft of the interface and "steal" all the coordinates and size attributes that are used by the XML definitions from the Info panel.

In the source files provided, you can also find a proto01.fla file that has been used as a prototype for generating the XML data for the sample01.xml file. If you open it, you will notice that even a simple graphic shape is sufficient to obtain the information about the position and size of a form.

However, you must take care when reusing the coordinates shown in the Info panel since they are expressed in stage terms.

Let us verify what that means.

Figure 6-4 shows the contents of the Info panel after you have opened the proto01.fla file and selected the graphic shape corresponding to the form defined by the following XML line:

```
<form name="DefaultForm" x="25" y="25" width="840" height="200"
      transparentBackground="false" styleName="xleffForm">
```

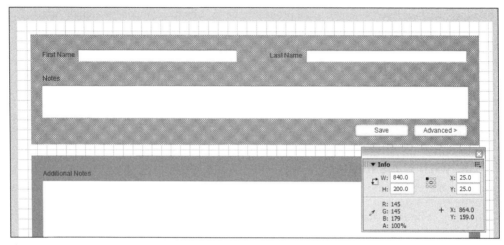

Figure 6-4. Using the Info panel, stage level

As you can see, the values of x, y, width, and height are exactly the same both in the Info panel and in the XML data.

However, if you select the Save button, you will notice a discrepancy between the information in the Info panel, shown in Figure 6-5, and the XML data that will generate that button in its intended position:

```
<button name="SaveButton" styleName="xleffNormal" x="607" y="162"
        width="100" height="22" label="Save" />
```

While width and height are still the same, the (x, y) coordinates are numerically different. The Info panel shows the values (632, 187), while the XML data defines (x, y) as (607, 162), respectively.

The XML data compensates for the fact that the SaveButton will be created as a child of DefaultForm and, therefore, subtracts the values (25,25) from the values shown in the Info panel to express the button coordinates relatively to its container. If you are wondering where the values (25, 25) come from, look back at the Info panel in Figure 6-4: they are the coordinates of the form itself that required no adjustment, because in the structure of the user interface this form is contained by the stage itself.

The conclusion is that when a component instance is within a container, its position must be expressed in coordinates that are relative to the container itself.

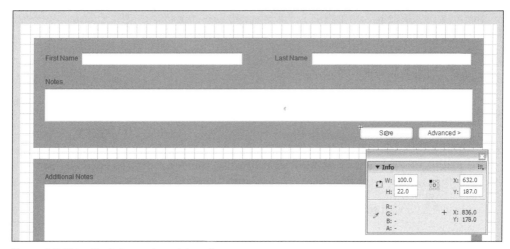

Figure 6-5. Using the Info panel, container discrepancy

If you do not want to spend time with the calculations, a trick to get the right information in the Info panel is to group all the objects belonging to a container inside a symbol (which, as a matter of fact, is itself a container) and then use the option Edit in Place to navigate among its objects to obtain their relative coordinates from the Info panel, as shown in Figure 6-6.

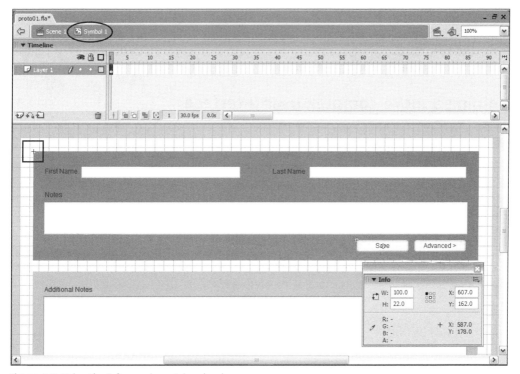

Figure 6-6. Using the Info panel, container level

Note that in Figure 6-6 the SaveButton is still selected, while the Info panel is showing the relative coordinates that we need to include in the XML data.

Figure 6-6 contains two callouts that highlight two fundamental aspects that allow us to obtain the proper relative coordinates from the Info panel:

- Although the whole stage is still visible, we are now inside a symbol (namely Symbol 1) containing the SaveButton and every other object that is supposed to be inside the DefaultForm container.

- The objects inside Symbol 1 have been positioned so as to have the top-left corner of the graphic shape representing the form area coinciding with the registration point of the symbol. As you may already know, you can easily achieve such a result in one step by selecting all the objects to be contained in the symbol and then clicking the top-left point of the registration grid in the Convert to Symbol dialog box, as indicated in Figure 6-7.

Figure 6-7. Defining the top-left registration point

Applying this technique and properly grouping related objects into a symbol, which acts as their container, allows you to manage relative coordinates in nested structures efficiently through visual feedback of the their properly defined numerical values.

Examining a more complex user interface

The file example02.xml, which you can find among the source files associated with this chapter, describes a more complex interface than the one discussed earlier.

In order to generate the interface described in example02.xml, you must edit the XLEFFsampler.html file and replace the two occurrences of sample01.xml in it with the name of the new XML file (sample02.xml). The sampler will display the new user interface once the modified HTML file is loaded in your browser.

Once again, to quickly grab the main structure of the user interface, we start looking at an incomplete version of the XML data on the stage. The following XML block has been produced from the original in sample02.xml after removing all of the attributes and some of the inner elements. What remains is an XML description of the core structure of the user interface.

```
<stage>
    <form>
        <menubar></menubar>
        <accordion></accordion>
        <button />
        <button />
    </form>
</stage>
```

The previous XML block is much easier to read than the entire `sample02.xml`, since that file contains 250+ lines of XML data. The simplified XML block allows you to easily see that the user interface has been based on a main form that contains four component instances: a MenuBar instance, an Accordion instance, and two Button instances, combined together to create the layout displayed in Figure 6-8.

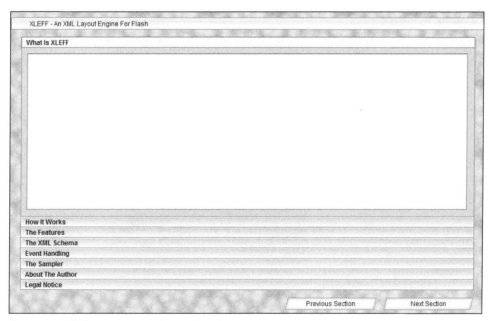

Figure 6-8. Defining a more complex user interface

This user interface was designed using a pattern that can be reused in more than one application.

User interface patterns

The user interface described in `sample02.xml` has been designed to allow intuitive access to a content-based application while offering several ways to navigate such content. It is the first draft of XLEFFdoc, a guide to XLEFF produced by the same technology being documented.

The content is structured in sections, each of them displayed inside a child of the Accordion instance. The sections can be accessed directly by clicking the Accordion headers or, alternatively, by selecting the respective menu item in the MenuBar instance.

A couple of Button instances provide the means for navigating the sections sequentially by moving to the next (or the previous) one.

Since a user interface so defined is independent from both the actual content and the logic of the application, you may be able to reuse it as a starting point for several different applications.

The point made is not that you have found a good user interface pattern, but that an XML layout engine such as XLEFF allows you to easily capture user interface patterns for later reuse.

A first look into the substructures

The content of XLEFFdoc has been divided in eight sections and, therefore, the Accordion instance has a total of eight children.

The simplified structure of the XML block describing the Accordion (stripped of attributes and inner elements) shows that each child is, in fact, a form:

```
<accordion>
    <form></form>
    <form></form>
    <form></form>
    <form></form>
    <form></form>
    <form></form>
    <form></form>
</accordion>
```

Going further down a level in the Accordion structure, you will realize that each Accordion child is a form that contains a TextArea instance only, as in the still-simplified XML block:

```
<form>
    <textarea></textarea>
</form>
```

Of course, it is likely that in the final version of the user interface, the sections may differ somewhat from each other and, consequently, the substructures of the forms acting as Accordion children may well be redefined in different ways.

The important thing to notice here is that even a large XML description made of hundreds (or even thousands) of lines can eventually be simplified and described in a few lines. This is one of the reasons XML is so convenient to formally describe user interfaces that can then be generated dynamically.

The same concept applies to the MenuBar instance that contains a pop-up menu, as shown in Figure 6-9.

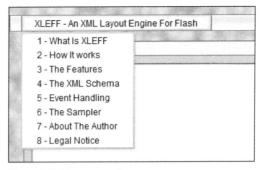

Figure 6-9. Menu example

The simplified XML block of the MenuBar instance is as follows:

```
<menubar>
    <menu>
        <menuitem />
        <menuitem />
        <menuitem />
        <menuitem />
        <menuitem />
        <menuitem />
        <menuitem />
        <menuitem />
    </menu>
</menubar>
```

The last XML block clearly shows that the MenuBar instance contains a single pop-up menu that is made of eight menu items (not surprisingly, one for each Accordion child).

Using custom classes

The user interface currently being examined contains two Button instances that are an example of

- How to skin the Button component
- How to utilize new component classes in XLEFF

Although customizing the Button component is the topic of Chapter 11, we must now anticipate one of the issues demonstrated in Part 3 of the book: not every component can be skinned by simply replacing its graphic assets.

In order to skin certain components, we must create a new class based on the original component class and provide some added functionality. This process is usually defined as **subclassing**.

Eventually the new class will be associated with a new component, inheriting most of its functionality from the component that it is based upon.

This is the case of the Button instances in our example. In fact, those buttons are actually instances of the XleffButton class, which is a class derived from the Button class and belonging to XLEFFtheme. A **theme**, like XLEFFtheme, is a collection of styles and skinned/customized components that share a common look and feel.

The creation of a new component based on the original Button class was required to obtain the skewed look displayed in Figure 6-10.

Figure 6-10. Skewed-looking buttons

Since the component architecture defines the outline of most components programmatically via the RectBorder class, Button included, it would have been not possible to achieve the skewed look without creating a new component based on the Button class and using a custom implementation of the RectBorder class.

Do not worry if the described technique sounds obscure at the moment, since it will be explained in detail in Part 3 of the book. What is relevant at this point is to look at the following XML block, extracted from sample02.xml, and understand that it creates a customized button by specifying a customized class via the cls attribute:

```
            <button cls="XLEFFtheme.subclassed.XleffButton"
➡ name="PrevButton"
                styleName="xleffNormal" x="520" y="519" width="160"
                label="Previous Section" />
```

Although the instance described by the previous XML block belongs to the functional class of buttons, the cls attribute of the XML element specifies that the instance must be generated dynamically by using the class XLEFFtheme.subclassed.XleffButton instead of the original Button class.

The conclusion is that, in addition to dynamically generating any preexisting component in the architecture, XLEFF also provides an easy way for dynamically creating new components that are customized versions of the preexisting ones.

Events to be handled

When using the sampler to generate the latest interface, you may notice that the interface reacts to some but not all the events generated by the user interaction. In particular:

- The proper Accordion child is shown when clicking an Accordion header.
- The pop-up menu is shown when clicking the sole menu in the MenuBar.
- Nothing happens when you click one of the menu items in the pop-up menu. Following the intuitive logic, the proper Accordion child should be displayed, but it is not.
- Nothing happens when you click the Previous Section or Next Section buttons. Following the intuitive logic, the proper Accordion child should be displayed, but it is not.

There is nothing wrong here, because the dynamically generated user interface is completely separated from the application logic, and therefore it triggers no particular action until you implement its associated application.

An Accordion header reacts, displaying its associated Accordion child menu because that functionality is already implemented in the component and represents its default behavior. The same holds for the pop-up menu in the MenuBar that reacts to the user click by displaying its menu items.

Some components respond to some user-generated events, such as the mouse click on an Accordion header, in a standard way. Those events are intracomponent communications: they are handled internally by the specific component instance.

Other events, such as clicking a specific menu item or a button, are not handled internally by the component. In our example, we would like the proper Accordion child to be displayed when the user clicks a menu item or a navigation button. But these events are not fired by the Accordion instance in the interface; they are fired by the MenuBar instance and from the Button instances, respectively. These are examples of communication between different component instances (intercomponent communication), and it is your task to implement their functionality.

Summary

In this chapter, you learned how convenient XML can be when it comes to describing a user interface that is generated dynamically.

You also played with a couple of examples that concretely demonstrated benefits that were firstly introduced as abstract ideas in the previous chapter.

The next chapter shows you how easily you can implement intercomponent event handlers and, in doing so, build component-based applications whose user interfaces are generated dynamically.

Chapter 7

EXTENDING THE APPLICATION FRAMEWORK

Opportunities multiply as they are seized.

Sun Tzu

In this chapter, we will focus on several essential considerations for the completion of a component-based application. In particular, you will learn

- How to define an FLA template, capturing the most essential structure of a component-based application
- How to build a folder structure that can be scalable and convenient enough to support several applications at the same time
- How to increase your efficiency when building component-based applications by implementing a Main class for each of them, acting as an entry point to the application logic
- How the process of implementing an event handler for a dynamically generated user interface can be dramatically simplified
- How to keep the user interface, the application logic, and the content used by the application well separated from each other

> *The completed source code introduced in this chapter is included in the file* src07.zip, *downloadable from this book's page at* www.friendsofed.com.

Defining an FLA template

FLA files can be structured in an infinite number of different ways by arranging frames, layers, and even scenes.

In this chapter, you will build a component-based template (ComponentBasedApp.fla) that can be reused when developing applications based on the component architecture and utilizing your own libraries (XLEFF is utilized in the template as an example of a larger library). Such a template does not limit the use of Flash's amazing graphic capabilities in any way, since you can always encapsulate animations and other graphic assets in symbols that can be added to the stage when needed.

The structure captured in the following template is the result of intense experimentation and represents a working solution to critical issues such as adding an effective preloader to a component-based application and having all of the classes available whenever needed.

The template exploits scenes, a feature of the Flash document that is not very popular among developers, probably because it is thought to be useful in the case of long animated clips only.

However, the scenes functionality can also be very useful within large applications such as those based on components. Scenes can break the higher-level structure of an application into separate modules, each having its own timeline and a specific purpose.

The component-based template will define three scenes:

- **Scene 1: Preloader scene**: The purpose of this scene is to host a custom preloader. A **preloader** is some sort of visual feedback displayed while the SWF file is being loaded. Good preloaders are capable of keeping the user informed about how much time is needed to complete the ongoing loading process. In the case of component-based applications, a good preloader is essential; SWF files tend to be rather large, and the absence of a good preloader would leave the user in front of an unpleasant blank screen for several seconds, possibly making them think that the application is not responding. This scene is only visible while the movie is loading and for one instant only, if the SWF has already been stored in the browser's cache (indicating that the user has already loaded the application once).

- **Scene 2: Dynamic Assets scene**: This scene is never visible because, once the preloading phase is terminated, the preloader jumps directly to the third scene. However, this scene is very important since it includes an instance of every component, allowing the components' classes to be correctly compiled and properly initialized before being utilized in the third and main scene.

- **Scene 3: Main scene**: The third scene becomes permanently visible after the preloading phase is completed. This scene hosts your application, while the previous two scenes were only needed to implement a good preloader and initialize the components properly without affecting the efficiency of the preloader.

Using scenes

The template defines three scenes, which are displayed in the Figure 7-1.

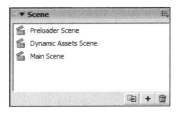

Figure 7-1. The three scenes in the ComponentBasedApp.fla template

Scenes are ideal for neatly separating the distinct parts of the structure of a component-based application, facilitating the easy implementation and maintenance of different functional units.

The template's structure is based upon the component architecture and will also include the support for using XLEFF as the most important (and reusable) concrete example provided in this book.

The first two scenes prepare the runtime environment of the specific component-based application that is actually encapsulated in the third scene.

The role of the first scene is to display the progress of loading the movie's content; by looking at its implementation, you will also learn the most critical issues associated with the preloading of a component-based application.

The Preloader scene

The preloading concept is very popular among Flash designers and developers.

The high-quality user experience usually associated with Flash applications can be somewhat hindered by the absence of visual feedback showing the progress of the movie being loaded. Depending on the size of content to be loaded, the user may have to wait a significant amount of time before being able to interact with the application. A preloader animation must be capable of providing a display of the loading progress to improve the user experience during that initial step.

However, implementing an efficient preloader can become a daunting task when components are included in the Flash movie due to several factors that will be addressed in the template being defined.

Basically, once compiled, the Flash movie of a component-based application can end up with lots of content transparently included in the first frame. This is mostly due to the fact that classes are exported in the first frame by default and, as you know by now, the component architecture comes with lots of classes.

Such a bad scenario is shown in Figure 7-2.

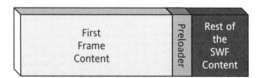

Figure 7-2. Bad scenario: lots of content to be loaded before the preloader

Whatever content included in the first frame will be loaded before anything else, even before the pre-loader, so it will not be able to provide any visual feedback to the user during this first phase of the loading process.

The structure of an FLA file must be carefully defined to minimize the part of the movie loaded before the preloader; reducing the size of this initial section will allow the preloader to quickly and more accurately display its visual feedback. Figure 7-3 shows an example of a good scenario in which most of the content is loaded after the preloader.

Figure 7-3. Good scenario: the majority of content is loaded after the preloader

Building an effective preloader is a task made complicated by the fact that components need to be initialized properly and to have the ActionScript classes loaded as soon as possible and certainly before they are utilized in the code.

Figure 7-4 is a glimpse of the first scene in our template; named the Preloader scene, it is dedicated to the preloader functionality only. It includes a very simple preloader that is a countdown synchronized with the loading process.

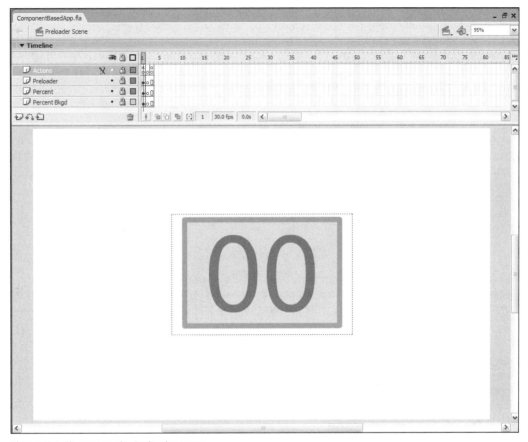

Figure 7-4. First scene: the Preloader scene

Of course, you can customize this preloader radically to suit your designs. Whenever you do it, take note of the following guidelines that should be followed when implementing the simple preloader:

- **Guideline 1**: Do not use components or classes in the preloader.
- **Guideline 2**: Include your preloader in the first of the three frames present in the first scene.
- **Guideline 3**: Once the loading process is complete, your preloader should jump to the third scene by invoking _root.jumpToMain();.

The first guideline is a recommendation suggested by the fact that if you do use classes or components in the preloader, then those classes will have to be loaded before being used. If the size of the classes is insignificant compared to the size of the whole movie, then you may not follow the first guideline, since the loss of accuracy of the preloader would be imperceptible. However, by following the first guideline, you can maximize the accuracy of the preloader and therefore the user experience deriving from it.

The second guideline recommends keeping the three-frames structure of the first scene that includes the implementation of the jumpToMain function. This structure has been tested thoroughly and revealed to be a bulletproof pattern that works particularly well when scenes are involved. When mixing scenes and components and then altering several default aspects of the FLA file in order to maximize contrasting features such as the preloading of components, it becomes easy to end up with unexpected behaviors. You are encouraged to try different structures and improve the existing one, but if problems should arise from your experiments, you can always roll back to the efficient solution discussed here.

The third guideline is just a note informing you of the presence of the jumpToMain function, implemented in the first frame of the scene. Your preloader should invoke this function once the loading process is completed to move to the Main scene according to the pattern embedded in the ComponentBasedApp.fla template.

The body of the jumpToMain function, declared in the first frame, is very simple:

```
function jumpToMain() {
    _root.gotoAndPlay(2);
}
```

When that function is invoked by your preloader, at the end of the preloading process, the playhead leaves the first frame where it was stopped during preloading, "takes a breath" on the second frame, and moves to the third frame, where it encounters the code that moves it to the third and Main scene:

```
gotoAndPlay("Main Scene",1);
```

After the process of loading the movie has completed, the jumpToMain function moves to the third scene, skipping the second one. As a matter of fact, the second scene never gets played. Let's have a look at what it contains and why it is included in the template.

The Dynamic Assets scene

The playhead never moves to the frames in the second scene, the Dynamic Assets scene. Nevertheless, this scene plays a very important role in the structure of the ComponentBasedApp.fla template.

The second scene contains an instance of every symbol involved in the creation of the components used in the movie. Having each of those symbols included in the second scene ensures that their classes are compiled and properly initialized, ready to be used whenever needed during the third and main scene.

Figure 7-5 shows the two layers in the second scene containing several component instances.

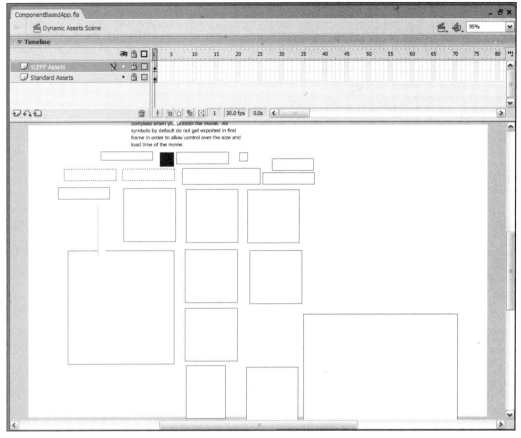

Figure 7-5. Second scene: the Dynamic Assets scene

The bottom layer, named Standard Assets, includes a symbol called firstFrameExporter that allows you to add in a single step every asset required by the standard components in the architecture. You will add this symbol to the template by dragging it from the library of the StandardComponents.fla file included with the source code of the component architecture. (See Appendix A for locating the source code of the component architecture on your machine.) The purpose of the firstFrameExporter is suggested by its name and clearly stated in the comments included within the symbol: it should be included in the first frame of the movie in order to have all the symbols in it immediately compiled and then available for use throughout the rest of the movie from then on.

Unfortunately, having such a symbol in the first frame of the movie would completely spoil the pre-loader functionality as we saw earlier. That's why our template includes it in the second scene, forcing its compilation before the third scene, the sole scene that actually uses the components.

In addition to hosting all the assets of the component architecture in the Standard Assets layer, the Dynamic Assets scene also includes a second layer called XLEFF Assets. This layer includes the assets of XLEFF that will also be used in the main scene. More generally, you should utilize the second scene as a storage area for the assets of any other component that you may use in your application to ensure their proper compilation and initialization.

The Main scene

The third and last scene in the `ComponentBasedApp.fla` template, the Main scene, contains the actual application.

At authoring time, the stage shows the "creating cover" (a sort of splash screen that appears for a few seconds after the movie has been fully loaded and while the components in the user interface are being created dynamically), which you can see in Figure 7-6.

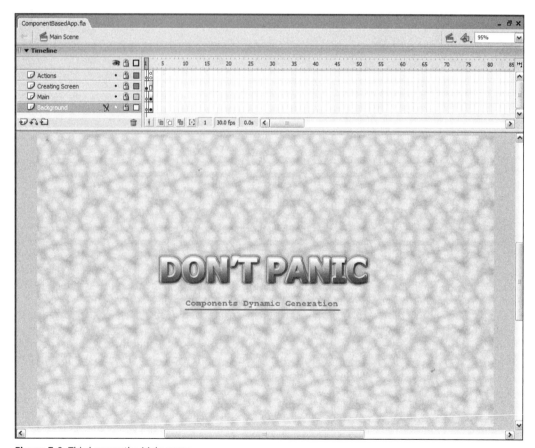

Figure 7-6. Third scene: the Main scene

The process of dynamically creating the components in the user interface may take a few seconds depending on the number of instances being created and the power of the machine running the application. Of course, you can customize such a screen in any way you like, changing the graphics or message as you see fit.

The three scenes in the structure of the `ComponentBasedApp.fla` template, plus a few expedients discussed later on in this chapter, make sure that

- The component-based application can have an efficiently working preloader mechanism.
- The classes and assets needed by the component-based application are loaded and compiled properly and, therefore, available whenever needed by the application code.

Licensing issue

The Flash authoring environment contains the source code of the whole component architecture, including the FLA structure of every standard component in it. The availability of such source code is what makes those components highly customizable: without it, some customizations would just not have been possible.

Being the owner of a licensed Flash authoring environment, you can customize the component to fit into your designs, include the component sources in your projects, modify the skins, and so on. But the license coming with the product does not allow you to distribute the original source code: every original source included in your project must be distributed in compiled format.

Please note that this is the author's interpretation of the license terms defined at the moment of writing. You are invited to read the actual terms, as the vendor defined them, by visiting the following site:

www.macromedia.com/software/eula/tools/flash_components.html

In order to respect the "Supplemental License Terms Relating to Components" available at the vendor's website, I did not include the source code of the standard components in the `ComponentBasedApp.fla` template.

However, the template must include such source code in order to generate the components dynamically while being able to customize them thoroughly.

The solution to this issue is pretty neat, since you can include the standard components source code manually in the template by using the source code found in your own installation of the Flash tool, with the added bonus of learning the remaining expedients required to make everything (preloader, classes, etc.) work as expected.

Including the standard components source code

Importing the standard components source code in the `ComponentBasedApp.fla` template is an easy and fast operation once you find where the `StandardsComponents.fla` file is on your machine (see Appendix A to locate the component architecture source code).

Figure 7-7 shows the library of the `ComponentBasedApp.fla` template before you add the source code of the standard components to it. At this time, the library includes only two main folders:

- `Template Assets`: A folder including the assets specifically created for the template. This folder includes only one movie clip symbol, named Preloader: an empty symbol utilized for implementing the preloader in the first scene by attaching some code to its instance.

- `XLEFF Assets`: A folder including the assets of XLEFF, the XML Layout engine also utilized by the component-based template.

Figure 7-7. The template's library before adding the source code of the standard components

The following steps describe what you must do to complete the `ComponentBasedApp.fla` template by including the standard components source code in it:

1. Open the `ComponentBasedApp.fla` template that you will find in the code associated with this chapter.

2. Open the `StandardsComponents.fla` file as an external library by using the command File ➤ Import ➤ Open External Library.

3. Drag the `firstFrameExporter` symbol from the external library into the first frame of the Standard Assets layer in the second scene of the component-based template, named Dynamic Assets.

Dragging the `firstFrameExporter` symbol contained in the `StandardsComponents.fla` external library onto the stage of the template's second scene allows you to transfer all the assets of the component architecture to the template in a single step.

Figure 7-8 shows the contents of the template's library after completing the previous task.

Name	Kind
firstFrameExporter	Movie Clip
Flash UI Components 2	Folder
Template Assets	Folder
XLEFF Assets	Folder

Figure 7-8. The template's library after adding the source of the standard components

The template's library now contains two additional objects at its topmost level:

- firstFrameExporter: The symbol that you imported from the StandardComponents.fla external library.
- Flash UI Components 2: A folder that was invisibly included when importing the firstFrameExporter symbols and that contains almost 200 symbols: the source and assets of the standard components in the architecture.

After the inclusion of the standard components' source code and assets, the ComponentBasedApp.fla template is ready to be used for generating component instances dynamically via XLEFF.

You can easily customize the ComponentBasedApp.fla template by adding further components and external libraries whenever needed. All you have to do is to follow the guidelines illustrated here and applied to both the standard components and XLEFF as examples.

In the remaining part of the chapter and in the rest of the book, the presence of XLEFF will act as a significant example for concretely extending your template and learning how to customize the appearance and behavior of each standard component.

Progressive update of the template

The presence of the source code of the standard components in the ComponentBasedApp.fla template is due to a couple of reasons:

- It allows you to customize the appearance and behavior of the standard components and therefore have full control over the component instances.
- It makes it possible to implement an effective preloader in the case of a component-based application.

During Part 3 of the book, you will learn how to implement fully customized versions of the standard components that can be included in a new template created by progressively updating a copy of the ComponentBasedApp.fla template. The inclusion of the source code of the standard components will ensure that every customization will work properly.

Analyzing the size report

You may well find it interesting to publish the SWF file of the template with the Generate size report option set. Figure 7-9 shows the significant output of such a report.

```
ComponentBasedApp.swf Movie Report
-----------------------------------
Frame #    Frame Bytes    Total Bytes    Scene
-------    -----------    -----------    -----------------
      1            594            594    Preloader Scene
      2              5            599
      3         175073         175672    (AS 2.0 Classes Export Frame)
      4          18000         193672    Dynamic Assets Scene
      5          28275         221947    Main Scene
      6          20694         242641
```

Figure 7-9. Main output of the size report

The very first lines of the size report describe an ideal scenario: the movie size (including all the standard components plus the XLEFF components) is approximately 236KB large. More importantly, only 594 bytes are loaded in the first frame!

The preloader can provide very efficient visual feedback, since less than 1% of the overall movie size is loaded in the first frame.

The ComponentBasedApp.fla template clearly captures a pattern for taking full control of the loading process in the case of component-based applications.

This result is achieved by effectively keeping both the symbols and the ActionScript classes away from the first frame. The template's structure is defined to maximize such an effect by applying a couple of techniques described in the next section.

Moving the symbols after the first frame

The components are exported symbols, and every exported symbol is usually included in the first frame unless the Export in first frame option of the Linkage Properties dialog box is unchecked, as illustrated in the example of Figure 7-10.

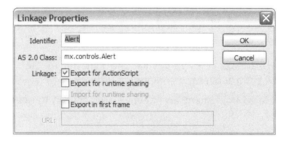

Figure 7-10. Note the unchecked Export in first frame option.

Luckily, both the standard and the XLEFF symbols already have that option unchecked and, therefore, there isn't much you have to do about it apart from remembering to uncheck the option when adding new exported symbols to the template.

Unchecking the Export in first frame option for a symbol means that the symbol in question is no longer included in the first frame of the main timeline. However, that also means the symbol will not be included in the SWF file at all, unless present somewhere else on the timeline.

This aspect exposes yet another reason why the Dynamic Assets scene contains an instance of every exported symbol (components included): to ensure that those symbols are still included in the SWF file once we uncheck their Export in first frame options.

Although applying this technique is necessary to reduce the number of bytes loaded with the first frame, it is not sufficient to minimize it because the ActionScript classes are still loaded in the first frame by default. The next section will show you how to postpone the inclusion of the ActionScript classes so that they will be loaded with the same frame of the Dynamic Assets scene that contains the exported symbols and, therefore, be available when the playhead reaches the Main scene without negatively affecting the preloading mechanism.

Moving the classes after the first frame

Taking control of the loading process of a component-based application requires a careful approach not only because of various issues that we have already examined, but also because exported symbols are not the only objects to be included in the first frame by default.

ActionScript classes, introduced with AS 2.0, are included in the first frame by default as well, and since the component architecture is based upon numerous classes, it is not a surprise that the size report in Figure 7-9 clearly indicates that the AS 2.0 Classes Export Frame was by far the "fattest" frame in the template structure.

When creating the template, I utilized the Export frame for classes option of the ActionScript settings dialog box shown in Figure 7-11. This dialog box is accessible via the Publishing Settings option of the movie (File ➤ Publishing Settings ➤ Flash ➤ ActionScript 2.0 Settings).

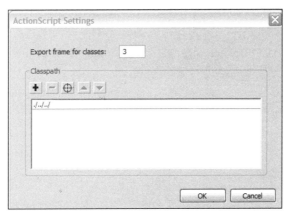

Figure 7-11. Setting a new export frame for classes

Defining the Export frame for classes setting as the third frame (3) ensures that

- The classes are not exported in the first frame.
- The classes are exported before any exported symbols and, therefore, available when those symbols were compiled.
- The classes are exported before the main scene and, therefore, available when utilized by application code.

It is now more evident that the techniques we just examined can achieve a neat result when working in conjunction with an FLA structure like the one defined for the ComponentBasedApp.fla template.

Defining a folder structure

Object orientation is a successful paradigm mostly because of its ability to capture complex designs in a simple way.

183

In the case of the Flash authoring environment, the introduction of classes in ActionScript has been revolutionary, going far beyond the common significance of the most essential object-oriented mechanisms, since classes can be individually associated with symbols in the library: a class is now the most natural implementation of a symbol's behavior and can also define its appearance, either partially or completely.

The availability of such powerful features has vastly expanded the horizon of Flash, and the most popular browser plug-in has become a developer's dream, sought after now that the technology, already well known for being actually capable of running the same application everywhere, has been bestowed with the functionality required for large-scale developments.

In this section, we are going to define a scalable folder structure that conveniently separates the most important parts of a Flash component-based application.

Among the several benefits of such a structure, the most important one is that subsystems (such as XLEFF) and themes can be reused by several applications, making the maintenance of such applications much cheaper.

Figure 7-12 shows the main branches of the recommended folder structure. The main folder is given the name root and contains three subfolders:

- The apps subfolder, which contains the component-based applications
- The org subfolder, which contains one or more subsystems
- The yourTheme subfolder, which contains a theme

Figure 7-12. Main branches of the folder structure

Once you get used to the implementation reasoning behind the definition of this folder structure, you will find it very natural to extend it by adding further themes or even new subsystems starting from the root folder.

Figure 7-13 provides an in-depth view of the apps subtree. The apps folder is supposed to contain a subfolder for each component-based application that you are developing. Of course, you can give more meaningful names to the folders containing the actual applications instead of the sample names shown in Figure 7-13 (application1, application2, application3). Thanks to the folder structure that we are defining, all of the applications in the apps folder will be able to use the same themes and subsystems included under the root folder.

Figure 7-13. Example of the apps subtree

XLEFF implements an XML layout engine, a functionality well separated from the application itself and, as such, reusable by several applications at the same time. Because of this, XLEFF is a significant example of a subsystem that can be included under the root folder as described in Figure 7-14. In the proposed folder structure, you can add as many folders as you like under the root folder to make the subsystems included in those folders reusable for the applications inside the apps folder.

Figure 7-14. XLEFF as an example of a subsystem

The folder structure in Figure 7-14 also includes a folder named yourTheme as a placeholder for a theme that you may create by subclassing the standard components while learning the techniques exposed in Part 3 of the book.

A **theme** is a collection of several assets that may include color schemes, styles, and even ActionScript classes in order to customize the appearance and behavior of the components in the architecture. A theme can give an application a consistent look and feel that can also be shared with other applications.

Adding further themes under the root folder is an easy way of extending the folder structure, allowing you to quickly select, or even change, a theme when building a component-based application.

Properly grouping the applications in a folder structure that includes their subsystem and themes can significantly reduce development costs and facilitate maintenance of both the applications and their parts.

But how can an application be aware of the presence of a subsystem or even a theme in the folder structure? The answer to that question is in the **classpath** concept.

The role of classpath

A classpath is a collection of paths that is used by the compiler in the authoring environment to locate external ActionScript files. Because of this, ActionScript class files are usually grouped in folders usually referred as **packages**.

The folder structure previously defined distinguishes among three different kinds of packages, applications, subsystems, and themes, defining a convenient and scalable organization of the classes used by a component-based application.

When in the Flash authoring environment, you can define the collection of paths that define the classpath globally and locally.

Paths added to the global classpath via the menu option Edit ➤ Preferences ➤ ActionScript ➤ ActionScript 2.0 Settings are always searched by the compiler, whatever FLA file you are working on.

Paths added to the local classpath via the menu option File ➤ Publish Settings ➤ Flash ➤ ActionScript 2.0 Settings are stored locally in the FLA file and searched only when compiling that particular file.

If you have the chance of defining the folder structure of your Flash projects and you are willing to give the one recommended in this chapter a try, you will discover that setting the classpath locally can be more convenient than its global counterpart for the following reasons:

- The classpath required by the recommended structure is made of a single path.
- This single path is a relative path that allows you to easily move the root folder around in your file system without having to do any modification to the classpath: everything will still be compiled successfully.
- Being that the classpath is local, and therefore stored in the application's FLA files, it is easier to move or copy the root folder to a different system without having to define a global classpath for the authoring environment in that system.

So what is the single path to be included in the local classpath of an application FLA belonging to the recommended folder structure? This path is

```
./../../
```

which was already shown in Figure 7-11, since the ActionScript Settings dialog box that allows you to define the export frame for classes is the same dialog box used to define the local classpath.

Thanks to the dot-based notation available for paths, this very simple setting is all you need to make the packaged subsystem and themes included in the folder structure visible to the compiler when it builds the application. You can keep adding further subsystems and even themes to the structure without having to change anything.

For example, let's consider the following import statement:

```
import org.XLEFF.XMLStage;
```

Thanks to the local classpath definition, the compiler starts looking from the root folder and, from there, into the org folder, then the XLEFF folder to eventually find the XMLStage.as file that implements the XMLStage class. Very similarly, the compiler will be able to locate the classes of any other subsystem and theme starting from the root folder.

Facilitating event-driven programming

Once you have a good grasp of how to organize the initial development of a component-based application conveniently, by structuring its FLA file and the folders containing the necessary ActionScript classes, we can move on to looking at how to efficiently utilize a dynamically generated user interface.

In the last chapter, I showed you that the component instances in the user interface are inherently capable of handling certain user interaction: the MenuBar instance knows how to hide/show its menus, the Accordion instance knows how to display the proper child instance reacting to the user clicking one of its headers, and so on.

We called those events **intracomponent events** to indicate that they are handled by the functionality already implemented in the component. The good thing about these events is that you don't have to write any code to support them, unless you want to change the component's default behavior.

You also discovered that some events cannot be implemented in the component functionality such as, for example, the user clicking a Button instance. In those cases, the reaction depends on the specific application that you are implementing and, therefore, it is your responsibility to provide the ActionScript code to be executed when the event is triggered.

Such responsibility actually identifies a repeating pattern: writing code to handle the events triggered by the user interface. This pattern is so central to the development of component-based applications that XLEFF was designed to include further functionality to make it easier to program and maintain event handlers.

The FLA structure of the `ComponentBasedApp.fla` template, the folder structure we saw earlier, and the repetitive task of coding event handlers (facilitated by XLEFF) find a perfect marriage in the Main class, which I introduce next.

The Main class

Going back to the third scene of the `ComponentBasedApp.fla` template, the Main scene, you may notice that the most important layer in its structure is the one called Main.

This layer contains only a single instance of a component called Main. In Figure 7-15, you can see that this component is included in the XLEFF folder of the template's library.

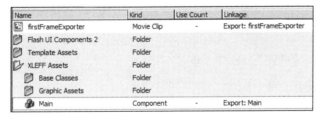

Figure 7-15. The Main component

Although the Main component is included by the XLEFF implementation, the name of the ActionScript class associated with the component is defined without any package prefixes as you can see in the dialog box in Figure 7-16, which presents the linkage properties of the Main component.

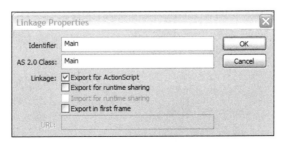

Figure 7-16. Linkage properties of the Main component

The absence of package information indicates that the `Main` class is supposed to be found in the same folder where the application is being developed. In fact, you can find a `Main.as` file, containing the `Main` class, in the same folder where the `ComponentBasedApp.fla` template is.

This is because the `Main` class represents the entry point of the application logic, the class where you will implement what must happen whenever the user triggers events via the user interface dynamically generated by XLEFF. It follows that every component-based application must provide its own implementation of the `Main` class, since all the code in that class will be application specific.

Thanks to this design, the whole process of creating a component-based application has been simplified to the following:

1. Creating an XML description of the user interface
2. Providing an implementation of the `Main` class, including the event handlers that are specific to each particular application

Let's examine how strikingly easy and direct the implementation of an event handler is in the `Main` class compared to the approach we studied in Part 1 of the book where we used listener objects.

Note that the last statement is not criticizing the approach of handling events via listener objects. Listener objects are highly generic and, as such, useful in all the cases where there isn't a pattern that can be optimized.

A concrete example

In order to have a concrete example of the `Main` class, we now continue to implement the XLEFFdoc example introduced in the previous chapter.

We are actually going to see that, starting from the `ComponentBasedApp.fla` template, the whole process of building a component-based application as been reduced to these two steps:

1. Produce an XML description of the user interface.
2. Produce an implementation of the `Main` class.

We continue from the XLEFFdoc example since it already includes a significant XML description of a user interface, which is redisplayed in Figure 7-17.

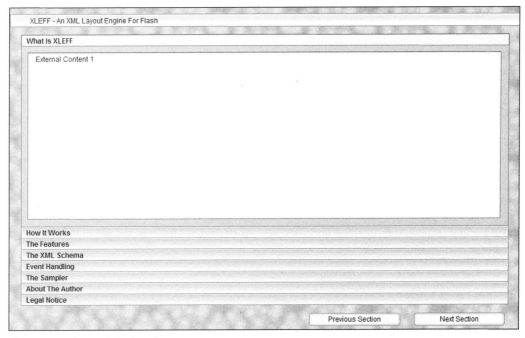

Figure 7-17. The XLEFFdoc interface

Skeleton of the Main class

The skeleton of the Main class of a component-based application capable of generating the user interface dynamically via XLEFF is very simple:

```
import mx.controls.*;
import org.XLEFF.*;
import org.XLEFF.managers.*;
import org.XLEFF.utils.*;

class Main extends MainBase {

    public function Main() {
    }

}
```

The base class MainBase provides the implementation of the XML Layout parameter that you can set via the authoring interface to specify the name of the XML file providing the description of the user interface to be generated dynamically.

The third scene of the `ComponentBasedApp.fla` template contains a layer called Main, which hosts an instance of the Main component in its second frame. This instance is physically located on the top-left corner of the stage and, once selected, you will be able to notice its name, mc_main, and the default setting of its XML Layout parameter, XLEFFdoc.xml, as shown in Figure 7-18.

Figure 7-18. Setting the XML Layout parameter

Changing the value of the XML Layout parameter allows you to use a different XML file as the descriptor of the user interface to be dynamically generated by XLEFF. Figure 7-19 shows how the folder structure of your drive should look after making a copy of the `Component Based Template` folder and renaming the new folder XLEFFdoc.

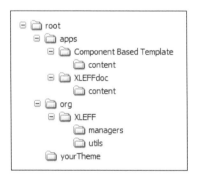

Figure 7-19. Folder structure for the XLEFFdoc application example

Your next task is to flesh out the skeleton of the Main class in the XLEFFdoc folder by adding the event handlers required by the dynamically generated user interface of our specific application example.

Handling the user interface events

In the previous chapter, we saw that the user interface of the XLEFFdoc example generated by the "XLEFF sampler" would not handle some application-specific events.

In particular, the user interface was designed with a couple of navigation buttons and a drop-down menu as alternatives to the navigation offered by the Accordion header.

The intended functionality associated with those components can be easily implemented via a Main class, whose code is also very readable, as shown in the following lines:

```
import mx.controls.*;
import org.XLEFF.*;
import org.XLEFF.managers.*;
import org.XLEFF.utils;
```

```
class Main extends MainBase {
    private var MainForm:MovieClip;

    public function Main() {
    }

    private function onPrevButton_Click(eventObject:Object):Void {
        if ( MainForm.MainAccordion.selectedIndex > 0 ) {
            MainForm.MainAccordion.selectedIndex =
                MainForm.MainAccordion.selectedIndex - 1;
        } else {
            MainForm.MainAccordion.selectedIndex =
                MainForm.MainAccordion.numChildren - 1;
        }
    }

    private function onNextButton_Click(eventObject:Object):Void {
        if ( (MainForm.MainAccordion.selectedIndex + 1) <
                MainForm.MainAccordion.numChildren ) {
            MainForm.MainAccordion.selectedIndex =
                MainForm.MainAccordion.selectedIndex + 1;
        } else {
            MainForm.MainAccordion.selectedIndex = 0;
        }
    }

    private function onMenuWhatIs_Change(eventObject:Object):Void {
        MainForm.MainAccordion.selectedIndex = 0;
    }

    private function onMenuHowItWorks_Change(eventObject:Object):Void {
        MainForm.MainAccordion.selectedIndex = 1;
    }

    private function onMenuFeatures_Change(eventObject:Object):Void {
        MainForm.MainAccordion.selectedIndex = 2;
    }

    private function onMenuSchema_Change(eventObject:Object):Void {
        MainForm.MainAccordion.selectedIndex = 3;
    }

    private function onMenuEventHandling_Change(eventObject:Object)
➥ :Void {
        MainForm.MainAccordion.selectedIndex = 4;
    }
```

```
    private function onMenuTheSampler_Change(eventObject:Object):Void {
        MainForm.MainAccordion.selectedIndex = 5;
    }

    private function onMenuTheAuthor_Change(eventObject:Object):Void {
        MainForm.MainAccordion.selectedIndex = 6;
    }

    private function onMenuLegalNotice_Change(eventObject:Object)
➡ :Void {
        MainForm.MainAccordion.selectedIndex = 7;
    }

}
```

The Main class declaration includes a MainForm private member declared as an instance of the MovieClip class. Where does it come from?

As for all the other instances of objects belonging to the user interface, MainForm will be generated dynamically by XLEFF because it can be found in XLEFFdoc.xml, the XML file containing the description of the user interface:

```
<form name="MainForm" styleName="xleffNormal" x="0" y="0">
```

MainForm is indeed the main form in the user interface of the XLEFFdoc example and its name has been declared in the previous XML line. Note also that a few lines below that line there is another significant XML element:

```
<accordion cls="Accordion" name="MainAccordion" x="20" y="45"
 width="850" height="460">
```

This element refers to an Accordion instance, contained inside MainForm, not very originally named MainAccordion. How does that translate in the ActionScript code of the Main class? Very intuitively, as is shown by the following line:

```
MainForm.MainAccordion.selectedIndex = 0;
```

XLEFF has dynamically created a very intuitive object model that matches the description contained in the XML file.

Once you know the instance names that you defined in the XML description and their containment relationships, you are able to access every component instance generated dynamically utilizing the same notation common to all the powerful object-oriented programming languages.

As a result, the code you write is almost self-descriptive, as demonstrated in the following example, implementing the event handler that synchronized the Accordion instance with the choice made by the user when selecting a menu item:

```
    private function onMenuWhatIs_Change(eventObject:Object):Void {
        MainForm.MainAccordion.selectedIndex = 0;
    }
```

The name of the menu item is MenuWhatIs, as you can check by looking for the following line in the XML file:

```
<menuitem label="1 - What Is XLEFF" instanceName="MenuWhatIs" />
```

So the name of the function implementing the related event handler is actually onMenuWhatIs_Change.

The only detail in the name of the event handler that may confuse you is the use of the word "Change" instead of "Click", a term that derives from the name given in the component architecture for the event triggered when the user selects a menu item. In this case, the menu item triggers a change event instead of a click event!

By default, XLEFF sticks to the names defined by the component architecture consistently to allow you to learn it quicker.

What happens then when the user selects the MenuWhatIs menu item and the change event is raised by the component architecture? The onMenuWhatIs_Change event handler is invoked by XLEFF and the following line is executed:

```
MainForm.MainAccordion.selectedIndex = 0;
```

This line asks the accordion instance to display its first child (accordion's children are numbered starting from zero) since the MenuWhatIs menu item is, in fact, the first menu item in the menu.

Just slightly more complex is the implementation of the event handler associated with the NextButton instance:

```
private function onNextButton_Click(eventObject:Object):Void {
    if ( (MainForm.MainAccordion.selectedIndex + 1) <
         MainForm.MainAccordion.numChildren ) {
       MainForm.MainAccordion.selectedIndex =
       MainForm.MainAccordion.selectedIndex + 1;
    } else {
       MainForm.MainAccordion.selectedIndex = 0;
    }
}
```

The event handler name is now even more intuitive (onNextButton_Click) since buttons do trigger click events while the code uses a couple of properties of the Accordion class (selectedIndex and numChildren) to verify whether there actually is a next child of the Accordion to be displayed or whether it is the case to restart from the first one.

Utilizing the user interface generated dynamically by XLEFF could not be more intuitive once you have understood the following points:

- The Main class will have access to an object model that is the faithful copy of the one specified in the XML description.

- You can implement event handlers by simply following a naming convention.

Let's then formalize the naming convention supported by XLEFF in the case of the names of event handlers.

Event handler naming convention

In order to implement an event handler for an event triggered by a component instance, you must implement a method in the Main class with the following name:

    onInstance_Event

In the previous syntax, [Instance] is the name of the component instance, as it was declared in the XML description of the user interface, and [Event] is the capitalized name of the event being handled. The on prefix and the underscore character for separating the instance name from the event name have been added to increase the readability of the event handler name.

Table 7-1 illustrates a few valid examples of event handler names.

Table 7-1. Examples of event handler names

Event Handler	Instance Name	Event Name
onButton1_Click	Button1	click
onButton2_Click	Button2	click
onMenuItem1_Change	MenuItem1	change
onComboBox1_Enter	ComboBox1	enter
onComboBox1_Change	ComboBox1	change

Assuming that Button1 is the name of an instance of the Button component, the following is an example of an invalid event handler name since the Button class does not support the change event:

    onButton1_Change

The fact that writing component-based applications using XLEFF is very easy is what makes it particularly good as a unifying example for navigating in the vastness of the component architecture, understanding its functionality, and testing its applicability.

You may then decide to use and extend it for your own applications or as a prototyping tool for statically produced user interfaces.

The benefits of XLEFF, however, extend even beyond the ability to generate a user interface starting from an XML description and its help in making event-driven applications easy to program and maintain. It can also facilitate the content management of your component-based applications.

Managing content

Software internationalization is a term describing the process of porting an application to other languages.

Whether you have to port your application in several languages or not, software internationalization represents a good study case to test how well the content is managed by the framework being used for developing your applications.

Figure 7-20 shows the user interface of the example we are working on (XLEFFdoc) after having been translated in Italian.

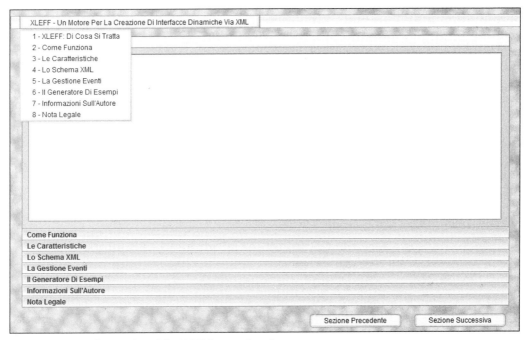

Figure 7-20. An Italian version of the XLEFFdoc user interface

In the case of a static user interface designed in the authoring environment, you would have to select each component instance one by one, possibly opening several containers in the process, in order to set the text in each related parameter according to the Italian language: a process that is as easy as it is tedious. This process would also be rather error prone, since it makes it so easy to forget some label buried deep inside the component parameters (think of the menu items within a MenuBar that are invisible at design time, for example).

Furthermore, once you have finished with the FLA file, you must recompile it and from there on manage two FLA files (one for each language version) that, as you will have realized by now, usually have a much more complicated structure than text files.

Contrast this to the approach when the user interface is generated dynamically via an XML description. Internationalizing the interface is as simple (and quick) as going through the XML file and replacing the content of every label, as in this example:

```
<menuitem label="3 - Le Caratteristiche" instanceName="MenuFeatures" />
```

Or this one:

```
<button name="PrevButton" styleName="xleffNormal" x="520" y="519"
        width="160" label="Sezione Precedente" />
```

Modifying the contents of the XML file does not require recompiling the Flash document to produce a new SWF file, meaning that you can redefine the existing user interface without having to touch the Flash document at all.

In some cases, you may wish to use an XML file with a different name, in which case all you need to do is to change the XML Layout parameter of the Main class to specify the name of the new XML file to be used.

Evidently, XLEFF can be a big time saver, especially when it comes to maintenance, since changes can be easily applied. And there is more to come—XLEFF also supports internal and external content.

Pushing the separation paradigm further

In our current example (XLEFFdoc), the layout of the user interface is rather simplified since each Accordion child contains a single instance of the TextArea component.

The content of the TextArea component instances can be defined internally to the XML description as in the following example:

```
<textarea name="WhatIsTextArea" x="10" y="10" width="825" height="284">
    <content>Some internal content.</content>
</textarea>
```

However, unlike labels, the content of the TextArea component can include several lines and potentially increasing the size of the XML file significantly while decreasing its readability and the overall performance of the parser.

The separation paradigm, which has already shown its numerous benefits in many other areas of our developments, once again suggests a neat solution: utilizing external content.

Alternatively, to supporting the content XML element, XLEFF also supports the externalContent element, as demonstrated by the following example:

```
<textarea name="WhatIsTextArea" x="10" y="10" width="825" height="284">
    <externalContent>content/content01.xml</externalContent >
</textarea>
```

While the content element was used to specify the actual content to be included in the TextArea instance, the externalContent in the previous example element provides a relative URL to an XML file that contains the content to be loaded in the component instance.

XLEFF supports the loading of content embedded in separated XML files having the structure described in the following example, taken from the content01.xml file, which you can find in the source code associated with this chapter:

```
<?xml version="1.0"?>
<content><![CDATA[External Content 1]]></content>
```

The XML structure of external content files is very simple, since it constitutes a single XML element (content).

Embedding the actual content in a CDATA section is not mandatory, but it is strongly recommended because of the important role of this XML feature.

The role of CDATA

The purpose of a CDATA section is to include text that will not be parsed by the XML parser.

A CDATA section starts with

```
<![CDATA[
```

and ends with

```
]]>
```

CDATA is not always necessary, but it becomes essential in the case of text containing special characters like < or >. Those characters would generate parsing errors that would eventually lead to an unexpected behavior in your application.

Basically, CDATA sections give you the freedom to use whatever character you wish when defining text content within an XML file (with the sole exception of the]]> sequence, since nested CDATA sections are not allowed by XML).

Also, using a CDATA section to describe your text content will allow you to faithfully reproduce the line breaks in the text. For example, the following external content:

```
<?xml version="1.0"?>
<content><![CDATA[First line.
Second line.
Third line.
Fourth line.
Fifth line.]]></content>
```

would be displayed in a TextArea instance with line breaks reproduced as follows:

```
First line.
Second line.
Third line.
Fourth line.
Fifth line.
```

Summary

This chapter covered a topic that has a very wide scope, since component-based applications can be designed for almost any purpose one may think of.

You have learned how a good organization of several different aspects can act synergically, eventually increasing a developer's efficiency and productivity dramatically.

Although some of the aspects in completing an application are too specific to be treated in a book, you have been given guidelines and techniques that allow you to integrate those aspects with the features that are to some extent present in the design and development of every component-based application.

By reading this chapter, you ended up with a set of best practices and a component-based template that encapsulates them. In particular, you have learned how to

- Take control of the loading process in component-based applications, determining when classes and exported symbols are loaded.

- Define the structure of a Flash document that properly compiles and initializes the components' symbols and their classes before they are generated dynamically.

- Define a folder structure capable of managing several applications, their shared subsystems, and their themes efficiently, and at a low cost of maintenance.

In the second part of the chapter, you learned the basics of developing an application based on an XML layout engine and the benefits that come with it. Many of those benefits depend on mastering the use of XML within a component-based application framework.

The next chapter will show you how to take full control over XML parsing in order to be able to extend the framework by adding new features to existing components or even expand it by adding support for brand new components.

Chapter 8

MAKING YOUR XML LIFE EASIER

He that would perfect his work must first sharpen his tools.

Confucius

Before being considered for describing user interfaces, XML had already become a very popular choice for capturing information across multiple applications, on account of the many benefits deriving from its inherent ability to represent content via a simple, yet highly interoperable format.

XML has been available in ActionScript via a built-in class, originally called XML, since Flash 5. However, it was not until the next version of the player (version 6) that the class was moved into the core of the language with a significant gain in performance.

The XML class built into ActionScript provides many different services:

- It is capable of loading an XML document and parsing it.
- It can send an XML document to a specific URL.
- It can build an XML document dynamically.
- It can alter the structure of an existing XML document.

However, if you tried to parse an XML document using the XML class, you will be aware that writing the necessary parsing code is not only tedious, but also generates overcomplicated, almost unreadable code.

In this chapter, you will find a neat approach to overcoming the limitations of the XML class. In order to fully grasp the design and benefits of the exposed solution, you need to first review how the XML class implements the structure of an XML document (DOM) and how that affects the code you usually write for extracting data from an XML document.

> *The completed source code introduced in this chapter can be found in the package* `src08.zip`, *downloadable from this book's page at* www.friendsofed.com.

Parsing XML in ActionScript

If you already know how the built-in XML class works, you should find the following examples very simple. The purpose of these examples is to point out the limitations of the XML class and how to improve upon them.

When using the XML class, the process of parsing an XML document happens behind the scenes. You start with an instance of the XML class that becomes somewhat "larger" after it loads an XML document from a specific URL because the structure of the loaded XML document will be re-created inside the instance of the XML class.

The following ActionScript code, run by the `XML_00a.fla` file that you can find in the source code associated with this chapter, shows the basic process of loading an XML document via an instance of the XML class and how such an instance (called xmlObj) has indeed changed after the loading process is completed:

```
var xmlObj:XML = new XML();
xmlObj.ignoreWhite = true;
xmlObj.onLoad = function(success:Boolean) {
    if (success) {
        trace("AFTER: " + xmlObj.toString());
    }
}

trace("BEFORE: " + xmlObj.toString());
trace("-------------------------------");
xmlObj.load("../../XMLdata/example.xml");
```

Note that, unless otherwise specified, we will be using the same XML document throughout all the examples in this chapter for the sake of consistency when comparing different parsing code.

The chosen XML document is stored in the example.xml file and contains the following description of a very simple user interface:

```
<?xml version="1.0"?>
<xleff>
    <stage>
        <form name="MainForm" x="0" y="0">
            <button name="YesButton" label="Yes"
                x="270" y="280" width="160" />
            <button name="NoButton" label="No"
                x="470" y="280" width="160" />
        </form>
    </stage>
</xleff>
```

If you run the example XML_00a.fla, you will notice that the outcome of the ActionScript code, shown previously, will be displayed in the Output window as follows:

```
BEFORE:
---------------------------------
AFTER: <?xml version="1.0"?><xleff><stage><form name="MainForm" x="0"
y="0"><button name="YesButton" label="Yes" x="270" y="280" width="160"
/><button name="NoButton" label="No" x="470" y="280" width="160"
/></form></stage></xleff>
```

The string resulting from the call to xmlObj.toString is empty before loading the XML document, while it contains the whole document after the XML document has been loaded.

However, at the same time, something more complicated than just having the XML document in a single string has happened: the XML document has been parsed, and a tree-like structure has been added to xmlObj, as displayed in Figure 8-1.

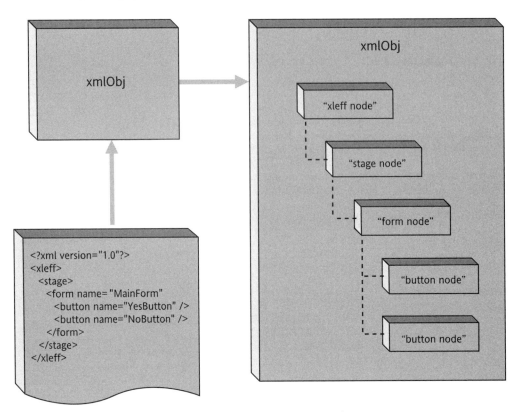

Figure 8-1. The xmlObj tree-like structure "grows" after loading an XML document.

But where does this tree-like structure come from and what is the cost of accessing it via the API implemented by the XML class built into ActionScript?

Object models and trees

The widespread diffusion of the object-oriented paradigm has involved the frequent use of the term "object model" in a variety of contexts.

Although there isn't an "official" definition of what an object model is, an object model usually refers to the deconstruction of a macro object in subobjects.

In Chapter 6, we considered a user interface as a macro object and deconstructed it into several objects (stage, forms, accordions, buttons, etc.). Basically, the XML syntax defined by XLEFF is a representation of the object model of a user interface.

Going further, it should not be too difficult to realize that an XML document can also be considered a macro object and deconstructed into several subobjects.

There is an "official" object model for XML documents, and it is called the W3C DOM (**D**ocument **O**bject **M**odel) Level1 recommendation. This recommendation has been produced by W3C, a consortium promoting standards for the Web, and can be found online at http://www.w3.org/TR/REC-xml/.

The XML class that we find in ActionScript is loosely based on the W3C DOM Level1 recommendation, and that is where the tree-like structure created after parsing an XML document comes from.

If you look back at Figure 8-1, you will notice that there is a one-to-one relationship between each XML element in the XML file and the nodes in the tree-like structure created in the xmlObj after parsing the XML document.

The tree-like structure implemented by the XML class reflects the containment relationships present in the XML document, and each node in the tree is an instance of the XMLNode class, another ActionScript built-in class.

In Figure 8-1, the nodes in the tree structure were labeled figuratively to facilitate recognizing the one-to-one correspondence with the elements in the document.

By using the common properties of the XML and XMLNode classes, you can access the nodes of the tree-like structure, generated after parsing an XML document, in several ways.

Figure 8-2 shows the same tree displayed in the previous xmlObj diagram after replacing each node's label with the actual ActionScript statement required to access that node by using the childNodes property.

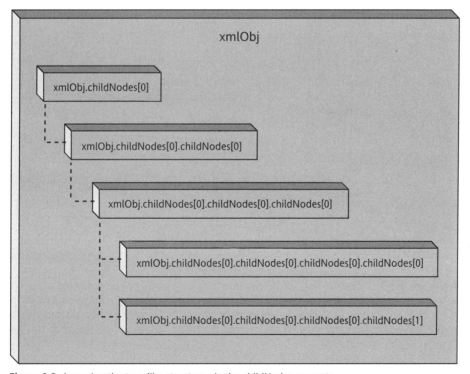

Figure 8-2. Accessing the tree-like structure via the childNodes property

The childNodes property of each XMLNode instance is a read-only array that contains the children of the node that in turn are instances of XMLNode as well.

Without comparing Figure 8-1 with Figure 8-2, it is very difficult, if not impossible, to recognize what node of the XML document is accessed by the following ActionScript statement:

```
// a not very readable reference to the 'form node'
xmlObj.childNodes[0].childNodes[0].childNodes[0]
```

The XML and XMLNode classes define five additional properties that you may use as an alternative to childNodes in order to browse the tree-like structure of an XML document. Their names intuitively suggest their purpose: parentNode, firstChild, lastChild, nextSibling, and previousSibling.

Figure 8-3 maps the tree-like structure of our current example into the ActionScript statements required to access its nodes using some of the alternative properties.

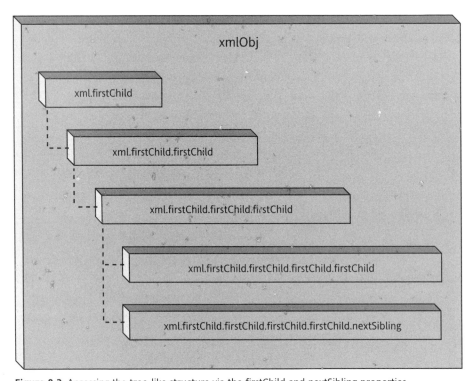

Figure 8-3. Accessing the tree-like structure via the firstChild and nextSibling properties

Each of the parentNode, firstChild, lastChild, nextSibling, and previousSibling properties references a single node that is somewhat related to the current node. Using them instead of the childNodes array can slightly improve the performance of your code, since there is no index processing, but the resulting ActionScript statements are still not very readable, as in the case of the following:

```
// another not very readable reference to the 'form node'
xmlObj.firstChild.firstChild.firstChild
```

Of course, you can declare variables with names that are better related to the domain problem of your application and use them as pointers to the tree-like structure in order to make your code more readable. In fact, that is what wise developers do every time they have to use the XML class to access the data in an XML document.

The typical job of an XML developer

When wearing the hat of the XML developer, we define one or more XML schemas (or receive them as part of the application's requirements) that model the information within the problem domain of an application, and we usually end up writing lots of parsing code to access the data present in XML documents created respecting those schemas.

The larger the project, the more important it is that the source code be readable in order to reduce the costs of debugging, maintaining, and extending the software being developed.

That is the one of the major reasons why any typical multitier architecture includes at least one tier for the business logic in the application. In cases like these, developers spend a lot of time implementing intermediate objects that are much closer to the business logic than the tree-like structure included in the XML class.

The benefits of such intermediate objects become more evident if you compare the tree-like structure shown in Figure 8-4 with those displayed in the previous two diagrams (Figures 8-2 and 8-3).

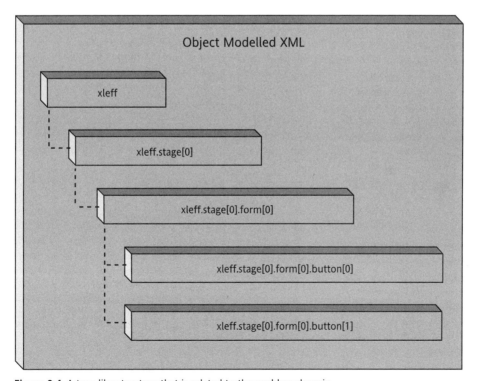

Figure 8-4. A tree-like structure that is related to the problem domain

Let's compare the three statements in those three figures that are associated with the same "form node" of the current XML example:

```
// a not very readable reference to the 'form node'
xmlObj.childNodes[0].childNodes[0].childNodes[0]
// another not very readable reference to the 'form node'
xmlObj.firstChild.firstChild.firstChild
// do you really need a comment to know what the next line is about?
xleff.stage[0].form[0]
```

Of course, the line

```
xleff.stage[0].form[0]
```

not only tells you about what kind of the object being referred (form), but also tells you more about the two objects that contain it (xleff and stage).

The point here is about how many steps you have to make to access the information stored in the XML document and how readable those steps are. The comparison is between the anonymous structure created by the XML class, depending on properties such as firstChild and childNodes, and an object model that is based on the specific XML document that you are dealing with. So far, we have been reusing the same XML document illustrated in Figure 8-1. An example that uses a completely different XML document will further clarify the points being made here. Let us consider another simple XML document:

```
<?xml version="1.0"?>
<forest>
    <tree>
        <branch>
            <apple />
            <apple />
        </branch>
    </tree>
    <tree>
        <branch>
            <orange />
            <orange />
        </branch>
        <branch>
            <orange />
        </branch>
    </tree>
</forest>
```

Here we are simply describing a forest with two trees (an apple tree and an orange tree). Accessing the orange in the second branch of the orange tree following the three different approaches illustrated so far would produce the following three statements:

```
// a not very readable reference to the 'form node'
xmlObj.childNodes[0].childNodes[1].childNodes[1].childNodes[0]
// another not very readable reference to the 'form node'
xmlObj.firstChild.firstChild.nextSibling.firstChild \\ continues below
    .nextSibling.firstChild
forest.tree[1].branch[1].orange[0]
```

Once again the statement

```
forest.tree[1].branch[1].orange[0]
```

tells us immediately that we are dealing with the first orange on the second branch of the second tree in the forest (read it from right to left and consider that arrays are zero-based).

You can choose slightly different strategies to implement your "business objects" starting from the highly generic tree-like structure returned by the XML class, but no matter what you will always end up doing a lot of repetitive work.

Wouldn't it be wonderful if the XML class automatically returned an object matching not the generic DOM of an XML document, but the more application-specific object model defined by the XML schema upon which the XML document is based?

That is what the XModel class included in XLEFF does.

Simplifying the parsing process

Being able to write parsing code that is at the same time more compact and readable can make a huge difference in the case of applications that severely rely on XML.

When implementing the very first version of XLEFF, all the limitations of the anonymous tree-like structure of the XML class becomes immediately evident, and the need to extend such a class becomes mandatory in order to effectively produce and maintain the XML layout engine.

The sort of code being written by using the XML class is very repetitive, and that suggests that there is a pattern hidden in such code:

> *The developer is constantly transforming the generic object model of the XML DOM into an application-specific object model.*

A second fundamental aspect of such pattern is that

> *The application-specific object model (or a significant part of it) is described by the XML schema(s) of the XML document(s) being used in the application.*

209

Both aspects firmly suggest the way to go: extend the XML class by implementing a new class (XModel) capable of returning a macro object modeled following the object model defined by the application-specific schema inside the XML documents.

The use of the XModel class in the XLEFF project makes the parsing code so much more readable and compact that it is not an exaggeration to say that XLEFF may have not existed without the help of such functionality.

Although the XModel class was purposely created for XLEFF, its functionality is logically independent from it, and it would be as useful in any other project requiring you to produce a lot of XML parsing code.

Since the scope of the XModel class is made so clear by the necessity of having a more readable parsing code while writing less and less of it, every feature in the class has been added with such benefits in mind.

Let's then compare the parsing code deriving from the use of XModel with the options offered by the XML class.

Parsing an XML document

Parsing an XML document using the XML class involves the implementation of the onLoad event handler, as we saw in our earlier example in this chapter.

The XModel class defines a new onModelledObject event that is handled via a listener object following the standard approach for custom events discussed in the first part of the book. The following code sample illustrates a typical use of the XModel class:

```
var listener = new Object();
listener.onModelledObject = function(eventObject:Object) {
    var xleff:Object = eventObject.modelledObject;
    // the xleff variable now refers to the modelled object
    // resulting from parsing the example.xml document
}

xModel.addEventListener("onModelledObject", listener);
xModel.load("../../XMLdata/example.xml");
```

The onModelledObject event handler receives an eventObject that has a property called modelledObject: this property provides access to the macro object created by the XModel class after parsing the XML document.

Note that following the declaration of

```
var xleff:Object = eventObject.modelledObject;
```

the variable xleff represents the root of such a macro object that has the expected structure, which was described in the statements we previously saw in Figure 8-4.

As you may notice, there is a one-to-one correspondence between the XML elements in the XML document and the subobjects of the macro object. You may also notice that the root element (coinciding with the modelledObject property returned by the onModelledObject event) is the only node not implemented as an array—this is because the root element of an XML document is slightly different from the other nodes in the document.

Document root and other nodes

The XModel class implements the root element of an XML document as an object and any other node underneath it as an array. This is because an XML document can have only one root element, but this root element can have any number of children.

The root element of the XML document is also the only node that has an anonymous name (modelledObject), unrelated to the specific schema of the XML document, since it is a property of the object returned from the onModelledObject event.

To further clarify this point, the following code illustrates the declaration you may write if you are using the XModel class to create a macro object for the XML example describing a forest that we saw earlier:

```
var forest:Object = eventObject.modelledObject;
```

Following this declaration, you would be able to access the node using the following line:

```
forest.tree[1].branch[1].orange[0];
```

since the macro object created by the XModel class would reflect the contents of that XML document.

Identifying a node name

We already know that whenever we use the anonymous tree-like structure returned from the XML class, we are unable to recognize the name of the XML element associated with a node by just looking at the structure, as in this example:

```
xmlObj.childNodes[0].childNodes[0].childNodes[0]
```

In order to identify the element name, we must read the value of the nodeName property of the XMLNode class. The following statement:

```
trace(xmlObj.childNodes[0].childNodes[0].childNodes[0].nodeName);
```

would print the text

```
form
```

in the Output window, assuming that the XML document being parsed is the first one we introduced in this chapter, which is the default for the our current examples.

However, the nodeName property of a node would not tell us the names of the parent nodes. In the case of the macro object returned by XModel, we don't need to test the value of any property to know the name of a node and also the names of its parents, as demonstrated in the following example:

```
xleff.stage[0].form[0]
```

The previous statement is clearly more readable and compact than any alternative statement built by using the properties provided the XML and XMLNode classes.

Identifying a node type

The W3C DOM Level 1 recommendation defines 12 different types of node, each of them identified by an integer:

1. ELEMENT_NODE
2. ATTRIBUTE_NODE
3. TEXT_NODE
4. CDATA_SECTION_NODE
5. ENTITY_REFERENCE_NODE
6. ENTITY_NODE
7. PROCESSING_INSTRUCTION_NODE
8. COMMENT_NODE
9. DOCUMENT_NODE
10. DOCUMENT_TYPE_NODE
11. DOCUMENT_FRAGMENT_NODE
12. NOTATION_NODE

However, the XML class supports only two types of node: the ELEMENT_NODE (1) and the TEXT_NODE (3).

All the nodes that we have been dealing with in this chapter until now were of type 1 (ELEMENT_NODE), since the respective XML documents did not contain any node of type 3 (TEXT_NODE).

Let's extend our default XML document in order to have a node of type 3 in the tree-like structure created by the XML class:

```
<?xml version="1.0"?>
<xleff>
    <stage>
        <form name="MainForm" x="0" y="0">
            <button name="YesButton" label="Yes"
                        x="270" y="280" width="160" />
                    <button name="NoButton" label="No"
                    x="470" y="280" width="160" />
                    <textarea name="TextArea1"
➥ x="270" y="400"

                        width="400" height="200">
                        <content>
```

```
                              This text creates a TEXT_NODE
                              type in the XML class tree-like
                              structure
                            </content>
                            </textarea>
                      </form>
                 </stage>
            </xleff>
```

Note that, following the syntax supported by XLEFF for the description of user interfaces, we added another node of type 1 (associated with the textarea element) containing an additional node of type 1 (associated with the content element). The content element, however, contains some text; text inside an element generates an unnamed node of type 3 in the tree-like structure created by the XML class when parsing that XML document.

When considering node types, writing parsing code by using the XML class becomes even more awkward, and the outcome is even less readable because of the following:

- An additional nodeType property of the XMLNode class is provided to check the actual type of a node (returning an integer value of 1 or 3, according to the node's type).
- The nodeName property makes sense only for nodes of the type 1. In fact, in the case of type 3 nodes, this property has a value of null.
- The XMLNode class defines another cumbersome property named nodeValue to allow retrieving the text of a node of type 3. To make things worse, this property has no significance in the case of type 1 nodes and, in fact, its value is set to null when the node is of type 1.

Basically, when writing parsing code by using the XML class, you will frequently have to test the nodeType property to verify the type of a node and, depending on its actual type, access a different property (nodeName for nodes of type 1, nodeValue for nodes of type 3).

Assuming that you know the exact structure of the XML document in our example, a single statement accessing the text inside the content element would look something like the following:

```
xmlObj
  .childNodes[0]
    .childNodes[0]
      .childNodes[0]
        .childNodes[2]
          .childNodes[0]
            .childNodes[0]
              .nodeValue
```

The previous ActionScript statement is not only very long, but also cryptic, since the childNodes property does not tell us much about the XML structure that we are navigating. Furthermore, by looking at the previous line, you cannot tell the type of the node that you are accessing (text node or element node), which can be particularly significant since the nodeValue property is null in the case of element nodes, and verifying the type of the node, by checking the nodeType property, makes your code more robust but also more complex.

Compare the previous approach with that of the XModel class in a similar situation. The XModel class does not distinguish among different node types since it is not a DOM (**D**ocument **O**bject **M**odel). As you have learned, the XModel class creates a macro object matching the object model described by the XML schema of the XML document.

When text is included inside an XML element, the XModel class just adds a text property to the specific subobjects and assigns the text value to it. Accessing the text inside the content element of our XML document in a single statement would then be done using the following code:

```
xleff.stage[0].form[0].textarea[0].content[0].text
```

This is considerably more compact and readable than any single statement you may create to access the same text value by using any combination of the properties made available by the XML and XMLNode classes!

Accessing the attributes of a node

As you may well know, XML elements can have attributes whose values can be enclosed in single or double quotes, as in the following example:

```
<button name="YesButton" label="Yes"
        x="270" y="280" width="160" />
```

The former line shows a button element that has five attributes (name, label, x, y, and width). In the following example, where xmlObj is supposed to be the instance of the XML class, a variable n was utilized to have a short reference to the node corresponding to the button element in order to demonstrate how its attributes can be accessed via the XMLNode class:

```
var n:XMLNode =
xmlObj.childNodes[0].childNodes[0].childNodes[0].childNodes[0];
trace(n.attributes.name);
trace(n.attributes.label);
trace(n.attributes.x);
trace(n.attributes.y);
trace(n.attributes.width);
```

When executed, the previous code would display the following values in the Output window:

```
YesButton
Yes
270
280
160
```

It follows that, when using the XML class to parse an XML document, the attributes of an XML element are accessed via the attributes property of the respective XMLNode instance. The attributes property is implemented as an associative array in which the keys are the names of the element's attributes and the values are the respective attribute's values.

Even when accessing attributes of an XML element, the XModel class provides a more compact and readable option, as explained by the following example:

```
var n:XMLNode = xleff.stage[0].form[0].button[0];
trace(n.name);
trace(n.label);
trace(n.x);
trace(n.y);
trace(n.width);
```

The XModel class does not introduce an intermediary subobject and, in doing so, assigns the attributes as values in a more intuitive way, which can also be demonstrated by accessing an attribute's value via a complete reference to the attribute, like so:

```
xleff.stage[0].form[0].button[0].name
```

This accesses the name attribute of the first button in the form in a very readable manner.

Browsing the structure of an XML document

We have been focusing on the most elemental steps in writing XML parsing code to show how clearly the suggested approach, implemented by the XModel class, provides a way to increase the readability of the code and the productivity of the developer.

Still there are infinitely more complex cases that may benefit from such an approach. Considering the steps to take when browsing the structure of an XML document can provide an even more significant example of those we have seen so far.

Let's reconsider the extended version of our default XML example after we added the textarea element to it. The following fragment shows a form element containing two button elements and a textarea element:

```
<form name="MainForm" x="0" y="0">
    <button name="YesButton" label="Yes"
            x="270" y="280" width="160" />
    <button name="NoButton" label="No"
            x="470" y="280" width="160" />
    <textarea name="TextArea1" x="270" y="400"
            width="400" height="200">
        <content>
        This text creates a TEXT_NODE
        type in the XML class tree-like
        structure
        </content>
    </textarea>
</form>
```

215

In the tree-like structure resulting from the use of the XML class, the node corresponding to the form element would be accessed via the following code:

```
var n:XMLNode = xmlObj.childNodes[0].childNodes[0].childNodes[0];
```

We already know that this code isn't very readable, but this is not the point we are trying to demonstrate here. If executing the following code

```
trace(n.childNodes.length);
```

we would find out that the node associated with the form element has three children. It is to be expected, since we know that the form element contains two button elements and one textarea element—a total of three (3) children.

The problem is that when programming actual parsing code, we would not know what the XML document would contain at runtime. All we would know programmatically is that the n node is a form element (by checking its nodeName property) and that its childNodes property contains three additional nodes. The research for further information is still possible, but it requires more and more checking.

When using the XModel class, we not only obtain more readable and compact code, but also a macro object in which information is already arranged in a better way.

We already know that the subobject corresponding to the form element would be accessed via the following statement:

```
var n:XMLNode = xleff.stage[0].form[0];
```

What we have not appreciated yet is that such a subobject would not have a single property with three children; rather it would have two different properties: one named button containing two children, and the other named textarea containing the third child. The following code would show a 2 followed by a 1 in the Output window:

```
trace(n.button.length);
trace(n.textarea.length);
```

Having the children already grouped in arrays in a way that is consistent with their XML elements simplifies the code that you must write for your applications even more than before.

The more complex the parsing code to be produced, the greater the benefits from such object-modeled organization of the information.

In the next few chapters, XLEFF will be used as a complex example, allowing you to fully appreciate the benefits of the approach captured in the XModel class. Every time you see XML parsing code in XLEFF, ask yourself how you would have done that by using the XML class—you would certainly end up with a significant increase in the complexity of your code.

A few notes on the use of XModel

The approach encapsulated in the XModel class offers so many benefits and can play such an important role in developing XML-based applications that you will certainly be interested in investigating whether there are holes in its strategy.

It may help your investigations to first consider that the XModel class works pretty well in the case of XLEFF—XML layout engines are naturally required to produce lots of XML parsing code in order to implement and maintain their functionality.

Also, it would be a severe misreading to interpret the approach suggested here as a criticism to the XML class implemented in ActionScript. On the contrary, the fact that XModel extends the XML class represents a very significant example of how conveniently built-in classes can be extended to give a competitive edge to your applications.

Finally, since the XModel class does not override any functionality implemented by the XML class, it is compatible with any code that you may have already written using the default built-in class.

Summary

In this chapter, you learned how to save a lot of time when it comes to writing XML parsing code.

Such a result is achieved by realizing that most of the time spent writing code to access the content of XML documents goes into translating the generic XML DOM supported by the XML class into an object model that is specific to your application.

You also learned how to use the XModel class—a huge time-saver since

- It automatically shapes the information inside an XML document in an object-oriented way by returning a macro object that very intuitively captures the application-specific contents of the document.
- It allows you to write code that is both more compact and more readable, facilitating the development and maintenance of your XML-based applications.

The next chapter will complete the second part of the book dedicated to mastering the techniques for exploiting the component architecture by introducing the customization process.

Chapter 9

THE CUSTOMIZATION PROCESS

Wisdom and beauty form a very rare combination.

Petronius

Quite often you will have to customize one or more aspects of a component in order to meet your customer's specifications.

The complexity of customizing a single aspect of a component can range from the simple replacement of a few graphic symbols to a rewrite of part of its functionality, the latter requiring a complete understanding of its implementation.

The appearance and behavior of components are influenced by several intertwined concepts: to understand the way they work and interact, you must learn the choices that were made when designing and implementing the architecture. Only then will you be able to select the technique that best suits a requirement among those that you will learn in this chapter.

The architecture supports two different functionalities for customizing the appearance of a component: **styles** and **skins**.

Although both can contribute to developing a uniform look among different components, styles usually act on a more global context than skins, and because of this they tend to define aspects that you can find in almost any component, such as color and text.

Conversely, because of its nature, a skin is usually strictly related to a specific component; artistic skills are required in order to create a set of skins that can give two different components a consistent look and feel.

Styles and skins are grouped in sets called **themes**. A theme is a collection of styles and skins that, working together, confer a similar look to a set of components.

Those are the basics. Now you need to learn the details.

> *The completed source code introduced in this chapter can be found in the package* src09.zip, *downloadable from this book's page at* www.friendsofed.com.

Working with styles

We first met styles in Chapter 6, when they were included in the XML description of a user interface to be dynamically generated by XLEFF. Those XML definitions were based upon the architecture's implementation of styles.

You may recall the presence of color names, colors, and text properties. In this section, we are going to examine how to use styles programmatically with ActionScript and, in more general terms, how styles have been implemented in the architecture.

The support for styles is implemented in the UIObject class, the root of the component architecture, and therefore it is available to any standard component.

A style is uniquely identified by its name. Of course, a specific style has an effect on a certain component only if that component supports it. By implementing a specific style, a component also defines how that style influences its appearance.

Parameters controlled by styles

Styles provide control over certain parameters of a component's appearance such as color, text, and behavior. Styles can also provide a limited control on the graphic design of a component instance.

Styles can then be classified into four general categories:

- **Color styles**, used to tell a component what colors to use. Color styles can also affect the skin and the text inside a component instance.
- **Text styles**, used to define formatting attributes (font family, font weight, etc.) of the text inside a component instance.
- **Behavior styles**, related to the dynamics of a component and affecting some components, such as the ComboBox or the Accordion, that display state transitions via animations. Behavior styles can affect the speed and accelerations of such animations.
- **Graphic styles**, affecting a component design in a limited way. The border style property is the most typical example of a graphic style. Components supporting the border style property can have several types of border (inset, outset, etc.).

The style lookup process

A component instance reads a style's value while drawing itself to synchronize its appearance accordingly with the style definition. However, the same style can be defined in more than one context: Figure 9-1 shows the priorities of the style lookup process as they have been implemented in the component architecture.

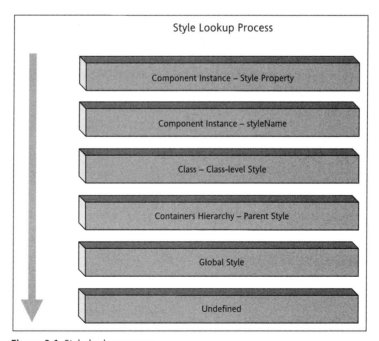

Figure 9-1. Style lookup process

Figure 9-1 is telling us that styles defined as properties of a component instance are given priority above any other definition and that global styles are the last context to be searched, after which the style property is considered undefined.

Figure 9-1 also lists all the options made available by the architecture when it comes to defining a style. Let us examine them one by one, starting from the highest priority.

Styles as properties of a component instance

If a style name is defined as a style property of a component instance, then its value takes precedence over any other definition of the same style name.

The best way to see how to set a style property of a component instance is to look at the code:

```
comboBox1.setStyle("backgroundColor", 0xaaaaff);
```

In the previous line, comboBox1 is an instance of the ComboBox component that you may have dropped on the stage of a newly created Flash document and named as suggested.

The setStyle method allows you to define the value of a specific style property. The first parameter specifies the style name of the style property being defined (backgroundColor in the example). The second parameter specifies the value being assigned to the style property (0xaaaaff, being a bluish color in the example).

It is just as simple as that. Note that a complementary method, named getStyle, can be used to retrieve the value of a style programmatically. Interestingly, running the following code in a Flash document containing nothing else but the comboBox1 instance of the previous example would show that the backgroundColor style is initially undefined and, after the execution of the setStyle method, would be defined by the value specified programmatically:

```
trace(comboBox1.getStyle("backgroundColor"));
comboBox1.setStyle("backgroundColor", 0xaaaaff);
trace(comboBox1.getStyle("backgroundColor"));
```

If you delete the comboBox1 instance from the stage of the former example and replace it with the one that follows, you can verify that the setStyle and getStyle methods still work as expected in the case of a dynamically generated component:

```
import mx.controls.ComboBox;

var comboBox1:ComboBox = createClassObject(ComboBox, "comboBox1", 1);
trace(comboBox1.getStyle("backgroundColor"));
comboBox1.setStyle("backgroundColor", 0xaaaaff);
trace(comboBox1.getStyle("backgroundColor"));
```

By using the setStyle method, you can define the style properties of a component instance one at a time. Note that the styles defined programmatically by using this technique will affect that specific component instance only.

When using XLEFF, you can set a component instance's style property by including its XML element within the component XML element, as in the following example:

```
<combobox name="comboBox1">
  <style>
    <property name="backgroundColor">
      <value type="Number">0xaaaaff</value>
    </property>
  </style>
</combobox>
```

Note that you can set more than one style property of the same component instance by adding further property elements inside the style element.

The styleName property

Defining the style properties of a component instance one by one gives you greater control since you may specify different settings for each component, although overusing this option is likely to produce a user interface with an irregular look. Also, in the absence of other options, your source code would grow with numerous calls to setStyle in order to define each style property individually for each component instance.

Grouping style properties into sets can provide significant help in enforcing a consistent look and feel while writing much less code. Because of this, the architecture supports grouping style properties in four different ways.

The first and most intuitive grouping technique allows collection of a number of style properties into a single style object so that you are able to assign all its properties to a component instance in a single step via the styleName property.

Once again, we may reuse the previous example made of a Flash document containing a single instance of a ComboBox component named comboBox1 to illustrate this technique with simplicity. The following lines create a style object named style:

```
import mx.styles.*;

var style = new CSSStyleDeclaration();
style.styleName = "Style4MyCombos";
```

What you should learn from the previous line is that style objects are instances of the CSSStyleDeclaration class, yet another class implemented by the component architecture. We define a name (Style4MyCombos) for the style object that indicates our intention to reuse it for any ComboBox instance in our application.

Once we have the style object, we can add to it as many style properties as we like. Imitating our previous example, we only add the backgroundColor property, but you may experiment by adding more of them:

```
style.setStyle("backgroundColor", 0xaaaaff);
// you can set other style properties here
// by adding further calls to style.setStyle
```

In order to make this style object accessible globally, we add it to the global styles collection created and maintained by the component architecture:

```
_global.styles.Style4MyCombos = style;
```

Note that we globally define the name of the style object according to the definition of its styleName property.

From there on, you can use the new, globally defined style object to assign all its style properties to a component instance in a single step, as in the following example:

```
comboBox1.setStyle("styleName", _global.styles.Style4MyCombos);
```

Since the style object as been added to the global collection of styles, you can refer to it anywhere in your application. The technique explained here can work also if we include its whole source code in the first frame of the Flash document:

```
import mx.styles.*;

var style = new CSSStyleDeclaration();
style.styleName = "Style4MyCombos";
style.setStyle("backgroundColor", 0xaaaaff);
// you can set other style properties here
// by adding further calls to style.setStyle
_global.styles.Style4MyCombos = style;

comboBox1.setStyle("styleName", _global.styles.Style4MyCombos);
```

Note that if you apply the best practice of enforcing strict typing by changing the line where the style object is declared:

```
var style:CSSStyleDeclaration = new CSSStyleDeclaration();
```

the example will stop working because the compiler will tell you that the setStyle method is not defined; the error message will be as follows:

```
There is no method with the name 'setStyle'
```

This is due to a potential flaw in the design of the CSSStyleDeclaration class. If you open the class file provided with the source code of the component architecture, you will find that there is no setStyle method declared in there, nor is the class derived from a base class that defines such a method.

The compiler is quite right, although we know that the setStyle method must have been added somehow to the class; otherwise, the previous code would not work at all. In fact, the setStyle method is implemented as a class (CSSSetStyle) and added to the CSSStyleDeclaration class via its prototype property. Find the following line:

```
CSSStyleDeclaration.prototype.setStyle = ui._setStyle;
```

In the implementation of the `classConstruct` method of the CSSSetStyle class, this demonstrates how the `setStyle` method eventually ends up being added to the CSSStyleDeclaration class. Unfortunately, such an exotic method clashes with the type checking mechanism implemented by the Flash compiler that cannot validate at compile time properties and methods added at runtime.

I spent a few lines on this issue to show that although best practices are a good thing, sometimes you have to forget them in order to achieve a result. Hopefully, in the next version of the component architecture, the implementation of the CSSStyleDeclaration class will be cleaner, and strict typing will not be a problem for it.

Note that the XLEFF equivalent of the `style` object option is to define a style in the Styles section of the XML schema like so:

```
<style name="Style4MyCombos">
    <property name="backgroundColor">
        <value type="Number">0xaaaaff</value>
    </property>
</style>
```

and then assign it to a component instance via the `styleName` attribute, as in the following:

```
<combobox name="comboBox1" styleName="Style4MyCombos" />
```

Even in this case, XLEFF follows very closely the design of the component architecture.

Class-level styles

Style objects could be used in a broader context than the one showed in our last example. For example, you may define a `BlueStyle` object that can be applied to component instances belonging to different classes but that support the same style properties (such as backgroundColor). This is achieved through a shortcut, used when you must address a specific component class: class-level style properties.

If the global `styles` collection contains a style object whose name is exactly the same as that of a component class, its style properties are automatically defined in every instance of the component in question. That may sound more complex than it actually is, so let us look at an example:

```
_global.styles.ComboBox.setStyle("backgroundColor", 0xaaaaff);
```

This single line is sufficient to define the `backgroundColor` style property for all the ComboBox instances in your application, since it adds the style property's definition to the ComboBox global style included in the `styles` global collection.

If all the ComboBox instances in your application must have the same look, this is probably the best option to consider when defining their style properties in your application.

Note that if a certain style object for a specific component class is not implemented, you can add it to the global styles collection and it will start working, assuming that it has the exact same name of its associated component class. However, you must act carefully, as demonstrated by the following example:

```
if (_global.styles.MyComponentClass == undefined) {
    _global.styles. MyComponentClass =
                            new mx.styles.CSSStyleDeclaration();
}
```

Before adding the MyComponentClass global style object to the global styles collection, check whether it is already defined; otherwise, you will risk losing all its preexisting definitions.

XLEFF support of class-level styles is very intuitive also. You can define style classes in the same XML section where you define style objects. The only difference is that class-level styles will have the name of an existing component class, as in the following example:

```
<style name="ComboBox">
    <property name="backgroundColor">
        <value type="Number">0xaaaaff</value>
    </property>
</style>
```

Inheriting styles from a container

The third way of grouping style properties may be less intuitive than using style objects or class-level styles, but it can still be effective in several circumstances: it works by inheriting the style properties of a component instance's container, if any.

Not every style property can be inherited, though, since a style property must be implemented as inheritable in order to be inherited.

Although the official documentation claims that the component architecture already implements certain style properties as inheritable, concrete testing shows that this feature is not yet consistently supported throughout the architecture. Since it is also likely that the number and name of the style properties that are inheritable will change in the feature, I recommend using the StyleManager class to verify whether a specific style property is actually inheritable by using its static isInheritingStyle method, for example:

```
import mx.styles.*;

trace(StyleManager.isInheritingStyle("backgroundColor"));
```

At the moment of writing, the backgroundColor is not an inheritable style property and, therefore, the previous example would display the value false in the Output window if executed in the authoring environment.

Note that, when implementing new styles for new components, you can make them inheritable by using a complementary method of the StyleManager class, called registerInheritingStyle, that works as in the following example, which shows a style property called MyNewStyleProperty being registered as inheritable:

```
import mx.styles.*;

StyleManager.registerInheritingStyle("MyNewStyleProperty"));
```

By using the registerInheritingStyle method, you may also try to change the existing inheritance rule in the component architecture, although the use of this method for this purpose is currently undocumented and, therefore, should be considered a hack and used with care.

In the case of XLEFF, the layout engine has nothing to do with implementing inherited styles, since they are inherited transparently at runtime depending on the containers that will be dynamically created in the interface. Conclusion: if an inheritable style property works for the component architecture, it will also work in XLEFF.

Global styles

Global styles are the fifth and last technique that allow you to define a style property. They can be loosely considered the fourth "grouping" technique since, like the previous three techniques, global styles allow you to apply style properties to more than one component instance at a time.

Global styles come last in the priority order of the style lookup process illustrated earlier in Figure 9-1. If, at runtime, a style property definition cannot be found even among the global styles, its value remains undefined.

Global style properties are added to the global style object, which is an instance of the CSSStyleDeclaration class like any other style object considered so far.

In the case of the example we have been using for our examination of the five different options for defining style properties, one line of code is sufficient to set the bluish background for the comboBox1 instance of the ComboBox class:

```
_global.style.setStyle("backgroundColor", 0xaaaaff);
```

Notice that the last statement defines the backgroundColor style property globally by using the _global.style object implemented by the component architecture. As a result of this, the statement affects every component instance in the application, not just comboBox1, unless the backgroundColor has been also defined by using some of the previous four techniques; if this is the case, the process outlined in Figure 9-1 determines how multiple definitions of the same style property are prioritized and which one will prevail.

XLEFF supports a globalstyles XML element that you can add to the Styles section of the XML schema to declare style properties that must be implemented globally, as in the following example:

```
<globalstyles>
    <property name="backgroundColor">
        <value type="Number">0xaaaaff</value>
    </property>
</globalstyles>
```

Analyzing skins

As you saw earlier, the use of style properties allows you to customize certain aspects of a component instance, including its graphic design to a limited extent.

However, most of the standard components in the architecture owe much of their appearance to skins, and you will have to consider various techniques to replace them if you really want to take full control of how components look.

What is a skin?

Generally speaking, a **skin** is ultimately an exported symbol. The component architecture implements skins in several different ways, depending on the specific component. The common denominator of those implementations is that skins are, in any case, movie clips with a linkage identifier and, by extension, are symbols exported for ActionScript.

Working with skins can be hard even for a seasoned developer because some skins are implemented by coding rather complex algorithms. We will start looking at the commonalities and differences among various skins so we can define an abstract process for selecting the proper technique when customizing them.

Apart from being exported symbols, skins share another common feature: each skin is somewhat associated with a specific state of a component.

Components can assume different states over time depending on the user interaction or as the result of programming. For example, think of a Button instance that can present several states such as button up, button over (when the mouse point is over it), button down (while the button is being clicked), and so on.

When considering a particular skin, do not forget that it is associated with one state of a component, and its purpose is to visualize that state.

A skin may, of course, be associated with more than one state at a time, but providing different skins for each state of a component makes that component instance much more lively, since the user will be able to recognize each of those states visually. Associating the same skin to two different states of a component may well make those states look very similar, if not identical.

Now that you understand all skins are exported symbols with a linkage identifier and associated with (at least) a component state, it makes sense for me to introduce you to the three major categories of skins: handcrafted skins, mixed skins, and purely coded skins.

Handcrafted skins

A **handcrafted skin** is an exported symbol that is not empty: it contains graphics designed by an artist to visualize a particular state of the associated component.

The StandardComponents.fla file that we examined earlier in the book contains not only the physical structure of the standard component, but also their default skins. After locating the file (see Appendix A for instructions), you can open it and start examining the skins that you can find in its library.

The file library contains several folders, and you can access the skins by selecting Flash UI Components 2 ➤ Themes ➤ MMDefault. Once in the MMDefault folder, you will find several folders, each having a name associated with a certain standard component.

Let us focus on the CheckBox Assets subfolder to find examples of handcrafted skins. Remember that skins are associated with a component states, which is indicated by the presence of a States subfolder containing the skins of the CheckBox component, as displayed in Figure 9-2.

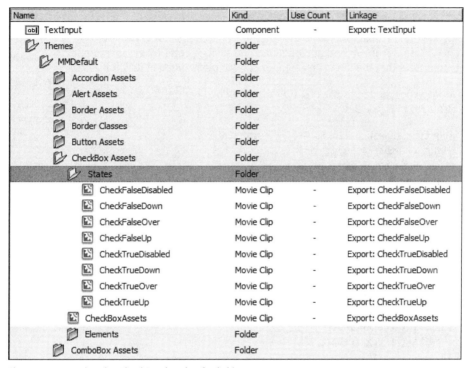

Figure 9-2. Locating the CheckBox handcrafted skins

Figure 9-2 also shows that each of the skins in the States folder has a linkage identifier as expected (CheckFalseDisabled, CheckTrueDisabled, etc.).

The state of a CheckBox instance is determined by several factors at the same time:

- The mouse interaction (over, out, click)
- The instance enabled status (enabled, disabled)
- The instance selected status (true, false)

It is interesting to note that the CheckBox component comes with eight different skins, each of them associated with a different state of a component instance.

229

Figure 9-3 shows each of the eight skins alongside the names chosen for both the symbols and their linkage identifiers.

The linkage identifiers chosen for the CheckBox skins are rather intuitive; you may well guess that the skin name CheckTrueOver is associated with the state of the CheckBox instance when the mouse rolls over it and its selected and enabled properties are both true. However, concrete confirmation of what state a skin represents will come when we investigate the CheckBox class throughout this chapter.

You can generate the image captured in Figure 9-3 via ActionScript code by creating a new Flash document and adding/deleting a single CheckBox instance on its stage to ensure that the CheckBox component will be included in its library.

The following code, added to the first frame of the document, will generate the image displayed in Figure 9-3:

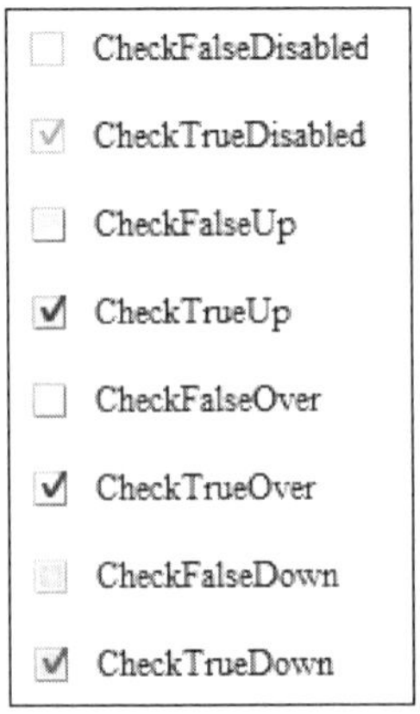

Figure 9-3. The eight skins of a CheckBox and their linkage identifiers

```
function showSkin(linkId:String, idx:Number) {
  var x:Number = 50;
  var y:Number = 10 + 30*idx;
  attachMovie(linkId, "cb" + idx, getNextHighestDepth(),➥
    {_x: x, _y: y});

  createTextField("cb" + idx + "txt", getNextHighestDepth(),➥
    x + 20, y - 4, 100, 20);
  eval("cb" + idx + "txt").text = linkId;
}

showSkin("CheckFalseDisabled", 0);
showSkin("CheckTrueDisabled", 1);
showSkin("CheckFalseUp", 2);
showSkin("CheckTrueUp", 3);
showSkin("CheckFalseOver", 4);
showSkin("CheckTrueOver", 5);
showSkin("CheckFalseDown", 6);
showSkin("CheckTrueDown", 7);
```

What is interesting in the last example is

- It shows that skins are included in the compiled (SWC) version of the CheckBox component. To include the component in the document's library is enough to start generating those skins dynamically.

- The function showSkin implemented in the example uses the attachMovie method to create a skin dynamically. Although the component architecture implements the basic skin functionality in the UIObject class via several methods, skins are exported symbols because, eventually, they are created dynamically in the same way: by calling attachMovie.

The skins of the CheckBox component prove to be a good starting point since they provide us with examples of the simplest type of skins:

- These handcrafted skins are individually linked with a specific state of a component.
- Each state of the component is associated to one skin only. As a result, only one skin is visible at any moment.
- Each state of the component can be wholly previewed in the library by looking at the respective skin.

The remaining two major categories of skins are usually much more complicated, and not just because of the presence of ActionScript code, as you are going to see in the examples in the next two sections.

Mixed skins

It is not always possible to implement a component appearance by using a single handcrafted skin for each of its states. In the case of the CheckBox component, its sole content is a label that is always placed well apart from the component's skin regardless of whatever option we choose for the labelPlacement property (right, left, top, or bottom), as shown in Figure 9-4.

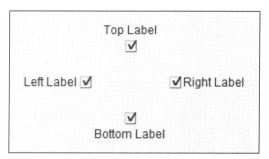

Figure 9-4. The four positions available for a CheckBox's label

Positioning the CheckBox label does not require any change to the skin design, and this ultimately is what allows it to be implemented following the simplest option: one graphic symbol for each of the component states.

However, there are cases when accommodating a component's content requires a more flexible, and therefore more complex, implementation of its skins.

Mixed skin is a term that I use in this book to indicate a skin that is built by combining not just one, but several exported symbols at the same time in order to visualize the current state of a component. The adjective "mixed" also indicates that the various symbols are controlled and coordinated via algorithms implemented using ActionScript. The implementation of a mixed skin, therefore, involves a combination of several graphic symbols plus frequently complex coding. As you can imagine, customizing a component that has a mixed skin is not as easy as changing the skins of a handcrafted component.

The component architecture includes several examples of mixed skins. Arguably, the UIScrollBar component implements the most complex example of mixed skin in the architecture, since 26 different graphic symbols are required to draw its skin.

In the architecture, scrollbars are frequently subcomponents of containers like the ScrollPane component, and they are also available as the UIScrollBar standard component.

The 26 graphic symbols requested to display the states of the UIScrollBar component can be found in the StandardComponents.fla file's library by selecting Flash UI Components 2 ➤ Themes ➤ MMDefault ➤ ScrollBar Assets ➤ States. I have displayed these symbols in Figure 9-5 for your convenience.

Figure 9-5. The 26 exported graphic symbols required by the UIScrollBar skin

The graphic symbols used in the UIScrollBar implementation deconstruct the component structure into four logical entities:

- **Up arrow button**: The button of a scrollbar that the user clicks to scroll backward
- **Down arrow button**: The button of a scrollbar that the user clicks to scroll forward
- **Thumb**: The handle of a scrollbar that the user drags back and forth to scroll accordingly
- **Track**: The background of the area constraining the movement of the thumb

Figure 9-6 shows the skin of a scrollbar deconstructed into these four subobjects.

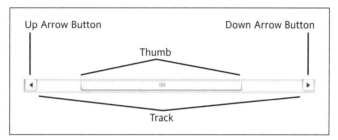

Figure 9-6. A scrollbar's skin deconstructed

Both the up arrow and down arrow buttons take four skins each to represent their four states (Disabled, Down, Over, and Up). Although belonging to a subcomponent, these skins can be considered handcrafted ones since each of them corresponds to a specific state of the subcomponent.

The thumb is treated similarly to a button; however, although it only has four states (Disabled, Down, Over, and Up) like the other buttons, it takes 16 skins to be represented. This is because the skin of each state of the thumb is visualized using not just one, but four graphic symbols (ScrollThumbBottomUp, ScrollThumbGripUp, ScrollThumbMiddleUp, and ScrollThumbTopUp in the case of the Up state). Figure 9-7 shows the skin of the thumb deconstructed into the four subskins.

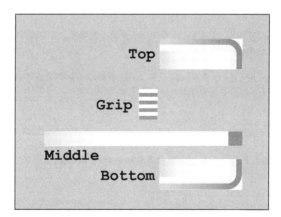

Figure 9-7. A scrollbar's thumb deconstructed

When scrollbars are used inside containers such as the ScrollPane component, the size of the thumb in the scrollbar matches the percentage of content currently visible in the container. Because of its variability, the state of the thumb cannot be visualized by a single graphic component. The combination of the four skin parts shown in Figure 9-7, controlled via code, allows the creation of a thumb whose size is variable while certain visual aspects (like the grip and the extremes of the thumb) remain unchanged. In the case of a horizontal scrollbar, like the one shown in Figure 9-6, all of the four skin parts are rotated to match the horizontal design.

The two skins still unaccounted for (ScrollTrack and ScrollTrackDisabled) belong to the scrollbar's track. They also may be considered handcrafted skins, since each of them corresponds to a state of the track (enabled or disabled). However, such skins are evidently stretched to match the length of the scrollbar, as required.

In the end, the scrollbar example provides us with a mixed skin made of several skin parts that also belongs to four different elements of a scrollbar (up/down buttons, thumb, and track).

To customize a mixed skin not only is a lengthy process (26 graphic symbols to be redesigned), but also requires the understanding of how certain skin parts are controlled, resized, and rotated by the skin algorithms implemented for the component in order to create an apparently seamless skin. The complete process of customizing the skin of the UIScrollBar component is described in Chapter 21.

However, in the case of mixed skins, you only need to know how the skin parts are used by those algorithms in order to replace them with compatible graphics. Therefore, you are not requested to implement or change a skin algorithm when you customize a mixed skin.

Purely coded skins

As you may be guessing by now, the third category of skins, **purely coded skins**, is even more complex and does require you to write a skinning algorithm if you want to customize this kind of skin.

The designs of the skins considered so far were defined by a single graphic symbol (handcrafted skins) or from the arrangement of several graphic symbols duplicated, resized, or even rotated via code to achieve the final result (mixed skins).

In both cases, however, you could find some kind of graphic asset inside the exported symbol representing the whole skin or just a part of it.

In the case of purely coded skins, you are still dealing with exported symbols that, as you know, are movie clips with a linkage identifier. However, in the case of purely coded skins, those movie clips are empty!

The most commonly used purely coded skin in the component architecture certainly is that associated with the Button component. That is right—the appearance of instances of the Button component does not depend on any graphic assets, and it is fully created at runtime via the Drawing API available in ActionScript.

Let us then look at what assets you can find in the StandardComponents.fla file in the folder associated with the Button component. You can find the folder in the document's library by selecting Flash UI Components 2 ➤ Themes ➤ MMDefault ➤ Button Assets. Figure 9-8 shows the contents of this folder.

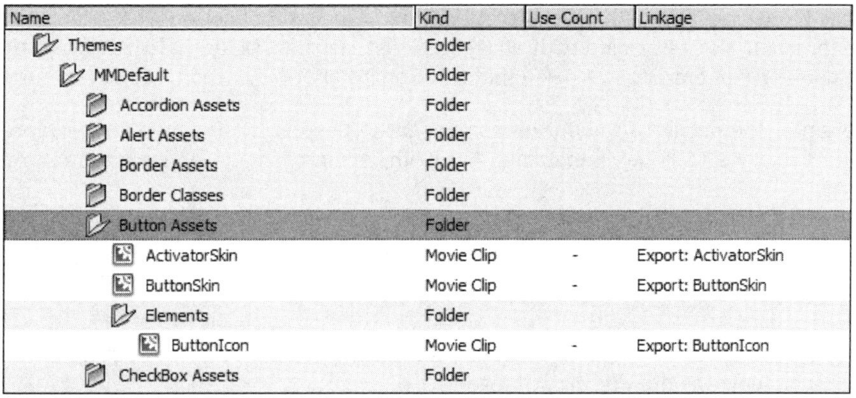

Figure 9-8. The contents of the Button Assets folder

The first detail worthy of notice is the absence of a `States` subfolder that should have contained the skins associated with each state of the Button component.

The Button component skin is implemented by only one symbol (ButtonSkin) that you can find directly inside the `Button Assets` folder.

Do not get confused by the presence of another symbol, called ActivatorSkin. This symbol is a skin, but it is only used in the case of menus objects, and probably should have been included in a different folder (occasionally we may find other discrepancies in the component architecture source code).

So, in the case of the Button component, each of its several states is implemented by one symbol only. To make things even more mysterious, at first, if you open that symbol (ButtonSkin), you will find that it is, indeed, empty!

This is just a further confirmation of what was already stated: purely coded skins do not use any graphic assets. The key in the implementation of this "magic" skin can be found if you examine its Linkage Properties dialog box, shown in Figure 9-9.

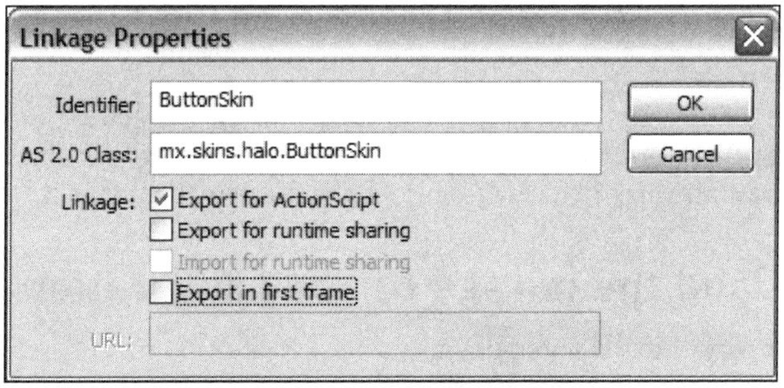

Figure 9-9. Linkage properties of the ButtonSkin symbol

The Linkage Properties dialog box reveals that the ButtonSkin symbol not only has a linkage identifier as expected, but is also associated with an ActionScript class: mx.skins.halo.ButtonSkin. It is this class that takes care of drawing every skin that a Button instance may need to display its current state.

We will examine the details of the Button component in Chapter 11. For the scope explored in this chapter, all you need to know is that this skin is implemented by an ActionScript class using the Drawing API.

Implementing a skin like that of the Button component involves numerous calls to methods such as lineTo, curveTo, moveTo, and, of course, the mathematics required to draw lines and curves according to the intended design.

This is why purely coded skins are certainly the most difficult skins to be customized—they require altering or even replacing drawing algorithms.

Now that you know the several kinds of styles and skins, you are ready to move on the theme concept and learn the techniques available for customizing the appearance and behavior of the standard components in the architecture.

Working with themes

The **theme concept** satisfies the need to have user interfaces with a consistent look and feel. Although artistic freedom is important, user interfaces designed using a variety of fonts and no set color scheme are likely to confuse users.

The purpose of a theme is to group styles and skins that are visually well balanced in order to facilitate their use when customizing the appearance and behavior of the components included in the architecture.

The current component architecture includes only two themes: the default **Halo** theme, and a rather anonymous, if not incomplete, alternative called the **Sample** theme.

Producing a theme for the component architecture is a task of substantial complexity that should not be underestimated. Regardless of the huge popularity of the Flash technology, web resources on themes have not appeared yet, even though themes were first introduced in 2003.

Before delving into the various techniques available to produce and apply a theme, it is worth reviewing the design choices that were made when producing the current version of the component architecture in order to grasp the major challenges of designing a new theme for it.

Changing skins and the mirage of code separation

As we saw in the first part of this chapter, defining styles for the component architecture is a straightforward process involving very little coding, regardless of whatever option you choose among those made available by the architecture.

Unfortunately, producing new skins for components is not as simple.

The idea of skinning components was initially born to separate a component appearance from its implementation, but, as you learned earlier, that ideal is respected by a certain kind of skin only (handcrafted skins), while there are two other categories of skins (mixed skins and purely coded skins) that substantially, or even totally, rely on coding.

The lack of uniformity may well be subject to criticism, but at the same time it represents a huge opportunity for the accomplished ActionScript developer to learn and compare three different implementations, each of them with their own specific benefits.

Furthermore, an attentive examination of the component architecture at its higher level of abstraction will reveal one important aspect shared by all skins: in all cases, a skin is an exported symbol dynamically created and manipulated by the component class, so to a certain extent it is well separated from the component logic.

Because of this, theoretically you can replace a purely coded skin with a handcrafted (or mixed) one. Of course, this is not an easy task and may not be convenient compared with other options. However, considering alternative implementations for the existing skins will help you in appreciating the pros and cons of their current implementation.

Let us now start exploring what techniques you can concretely apply to change the skin of a component depending on the nature of the skin being replaced.

Changing skins at authoring time

Changing a skin at authoring time, whenever possible, is certainly the easiest among the techniques available, although it has limitations that some of the more complex techniques do not have.

This technique is based on an essential principle: if you add an exported symbol having the same linkage identifier of a skin used by a certain component to the Flash document's library, then every instance of that component will start using the new symbol instead of the one embedded in the compiled version of the component.

If that concept sounds complex, you will be surprised to find how simple it actually is, as the following example illustrates:

1. Create a new Flash document and save it as `CheckBoxSkinTest.fla`.
2. Drag the CheckBox component on stage to create an instance of that component.
3. Using the Oval tool, draw a small red circle with a black border approximately as big as the box of the CheckBox (12 by 12 units).
4. Double click the circle shape to select it and convert it to a movie clip named `CheckFalseUp`. Before closing the Convert To Symbol dialog box, check the Export for ActionScript option so you have a linkage identifier with the same name as the one you just defined for the symbol. Delete the circle shape on the stage, which has become an instance of the `CheckFalseUp` exported symbol.
5. Save the Flash document.

Earlier in this chapter, in the example of a handcrafted skin, you saw that the CheckBox component uses eight skins, one for each of its states. In fact, what we just did was to manually draw one of those skins, the one associated with the initial state of the CheckBox (not selected, up).

Figure 9-10. Espresso skinning of the CheckBox

If you test this last example, you may be surprised to see the red circle you have just drawn being used by the CheckBox instance, as displayed in Figure 9-10, without your having to write any code at all.

That happened automatically since the circle had been converted into an exported symbol whose linkage identifier (CheckFalseUp) is the same as the CheckBox skin in use by the CheckBox class. Figure 9-11 shows how the document library of our example contains two objects only: the compiled CheckBox component and our newly created symbol.

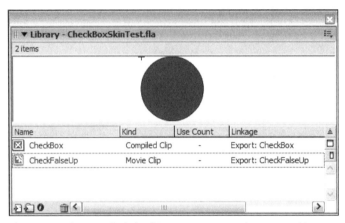

Figure 9-11. The compiled CheckBox component and a custom skin

While testing the last example, notice that the red circle encapsulated in the new skin (CheckFalseUp) is displayed only when the checkbox is in its initial state (not selected, up). If you roll the mouse pointer over the component instance or even click it, other original skins are displayed according to the component's other states.

When planning to fully customize a component, you should provide an alternative for each of its skins. In the case of the CheckBox component, you already saw that eight skins are requested to visualize each of the component's states.

The HaloTheme.fla file, which you can find in the same folder as the StandardComponents.fla file, contains all the assets of the Halo theme. Reusing these assets as a starting point in customizing the skins of a component can significantly speed up your operation, as you can appreciate in the following example:

1. Open the Flash document we created in the previous example and save it as CheckBoxSkinTest2.fla.

2. Delete the symbol CheckFalseUp from the document's library. We will replace it with a copy of its original version in the next steps.

3. Open the HaloTheme.fla file as an external library by selecting File ➤ Import ➤ Open External Library.

4. Look for the folder containing the CheckBox assets in the `HaloTheme.fla` file. You can find it by selecting Flash UI Components 2 ➤ Themes ➤ MMDefault ➤ CheckBox Assets.

5. Drag the file folder named `CheckBox Assets` from the `HaloTheme.fla` library into the `CheckBoxSkinTest2.fla` library. This creates a copy of the folder and its contents in the Flash document of our new example.

In a few steps you have included a copy of all the original skins required by the CheckBox component in the `CheckBoxSkinTest2.fla` file and you can now edit all of them as you like to alter the look and feel of the CheckBox component.

Figure 9-12 shows the library of the `CheckBoxSkinTest2.fla` file, underscoring the advantage deriving from this quick approach.

Name	Kind	Use Count	Linkage
CheckBox	Compiled Clip	-	Export: CheckBox
CheckBox Assets	Folder		
States	Folder		
CheckFalseDisabled	Movie Clip	-	Export: CheckFalseDisabled
CheckFalseDown	Movie Clip	-	Export: CheckFalseDown
CheckFalseOver	Movie Clip	-	Export: CheckFalseOver
CheckFalseUp	Movie Clip	-	Export: CheckFalseUp
CheckTrueDisabled	Movie Clip	-	Export: CheckTrueDisabled
CheckTrueDown	Movie Clip	-	Export: CheckTrueDown
CheckTrueOver	Movie Clip	-	Export: CheckTrueOver
CheckTrueUp	Movie Clip	-	Export: CheckTrueUp
CheckBoxAssets	Movie Clip	-	Export: CheckBoxAssets
Elements	Folder		

Figure 9-12. The library of our example after you add a copy of all the CheckBox assets

The document's library of our example now contains the compiled CheckBox component and all the exported symbols associated with its skins with their original linkage identifiers.

You can easily redesign the appearance of the CheckBox component by altering the symbols in the document's library, since they are working copies that also remind you what skins you have to provide to complete the job.

For instance, you may use the Free Transform tool to quickly rotate the squares of every skin 45 degrees and obtain a CheckBox that looks like the one displayed in Figure 9-13.

Figure 9-13. Altered CheckBox skin

The technique that you have just learned demonstrates that it is possible to change a component's skins without having to write a single line of code, making this technique attractive to designers who do not have time to learn the necessary skills for advanced programming.

However, this technique should be considered a "quick-and-dirty" option because of several limitations:

- Once added to the library, the new skin overrides the existing one, and it is applied indiscriminately to every instance of the related component: you are unable to apply different skins to different component instances.

- It works conveniently in the case of handcrafted skins only. It can also work with mixed skins, but it requires a perfect understanding of how the skin parts are assembled together via code in order to produce a whole skin. It cannot work with purely coded skins, since they require coding to work as expected.

- Sometimes a component's functionality does not meet your requirements in full, and you may need to customize its behavior. You cannot achieve that goal without coding.

While this technique can be useful in several cases when creating small applications, it is basically unsuitable for large projects due to its inherent limitations. However, it is a significant example of the close relationship between the linkage identifiers of symbols and the component classes that use them to implement their skins.

Let us now examine techniques that can provide you with more control via coding.

Changing skins programmatically

You have learned how to change handcrafted skins, and possibly mixed skins, by simply providing alternative graphics in the form of an exported symbol.

You have also learned of the limitation of this technique, and, being a developer, you may have already guessed that in order to take full control of the skinning process some coding will be required.

In this section, we will examine how to change skin programmatically. This will remove the first limitation previously considered: you will be able to define different skins for component instances belonging to the same class.

In order to implement skinning, components must store the linkage identifiers associated with the symbols used to implement them.

Even if there is no exact naming convention established for them, those linkage identifiers are stored inside the component classes as properties. The following lines of code are a few examples of those properties that you can find in the implementation of the respective classes:

```
// from the implementation of the RadioButton class
var falseOverIcon:String = "RadioFalseOver";


.....


// from the implementation of the NumericStepper class
var downArrowUp:String = "StepDownArrowUp";


.....


// from the implementation of the Window class
var skinTitleBackground:String = "TitleBackground";
```

As you can see from the names of the properties selected for the previous example, similarities are rare, and to locate the property associated to a specific skin may require a careful study of the source code, especially in the case of subcomponents' skins. The chapters dedicated to each component in Part 3 will help you locate every specific property associated with a skin.

In this context, we are going to examine the technique that you may apply once you know which property is associated with a certain skin.

Having already worked with the CheckBox component in the previous examples makes this class ideal for presenting this new technique. The CheckBox component stores the linkage identifier associated with the CheckFalseUp state that we customized earlier in the falseUpIcon property of the CheckBox class, as you can verify by finding the following line in the source code of the class:

```
var falseUpIcon:String  = "CheckFalseUp";
```

> Note that, although difficult to believe, the CheckBox class also includes the declaration of a falseUpSkin property, which is **not** used by the class implementation. Several unnecessary and confusing declarations appear in the source code of the component architecture that will probably be removed in its next version. They are mostly harmless, as long as you realize they are unused and ignore them.

Going back to the objective of programmatically changing the skin of the CheckBox component, let us build an example showing how to do it:

1. Open the Flash document created in our first example (CheckBoxSkinTest.fla), which is the one with the red dot skin, and save it as CheckBoxSkinTest3.fla.

2. Using the Info Panel, place the CheckBox instance already on stage at x: 100, y: 100.

3. Select the CheckFalseUp symbol in the document's library and change its linkage identifier from CheckFalseUp to CustomCheckFalseUp by right-clicking the symbol and selecting the Linkage option. The name of the identifier is in the first field of the Linkage Properties dialog box. By renaming the linkage identifier, that symbol will not be associated to the skin of CheckBox instances automatically anymore. If you run a test at this point, you will notice that the skin of the CheckBox instance is back to its default appearance.

4. Select the first frame in the document and add the following code:

```
#include "test.as"
```

5. Create an ActionScript file and save it as test.as in the same folder as the Flash document you are working on.

6. Add the following code to the newly created ActionScript file:

```
import mx.controls.CheckBox;

var initObj:Object = {
    _x: 100,
    _y: 140,
    _width: 200,
```

```
        label: "Custom CheckBox",
        falseUpIcon: "CustomCheckFalseUp"
    }
    var cb1:CheckBox = createClassObject(CheckBox, "cb1",
                                getNextHighestDepth(), initObj);
```

7. Save the ActionScript file.

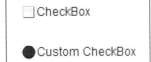

If you test the file, you will find that the movie now shows two CheckBox instances, but only one uses the custom skin that we designed for the example. Figure 9-14 shows the expected result.

The last technique demonstrates that different customizations of the same component can coexist in the same application. It is based on an initialization object (named initObj in the example) that is passed to the instance to be customized when the instance is created dynamically via a call to the createClassObject method.

Figure 9-14. Customizing the skin of a specific instance

The core attribute of the initialization object used to implement this technique is the falseUpIcon property of the CheckBox class that is utilized to store the linkage identifier (CustomCheckFalseUp) of the CheckFalseUp symbol in the document library. Not using the default name (CheckFalseUp) for the linkage identifier ensured that every other CheckBox instance would not be affected by automatic changes, retaining its default appearance as demonstrated by the instance already on stage.

You may be now wondering "We just saw how to customize a specific instance created dynamically, but what if the instance was creating at authoring stage and, therefore, already on the stage?" Since the initialization object technique cannot be applied in that case, let us look at another example that fixes this:

1. Open the Flash document created in our previous example (CheckBoxSkinTest3.fla) and save it as CheckBoxSkinTest4.fla.

2. Select the CheckBox instance on the stage and add the following movie clip event handler to it:

```
onClipEvent (initialize) {
    falseUpIcon = "CustomCheckFalseUp";
}
```

3. Save the Flash document.

If you now run a test on this new example, the output will show that both of the CheckBox instances are using the custom symbol that we defined for its skin (see Figure 9-15).

We customize the CheckBox instance on stage by using a different technique in order to be able to modify the value of the falseUpIcon property of the CheckBox class at the right time, which is before the component instance would be created on stage by the Flash player.

Figure 9-15. Two different techniques, the same result

In order to do this, we had to utilize an undocumented event called initialize. This event runs before the component is created on stage and, therefore, fits well our purpose of customizing the skin of that specific instance programmatically.

The initialize event is undocumented, so it is not listed among the onClipEvent candidates when you write the example code in the authoring environment.

The candidate events suggested by the authoring environment when writing onClipEvent statements are load, unload, enterFrame, mouseDown, mouseMove, mouseUp, keyDown, keyUp, and data. For each of these events, you can find an alternative in the MovieClip class in the form of an event handler (onLoad, onUnload, etc.).

Generally, it is good practice to avoid using the onClipEvent statement if a more object-oriented alternative is available; but since the initialize event is undocumented, the MovieClip class does not offer an event handler such as onInitialize and, therefore, there are no alternatives to its use in the case of component instances added at authoring time. When component instances are created dynamically, you can apply the initialization object technique you saw before that provides yet another reason to favor dynamic creation whenever possible.

Skins that reflect styles

You can achieve greater control over a component's appearance when certain aspects of its skin, like the color, can be altered via style properties.

The standard components in the architecture support several styles that we will examine in detail in the chapters dedicated to each component in Part 3.

In this section, you will learn a simple but powerful technique that shows you how to add the support of a color style to the skins that you create when customizing a component.

In the following example, we rebuild the custom skin that we defined in our previous examples to make it more suitable for supporting two custom color styles: boxColor and boxBorderColor.

1. Create a new Flash document and save it as CheckBoxSkinTest5.fla.
2. Drag the CheckBox component on stage to create an instance of that component.
3. Create a new movie clip symbol by selecting Insert ➤ New Symbol, and give it the name CheckFalseUp and the linkage identifier CustomCheckFalseUp. (Remember to check the Export for ActionScript option to be able to define the linkage identifier.)
4. Add two additional layers in the newly created CheckFalseUp symbol and then rename its three layers as actions, sub-skin box, and sub-skin border, starting from the topmost layer.
5. Select the first frame in the topmost layer (actions) and add the following ActionScript code:

```
box_mc.boxColor = getStyle("boxColor");
border_mc.boxBorderColor = getStyle("boxBorderColor");
```

6. Draw a borderless shape using the Oval Tool in the first frame of the sub-skin box layer. Once done, set the position and size of the shape as follows: X = 1.0, Y = 1.0, H = 10.0, W = 10.0, by using the Info panel. Set the shape color as red.

7. Draw a borderless shape using the Oval tool in the first frame of the sub-skin border layer. Once done, set the position and size of the shape as follows: X = 0.0, Y = 0.0, H = 12.0, W = 12.0, by using the Info panel. Set the shape color as black.

8. Select the shape in the sub-skin box layer and convert it into a symbol named CheckFalseUpBox and a linkage identifier of CheckFalseUpBox.

9. Select the shape in the sub-skin border layer and convert it into a symbol named CheckFalseUpBorder and a linkage identifier of CheckFalseUpBorder.

10. Select the symbol instance in the sub-skin box layer and give it the instance name of box_mc.

11. Select the symbol instance in the sub-skin border layer and give it the instance name of border_mc.

12. Edit the box_mc symbol instance and add the following code to its first frame:

```
mx.skins.ColoredSkinElement.setColorStyle(this, "boxColor");
```

13. Edit the border_mc symbol instance and add the following code to its first frame:

```
mx.skins.ColoredSkinElement.setColorStyle(this, "borderColor");
```

14. Select the CheckBox instance on the stage and attach the following ActionScript code to it:

```
onClipEvent (initialize) {
    falseUpIcon = "CustomCheckFalseUp";
    boxColor = 0x008800;
    boxBorderColor = 0xff0000;
}
```

15. Save the Flash document.

The CheckFalseUp skin of the current example looks similar to the ones in our previous examples, but it contains two subskins (an instance of CheckFalseUpBox named box_mc and an instance of CheckFalseUpBorder named border_mc).

Introducing two subskins for the box and the border is necessary for being able to set their color separately via two different styles (boxColor and boxBorderColor).

The few lines of code in this example are worth a thorough examination since they demonstrate a technique for breaking down a skin into several subskins (two in the example, but this can be replicated with any number) while implementing a style for defining the color of each subskin.

Let us first examine the sole lines present in each of the two subskins:

```
// present in the CheckFalseUpBox
mx.skins.ColoredSkinElement.setColorStyle(this, "boxColor");
// present in the CheckFalseBorder
mx.skins.ColoredSkinElement.setColorStyle(this, "borderColor");
```

Those lines both use the ColoredSkinElement mix-in class provided by the component architecture that does most of the job transforming a skin (or subskin) into a colorable skin. The only difference comparing the two lines is given by the style that influences the color of each specific subskin.

There is some code in the CheckFalseUp symbol as well:

```
box_mc.boxColor = getStyle("boxColor");
border_mc.boxBorderColor = getStyle("boxBorderColor");
```

The CheckFalseUp skin is one of the skins of the CheckBox component and, as such, it receives the style definitions from the component architecture. Both the lines of code included in this skin have the effect of propagating those style settings to its subskins that, being colorable skins, have a good use for them.

Basically the CheckFalseUp skin can support two color styles, because each of those colors is supported by one of its subskins. This way we have bypassed the limitation imposed by the movie clip color that a skin could support one color only. Note that by replicating this technique, you can now build skins that support any number of colors via their subskins.

Finally, let us examine the code attached to the CheckBox instance on the stage:

```
onClipEvent (initialize) {
    falseUpIcon = "CustomCheckFalseUp";
    boxColor = 0x008800;
    boxBorderColor = 0xff0000;
}
```

This code applies the technique associated with the initialize event that you learned earlier on. You already have all the elements for replacing this approach with the one using an initialization object in the case of a dynamically generated component instance.

In the current example, the initialize event handler does a bit more than just redefining the linkage identifier of the skin. It also defines the values to be used for the two custom styles that we have just implemented in the new skin: boxColor and boxBorderColor.

If you test the movie, you will see an output similar to that of Figure 9-10, with the main differences being that the inner part of the rounded skin has a dark green color (0x008800) while the border has a lighter green color (0xff0000) as defined by the values of the custom style properties boxColor and boxBorderColor.

Thanks to this technique, you can now have fun drawing stylized skins that sport as many colors as you like.

In search of a unified approach: subclassing

The techniques you learned so far address important but varying issues. Although they are very useful and allow you to take customize several aspects of a component's appearance, what is still missing is a unifying approach in which you can blend them whenever needed.

That approach has to come from coding, since in the wide majority of cases you cannot satisfy your requirements by simply replacing one or more graphic symbols.

Being a developer, you will be pleased to know that there is indeed an object-oriented approach that can integrate each of the techniques presented and even provide more control on the customization of a component. Such an approach is called **subclassing**.

245

The term "subclassing" highlights the fact that what you do when customizing a component is create a new component whose class is derived directly from the class of the component that you are customizing. Subclassing a component then becomes a synonym of customizing it through extending and/or overriding some of its functionality by adding properties and methods to its derived class.

In order to customize a component, you need to include the component's source in the Flash document of your project. As you already saw, the source of all standard components can be found in the file `StandardComponents.fla`.

Since the CheckBox component accompanies all the examples in this chapter, we are going to subclass it in the following example to start exploring the benefits of this approach:

1. Create a new Flash document and save it as `CheckBoxSkinTest6.fla`.

2. Create a folder called `Flash UI Components 2` in the document's library. You will use it as the container of the source of the components to be customized.

3. Create another folder called `Customized Components` in the document's library. You will use this as the container of the customized components and their assets.

4. Open the `StandardComponents.fla` file as an external library by selecting File ➤ Import ➤ Open External Library.

5. Drag the CheckBox component that you find in the `Flash UI Components 2` folder of the `StandardComponents.fla` library into the `CheckBoxSkinTest6.fla` file's `Flash UI Components 2` folder. This action will add to the document's library all the source symbols of the CheckBox component in one step.

6. Duplicate the CheckBox symbol in the document's library and rename its copy as CustomCheckBox.

7. Open the Linkage Properties dialog box of the new CustomCheckBox symbol and define both the linkage identifier and the AS 2.0 class as `subclassed.components.CustomCheckBox`. Also, verify that Export for ActionScript and Export in first frame are checked.

8. Create a `CustomCheckBox Assets` folder under the `Customized Components` folder in the document's library.

9. Open the `CheckBoxSkinTest5.fla` file of our previous example as an external library by selecting File ➤ Import ➤ Open External Library.

10. Drag the CheckFalseUp symbol from the `CheckBoxSkinTest5.fla` library into the `CustomCheckBox Assets` folder under the `Customized Components` folder in the document's library. This will also copy the other two symbols, CheckFalseUpBorder and CheckFalseUpBox, there. The document's library will now look like what is displayed in Figure 9-16.

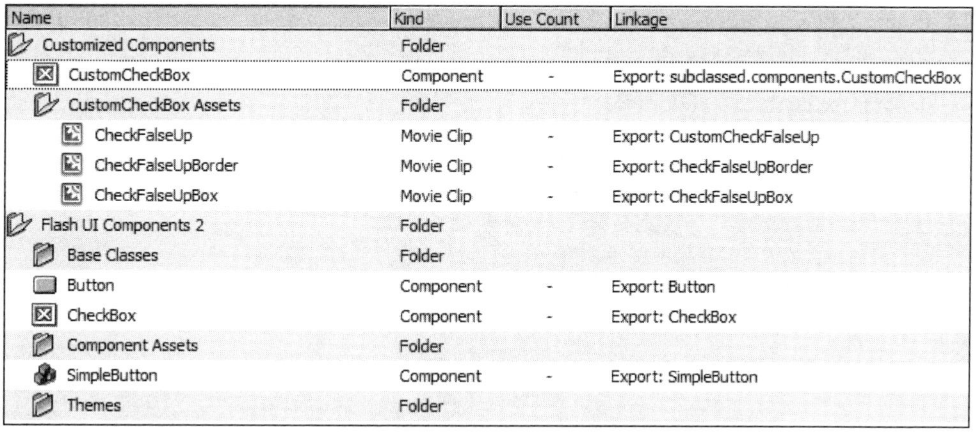

Name	Kind	Use Count	Linkage
Customized Components	Folder		
CustomCheckBox	Component	-	Export: subclassed.components.CustomCheckBox
CustomCheckBox Assets	Folder		
CheckFalseUp	Movie Clip	-	Export: CustomCheckFalseUp
CheckFalseUpBorder	Movie Clip	-	Export: CheckFalseUpBorder
CheckFalseUpBox	Movie Clip	-	Export: CheckFalseUpBox
Flash UI Components 2	Folder		
Base Classes	Folder		
Button	Component	-	Export: Button
CheckBox	Component	-	Export: CheckBox
Component Assets	Folder		
SimpleButton	Component	-	Export: SimpleButton
Themes	Folder		

Figure 9-16. Document library of the subclassing example

11. Select the first and only frame in the Flash document of the current example and add the following line of code to it:

```
#include "test.as"
```

12. Create an ActionScript file called `test.as` and save it in the same folder as the Flash document we are working on after adding the following code to it:

```
import subclassed.components.CustomCheckBox;

var initObj:Object = {
    _x: 100,
    _y: 140,
    _width: 200,
    label: "Custom CheckBox",
    boxColor: 0x008800,
    boxBorderColor: 0xff0000
}
var cb1:CustomCheckBox = createClassObject(CustomCheckBox, "cb1",
➥ getNextHighestDepth(), initObj);
```

13. Create a folder called `subclassed` in the same folder containing the Flash document of our example. Then create a folder named `components` inside the `subclassed` folder.

247

14. Create a new ActionScript file named CustomCheckBox.as, add the following code to it, and then save it in the components folder.

```
import mx.controls.CheckBox;

class subclassed.components.CustomCheckBox
➥ extends mx.controls.CheckBox {

    static var symbolName:String =
➥ "subclassed.components.CustomCheckBox";
    static var symbolOwner = subclassed.components.CustomCheckBox;

    var falseUpIcon = "CustomCheckFalseUp";

    function CustomCheckBox () {
    }

}
```

15. Save the Flash document of this example.

The output of this example will once again be similar to that of Figure 9-10, although the steps we have taken for obtaining the final results are rather different: we added the CheckBox source symbol (not compiled) to the document's library and implemented a class for a duplicate that we created and renamed as CustomCheckBox.

The presence of the falseUpIcon property in the implementation of the CustomCheckBox class indicates that the skin customization is applied at class level: every instance of this customized component will have the same skin. This is a design choice that assumes that a customized component is somewhat identified by its customized skin, whose appearance can be influenced at instance level by style properties like those added to the initialization object of this example (boxColor and boxBorderColor).

If you look at this example, the benefits of the subclassing approach are almost invisible: you end up writing more code (but not much more), and you have to do a few steps more than some of the previous approaches in order to prepare the document's library with the original source and its duplicate, which will become the customized component.

The extra work does not amount to much. The benefits at the moment can all be suggested by intuition: we have an ActionScript class (CustomCheckBox) that we can use for packaging the techniques discussed earlier, but also, and more importantly, we can override or even extend the existing functionality of a standard component.

The many benefits of subclassing will be exploited in Part 3 of the book when we apply it to real cases provided by each standard component.

An alternative to subclassing

Although subclassing is the approach recommended in this book, in particular circumstances you may prefer to have a faster, though "dirtier," technique that allows you to override some existing feature of a component.

The technique exposed here involves using the prototype property of a component class.

In the previous examples, you learned that there are two different techniques for customizing the skin of a component instance, depending on how the instance was created (dynamically or statically). One technique relied on an initialization object, while the other required writing an event handler for the undocumented initialize event.

By using the prototype property of a component class, you can affect components that are created either statically or dynamically; in fact, by using the prototype property you can affect each and every instance of a particular class. The following line is an example that would have set our custom skin for every CheckBox, regardless of how it would have been generated:

```
CheckBox.prototype.falseUpIcon = "CustomCheckFalseUp";
```

The previous line overrides the definition of the falseUpIcon property of the CheckBox class pointing to a skin related to a specific state (CheckFalseUp) of the component by using the prototype property. Of course, the prototype property can be used in the same way for overriding not only other skins, but also one or more specific features of a component class implemented via a property or method.

Summary

In this chapter, you have learned how the component architecture implements styles and skins.

You have also learned that there are three different kind of skins, and that for some of them the separation of code from representation cannot be achieved, because in several cases a skin's appearance is defined also, or exclusively, by ActionScript code.

You became aware of a set of different techniques that allow you to overcome any limitation you may encounter when customizing a component.

The approaches presented here can be applied in many different situations. The third part of the book, starting next, exploits the application of these techniques in the context of each standard component, providing plenty of concrete and different examples.

Part Three

CUSTOMIZING THE COMPONENTS

Chapter 10

THE ACCORDION COMPONENT

Accordion		
mx.containers.Accordion		

Frequency: Rare

Complexity: Simple

Stability: Robust

Maturity: Novelty

Popularity: Specific

The Accordion component is a container capable of structuring its contents into multiple segments, or children, that share the same space by being displayed one at a time. It provides each segment with a header that remains visible even when the segment's content is hidden. Displaying the content of a new segment is as easy as clicking its header; the content of that segment then replaces the content that was previously visible. The Accordion implementation that we will examine in this chapter nicely exploits the Flash technology by using a smooth animation for displaying the transition from one child of the Accordion to the other.

Due to its peculiar behavior, the Accordion component is not the sort of feature typically available in other component architectures. This chapter will help you to get the most from this component, and you will be pleasantly surprised to discover that its apparent complexity can be handled easily by using the proper techniques. The component's behavior is very consistent, making it a robust choice that can successfully meet a variety of requirements.

> *The completed source code introduced in this chapter can be found in the package* `src10.zip`, *downloadable from this book's page at* `www.friendsofed.com`.

A minimal example

In this section of the book, every chapter will include a minimal example that serves three purposes:

- Facilitate the identification of the discussed component's core features by showing the minimum number of steps required to implement an instance of the component.
- Provide a starting point to be reused when explaining the techniques that can be applied to this component later in the chapter.
- Introduce the XLEFF syntax for generating the same component instance via an XML description.

This chapter's minimal example will implement an Accordion instance that will look like the one shown in Figure 10-1.

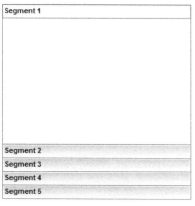

Figure 10-1. The Accordion instance implemented by the minimal example

You can implement the Accordion component using ActionScript code or by setting the component instance parameters in the authoring environment. We will explore and compare both approaches, starting with the code-based version.

Code-based version

The code-based version of our minimal example actually requires very few lines of code. Follow these steps to create it:

1. Create a new Flash document and save it as accordion01.fla.

2. Open the Document Properties dialog box, via the Modify ➤ Document menu option, and set the document's dimensions as 300 X 300 pixels.

3. Drag the Accordion component on stage in order to create an Accordion instance. Define its instance name as mainAccordion.

4. Select the mainAccordion instance and, via the Info panel, set its position at X: 0, Y: 0 and its dimensions as W: 300, H: 300. This way, the Accordion instance will coincide with the whole stage of the Flash document.

5. Create a new ActionScript file and save it as test.as in the same folder where you saved the accordion01.fla file.

6. Add the following code to the newly created test.as file:

```
import mx.core.View;

mainAccordion.createSegment(View, "s1", "Segment 1");
mainAccordion.createSegment(View, "s2", "Segment 2");
mainAccordion.createSegment(View, "s3", "Segment 3");
mainAccordion.createSegment(View, "s4", "Segment 4");
mainAccordion.createSegment(View, "s5", "Segment 5");
```

7. Select the first frame in the document and add the following ActionScript line to it:

```
#include "test.as"
```

8. Save the accordion01.fla and test.as files.

Testing the movie will demonstrate the live implementation of the Accordion instance, as shown earlier in Figure 10-1.

The implementation relies on the createSegment method of the Accordion class, invoked five times in similar fashion. The following line creates the first segment:

```
mainAccordion.createSegment(View, "s1", "Segment 1");
```

This line creates a segment with an instance name of s1 (second parameter), whose header has a text label showing Segment 1 (third parameter). In the first parameter, we provide a reference to the View class, which will be used to implement the content area of the segment being created. It is your responsibility to implement the content area of a segment by providing an object that usually inherits from the View class or, at least, is based on the UIObject class, as explained in the "Segment content area" section later in this chapter.

Could this example have been implemented in the authoring environment without writing a line of code? Yes, as you'll see in the next section.

Codeless version

There is lot of hype about deploying component-based applications without coding. However, as you will see, in any case where the two options—coded or codeless—are available and can be compared, a codeless option is frequently very limited compared to its counterpart.

Nonetheless, the fact that it is possible to produce codeless versions is useful when you want to experiment with a component's basic behavior or when building prototypes. You can learn quite a bit by examining how far a codeless implementation can go.

> *Although prototypes are frequently sold as applications, it is far too easy to distinguish them from the more versatile and robust solutions that have been produced with sapient coding. Quite simply, there will always be requirements that cannot be met without coding.*

Follow these steps to create the codeless version of the minimal example:

1. Create a new Flash document and save it as `accordion02.fla`.

2. Open the Document Properties dialog box, via the Modify ➤ Document menu option, and set its dimensions as 300 × 300 pixels.

3. Drag the Accordion component on stage in order to create an Accordion instance. Define its instance name as `mainAccordion`.

4. Select the `mainAccordion` instance and, via the Info panel, sets its position at X: 0, Y: 0 and its dimensions as W: 300, H: 300. This way, the Accordion instance will coincide with the whole stage of the Flash document.

5. Keeping the selection on the `mainAccordion` instance, open the Parameters tab in the Properties panel. Define five items in the `childLabels` parameter: Segment 1, Segment 2, Segment 3, Segment 4, and Segment 5. Also define five elements in the `childNames` parameter: s1, s2, s3, s4, and s5. After you've created those items, the Properties panel should look like Figure 10-2.

6. Save the Flash document.

Figure 10-2. The Properties panel after defining some of the Accordion's parameters

Testing the movie will show that you have implemented the same Accordion instance you saw previously, but this time, without writing a line of code.

However, by adding a single line of code in the first frame of our codeless example, you can extract some interesting information about how the component has been implemented via the authoring environment:

```
trace(mainAccordion.s1.className);
```

This line investigates the class used by the component environment by default when defining the content area of an Accordion's segment. The trace function will output the following information:

```
View
```

This visually confirms that the View class is the default choice made by the architecture when implementing an Accordion's content area. The authoring environment chooses the View class for implementing a content area to allow tabbing among the content areas. As you will learn in the next section, XLEFF supports the use of Form instances to implement the content areas of segments. Since the Form class inherits from the View class via its ancestors, the tabbing functionality is still available to navigate the Accordion instance's contents.

XLEFF version

The following XML block provides an XML description of the Accordion instance implemented by the minimal example:

```
<accordion name="mainAccordion" x="0" y="0"
           width="300" height="300">
    <form name="s1" x="0" y="0" label="Segment 1" />
    <form name="s2" x="0" y="0" label="Segment 2" />
    <form name="s3" x="0" y="0" label="Segment 3" />
    <form name="s4" x="0" y="0" label="Segment 4" />
    <form name="s5" x="0" y="0" label="Segment 5" />
</accordion>
```

Basically, the only difference to what you may have expected is the use of the <form> element instead of a <view> element, which is currently not supported by XLEFF. At the time of writing, XLEFF assumes that forms will be the standard container used in designing component-based interfaces. Therefore, Accordion segments are implemented via Form instances, whose label attributes will be displayed in the Accordion header.

The package associated with this chapter includes a preconfigured version of the XLEFF sampler, discussed in Chapter 6, that reuses the previous XML description to generate an Accordion instance similar to that implemented in the minimal example.

The component structure

The main subparts of an Accordion component are frequently called *children* in the official documentation. However, in several cases (as in the case of the createSegment method), they are referred to as *segments*. As you may have already noticed, the term *segment* is my choice, and the reason is rather intuitive: the term *child* is too generic—every component can have children. As you will see later, Tree and DataGrid components have children, too, but they are called more appropriately (and specifically) *nodes* and *cells*, respectively. The term *segment* quite simply is a better definition of an Accordion's subpart.

An Accordion instance must have at least one segment, although at least two segments are required to make transitions from one segment's content to the other. A segment is made of one header and one content area. Figure 10-3 shows an Accordion instance made of only one segment to emphasize the neat separation between a segment's header and its content area.

Figure 10-3. Structure of an Accordion segment

Segment header

The header of a segment plays an important role when navigating the contents of an Accordion instance. A segment's header is visible even when its content area is hidden. The user can ask the Accordion instance to display the content area of a segment by simply clicking its header.

Once a header has focus, a user can also move the focus among the headers using the arrow keys and change the selected header by pressing the ENTER key or the SPACEBAR. The key-based navigation among content areas can be faster. The PAGE UP and PAGE DOWN keys move the focus to a new segment in a single step. The TAB key moves the focus back and forth to other component instances (if any) or back and forth among the Accordion headers and content areas.

> *These keyboard commands largely work only in the stand-alone Flash Player, not the Flash Player in the actual Flash IDE that opens content when you are testing it.*

A segment's header can include an icon that is displayed on the left side of its label and can also be skinned, as discussed in the "Skinnability" section later in this chapter.

Segment content area

When implementing the content area of a segment you have two options: provide the constructor of a class or provide the linkage identifier of a symbol that you included in the Flash document's library.

You can provide the constructor of a class to create an instance that will implement the content area. The specified class must be compatible with the component architecture, meaning that it must be inherit from the UIObject class. Since every standard component inherits from UIObject, you may use any of the existing components to implement a content area. As noted earlier, the reason why the authoring environment chooses the View class by default for implementing a content area is to allow tabbing among the content areas. Therefore, if you want to maintain the tab order and related navigation inside an Accordion, you must implement the content areas with instances of the View class or of a class that inherits from it. Figure 10-4 shows the descendants of the View class as they have been implemented by the component architecture.

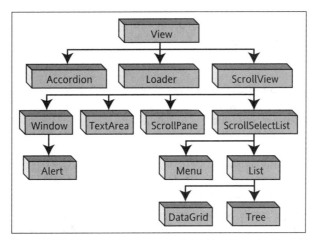

Figure 10-4. Classes and components inheriting from the View class

Alternatively, if you implement the content area by providing the linkage identifier of a symbol that you included in the Flash document's library, that symbol will be dynamically instantiated as a UIObject instance by the component architecture.

Now that you know more about a segment's structure, we can expand our minimal example to exploit some of the Accordion's features.

A richer example

Now, we will expand our minimal example to include icons for the Accordion's headers and symbol instances for its content areas. Once again, we will build both a codeless and a coded version, since both the options are still available. However, this time, we will start with the version that does not require any coding.

Codeless version

The following example continues from the one we built in the accordion02.fla Flash document. In that example, we defined a couple of parameters of the Accordion instance accessible via the Properties panel. We are now going to define the remaining two parameters that we previously left untouched.

Follow these steps to create the richer Accordion example:

1. Open the `accordion02.fla` file you created earlier and save it as `accordion03.fla`.

2. Create a new movie clip symbol via the Insert ➤ New Symbol menu option, and define both its name and its linkage identifier as `icon1`.

3. Edit the `icon1` symbol and, using the Oval tool, draw a round shape within it. Use the Info panel to define the shape position as X: 3.0, Y: 1.0 and its dimensions as W: 8.0, H: 8.0. Using the Properties panel, define the stroke height of the shape as 3. Also set the border color as dark gray and the fill color as light gray. The final shape should look like the one shown in Figure 10-5.

Figure 10-5. A quickly prepared icon for the Accordion's headers

4. Create yet another new symbol via the Insert ➤ New Symbol menu option, and define both its name and its linkage identifier as content1. We will now add some shapes to both of the newly created symbols to give them a basic appearance.

5. Edit the content1 symbol and, using the Rectangle tool, draw a square shape within it. Use the Info panel to define the shape position as X: 0.0, Y: 0.0 and its dimensions as W: 297.0, H: 192.0. Using the Properties panel, define the stroke height of the shape as 1. Also set the border color as red and the fill color as dark green. The final shape should look like the one shown in Figure 10-6.

Figure 10-6. Just a square with a thin, red border to fit into the content areas

6. Go back to the stage and select the mainAccordion instance. Open the Parameters tab in the Properties panel and define five items in the childIcons parameter: icon1, icon1, icon1, icon1, and icon1. Then define five elements in the childSymbols parameter: content1, content1, content1, content1, and content1. After you've created those items, the Properties panel will look like Figure 10-7.

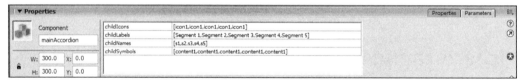

Figure 10-7. The Properties panel after further defining the Accordion's parameters

7. Save the Flash document.

Testing the movie will result in an Accordion implementation that is slightly richer in detail, as shown in Figure 10-8.

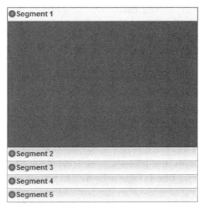

Figure 10-8. A more detailed implementation of an Accordion instance

It should be obvious that you can draw five different icons and five different symbols and assign them to each Accordion segment via the childIcons and childSymbols parameters in the Properties panel, although all we did in this example was assign the same icon (icon1) and the same symbol (content1) five times to those parameters.

Even though it wasn't elaborate, we gave some attention to the simple graphic of the content1 symbol. In particular, we defined the shape's size to fit perfectly into the content area and designed its thin, red border to visually display this fit.

But how did I know that this content area would be 297 pixels wide and 192 pixels tall? Unfortunately, you cannot determine the content area's precise size within the authoring environment. To discover the size, I captured a screen of this example and measured the size of the content area using Photoshop. Basically, you can follow the same empirical procedure or a variant of it, based on the tools you know. You need to determine the dimensions of the content area so that you can match them when defining the dimensions of the instance implementing it. If you don't, the Accordion content will look patched with holes, or it will look cropped if the content instance is too big.

Let's now see how to build an equivalent version of the richer example by coding it.

Code-based version

The code-based version of the example will replicate the same functionality of the codeless version that we just implemented. Follow these steps to create this version:

1. Open the accordion01.fla file you created earlier and save it as accordion04.fla in a new folder. Also copy the test.as file associated with the accordion01.fla file into the new folder.

2. Open the accordion03.fla file as an external library via File ➤ Import ➤ Open External Library menu option. Import both the icon1 and content1 symbols from the accordion03.fla library into the accordion04.fla library by dragging and dropping them (so you do not need to re-create them).

3. Open the copy of the `test.as` file that is in the current document's folder and replace the ActionScript lines in the file with the following:

```
mainAccordion.createSegment("content1", "s1", "Segment 1", "icon1");
mainAccordion.createSegment("content1", "s2", "Segment 2", "icon1");
mainAccordion.createSegment("content1", "s3", "Segment 3", "icon1");
mainAccordion.createSegment("content1", "s4", "Segment 4", "icon1");
mainAccordion.createSegment("content1", "s5", "Segment 5", "icon1");
```

4. Save both the Flash document and the `test.as` file.

Testing the file will display an Accordion instance that is identical to the one implemented in the previous codeless version, as shown earlier in Figure 10-8.

Five repetitive lines of code are sufficient to generate the five segments in the Accordion instance, including the definition of their content areas and the labels and icons for their headers. Each line uses the `createSegment` method that was discussed earlier. In this version, we added a fourth parameter that is the linkage identifier of the header's icon, and we replaced the constructor of the `View` class in the first parameter with the linkage identifier of the content symbol in the document's library.

Now that you have learned how to implement Accordion instances with and without coding, let's move on and see how to customize their appearance and behavior. Every customization option will require a certain amount of coding, so we will not build any other codeless examples in this chapter. As I noted earlier, the codeless approach has limits, and one of those is that it cannot be used to customize a component. The codeless approach is suitable only for prototyping or small-scale implementations.

Supported styles

Styles can be highly productive, and they certainly contribute to creating a consistent look and feel among component instances and even different components.

In this section of the book, when listing the styles supported by a component, I will distinguish between two different kinds of styles:

- **Common styles**: These are the styles that are supported by several component classes. They not only affect the same aspects of a component, but they also are the only styles that allow a certain consistency among instances of different components, because they are implemented universally within the component architecture.

- **Specific styles**: These are that styles that make sense only in the context of a particular component. Certain features are necessarily component-specific. These styles allow a certain consistency among instances of the same component.

Let's first examine the common styles supported by the Accordion component.

Common styles

The Accordion component supports several common styles, grouped by their respective functional context as follows:

- **Color styles**: themeColor, backgroundColor, color, disabledColor, and all the border-specific color styles (borderCapColor, borderColor, buttonColor, highlightColor, shadowCapColor, and shadowColor)
- **Border styles**: borderStyle
- **Font styles**: embedFonts, fontFamily, fontSize, fontStyle, and fontWeight
- **Text styles**: textDecoration

Most of the common styles have names that indicate which aspects of a component's appearance they affect. In order to avoid repeating the same information in every chapter dedicated to a specific component, I'll address each category in the chapter where they are most applicable. Color and border styles will be examined in Chapter 11, which covers the Button component, and font and text styles will be discussed in greater detail in Chapter 18, which covers the TextArea, TextInput, and Label components.

Sometimes, common styles do not behave as expected because of holes in the official documentation or bugs in the component and/or in the architecture implementations. I'll point out those cases and, whenever necessary, provide techniques and workarounds in the "Solved mysteries" section in the appropriate chapter.

Generally, however, you should also test each style for yourself, since future versions of the component architecture may modify the way they work. You can easily test the styles of the Accordion component by expanding one of our previous examples as follows:

1. Open the accordion04.fla file you created earlier and save it as accordion05.fla in a new folder. Also copy the test.as file associated with the accordion04.fla file in the new folder.

2. Edit the content1 symbol in the document library and delete the shape in it. Once the content1 symbol is empty, drag an instance of the TextArea component into it. Give it the instance name of textarea_mc.

3. Select the textarea_mc instance and, using the Info panel, define its position as X: 0.0, Y: 0.0 and its dimensions as W: 298.0, H: 193.0.

4. Keeping the textarea_mc instance selected, set the text parameter in the Properties panel with the following text:

   Some text content, added to test style options.

5. Open the test.as file copy in the same folder where the current Flash document is and replace the ActionScript lines in the file with the following:

   ```
   function setAccordionStyles(accordion) {
       accordion.setStyle("themeColor", "red");
       accordion.setStyle("fontFamily", "Courier New");
       accordion.setStyle("fontStyle", "italic");
       accordion.setStyle("color", "red");
   }
   ```

```
setAccordionStyles(mainAccordion);

mainAccordion.createSegment("content1", "s1", "Segment 1", "icon1");
mainAccordion.createSegment("content1", "s2", "Segment 2", "icon1");
mainAccordion.createSegment("content1", "s3", "Segment 3", "icon1");
mainAccordion.createSegment("content1", "s4", "Segment 4", "icon1");
mainAccordion.createSegment("content1", "s5", "Segment 5", "icon1");
```

6. Save both the Flash document and the `test.as` file.

The `setAccordionStyles` function implemented in our example is clearly the entry point for testing the styles supported by the Accordion component. It contains several calls to the `setStyle` method implemented by the component architecture in the `UIObject` class and, therefore, available to any component instance. By adding further `setStyle` calls, you can easily make your own style tests.

We replaced the shape in the `content1` symbol with an instance of the TextArea component to see how styles set on the Accordion instance can also affect the content areas of its segments.

Figure 10-9 shows the result of testing the movie, visually demonstrating the styling effects:

- The `themeColor` style affects the Accordion headers, giving a reddish color to the currently selected one and a red border to the other headers when you roll the mouse over one of them.

- The `fontStyle`, `fontFamily`, and `color` styles affect both the headers and the content areas of the Accordion segments. You can see that the headers and the TextArea instances display their text using the red color, italics, and the Courier New font.

Figure 10-9. A stylized Accordion instance

At the time of writing, testing the `fontWeight` and the `fontSize` styles will not give the expected results. Also, what if you wanted to affect the appearances of a segment's header and content area separately? These are the sorts of unexpected situations and special requirements that I will address in the "Solved mysteries" section later in this chapter.

Next, let's examine the styles that are specific to the Accordion component.

Specific styles

The Accordion component supports three specific styles, including two animation styles that are also implemented by a couple other components (ComboBox and Tree) that use animations to display their state transitions.

The Accordion-specific styles are as follows:

- **Header height**: The headerHeight style defines the height of the Accordion's headers in pixels. The default height of an Accordion header is 22 pixels.
- **Animation styles**: The openDuration and openEasing styles can influence the animated state transitions of a component instance. See Appendix B for a list of the easing methods that can be assigned to both of these style properties.

Styles are very useful up to a certain customization level. In some cases, you may need to implement a design that quite simply cannot be achieved with styles alone. The Accordion component is also skinnable, which provides another level of customization. Let's see how.

Skinnability

Looking at a component from the perspective of its skins can add a further dimension to it. You have already seen that the logical structure of an Accordion is defined by its segments and that each segment is made of a header and a content area. When it comes to skins, however, the content area disappears, since it is just an abstract concept that becomes concrete only when somehow populated by an actual instance.

Focusing on skins, we discover that the physical framework of an Accordion component is made of two parts: the component's border and its headers.

The border

Most standard components owe the implementation of their border to the RectBorder class. The RectBorder class supports the border styles you saw earlier in the section about styles, and you should consider this class as a purely coded skin that can be stylized using those border styles.

The existing implementations of the RectBorder class are associated with the two available themes: the Halo theme and the Simple theme. Both implementations use the drawing API, although the Simple theme implementation provides a much simpler implementation, as suggested by its name. In this case, simpler also means that it does not support all of the border styles listed earlier.

So, the only RectBorder class that really counts is the one provided with the Halo theme. Since it affects, by default, almost every standard component, we will examine it in greater detail in Chapter 11, which is dedicated to the Button component, where you will also see how to replace it with a customized version.

The headers

The Accordion component headers extend the Button class and, because of that, you may consider them as Button subcomponents. This also implies that the Accordion headers are originally implemented with purely coded skins, as the Button class is. This fact makes the Accordion component a very good case for purely coded skins to be replaced by handcrafted (purely graphic) skins, since the Accordion class provides eight skin properties, initially undefined, which are capable of overriding the purely coded skin of the headers:

- falseUpSkin
- falseDownSkin
- falseOverSkin
- falseDisabledSkin
- trueUpSkin
- trueDownSkin
- trueOverSkin
- trueDisabledSkin

These eight skin properties can be grouped into two sets of four, depending on the state of the header (true means selected, and false means not selected). Each group, then, provides four skins for each button state: up, down, over, and disabled.

In the following example, we will skin the headers of an Accordion instance by replacing their purely coded default version with a handcrafted version. Once again, the minimal example we implemented earlier in this chapter will represent the ideal starting point for testing this option. Follow these steps to create the skinning example:

1. Open the accordion01.fla file you created earlier and save it as accordion06.fla in a new folder. Also copy the test.as file associated with the accordion01.fla file in the new folder.

2. Open the document's library and create a folder called Accordion Assets. Inside that folder, place two subfolders: Images and Skins. Figure 10-10 shows the folder structure, including the symbols that you must add in the next steps.

3. Create a new movie clip symbol named falseDisabledSkin with a linkage identifier identical to the symbol's name. Using the option File ➤ Import ➤ Import To Stage, import the image file falseDisabledSkin.png, which you will find in the source package associated with this chapter. This image has a size of 300 X 22 pixels. After selecting the image inside the new created symbol, use the Info panel to define its position as X: 0.0, Y: 0.0.

4. Repeat the previous step for each of the remaining seven skins, using the proper names that are associated with each specific skin. Once you have created a symbol, move it into the Skins folder of the document's library. Then move its associated image in the Images folder in the same library, to eventually build a library that has the structure shown in Figure 10-10.

Name	Kind	Use Count	Linkage
Accordion	Compiled Clip	-	Export: Accordion
Accordion Assets	Folder		
Images	Folder		
falseDisabledSkin.png	Bitmap	-	
falseDownSkin.png	Bitmap	-	
falseOverSkin.png	Bitmap	-	
falseUpSkin.png	Bitmap	-	
trueDisabledSkin.png	Bitmap	-	
trueDownSkin.png	Bitmap	-	
trueOverSkin.png	Bitmap	-	
trueUpSkin.png	Bitmap	-	
Skins	Folder		
falseDisabledSkin	Movie Clip	-	Export: falseDisabledSkin
falseDownSkin	Movie Clip	-	Export: falseDownSkin
falseOverSkin	Movie Clip	-	Export: falseOverSkin
falseUpSkin	Movie Clip	-	Export: falseUpSkin
trueDisabledSkin	Movie Clip	-	
trueDownSkin	Movie Clip	-	Export: trueDownSkin
trueOverSkin	Movie Clip	-	Export: trueOverSkin
trueUpSkin	Movie Clip	-	Export: trueUpSkin

Figure 10-10. Header skins and related images in the document's library

5. Open the `test.as` file copy in the same folder where the current Flash document is and replace the ActionScript lines in the file with the following:

```
import mx.core.View;
import mx.containers.Accordion;

Accordion.prototype.falseUpSkin = "falseUpSkin";
Accordion.prototype.falseDownSkin = "falseDownSkin";
Accordion.prototype.falseOverSkin = "falseOverSkin";
Accordion.prototype.falseDisabledSkin = "falseDisabledSkin";
Accordion.prototype.trueDownSkin = "trueDownSkin";
Accordion.prototype.trueUpSkin = "trueUpSkin";
Accordion.prototype.trueOverSkin = "trueOverSkin";
Accordion.prototype.trueDisabledSkin = "trueDisabledSkin";

mainAccordion.createSegment(View, "s1", "Segment 1");
mainAccordion.createSegment(View, "s2", "Segment 2");
mainAccordion.createSegment(View, "s3", "Segment 3");
mainAccordion.createSegment(View, "s4", "Segment 4");
mainAccordion.createSegment(View, "s5", "Segment 5");
```

6. Save both the Flash document and the `test.as` file.

As you may have already noticed, we used the prototype technique described at the end of Chapter 9 to quickly override the skin properties of the Accordion component, which are originally undefined, providing the names of the linkage identifiers we defined for each of the eight skin states.

Note that using handcrafted skins works well only if you know the exact size of the headers (300 X 22 pixels in this example). Although Accordion instances that are implemented with headers of a different size could still use those skins, they would not look as good as they would in their intended dimensions.

Figure 10-11 shows the skinned version created in this example.

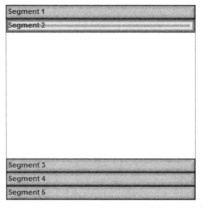

Figure 10-11. Skinned version of the minimal example

The next section examines several issues that are related to quirks in the current implementation of the Accordion component, explaining techniques that can be used to work around each issue.

Solved mysteries

Almost every component has its own unexpected behaviors, and the Accordion component is no exception. In the "Solved mysteries" section presented in almost every component-dedicated chapter, you will find hard-won knowledge that will help you in implementing component instances that can meet more stringent requirements.

Inheriting styles

The Accordion component is a container and, like any container in the component architecture, supports the mechanism of inheriting styles. A component instance can inherit style definitions from its container as long as the considered style is an inherited style. Officially, the following styles can be inherited:

- Single-value color styles such as color (Some color styles are not implemented as a single value.)

- Font styles like fontFamily, fontSize, fontStyle, and fontWeight

- Text styles like textAlign and textIndent

However, at the time of writing, the way that style inheritance works for the Accordion component is quite different from the specification of the component architecture. Here is a summary of how the styles work:

- Single-value color styles work as expected, affecting both the header and the content area of a segment.

- The fontStyle and fontFamily styles also work as expected, affecting both the header and the content area of a segment.

- The fontSize style affects the content area of a segment but not its header.

- The fontWeight style seems to affect neither the content area nor the header of a segment.

- The textAlign style, officially not supported by the Accordion header, affects the content area of a segment but not its header.

- The textIndent style seems to affect neither the content area nor the header of a segment.

As you can see, the behavior of the so-called inherited styles is rather inconsistent in the case of the Accordion component. Additionally, what if you want a style property to have different settings for the header and the content area of a segment?

Let's build an example that addresses these issues while exposing a technique that may be reused in other circumstances where you deal with the styles of a container and its children.

Since having a TextArea instance in the content area of a segment has proved to be useful for testing the styles applied to the content area of a segment, we will expand on the example we built earlier in the "Supported styles" section.

1. Open the accordion05.fla file you created earlier and save it as accordion07.fla in a new folder. Also copy the test.as file associated with the accordion07.fla file in the new folder.

2. We are going to change the height of the Accordion headers and reduce the number of segments from five to three. This will require refitting the TextArea instance in the content1 symbol. Edit the content1 symbol in the document's library and, after selecting the textarea_mc instance, set its new dimensions as W: 298.0, H: 181.0.

3. Open the test.as file copy in the same folder where the current Flash document is and replace the ActionScript lines in the file with the following:

```
function setAccordionStyles(accordion) {
    accordion.setStyle("headerHeight", 40);
    accordion.setStyle("fontFamily", "Courier New");
    accordion.setStyle("fontStyle", "italic");

    _global.styles.AccordionHeader.setStyle("fontSize", 30);
    _global.styles.AccordionHeader.setStyle("fontWeight", "bold");
}

function setContentAreaStyles(contentArea) {
    contentArea.setStyle("fontStyle", "normal");
    contentArea.setStyle("fontWeight", "bold");
}
```

269

```
setAccordionStyles(mainAccordion);

var s1 = mainAccordion.createSegment("content1", "s1", "Segment 1");
var s2 = mainAccordion.createSegment("content1", "s2", "Segment 2");
var s3 = mainAccordion.createSegment("content1", "s3", "Segment 3");

setContentAreaStyles(s1);
setContentAreaStyles(s2);
setContentAreaStyles(s3);
```

4. Save both the Flash document and the `test.as` file.

Testing the movie will result in a further customized version of the Accordion instance, as shown in Figure 10-12.

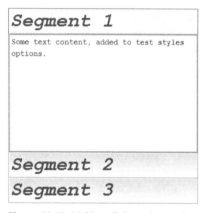

Figure 10-12. Making all the styles work

Every aspect of the solution illustrated here relies on the code in the `test.as` file. Let's first analyze the general procedure present in that code:

1. Set the Accordion instance styles via the `setAccordionStyles` function.

2. Create the Accordion's segments.

3. Set the content areas' specific styles via the `setContentAreaStyles` function.

The `setAccordionStyles` function does a bit more than just invoking the `setStyle` method on the Accordion instance. Such a method would not work for setting the `fontSize` and `fontWeight` styles of the Accordion's headers and, therefore, we define those styles as class-level styles of the `AccordionHeader` class, used by the component architecture to implement Accordion headers, as in the following line:

```
_global.styles.AccordionHeader.setStyle("fontSize", 30);
```

We already examined the technique of setting class-level styles in the previous chapter. The novelty is the existence of the undocumented `AccordionHeader` class used to set those troubled style properties.

That the class-level style properties defined for the headers are working is visually confirmed in Figure 10-12, where you can see the increased size of the bold text in the headers. (The headers' height was previously increased by setting the headerHeight style property of the Accordion calling setStyle, as usual.)

After the Accordion's segments have been created, three calls to the setContentAreaStyles function define their style properties. That way, we can override the setting defined for the Accordion instance and, for example, have a different setting for the fontStyle property. In fact, while the headers still show their text in italic, the content area text is now normal. Also, notice that we needed to specify the fontWeight as bold for the content areas, too, since they are not affected by the class-level styles of the AccordionHeader class.

By properly exploiting this approach, you can set any style for both the header and content area of an Accordion segment and even control their definitions separately.

However, we still have a limitation to overcome. The use of the AccordionHeader class-level styles means that every Accordion instance will have the headers responding to those same settings. What if you need to have a second Accordion instance on stage with much smaller headers (and therefore a smaller setting for the fontSize property)?

Creating header styles on a per-instance basis

Finding a workaround to create header styles on a per-instance basis requires a full understanding of the component architecture's current limitations and the nature of its quirks. The technique I found and will share here is a bit more complicated than what you have seen so far, but its application gives you further control of how to implement and customize component instances. Once again, let's build a concrete example that demonstrates the technique.

1. Open the accordion07.fla file you created earlier and save it as accordion08.fla in a new folder. Also copy the test.as file associated with the accordion08.fla file in the new folder.

2. Create a new movie clip symbol, via the Insert ➤ New Symbol menu command, and name it Formatter. This is an empty symbol that we will use to exploit its timeline by coding. Drag the newly created symbol on stage and name its instance as formatter_mc.

3. Open the test.as file copy in the same folder where the current Flash document is and replace the ActionScript lines in the file with the following:

```
function setAccordionStyles(accordion) {
    accordion.setStyle("headerHeight", 40);
    accordion.setStyle("fontFamily", "Courier New");
    accordion.setStyle("fontStyle", "italic");
}

function setContentAreaStyles(contentArea) {
    contentArea.setStyle("fontStyle", "normal");
    contentArea.setStyle("fontWeight", "bold");
}

setAccordionStyles(mainAccordion);
```

```
var s1 = mainAccordion.createSegment("content1", "s1", "Segment 1");
var s2 = mainAccordion.createSegment("content1", "s2", "Segment 2");
var s3 = mainAccordion.createSegment("content1", "s3", "Segment 3");

setContentAreaStyles(s1);
setContentAreaStyles(s2);
setContentAreaStyles(s3);

formatter_mc.accordion = mainAccordion;
formatter_mc.setHeaderStyles = function() {
    var header:Object;
    for (var i:Number = 0; i < this.accordion.numChildren; i++) {
        header = this.accordion.getHeaderAt(i);
        header.setStyle("fontSize", 30);
        header.setStyle("fontWeight", "bold");
    }
    mainAccordion.invalidate();
}

formatter_mc.onEnterFrame = function() {
    switch (counter) {
        case 0:
            this.setHeaderStyles();
            this.onEnterFrame = null;
            break;
        default:
            counter = 0;
    }
}
```

4. Save both the Flash document and the `test.as` file.

Once again, the solution is in the code of the `test.as` file. The first half of the script in the `test.as` file follows the approach we used in the previous example, with the sole exception that the class-level style definitions for the `AccordionHeader` class have been removed. We know that those definitions would have affected every Accordion instance, and that is exactly what we want to avoid here.

The technique implemented via the `Formatter` symbol allows you to set those style properties for the `mainAccordion` instance only, without affecting other Accordion instances that may be on stage at the same time.

The technique uses the `getHeaderAt` method of the `Accordion` class to retrieve a header instance and then invoke the `setStyle` method in its scope. Unfortunately, such a logical approach doesn't work if the method is invoked during the first frame of the main timeline. That's the purpose of the `formatter_mc` empty symbol. Its `onEnterFrame` method ensures that the `setStyle` method is invoked in the header scope during the second frame when the Accordion component instance is already up and running.

This is not only a nifty trick, but it is also a technique that you may need in many other cases when the process of initializing a standard component does not work because of limitations introduced by the current implementation of the architecture.

Reasons for subclassing

Now that you know all the quirks of the component and the best practices, techniques, and work-arounds to implement its instances, you can keep applying them again and again each time you need them in your project. Alternatively, you may decide to make a single extra effort by subclassing the component to create a new, better version of it, in which the quirks are fixed and best practices are observed. Typically, a subclassed component will also encapsulate a particular set of skins and style defaults that will be used homogeneously in your project.

Looking at how XLEFF handles the customization process provides a significant example of the convenience of creating a subclassed version of a component. The XML layout engine does not support any skinning but comes with a set of subclassed components that have been skinned consistently in order to make up a theme.

The following segment of XML code is almost identical to the one you saw earlier in the case of the XLEFF version of the minimal example:

```
<accordion cls="yourTheme.subclassed.Accordion"
          name="mainAccordion" x="0" y="0" width="300" height="300">
    <form name="s1" x="0" y="0" label="Segment 1" />
    <form name="s2" x="0" y="0" label="Segment 2" />
    <form name="s3" x="0" y="0" label="Segment 3" />
    <form name="s4" x="0" y="0" label="Segment 4" />
    <form name="s5" x="0" y="0" label="Segment 5" />
</accordion>
```

The only difference from the previous version is the presence of a cls attribute in the accordion element. The attribute's value (yourTheme.subclassed.Accordion) is the full class name of a subclassed version of the Accordion component that you may have implemented and saved in the /yourTheme/ subclassed/ path.

Since customizations are encapsulated within the subclassed component, XLEFF does not need to know anything about them, and you do not need to specify (or reimplement) them again and again. The XML layout engine just dynamically instantiates an instance of the subclassed component, and that's it.

Subclassing was explained in the Chapter 9, and you now know every technique to create a subclassed version of the Accordion component, encapsulating what you need to do to make it better suit your business requirements.

Chapter 11

THE BUTTON COMPONENT

Button	
mx.controls.Button	
Frequency:	Common
Complexity:	Simple
Stability:	Robust
Maturity:	Classic
Popularity:	Widespread

Buttons are present in every graphical user interface, and they represent the cornerstone of the point-and-click system introduced by that device oddly called the mouse.

It follows that they are frequently used in component-based applications, and utilizing instances of the Button component included in the architecture is pretty simple, even if its inner implementation is surprisingly complicated, which affects the complexity of customizing its appearance and behavior.

As usual, we will first explore a minimal example and start digging from there.

> *The completed source code introduced in this chapter can be found in the package* `src11.zip`, *downloadable from this book's page on* `www.friendsofed.com`.

Minimal example of the Button component

Actually using a Button instance is so simple that it's almost unbelievable how complicated things can get when it comes to customizing its appearance, as you will see later on in this chapter.

A consequence of the simplicity of implementing a Button instance is that our minimal example is truly minimal:

1. Create a new Flash document and save it as `button01.fla`.
2. Open the Document Properties dialog box by selecting Modify ➤ Document, and set its dimensions as 300×300 pixels.
3. Drag the Button component on stage in order to create a Button instance. Define its instance name as `mainButton`.
4. Select the `mainButton` instance and set its position at (X: 100.0, Y: 139.0) via the Info panel; this will place the Button instance in the center of the stage.
5. Create an ActionScript file and save it as `test.as`. Add the following lines to it:

```
mainButton.addEventListener("click", this);

function click(eventObject:Object):Void {
    if (eventObject.target._name == "mainButton") {
        trace("You clicked the mainButton instance");
    }
}
```

6. Select the first frame in the Flash document and add the following ActionScript line to it:

```
#include "test.as"
```

7. Save both the Flash document and the ActionScript file in the same folder.

Clicking buttons does not trigger any action unless you implement event handlers for their click events. This is what we do in our minimal example. First we register the _root object as a listener of the click event raised by the mainButton instance by using the addEventListener method available to all the instances inheriting from the UIObject class:

```
mainButton.addEventListener("click", this);
```

Then we implement in the top-level object (_root) a click function that will be automatically invoked by the component architecture whenever the mainButton instance raises a click event:

```
function click(eventObject) {
    if (eventObject.target._name == "mainButton") {
        trace("You clicked the mainButton instance");
    }
}
```

Testing the movie will result in a Button instance in the middle of the stage. Every time you click that button, the following message will be added to the Output window:

```
You clicked the mainButton instance
```

Our example is extremely simple. The only "excess" involves testing the name of the object that triggered the click event to be sure that it was indeed the mainButton instance. It is a good practice to verify what object triggered the event, since the listener object (in our case _root) could be listening to several instances at the same time and, therefore, its click function may be invoked, reacting to events triggered by different instances. Testing the name of the object that actually raised the event will allow you to execute the proper response.

Looking at how XLEFF implements the minimal example, it's worth very few words. The following XML segment should be included inside an XML file in order to dynamically generate a Button instance similar to the one present in the minimal example:

```
<button name="mainButton" x="100" y="139" label="Button" />
```

Now that you appreciate how little is required to implement a button instance and the response associated with it, we can move on to creating a slightly richer example that uses all the parameters accessible via the authoring environment.

A richer example

By selecting a Button instance on the stage, you can set up to five of its parameters via the Properties panel in the authoring environment:

- label: Certainly the most frequently used parameter, since it allows you to set the text label that appears in the Button instance.

- icon: An optional parameter that allows you to specify the linkage identifier of a symbol in the document's library that will be included as an icon inside the Button instance.

- labelPlacement: Makes sense only when you specify an icon for the Button instance. In that case, this property specifies the position of the text label in relation to the icon. Defined as right by default, it also supports left, bottom, and top.

- toggle: Boolean value that can modify how the Button instance works. Set to false by default, if true, it changes the Button instance default behavior into that of a toggle switch, meaning that the Button instance stays pressed after a click and it is released after the next click. Basically, when acting as a toggle switch, a Button instance becomes functionally very similar to a CheckBox instance.

- selected: Makes sense only when the Button instance is acting as a toggle switch. In this case, it indicates the state of the Button instance: pressed or released. Set to false by default, if true, it will display the Button instance as pressed.

Let's build an example that utilizes all these parameters by implementing an instance of a toggle button with an icon:

1. Open the Flash document created earlier, named button01.fla, and save it as button02.fla in a new folder. Also copy the test.as file associated with the button01.fla file into the new folder.

2. Open the copy of the test.as file that is in the current document's folder and replace the ActionScript lines therein with the following:

```
mainButton.addEventListener("click", this);

function click(eventObject) {
    if (eventObject.target._name == "mainButton") {
        trace("The selected state of the mainButton instance is: " +
            eventObject.target.selected);
    }
}
```

3. Create a new Movie Clip symbol by selecting Insert ➤ New Symbol, and define both its name and its linkage identifier as icon1.

4. Edit the icon1 symbol and, using the Oval tool, draw a round shape inside it. Use the Info panel to define the shape position as (X: 1.0, Y: 1.0) and its dimensions as (W: 8.0, H: 8.0). Using the Properties panel, define the stroke height of the shape as 3. Also set the stroke color as dark green and the fill color as light green. The final shape should look like the one displayed inside the Button instance later in Figure 11-2.

5. Go back to the stage and select the mainButton instance. Open the Parameters tab in the Properties panel and specify the five parameters of the Button instance as icon: icon1, label: Button, labelPlacement: left, selected: true, toggle: true. After you set these parameters, the Properties panel will look like the one in Figure 11-1.

Figure 11-1. The Properties panel after you further define the Button's parameters

6. Save the Flash document and the ActionScript file.

Testing the movie will result in a Button instance containing an icon on the right side of the text label like the one in Figure 11-2.

Figure 11-2. A Button instance with an icon behaving like a toggle switch and initially selected

Note that the Button instance has been implemented as a toggle switch and that it has been set as initially selected. The green border of the Button instance confirms that the instance is initially selected. If you keep clicking the Button instance, the selected state will pass from selected to released and so on. The Output window will display a message confirming the current value of the selected property of the Button instance, as in the following example:

```
The selected state of the mainButton instance is: false
```

Of course, you may implement the same Button instance via coding instead of setting the instance parameters in the authoring environment. The following code example does just that, and it is very readable since the names of the parameters in the authoring environment are identical to the names of the properties of the Button instance:

```
mainButton.label = "Button";
mainButton.icon = "icon1";
mainButton.labelPlacement = "left";
mainButton.toggle = true;
mainButton.selected = true;
```

Regardless, even when we added more detail to the implementation of an object instance and changed its behavior from the default (push button) to that of a toggle switch, using Button instances still proved to be very simple.

Let's increase the level of customization of this component by looking at how much we can alter its appearance via the supported style properties.

Supported styles

Styles allow an immediate customization of a component appearance that can be fine-tuned up to a per-instance basis. Styles can increase your productivity while contributing to creating a consistent look and feel in the appearance of your applications.

In this book, when listing the styles supported by a component, we will distinguish between two broad categories of styles:

- **Common styles**: Styles in this category are supported by several component classes. These styles not only affect the same aspects of a component, but also, as a matter of fact, are the only styles that allow promoting a certain consistency among instances of different components exactly because they are implemented universally within the component architecture.

- **Specific styles**: Styles in this category make sense only in the context of a particular component. Certain features are necessarily component specific, and the fact that they can be defined by using styles contributes to promoting a certain consistency among instances of the same component.

Let's first examine the common styles supported by the Button component.

Common styles

Almost all of the common styles supported by the Button component are dedicated to the appearance of the text label.

Following our practical approach, let's build a Button instance whose appearance is customized by using all of the common styles supported by the Button component:

1. Open the Flash document created earlier, named button01.fla, and save it as button04.fla in a new folder. Also copy the test.as file associated with the button01.fla file into the new folder.

2. Open the copy of the test.as file that is in the current document's folder and replace the ActionScript lines therein with the following:

```
mainButton.setSize(100,40);
mainButton.setStyle("themeColor", "haloBlue");
mainButton.setStyle("color", 0x00AAEE);
mainButton.setStyle("fontFamily", "Courier New");
mainButton.setStyle("fontSize", 20);
mainButton.setStyle("fontStyle", "italic");
mainButton.setStyle("fontWeight", "bold");
```

3. Save the Flash document and the ActionScript file.

Testing this movie will result in a Button instance appearing as shown in Figure 11-3.

The first line of this example uses the setSize to make the Button instance taller, creating the space required to conveniently host the enlarged text label. The use of several text-oriented style properties (color, fontFamily, fontSize, fontStyle, and fontWeight) determines the attribute of the text label visible in Figure 11-3.

Figure 11-3.
Stylized Button instance

Setting the themeColor style property to a cyan-like color (0x00AAEE) influences in a single step several states of the Button instance. The default Halo theme automatically defines the border styles and the component background color based on the value assigned to the themeColor style property. You can verify this by rolling over the Button instance or keeping it pressed by holding down the mouse click button: all of the Button states will be influenced by the cyan-like color assigned to the themeColor property in our example.

The Button component also supports another couple of common styles, textDecoration and disabledColor, which behave as expected: influencing the appearance of the text label by allowing underlined text and defining the text color of disabled Button instances.

The consistency of behavior that we find in the common styles supported by the Button component disappears once we dig into its so-called **border styles**.

Specific styles

Although we will discuss the border styles of the Button component here in the "Specific Styles" section, they may well have been included in the "Solved Mysteries" section of this chapter.

The major discrepancy that we find in the implementation of such styles is that they are not implemented by the Button component, but by the theme in use, and the two themes currently available in the component architecture provide a radically different implementation of these particular styles.

Finding out how border styles really work in the current version of the component architecture requires a thorough reverse-engineering analysis that jumps around several component classes, several other classes belonging to the architecture, and further classes added by the each specific theme.

Examining all of those relationships (most of them obscure and probably replaced in the next version of the component architecture) is beyond the scope of this chapter and, more importantly, unworthy of your time. As in other cases that were too specific, you can benefit from the author's hard-won knowledge and get directly to the point, which is how concretely border styles are affected by the Halo and the Sample themes.

Once again, the techniques will be demonstrated via concrete examples, starting with the simpler and less flexible Halo theme.

Halo theme case

As a matter of fact, you have already seen how the Halo theme affects border styles in the previous example: via the themeColor property.

In the "Solved Mysteries" section later on in this chapter, you will find an example showing how the implementation of the Halo theme works out the border styles starting from the theme color. In this section, we are going to implement a simple example showcasing what the Halo theme offers in terms of the border styles of a Button instance:

1. Open the Flash document created earlier, named button01.fla, and save it as button05.fla in a new folder. Also copy the test.as file associated with the button01.fla file into the new folder.

2. Open the copy of the test.as file that is in the current document's folder and replace the ActionScript lines therein with the following:

```
function setBorderStyles(s:String) {
    switch (s) {
        case "haloBlue":
            mainButton.setStyle("themeColor", "haloBlue");
            break;
        case "Reddish":
            mainButton.setStyle("themeColor", 0xFF0000);
            break;
        default:
            mainButton.setStyle("themeColor", "haloGreen");
    }
    mainButton.label = s;
}
```

```
function click(eventObject) {
    var b = eventObject.target;
    if (b._name == "mainButton") {
        switch (b.label) {
            case "Default":
                setBorderStyles("haloBlue");
                break;
            case "haloBlue":
                setBorderStyles("Reddish");
                break;
            case "Reddish":
                setBorderStyles("Default");
                break;
        }
    }
}

mainButton.label = "Default";
mainButton.addEventListener("click", this);
```

3. Save the Flash document and the ActionScript file.

Testing our movie will result in a Button instance whose label changes, rotating the values "Default", "haloBlue", and "Reddish" each time the button is clicked. A new themeColor is set each time.

The Halo theme comes with three predefined color names: haloGreen (acting as the default theme color), haloOrange, and haloBlue.

In our example, we rotate among the values of haloGreen (the default), haloBlue, and a custom color specified numerically as 0xFF0000 (red).

Keep clicking the Button instance so you will get an idea of how setting the themeColor to one of those three values affects several states of the Button instance dynamically and simultaneously.

This demonstrates both the advantage and the limitation of the approach implemented in the Halo theme: you don't need to do anything more to give a consistent look to each Button state apart from setting the themeColor style property. On the other hand, you cannot do anything more, meaning that you cannot set the colors of the Button instances separately.

As you are going to see, the implementation of the border styles in the case of the Sample theme is more complicated, but a bit more flexible.

Sample theme case

The Halo theme is the default theme of the component architecture: it is pre-added to the component instances, and you can use it straightaway without having to install it.

In the case of the Sample theme, you must add its Button assets to the Flash document in order to override the default theme (Halo). Let's do this while building our new example:

1. Open the Flash document created earlier, named button01.fla, and save it as button06.fla in a new folder. Also copy the test.as file associated with the button01.fla file into the new folder.

2. Open the copy of the test.as file that is in the current document's folder and replace the ActionScript lines therein with the following:

```
function setBorderStyles(s:String) {
    switch (s) {
        case "Custom":
            mainButton.setStyle("borderColor", 0x11ee00);
            mainButton.setStyle("buttonColor", 0xddeedd);
            mainButton.setStyle("shadowColor", 0x44bb22);
            mainButton.setStyle("highlightColor", 0x99ee99);
            break;
        default:
            mainButton.setStyle("borderColor", 0xd5dddd);
            mainButton.setStyle("buttonColor", 0x6f7777);
            mainButton.setStyle("shadowColor", 0xEEEEEE);
            mainButton.setStyle("highlightColor", 0xc4cccc);
    }
    mainButton.label = s;
}

function click(eventObject) {
    var b = eventObject.target;
    if (b._name == "mainButton") {
        if (b.label == "Default") setBorderStyles("Custom");
        else setBorderStyles("Default");
    }
}

mainButton.label = "Default";
mainButton.addEventListener("click", this);
```

3. Open the SampleTheme.fla file that you find in the same folder as the StandardComponents.fla file (see Appendix A) as an external library by selecting File ➤ Import ➤ Open External Library.

4. Copy the Button Assets folder that you find in the SampleTheme.fla library by dragging and dropping it into the library of the current Flash document. The Button Assets folder is located under the Flash UI Components 2 ➤ Themes ➤ MMDefault folder path. Simply copying this folder into the Flash document's library will apply the Sample theme to the instances of the Button component in the document.

5. Save the Flash document and the ActionScript file.

283

Figure 11-4. A Button instance utilizing the Sample theme

Testing the movie will result in a Button instance that looks pretty different from those implemented by the Halo theme. Figure 11-4 shows the initial appearance of a Button instance implemented using the Sample theme.

Similarly to our previous example, we implement a rotating algorithm to showcase different appearances. In this case, if you keep clicking the Button instance, you can visualize two different appearances, "Default" and "Custom".

Unlike the Halo theme, the Sample theme doesn't care about the themeColor style property. The Sample theme implements four border styles (borderColor, buttonColor, shadowColor, and highlightColor) that initially have the values displayed by the "Default" appearance. When setting the "Custom" appearance, our example mimics the greenish default color of the Halo theme by setting each of the four style properties as follows:

```
mainButton.setStyle("borderColor", 0xd5dddd);
mainButton.setStyle("buttonColor", 0x6f7777);
mainButton.setStyle("shadowColor", 0xEEEEEE);
mainButton.setStyle("highlightColor", 0xc4cccc);
```

By replacing one of those colors with red (0xFF0000 or "red") and testing the movie again, you will have visual feedback of what part of the component skin is affected by each specific style.

This example not only shows you how different the implementation of border styles is between the Halo and the Sample themes, but also, in part, how much of the definition of those styles depends on the specific theme: if you implement your own theme, you may well have to implement your own border styles or, as you will see later on, none of them!

Although very simple to use, the Button component is built upon a surprisingly complex implementation. Its skin, borders included, is purely coded. Every graphic feature of a Button instance is eventually implemented with calls to the drawing API. However, the purely coded implementation of the skin is the result of combining the functionality of several classes, some of them included in the package of a theme (Halo or Sample).

For a long time, the underlying implementation of the Button component has made the process of skinning the Button component nightmarish. Let's see how it is possible to make skinning a Button component a much simpler process without losing the flexibility required by designers who want to customize the appearance of a Button instance thoroughly.

Skinnability

Purely coded skins, like the default skin of the Button component, can be a very controversial choice for implementing the appearance of a component.

This is a book for developers and, therefore, it may sound surprising, at first, to find out that replacing a purely coded skin with a handcrafted one is, as a matter of fact, more convenient in the vast majority of cases.

However, regardless of purely coded skins having some benefits compared to their counterparts based on graphic assets, they clash with the most important among the core principles in designing and developing GUIs: the separation of code from representation.

That is what makes producing purely coded skins so expensive and ultimately inconvenient. We will go deeper into the issue, rather than avoid it, by showing a purely coded skin replacement for the Button instance later on in this chapter.

However, you may well consider and prefer the technique that we are going to examine immediately, one that allows you to easily replace the purely coded skin of a button with a handcrafted one. Undoubtedly, this technique will be your best choice in the vast majority of cases.

Replacing the purely coded skin

The beauty of the technique being introduced here is that it will allow you to replace the purely coded skin of the Button component with a handcrafted skin without losing any of the functionality of the Button class such as the handling of the text label and the icon.

While building the examples, we are going to use a few graphic assets that you will find in the source files associated with this chapter. Those assets have been designed to give a decent look to the Button instances but, of course, you are welcome to replace them and experiment with other skins that best suit your designs.

1. Create a new Flash document and save it as button07.fla.
2. Open the Document Properties dialog box by selecting Modify ➤ Document, and set its dimensions as 300×300 pixels.
3. Drag the Button component on stage three times in order to create three Button instances. Define their instance names as button1, button2, and button3.
4. Select the button1 instance and set its size as (W: 100.0, H: 50.0) and its position at (X: 100.0, Y: 42.0) using the Info panel; select the button2 instance and set its size as (W: 100.0, H: 50.0) and its position at (X: 100.0, Y: 125.0); select the button3 instance and set its size as (W: 100.0, H: 50.0) and its position at (X: 100.0, Y: 208.0).
5. Create an ActionScript file and save it as test.as. Add the following lines to it:

```
import mx.controls.Button;

Button.prototype.themeColor = 0x999966;
Button.prototype.disabledColor = 0xeeeeee;
Button.prototype.drawFocus = function() {};
Button.prototype.falseUpSkin = "btnFalseUpSkin";
Button.prototype.falseOverSkin = "btnFalseOverSkin";
Button.prototype.falseDownSkin = "btnFalseDownSkin";
Button.prototype.falseDisabledSkin = "btnFalseDisabledSkin";

button3.enabled = false;
```

6. Select the first frame in the document and add the following ActionScript line to it:

`#include "test.as"`

7. Create a new Movie Clip symbol (Insert ➤ New Symbol) called falseUpSkin with a linkage identifier set as btnFalseUpSkin. The graphic of this symbol, which is 100×50 pixels in size, appears as shown in Figure 11-5. You can find this graphic symbol in the library of the source file associated with this chapter.

Figure 11-5.
The falseUpSkin symbol

8. Create a new symbol (Insert ➤ New Symbol) called falseOverSkin with a linkage identifier set as btnFalseOverSkin. The graphic of this symbol has a similar shape and size to the previous one, but its colors are slightly different. Once again, refer to the library of the source file associated with this chapter to find this exact graphic asset.

9. Create a new symbol (Insert ➤ New Symbol) called falseDownSkin with a linkage identifier set as btnFalseDownSkin. The graphic of this symbol, which is approximately 108×62 pixels in size, appears as shown in Figure 11-6. You can find this graphic symbol in the library of the source file associated with this chapter.

Figure 11-6.
The falseDownSkin symbol

10. Create a new symbol (Insert ➤ New Symbol) called falseDisabledSkin with a linkage identifier set as btnFalseDisabledSkin. The graphic of this symbol is similar to that of the falseUpSkin symbol, but its colors are grayed out. Once again, refer to the library of the source file associated with this chapter to find this exact graphic asset.

11. Create a folder called skins in the document's library and drop the four newly created symbols (falseUpSkin, falseOverSkin, falseDownSkin, and falseDisabledSkin) into it. They are the handcrafted skins we will use in this example. After reorganizing it, the document's library should look like what you see in Figure 11-7.

Name	Kind	Use Count	Linkage
Button	Compiled Clip	-	Export: Button
Skins	Folder		
falseDisabledSkin	Movie Clip	-	Export: btnFalseDisabledSkin
falseDownSkin	Movie Clip	-	Export: btnFalseDownSkin
falseOverSkin	Movie Clip	-	Export: btnFalseOverSkin
falseUpSkin	Movie Clip	-	Export: btnFalseUpSkin

Figure 11-7. The document's library with our newly created skin

12. Save both the Flash document and the ActionScript file.

Figure 11-8 shows how the three Button instances look on stage at authoring time.

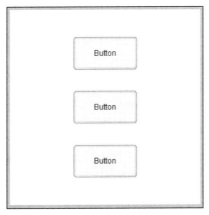

Figure 11-8. The Button instances as they appear at authoring time

The look of the three Button instances at authoring time is defined by the Halo theme. Compare this with the look of the same Button instances at runtime when testing the movie; as shown in Figure 11-9.

You will certainly notice that the look of the Button instances at runtime is very different, as they show the skins created for our example. Playing with the Button instances by using the mouse and/or the keyboard will also show the skins of the two button states that are initially not visible (over and down).

A Button instance usually has three states (up, down, and over) when enabled and only one state (disabled) when disabled.

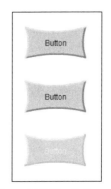

Figure 11-9. The Button instances as they appear at runtime

To implement these skins, we use the fast option offered by the prototype property, but we could also choose to subclass the Button component or to attach the skins to each instance via their undocumented initialize clip event (both the alternatives are explained in Chapter 9). The Button class implements four properties (falseUpSkin, falseOverSkin, falseDownSkin, and falseDisabledSkin) that allow us to install our skins using the following code:

```
Button.prototype.falseUpSkin = "btnFalseUpSkin";
Button.prototype.falseOverSkin = "btnFalseOverSkin";
Button.prototype.falseDownSkin = "btnFalseDownSkin";
Button.prototype.falseDisabledSkin = "btnFalseDisabledSkin";
```

Note that we use a btn prefix consistently when naming the skins' linkage identifiers in order to avoid name conflicts with similar skins that may be used by other components (after all, the Button component is not the only one to have states named up, over, down, and disabled).

The third button in our example is disabled in order to show the fourth skin via the ActionScript line:

```
button3.enabled = false;
```

The color of the text label of the disabled button is set via the disabledColor style property:

```
Button.prototype.disabledColor = 0xeeeeee;
```

We also define a themeColor style property that somewhat informs the component architecture about which base color of the color scheme is in use by our handcrafted skins:

```
Button.prototype.themeColor = 0x999966;
```

The component architecture would have used this color when drawing the focus rect around a button. However, such a rectangular focus rect would not look too good around our custom skins and, therefore, we disable it by overriding the drawFocus method with an implementation that does nothing.

```
Button.prototype.drawFocus = function() {};
```

Note that the user can easily notice when a Button instance obtains the focus via tabbing, since it shows the falseOverSkin in that case.

In the end, replacing the purely coded skins of the Button component with handcrafted ones can be done efficiently and quickly by replacing only 4 of the 32 skins supported by the Button class, as clearly demonstrated by our example. You will learn about the purpose of the remaining 28 skins in the next section.

By using handcrafted skins, you can design a vectorial skin by using the Flash drawing tools, or you can also import external bitmapped graphics in order to achieve additional effects.

In the source files associated with this chapter, you will find a second version (button08.fla) of the example in this section that uses bitmapped images as graphic assets that give to the three Button instances a look like the one displayed in Figure 11-10.

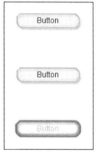

Figure 11-10.
The same example using bitmapped skins

Quite clearly, using the approach illustrated here allows you to change the Button component appearance via either vectorial or bitmapped skins in a snap to accommodate any kind of graphic requirement.

The only limit of handcrafted skins compared with purely coded skins is that they don't look as good when the component instance is stretched beyond its intended dimensions.

However, let's face it: in the case of well-designed user interfaces, buttons always have standard sizes. Most of the time you will need to implement only one size for your buttons, but even in the case of several standard sizes to implement, a few sets of skins (small, medium, and large, for example) are still more convenient than producing purely coded versions of the skins, as you will also appreciate later on in this chapter.

Let's now thoroughly examine the skin properties supported by the Button component: although we already covered what you need to know in the wide majority of cases, there may be requirements in which the following knowledge turns out to be useful.

The 32 skins of a button

The fact that the Button component supports the very large number of 32 skins has usually made developers reluctant to consider replacing purely coded skins with handcrafted versions.

As we saw previously, in most cases, you don't really need to care about 28 of the 32 skin properties to implement custom handcrafted skins that replace the purely coded versions.

Let's now examine why 28 out of 32 skins are not necessary in the majority of cases by seeing what cases they can actually be used in.

Implementing a toggle button

The component architecture provides a specific component (CheckBox) that acts as a toggle button. However, as you already saw in this chapter, the Button component is so flexible that it can be used for this purpose by setting its toggle property to true (in which case its selected property will store the state of the toggle button).

In the case of a toggle button, the four skins we created in our last example (falseUpSkin, falseOverSkin, falseDownSkin, and falseDisabledSkin) are no longer sufficient and, in fact, the Button class implements four similar skin properties to visualize the state of the toggle button when selected (trueUpSkin, trueOverSkin, trueDownSkin, and trueDisabledSkin). Pretty intuitively, it is the prefix in the name of the skin (false or true) that separates the two sets of skins and associates them with the toggle status (not selected or selected, respectively).

Emphasizing a button instance

The Button class supports another property named emphasized. The emphasized property should be set to true in the case of a Button instance that is the default button in the user interface.

If you want to improve the look and feel of your interface, you may well want to provide a slightly different set of skins for a Button instance that is emphasized.

Such an option will "cost" you another eight skins (falseUpSkinEmphasized, falseOverSkinEmphasized, falseDownSkinEmphasized, falseDisabledSkinEmphasized, trueUpSkinEmphasized, trueOverSkin➡ Emphasized, trueDownSkinEmphasized, and trueDisabledSkinEmphasized) since you must take care of the possibility of implementing a toggle button as we saw earlier. Toggle buttons can be emphasized, too.

Once again, it is rather intuitive to realize that the postfix Emphasized is the key in defining the new set of skin names.

Iconic buttons

So far, we have reached an overall number of 16 skins: the basic 4, another 4 skins added to handle the toggle state, and an additional 8 skins added to handle the emphasized state.

If we introduce a further element, we will be forced to double the skins set again, and we will reach the final set of the 32 skins supported by the Button component. You may have already guessed what this new element is by reading the title of this section: the Button icon.

If you want to provide a different skin for Button instances that include an icon, then you must provide it for all the cases that we have already examined, and that generates another 16 skin names:

- `falseUpIcon`, `falseDownIcon`, `falseOverIcon`, `falseDisabledIcon`: Associated with the four basic states of a Button instance

- `trueUpIcon`, `trueDownIcon`, `trueOverIcon`, `trueDisabledIcon`: Skins you may need if implementing a toggle button

- `falseUpIconEmphasized`, `falseDownIconEmphasized`, `falseOverIconEmphasized`, `false➡DisabledIconEmphasized`, `trueUpIconEmphasized`, `trueDownIconEmphasized`, `trueOverIcon➡Emphasized`, `trueDisabledIconEmphasized`: Skins you will need if you are mad enough to wish to emphasize the icon as well

It should appear clear, by now, why the four basic skins we implemented in the previous section are all you need in the vast majority of cases.

Quite rarely you will find it necessary to implement any of the remaining 28 skins supported by the Button component. However, whenever you need to, all you have to do is to draw the handcrafted skins and install them by using the respective skin properties in exactly the same way as we did it for the four basic skins in our last example.

Solved mysteries

The Button component is pretty robust, meaning that there are no known quirks in its functionality at the time of writing.

However, the complexity of its implementation is amazing, especially considering that buttons were native objects in Flash since its earlier versions.

Both the major techniques you learned earlier in this chapter (customizing the border styles implemented by the two themes available and replacing the purely coded skins of the Button component with handcrafted skins) could have easily been included in this section, since in both cases they unlock inner features of the component architecture.

What we have left here is to examine in greater detail the implementation of a purely coded skin. You will probably concede that handcrafted skins are a much better option but, nevertheless, this discussion will give you a better insight into the current implementation of the component architecture and food for thought about the different approaches available for skinning a component.

A purely coded classic: the pill button

We will proceed, as usual, by implementing a practical example. In this case, we are going to implement a purely coded skin in the style of the classic pill buttons that you find in various user interfaces.

The skin that we wish to implement is based on the Halo theme, and it is compared to the standard Halo appearance in Figure 11-11.

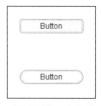

Figure 11-11. The default skin (top) compared with the new skin (bottom)

1. Create a new Flash document and save it as button09.fla.

2. Open the Document Properties dialog box by selecting Modify ➤ Document, and set its dimensions as 300✕300 pixels.

3. Drag the Button component on stage twice in order to create two Button instances. Define their names as button1 and button2.

4. Select the button1 instance and set its position at (X: 100.0, Y: 100.0) using the Info panel; select the button2 instance and set its position at (X: 100.0, Y: 178.0).

5. Select the button2 instance and add the following ActionScript lines to it by opening the Actions panel:

```
onClipEvent (initialize) {
    this.falseUpSkin = "ButtonPillSkin";
    this.falseDownSkin = "ButtonPillSkin";
    this.falseOverSkin = "ButtonPillSkin"
    this.falseDisabledSkin = "ButtonPillSkin";
    this.trueUpSkin = "ButtonPillSkin";
    this.trueDownSkin = "ButtonPillSkin";
    this.trueOverSkin = "ButtonPillSkin"
    this.trueDisabledSkin = "ButtonPillSkin";
}
```

6. Create a new Movie Clip symbol (Insert ➤ New Symbol) called ButtonPillSkin with a linkage identifier and an ActionScript 2.0 class name both set as ButtonPillSkin as well.

7. Create a folder called skins in the document's library and drop the newly created symbol into it (ButtonPillSkin). This empty symbol is the purely coded skin that will allow us to display pill buttons. After reorganizing it, the document's library should look like the one in Figure 11-12.

Name	Kind	Use Count	Linkage
Button	Compiled Clip	-	Export: Button
skins	Folder		
ButtonPillSkin	Movie Clip	-	Export: ButtonPillSkin

Figure 11-12. The document's library including the purely coded skin

8. Save the Flash document.

Note that the book does not list the complete source code of the ButtonPillSkin class; however, you can find it in the ButtonPillSkin.as file included in the source file associated with this chapter.

Before testing the movie, you must place a copy of the ButtonPillSkin.as file in the same folder as the Flash document that you created for this example. This file contains 117 lines of code, most of them repetitive, and we will only examine the most significant here.

Once tested, the movie will show the same two Button instances displayed in Figure 11-11.

By using the undocumented initialize event, we apply the purely coded skin only to one of the two instances (button2). You wrote the code inside the Flash document in the fifth step of the previous procedure. The most relevant bit of it is that every skin property is assigned the same skin regardless of the state: ButtonPillSkin.

It becomes obvious that the purely coded skin (ButtonPillSkin) must be able to recognize the current state of the Button instance and draw the proper skin at runtime.

That's why so many lines are required to implement the ButtonPillSkin class. Most of them are part of a single switch statement that tests the borderStyle style property to draw the proper skin at runtime, as in the following:

```
switch (borderStyle) {
    case "falseup":
        ...............
    case "falsedown":
        ...............
    case "falserollover":
        ...............
    case "falsedisabled":
        ...............
    case "trueup":
        ...............
    case "truedown":
        ...............
    case "truerollover":
        ...............
    case "truedisabled":
        ...............
}
```

Note that each case is associated with the value of a state. Those eight values are defined and set by the Button class and, therefore, are very important if you want to implement your own purely coded skin like we did in this example.

A purely coded skin must extend from the RectBorder class, as in the following:

```
class ButtonPillSkin extends RectBorder {
```

The RectBorder class implements the border of most, but not all, the components in the architecture. If you want to skin the border of those components, you must reapply a similar technique to the one displayed here for the Button component.

As mentioned previously, a purely coded skin is eventually implemented by calls to the drawing API. However, if we examine an example of how a button state is implemented by the ButtonPillSkin class, you will notice this is made of several calls to the drawRoundRect method, as in the case of the following:

```
case "falsedisabled":
    drawRoundRect(0,0,w,h,5 + radiusAdj,0xc8cccc,100);
    drawRoundRect(1,1,w-2,h-2,4 + radiusAdj,0xf2f2f2,100);
    drawRoundRect(2,2,w-4,h-4,3 + radiusAdj,0xd4d9d9,100);
    drawRoundRect(3,3,w-6,h-6,2 + radiusAdj,0xf2f2f2,100);
    break;
```

The drawRoundRect method is implemented by the Halo theme and is a rather large function (82 lines) that makes several calls to the drawing API in order to draw a rounded rect in the style that is typical of the Halo theme. You can find its implementation in the source code of the component architecture (in the default.as file included under mx\skins\halo).

Therefore, each implementation of a button's state usually requires many calls to the drawing API. In our example we were "lucky," since we managed to produce the pill button look by reusing the drawRoundRect method already implemented by the Halo theme.

The conclusion is that implementing a purely coded skin is likely to require hundreds (if not thousands) of lines of code in addition to reverse-engineering any functionality of the component architecture that may affect their implementation.

Purely coded skins are an interesting experiment, but it is very unlikely that they will find a future in component architectures that include skinnable components.

Reasons for subclassing a Button component

As usual, at the end of a chapter dedicated to a component, we consider what reasons you may have for subclassing it.

The Button component is very robust and, therefore, there aren't quirks or patches that would make subclassing it particularly appealing.

However, you may well find it still convenient if you want to encapsulate styles and skins that you widely reuse in your project.

In particular, if you produce several bitmapped versions of the same skins to fit various sizes (small, medium, large), you may find it convenient to be able to instantiate subclassed versions such as SmallButton, MediumButton, and LargeButton.

In the end, the better way of building new themes may well be creating a collection of subclassed components.

Chapter 12

THE CHECKBOX AND RADIOBUTTON COMPONENTS

CheckBox mx.controls.CheckBox	RadioButton mx.controls.RadioButton
Frequency: Common	Frequency: Common
Complexity: Simple	Complexity: Simple
Stability: Robust	Stability: Robust
Maturity: Classic	Maturity: Classic
Popularity: Widespread	Popularity: Widespread

The CheckBox and RadioButton classes, implementing the respective components, share the same base class, Button, and, therefore, all its functionality, which we examined previously.

Both CheckBox and RadioButton instances are utilized to offer selectable options with a difference: CheckBox instances are typically used in the case of one or more options that can be selected at the same time, while RadioButton instances are usually grouped to represent a set of mutually exclusive options: only one of them can be selected at any moment.

It follows that you select and deselect a CheckBox instance by clicking repeatedly over it, exactly like a toggle switch button, which we saw in the previous chapter. In the case of RadioButton instances, clicking one of them will always select it, while at the same time deselecting another RadioButton instance in the same group that was previously selected, if any.

Experimenting with the minimal example will clarify any doubts you may still have about the behavior of these two components.

> *The completed source code introduced in this chapter can be found in the package* `src12.zip`, *downloadable from this book's page on* `www.friendsofed.com`.

Minimal example of the CheckBox and the RadioButton components

Let's build a practical example that uses both components to compare their behavior:

1. Create a new Flash document and save it as `crbuttons01.fla`.

2. Open the Document Properties dialog box by selecting Modify ➤ Document, and set its dimensions as 300×200 pixels.

3. Drag the CheckBox component on stage three times in order to create three instances. Name those instances checkbox1, checkbox2, and checkbox3, respectively.

4. Drag the RadioButton component on stage three times in order to create three instances. Name those instances radiobutton1, radionbutton2, and radiobutton3, respectively.

5. Select the checkbox1 instance and set its position at (X: 40.0, Y: 45.0) via the Info panel; then select the checkbox2 instance and set its position at (X: 40.0, Y: 89.0); finally, select the checkbox3 instance and set its position at (X: 40.0, Y: 133.0).

6. Select the radiobutton1 instance and set its position at (X: 160.0, Y: 45.0) via the Info panel; then select the radiobutton2 instance and set its position at (X: 160.0, Y: 89.0); finally, select the radiobutton3 instance and set its position at (X: 160.0, Y: 133.0).

7. Save the Flash document.

Testing the movie will show three instances of the CheckBox component and three instances of the RadioButton component. By clicking over those instances, you will find out that you can select more than one CheckBox instance at the same time, while you can only select one RadioButton instance at a time, possibly ending with a configuration like the one displayed in Figure 12-1.

Figure 12-1. The minimal example after you selected some instances by clicking them

XLEFF version

The following XML description is the XLEFF equivalent for generating a user interface corresponding to the one in our minimal example:

```
<checkbox name="checkbox1" label="CheckBox" x="40" y="45" />
<checkbox name="checkbox2" label="CheckBox" x="40" y="89" />
<checkbox name="checkbox3" label="CheckBox" x="40" y="133" />
<radiobutton name="radiobutton1" label="RadioButton" group="radioGroup"
             x="160" y="45" />
<radiobutton name="radiobutton2" label="RadioButton" group="radioGroup"
             x="160" y="89" />
<radiobutton name="radiobutton3" label="RadioButton" group="radioGroup"
             x="160" y="133" />
```

You can find the XLEFF sampler configured to show the XLEFF version of the minimal example among the source files associated with this chapter.

The only attribute in the XML description that you should find unfamiliar at this point is the group attribute specifying the name of the group including the RadioButton instance. We will see more on the significance of the RadioButton group later on in this chapter.

Comparing the authoring parameters

By comparing the parameters that you can set at authoring time, you can find out more about the similarities and differences between the CheckBox and the RadioButton components.

Figure 12-2 shows the parameters of the checkbutton1 instance that you can see when selecting it in the authoring environment.

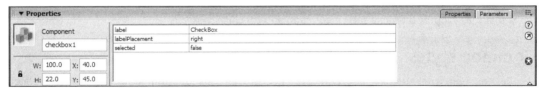

Figure 12-2. Parameters of the CheckBox component

Only three parameters are available:

- label: Defines the text appearing near the CheckBox instance.

- labelPlacement: Defines the position of the text label in relation to the CheckBox icon. Four options are available (left, right, top, and bottom), right being the default.

- selected: False by default. Whenever set to true, indicates that the CheckBox instance will initially appear as selected.

Figure 12-3 shows the parameters of the radiobutton1 instance that you can see when selecting it in the authoring environment.

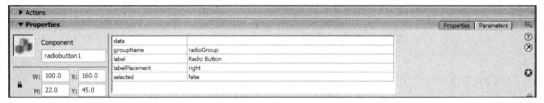

Figure 12-3. Parameters of the RadioButton component

Three of the five parameters available for RadioButton instances have the same names and function of the homonymous CheckBox parameters that we have just examined.

The remaining two parameters are as follows:

- data: Undefined by default. It allows you to specify a String data value associated with the RadioButton instance.

- groupName: Another String value, set to radioGroup by default. It stores the name of the radio group associated with the RadioButton instance. RadioButton instances belonging to the same radio group affect each other whenever selected: only one of them can be selected at any time, as you saw in the previously implemented minimal example.

Each of the parameters we have examined corresponds to a property with the same name that can be set via ActionScript. The only difference is in accessing those properties via ActionScript that reside in the data property of the RadioButton class. When assigned by coding, the value of the data property can be of any data type.

Supported styles

Another good reason for learning about the CheckBox and RadioButton components at the same time is that they support the same sets of common and specific styles.

Common styles

The common styles supported by both the CheckBox and RadioButton components are all related to the text label (color, disabledColor, embedFonts, fontFamily, fontSize, fontStyle, fontWeight, textDecoration), with the exception of themeColor, which, as usual, defines the color scheme of the components in the case of the Halo theme.

Their functionality is consistent throughout all the standard components in the architecture and will be examined in greater detail in Chapter 18.

Let's extend our minimal example to quickly experiment with some of the common styles applied to both components.

1. Open the minimal example stored in the Flash document `crbuttons01.fla` and save it as `crbuttons03.fla`.

2. Select the first and only frame on the document's timeline and add the following ActionScript lines to it:

```
import mx.styles.CSSStyleDeclaration;

_global.styles.CheckBox = new CSSStyleDeclaration();
_global.styles.RadioButton = new CSSStyleDeclaration();

function setGlobalStyles(style):Void {
    style.setStyle("themeColor", "red");
    style.setStyle("color", "red");
    style.setStyle("fontFamily", "Courier New");
    style.setStyle("fontStyle", "italic");
    style.setStyle("fontWeight", "bold");
}

setGlobalStyles(_global.styles.CheckBox);
setGlobalStyles(_global.styles.RadioButton);
```

3. Save the Flash document.

Testing the movie will display stylized, reddish versions of the CheckBox and RadioButton instances like those displayed in Figure 12-4.

Figure 12-4. Stylized version of the minimal example

Note that the symbols (squares for the CheckBox instances and circles for the RadioButton instances) will become reddish only when rolling over them or clicking them, whereas they remain grayish while in the up state.

The code used for implementing the stylized version of our minimal example is worth some comments.

We applied the style at class level using one of the techniques illustrated in Chapter 9. However, quite surprisingly, we had to work around the fact that the component architecture does not define class style objects in the case of some components, CheckBox and RadioButton included.

That's why we create these objects in the global styles collection as follows:

```
_global.styles.CheckBox = new CSSStyleDeclaration();
_global.styles.RadioButton = new CSSStyleDeclaration();
```

Note that you should always verify whether a particular class style has already been implemented before creating its object by checking if it is undefined, because by overriding an existing one you may involuntarily remove some preexisting style definitions. In our example, we do not make the test since, at the time of writing, the component architecture does not define global style objects for the CheckBox and RadioButton components. However, a longer but safer implementation would replace the previous two lines with

```
if (_global.styles.CheckBox == undefined) {
    _global.styles.CheckBox = new CSSStyleDeclaration();
}
if (_global.styles.RadioButton == undefined) {
    _global.styles.RadioButton = new CSSStyleDeclaration();
}
```

Going back to analyzing the code in our example, the last point worth our attention is the setGlobalStyles function, which was implemented with the sole purpose of applying the same style values to both the CheckBox and RadioButton classes.

We can now move on to examining the style properties that are specific to the CheckBox and RadioButton components.

Specific styles

The specific styles supported by both the CheckBox and RadioButton components are valid for the Sample theme only. Basically, the Sample theme implements and supports the following styles:

- symbolBackgroundColor
- symbolBackgroundDisabledColor
- symbolBackgroundPressedColor
- symbolColor
- symbolDisabledColor

These color styles affect the symbol of an instance, and its background and their names are mostly self-descriptive once you know that the symbol of the CheckBox component is the check symbol and the symbol of the RadioButton component is the large dot symbol.

In order to implement an example using some of the specific styles, you need to install the Sample theme, which is what we are going to do in the next example:

1. Open the minimal example stored in the Flash document crbuttons01.fla and save it as crbuttons04.fla.

2. Select the first and only frame on the document's timeline and add the following ActionScript lines to it:

```
import mx.styles.CSSStyleDeclaration;

_global.styles.CheckBox = new CSSStyleDeclaration();
_global.styles.RadioButton = new CSSStyleDeclaration();

function setGlobalStyles(style):Void {
    style.setStyle("color", "red");
    style.setStyle("fontFamily", "Courier New");
    style.setStyle("fontStyle", "italic");
    style.setStyle("fontWeight", "bold");

    style.setStyle("symbolColor", "red");
    style.setStyle("symbolBackgroundColor", 0xFFCCCC);
    style.setStyle("symbolBackgroundPressedColor", "red");
}

setGlobalStyles(_global.styles.CheckBox);
setGlobalStyles(_global.styles.RadioButton);
```

3. Open the SampleTheme.fla file that you find in the same folder as the StandardComponents.fla file (see Appendix A) as an external library by selecting File ➤ Import ➤ Open External Library.

4. Copy the CheckBox Assets and the RadioButton Assets folders that you find in the SampleTheme.fla library by dragging and dropping them into the library of the current Flash document. Both folders are located under the Flash UI Components 2 ➤ Themes ➤ MMDefault folder path in the SampleTheme.fla library. Simply copying this folder into the Flash document's library will not apply the Sample theme as usual, because the assets of both the CheckBox and RadioButton components have a further requirement. In the meantime, you can close the SampleTheme.fla library, since you will not need it anymore.

5. Find the CheckBoxAssets symbol inside the CheckBox Assets folder in the document's library and, after opening the Linkage Properties dialog box, check the Export in first frame option.

6. Find the RadioButtonAssets symbol inside the RadioButton Assets folder in the document's library and, after opening the Linkage Properties dialog box, check the Export in first frame option.

7. Save the Flash document.

The CheckBox and RadioButton assets of the Sample theme must be exported in the first frame to be utilized unless you structure your application in a way that ensures that those assets are loaded before being used.

We have already built a template that is capable of preloading any of the standard component assets in the second part of the book. Of course, for the sake of simplicity, we are not going to complicate the structure of our current example to avoid setting the dreaded Export in first frame option, since our example implements no preloader.

If, after testing the movie, you play with the instances on stage by clicking some of them, you will notice that the three specific styles utilized in this example (symbolColor, symbolBackgroundColor, and symbolBackgroundPressedColor) effectively influence the appearance of the CheckBox and RadioButton instances as expected, as you see in Figure 12-5.

Figure 12-5. A further stylized version of the minimal example

Now that you know everything about the styles of these two components, you can look into how to skin them in order to achieve an additional level of customization.

Skinnability

Both the CheckBox and the RadioButton components are very easy to skin, since their original skins are handcrafted. They both use some of the skin properties defined by their common base class: Button. In fact, they actually use the skin properties defined for the icon of the Button component.

The CheckBox component uses eight skin properties:

- falseUpIcon: Initially set as CheckFalseUp.
- falseDownIcon: Initially set as CheckFalseDown.
- falseOverIcon: Initially set as CheckFalseOver.
- falseDisabledIcon: Initially set as CheckFalseDisabled.
- trueUpIcon: Initially set as CheckTrueUp.
- trueDownIcon: Initially set as CheckTrueDown.
- trueOverIcon: Initially set as CheckTrueOver.
- trueDisabledIcon: Initially set as CheckTrueDisabled.

The RadioButton component uses only six of those eight properties:

- falseUpIcon: Initially set as RadioFalseUp.
- falseDownIcon: Initially set as RadioFalseDown.
- falseOverIcon: Initially set as RadioFalseOver.

- `falseDisabledIcon`: Initially set as RadioFalseDisabled.

- `trueUpIcon`: Initially set as RadioTrueUp.

- `trueDisabledIcon`: Initially set as RadioTrueDisabled.

The names of the style properties are once again readable. The prefix (`true` or `false`) is associated with the selected state that is common to both components. The middle part indicates the four states (`Up`, `Down`, `Over`, and `Disabled`) of a button instance, while the postfix (`Icon`) is always the same and does not have a particular meaning in relation to the component's state.

The names of the linkage identifiers assigned to the properties are intuitive, too. The prefix (Check or Radio) indicates whether it is a CheckBox or RadioButton linkage identifier. The middle part is associated with the `selected` state (`true` or `false`), and the last part is associated with the button states (`Up`, `Down`, `Over`, and `Disabled`).

In the source files associated with this chapter, you will find a Flash document (`crbuttons05.fla`) that skins both the CheckBox and RadioButton components, replacing the handcrafted skins with graphics provided by bitmapped images.

In this case, we are not going to examine the full procedure to create the file, since it is very repetitive, and only aim to create new symbols in the document's library.

In fact, in order to skin the CheckBox component, the document's library includes eight symbols defined by using the linkage identifiers we just listed; these also appear in Figure 12-6, which shows both the symbols used for the skin and the images used to implement their appearance.

Name	Kind	Use Count	Linkage
☒ CheckBox	Compiled Clip	-	Export: CheckBox
🗁 CheckBox Skins	Folder		
▨ CheckFalseDisabled	Movie Clip	-	Export: CheckFalseDisabled
▨ CheckFalseDown	Movie Clip	-	Export: CheckFalseDown
▨ CheckFalseOver	Movie Clip	-	Export: CheckFalseOver
▨ CheckFalseUp	Movie Clip	-	Export: CheckFalseUp
▨ CheckTrueDisabled	Movie Clip	-	Export: CheckTrueDisabled
▨ CheckTrueDown	Movie Clip	-	Export: CheckTrueDown
▨ CheckTrueOver	Movie Clip	-	Export: CheckTrueOver
▨ CheckTrueUp	Movie Clip	-	Export: CheckTrueUp
🗁 Images	Folder		
🖻 CheckFalseDisabled.png	Bitmap	-	
🖻 CheckFalseDown.png	Bitmap	-	
🖻 CheckFalseOver.png	Bitmap	-	
🖻 CheckFalseUp.png	Bitmap	-	
🖻 CheckTrueDisabled.png	Bitmap	-	
🖻 CheckTrueDown.png	Bitmap	-	
🖻 CheckTrueOver.png	Bitmap	-	
🖻 CheckTrueUp.png	Bitmap	-	
◉ RadioButton	Compiled Clip	-	Export: RadioButton
🗁 RadioButton Skins	Folder		

Figure 12-6. Symbols defined to skin the CheckBox component and the images used by them

Quite similarly, the document's library also includes six symbols, defined as specified earlier, in order to skin the RadioButton component. The definitions of those symbols are displayed in the Figure 12-7.

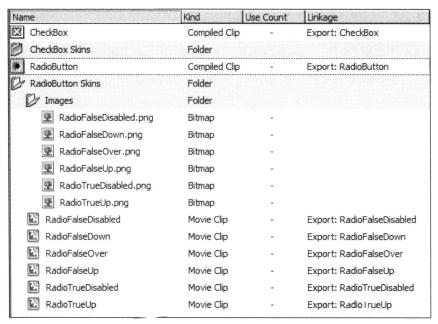

Name	Kind	Use Count	Linkage
☒ CheckBox	Compiled Clip	-	Export: CheckBox
📁 CheckBox Skins	Folder		
● RadioButton	Compiled Clip	-	Export: RadioButton
📁 RadioButton Skins	Folder		
📁 Images	Folder		
🖼 RadioFalseDisabled.png	Bitmap	-	
🖼 RadioFalseDown.png	Bitmap	-	
🖼 RadioFalseOver.png	Bitmap	-	
🖼 RadioFalseUp.png	Bitmap	-	
🖼 RadioTrueDisabled.png	Bitmap	-	
🖼 RadioTrueUp.png	Bitmap	-	
🎬 RadioFalseDisabled	Movie Clip	-	Export: RadioFalseDisabled
🎬 RadioFalseDown	Movie Clip	-	Export: RadioFalseDown
🎬 RadioFalseOver	Movie Clip	-	Export: RadioFalseOver
🎬 RadioFalseUp	Movie Clip	-	Export: RadioFalseUp
🎬 RadioTrueDisabled	Movie Clip	-	Export: RadioTrueDisabled
🎬 RadioTrueUp	Movie Clip	-	Export: RadioTrueUp

Figure 12-7. Symbols defined to skin the RadioButton component and the images used by them

No code is needed as long as the linkage identifiers used for the symbols are those shown in the images since, as we saw earlier, those are the default names assigned to the skin properties that both the CheckBox and RadioButton components use to implement their skins.

Testing the `crbuttons05.fla` file will give to the minimal example a new appearance, shown in Figure 12-8, due to a total of 14 exported symbols (8 for the CheckBox component plus 6 for the RadioButton component) added to its library.

Figure 12-8. The minimal example skinned by adding symbols to its library

Of course, you can also skin both the CheckBox and RadioButton components by applying any of the other skinning techniques explained in Chapter 9 (using the `initialize` undocumented clip event, using the prototype property, subclassing, etc.) and appearing in several other chapters whenever skinning more complex components.

It's now time to take a look at the (very few) mysteries of the CheckBox and RadioButton components.

Solved mysteries

Both the CheckBox and RadioButton components are very robust and easy to use, stylize, and skin. Because of this, there isn't much to discover or patch when using them in a component-based application.

However, the RadioButton component does have an associated class, the behavior of which is not completely documented: the RadioButtonGroup class.

Where to find the RadioButtonGroup instance

Every time that a RadioButton instance gets created, the component architecture looks at its groupName property (or parameter) to determine which radio group contains that instance. As we saw earlier, RadioButton instances are used for implementing mutually exclusive choices and grouped via the same value of their groupName property.

When the component architecture encounters a new value for the groupName property of a RadioButton instance, it automatically creates an instance of the RadioButtonGroup class whose instance name is the value of the groupName property. Furthermore, the RadioButtonGroup instance is created in the scope of the parent of the RadioButton instance.

As usual, building a practical example is helpful to fully grasp the importance of the functionality provided by the component architecture:

1. Open the minimal example stored in the Flash document `crbuttons01.fla` and save it as `crbuttons06.fla`.

2. Select the first and only frame on the document's timeline and add the following ActionScript lines to it:

```
radiobutton1.data = "Chris";
radiobutton2.data = "Julie";
radiobutton3.data = "Sam";

trace(radioGroup.selection);
radioGroup.selectedData = "Julie";
trace(radioGroup.selection);
```

3. Save the Flash document.

Lots of things are happening behind the scenes of the few lines of this example.

There are three RadioButton instances on stage (radiobutton1, radiobutton2, and radiobutton3). Their groupName property is assigned the value radioGroup via the groupName parameter in the authoring environment: that is what makes them related to each other, by belonging to the same radio group called radioGroup.

When the first RadioButton instance (radiobutton1) is created, the component architecture encounters the "radioGroup" name for the first time and therefore creates an instance of the RadioButtonGroup class with that name: radioGroup. This instance is created in the parent of the RadioButton instance, which is the _level0 object. The code in our example is attached to the first frame of the document and therefore in the scope of the _level0 object. That's why we can write a line like

```
trace(radioGroup.selection);
```

and find a radioGroup object in that scope. It is the component architecture that enables transparently creating such an object, which is an instance of the RadioButtonGroup class.

Knowing this, you can access two useful properties of the RadioButtonGroup class:

- selectedData: Returns the value of the data property of the currently selected RadioButton instance in the group. It can be assigned values of any data type as in the case of the data property. When assigned a value, it selects the RadioButton instance associated with that value.
- selection: Returns the object reference of the RadioButton instance currently selected. It can be assigned an object reference of a RadioButton instance in the group that becomes the currently selected instance.

The functionality of those properties may sound a bit obscure, but it is clarified and demonstrated by our example. In the first three lines of the example, we assign some data to each of the RadioButton instances on stage:

```
radiobutton1.data = "Chris";
radiobutton2.data = "Julie";
radiobutton3.data = "Sam";
```

We then verify the current value of the selection property of the RadioButtonGroup instance. The following trace will return an undefined value in the Output window of the authoring environment, since there is no RadioButton instance initially selected in our minimal example:

```
trace(radioGroup.selection);
```

Just after, we use the selectedData property of the RadioButtonGroup instance to select the second RadioButton instance (radiobutton2) programmatically by referring to the value of its data property:

```
radioGroup.selectedData = "Julie";
```

Finally, we check whether the selectedData property behaved as expected. Did our previous statement select the radiobutton2 instance? Of course, we can have a positive visual confirmation of it by looking at the initial state of the radiobutton2 instance in the movie, but we may also want to verify that the selection property of the RadioButtonGroup instance has been synchronized with the new state. The following trace will clarify all this:

```
trace(radioGroup.selection);
```

The same trace that was executed before now displays a different value in the same Output window of the authoring environment: _level0.radiobutton2. Yes, assigning a value to the selectedData property of the RadioButtonGroup instance sorted the expected result by selecting the radiobutton2 instance and also influencing the definition of the selection property of the same RadioButtonGroup instance.

With six lines of code, you tested and fully grasped what the component architecture does in the "mysterious" implementation of the RadioButtonGroup class, and you can reuse it to your advantage whenever needed.

Reasons for subclassing the CheckBox and the RadioButton components

The two components discussed in this chapter are among the simplest to use and the more robust in the component architecture. That reduces the number of reasons why you should consider subclassing them for your own purposes.

However, the possibility of packaging a set of skins and styles is still appealing whenever it comes to creating a theme or reusing those skins and styles in a large, distributed project.

By now, you know all the techniques and have all the information you need to create your own versions of the CheckBox and RadioButton components.

Chapter 13

THE LIST, COMBOBOX, AND DATAGRID COMPONENTS

List mx.controls.List
Frequency: Common
Complexity: Heavy
Stability: Robust
Maturity: Classic
Popularity: Widespread

ComboBox mx.controls.ComboBox
Frequency: Common
Complexity: Heavy
Stability: Robust
Maturity: Classic
Popularity: Widespread

DataGrid mx.controls.DataGrid
Frequency: Common
Complexity: Heavy
Stability: Robust
Maturity: Classic
Popularity: Widespread

This chapter is dedicated to discussing three rather complex components at once because of the very distinct similarities among them. Learning about these components at the same time can not only save you a lot of time, but also provide you with a better understanding of their logic design and proper utilization.

It is quite simple to explain the intimate relationships that bind these components: both the ComboBox and the DataGrid components are largely based upon the List component, although in different ways.

The ComboBox component aggregates an instance of the List component with an instance of the TextInput component to provide a sort of merged functionality. Both instances (the List and the TextInput) are subcomponents of the ComboBox component.

The DataGrid class is derived from the List class and, because of that, inherits all of its functionality and extends upon it to add a further dimension (columns) to the already existing one (rows).

Due to the relevance and "weight" of these components, this is certainly among the richest and largest chapters in the book. Nevertheless, its topics are structured following the pattern that we have consistently applied throughout Part 3 of this book. Our starting point will therefore be to build a minimal example implementing three instances, one for each component being examined in this chapter.

> The completed source code introduced in this chapter can be found in the package src13.zip, downloadable from this book's page at www.friendsofed.com.

Minimal example including the List, ComboBox, and DataGrid components

Let us build our minimal example by including an instance of each of the three components, to start comparing their functionality:

1. Create a new Flash document and save it as lists01.fla.
2. Open the Document Properties dialog box by selecting Modify ➤ Document and set its dimensions as 700×300 pixels.
3. Drag the List component on stage to create an instance of it and name it list1. Using the Info panel, define its position as (X: 462, Y: 66) and its dimensions as (W: 200, H: 200).
4. Drag the ComboBox component on stage to create one of its instances and name it combobox1. Using the Info panel, define its position as (X: 462, Y: 34) and its dimensions as (W: 200, H: 22).
5. Drag the DataGrid component on stage to create one of its instances and name it datagrid1. Using the Info panel, define its position as (X: 37, Y: 36) and its dimensions as (W: 400, H: 200).
6. Create an ActionScript file and save it as test.as. Add the following lines to it:

```
var colors = [
    {label: "White", data: 0xFFFFFF},
    {label: "Black", data: 0x000000},
    {label: "Red", data: 0xFF0000},
```

```
        {label: "Green", data: 0x00FF00},
        {label: "Blue", data: 0x0000FF}
    ];

    combobox1.dataProvider = colors;
    list1.dataProvider = colors;
    datagrid1.dataProvider = colors;
```

7. Select the first frame in the document and add the following ActionScript line to it:

```
    #include "test.as"
```

8. Save both the Flash document and the ActionScript file.

Testing the movie will show three instances, one for each of the three components being examined, each populated with the same data, as illustrated by Figure 13-1.

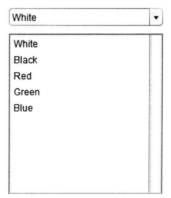

Figure 13-1. The minimal example

The dataProvider property, supported by all three components, plays a core role in feeding each component instance with data. In all the many examples in this chapter, we are going to feed the three instances with the same data using the same data object, as in the following:

```
    combobox1.dataProvider = colors;
    list1.dataProvider = colors;
    datagrid1.dataProvider = colors;
```

Of course, real-world applications usually provide different data to different component instances; however, by providing the same data in the examples displayed in this chapter, we have a better chance to analyze similarities and differences among the ComboBox, List, and DataGrid components. After all, to provide different data can be as easy as assigning different objects to the dataProvider property.

The dataProvider property accepts Array values or objects of any type supporting the **DataProvider API** (the purpose of which is to define an interface that allows you to manage an object interface in the same way as an Array instance).

Our minimal example defines the colors object, assigned to the dataProvider property of each component instance, as the array:

```
var colors = [
    {label: "White", data: 0xFFFFFF},
    {label: "Black", data: 0x000000},
    {label: "Red", data: 0xFF0000},
    {label: "Green", data: 0x00FF00},
    {label: "Blue", data: 0x0000FF}
];
```

The colors array contains five objects with a similar structure made of two properties: label and data. That is not a mere coincidence but an important requirement: the array in the example is assigned to a dataProvider property and, because of that, all of its elements must be objects of the same type (with the same properties). The {label, data} structure is a default that can and will be changed in most of the examples included in this chapter.

Regardless of the very few lines of ActionScript used in the minimal example, the final result shows us every essential aspect of the ComboBox, List, and DataGrid components' behavior. In particular, it provides a first glimpse about how they handle the dataProvider value.

The names of the properties of the objects in the colors array (label and data) have no special meaning for the DataGrid component, but they represent the default for an item of both the ComboBox and the List components.

The default behavior of the DataGrid instance is to display as many columns as the number of properties (two in our minimal example) and as many rows as the number of objects in the dataProvider array. It is part of its default behavior to include a header for each column with a text description that matches the name of each property (again, label and data in our example). Consider the following object with three properties:

```
{colorName: "Black", colorValue: 0x000000, colorSample:"Carbon"}
```

Assigning an array with objects of that type to the dataProvider property of the DataGrid instance would have resulted in a grid with three columns with headers of colorName, colorValue, and colorSample respectively, demonstrating that the DataGrid component can handle any object structure.

However, we utilized a {label, data} structure for our minimal example since that is the structure expected by both the ComboBox and the List components. Both components assume that there is a label property whose values are displayed in the rows of their lists (note that you must click the ComboBox instance's down arrow to see its list). The presence of a data property is also considered a default by both components when invoking their addItem method, as you will see later on.

So, we defined the structure of the objects in the colors array to be compatible with the defaults expected by both the List and ComboBox. Because of that, you are now able to compare how the same information is displayed by the three different component instances.

Now let us examine how XLEFF would generate a similar minimalist example.

XLEFF version

The following XML describes how to generate dynamically, via XLEFF, three instances that are similar to those in our minimal example:

```
<list x="550" y="200" width="200" height="200" name="list1" />
<combobox x="550" y="168" width="200" height="22" name="combobox1" />
<datagrid name="datagrid1" x="125" y="200" width="400" height="200" />
```

In real-world applications, you would probably populate these instances by assigning an object to their respective dataProvider properties via ActionScript.

However, XLEFF allows you to embed data in the XML description. In the case of the List instance, you can populate it as shown in the following example:

```
<list x="550" y="200" width="200" height="200" name="list1">
    <item label="Red">
        <value type="Number">0xFF0000</value>
    </item>
    <item label="Green">
        <value type="Number">0x00FF00</value>
    </item>
    <item label="Blue">
        <value type="Number">0x0000FF</value>
    </item>
    <item label="Black">
        <value type="Number">0x000000</value>
    </item>
</list>
```

Basically, you would include as many item elements as needed. Each item element would have a label attribute and include an additional element called value, like this:

```
<item label="Red">
    <value type="Number">0xFF0000</value>
</item>
```

Note that the value element may have a type attribute indicating the type of the value associated with each item. The String type is used if no type attribute is specified. The same itemized syntax would be used in the case of the ComboBox instance.

In the case of the DataGrid, the syntax is rather different to allow for its bidimensional nature. Implementing the colors array in XML requires something like this:

```
<datagrid name="datagrid1" x="125" y="200" width="400" height="200">
    <column name="ColorName" label="Color Name" width="190" />
    <column name="ColorValue" label="Color Value" width="193" />
    <row>
        <value>Red</value>
        <value type="Number">0xFF0000</value>
    </row>
```

```
<row>
    <value>Green</value>
    <value type="Number">0x00FF00</value>
</row>
<row>
    <value>Blue</value>
    <value type="Number">0x0000FF</value>
</row>
<row>
    <value>Black</value>
    <value type="Number">0x000000</value>
</row>
</datagrid>
```

As you can see, the datagrid element can contain two kinds of elements: column, dedicated to specifying the attributes of a column, and row, dedicated to including the data to be displayed in each row.

Via the column element, you can specify attributes such as the name of the column, the label to be displayed in its header, and its exact width.

The row element, unlike the item element that you saw earlier, can include more than one value element. In fact, it will include as many value elements as the number of columns. The syntax of the value element is the same as that used inside the item element.

You can find the XLEFF Sampler configured for generating the full XLEFF version of the current minimal example in the source files associated with this chapter.

Of course, there is much more to learn about these very structured components. Let us continue by building several richer examples.

Richer examples

The functionality provided by the List, ComboBox, and DataGrid components is very rich and, because of that, we will implement several richer examples, each of them focusing on a particular aspect of such functionality:

- The **Itemization** example will further analyze the differences between the structures of each component and the way they are related to DataProvider objects.

- The **Custom Label** example will demonstrate how to display processed values inside the List, ComboBox, and DataGrid components.

- The **Scrolling** example will examine how the scrolling behavior of each component can be defined programmatically.

- The **Sorting** example will delve into the issue of displaying the data inside a component instance in a specific, or even custom, order.

- The **Selection Management** example will show how to handle single and multiple selections of items within a component instance.
- The **Making It Editable** example will demonstrate how the ComboBox and DataGrid components can be used to interactively alter the data of a DataProvider object associated with a component instance.

Let us then start building the first of the richer examples.

Itemization

All of the three components examined in this chapter are influenced to some extent by the itemized structure defined for the List component and the similarly itemized structure of a DataProvider object.

A one-to-one relationship is established between each item in a list instance and each item in a DataProvider object, as displayed in Figure 13-2.

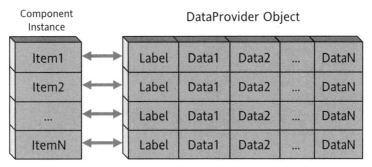

Figure 13-2. One-to-one relationship between list items and data items

Note that each data item is an object that can have one or more properties and, in the case of List and ComboBox instances, one of those properties plays a special role: the label.

Building a concrete example will better explain how the properties of data items are utilized by the List, ComboBox, and DataGrid instances:

1. Open the Flash document created earlier, named lists01.fla, and save it as lists03.fla in a new folder. Also copy the test.as file associated with the lists01.fla file in the new folder.

2. Open the copy of the test.as file that is in the current document's folder and replace the ActionScript lines there with the following:

```
function createItem(p1:String, p2:Number, p3:String):Object {
    return {A: p1, B: p2, C: p3};
}

var colors = [
    createItem("White", 0xFFFFFF, "Paper"),
    createItem("Black", 0xFFFFFF, "Carbon"),
    createItem("Red", 0xFF0000, "Rose"),
```

```
        createItem("Green", 0x00FF00, "Field"),
        createItem("Blue", 0x0000FF, "Sky")
    ];


    list1.labelField = "A";
    combobox1.labelField = "A";
    combobox1.dataProvider = colors;
    list1.dataProvider = colors;
    datagrid1.dataProvider = colors;

    colors.addItem(createItem("Yellow", 0xFFFF00, "Submarine"));
```

3. Save both the Flash document and the `test.as` file.

Figure 13-3 shows the result of testing our last example.

Figure 13-3. Instances in the Itemization example

We implemented a `createItem` function to populate the colors array. That gives us a bit more flexibility in defining the structure of objects inside the `DataProvider` object: you can easily change the name of one of the three properties that we defined for this example (A, B, and C):

```
    function createItem(p1:String, p2:Number, p3:String):Object {
        return {A: p1, B: p2, C: p3};
    }
```

The first evident result of having data items with three properties each is that the datagrid1 instance now shows three columns, one from each property (A, B, and C). The association of column to property can be easily recognized by looking at the name of the headers and to the values in each column. That is the default behavior of a DataGrid instance, and we did not have to add any code to achieve that apart, of course, from the line that assigns the colors array to the dataProvider property of the component instance:

```
datagrid1.dataProvider = colors;
```

A bit more work is required to reuse the same colors array in the case of the List and ComboBox instances. Unlike the minimal example that we implemented before, this time our data items do not have a label property, and, therefore, we must specify which of the available properties must be considered for that role. In both cases, we picked the A property and specified that it is indeed the property to be considered for the label role by using the labelField property of both the List and ComboBox instances:

```
list1.labelField = "A";
combobox1.labelField = "A";
```

The result of the previous two lines of code is that both list1 and combobox1 instances show the values of the A property in their list items.

We could have ended our example here, but with the last line we add to it, we further demonstrate the intimate relationship between the data items in a DataProvider object and the items in a component instance:

```
colors.addItem(createItem("Yellow", 0xFFFF00, "Submarine"));
```

With the previous line, we added an additional data item to the colors array, and that result is immediately reflected in all three instances of our example, as you can verify by testing the movie or looking back at Figure 13-3.

The role of the label can therefore be reassigned to a different property of a data item. But what if we want to display a processed value instead of the one available in the data item? In that case, we need to customize the label.

Custom labels

As you saw earlier, the default behavior of the DataGrid component is to render each value in the associated DataProvider object distributed in as many columns as the properties of the data items and as many rows as the data items themselves. The DataGrid component also reuses the name of those properties to define the text label of each column header.

You have also learned that both the List and the ComboBox components render only one of the properties in each data item: the label property or that of any other property that has been specifically assigned the "label" role.

What if you want to alter such default behavior and display some different text instead of the value of a specific property?

Our next example will demonstrate that you can take full control over the text displayed in each of the three components by using a very similar approach:

1. Open the Flash document created earlier, named lists03.fla, and save it as lists04.fla in a new folder. Also copy the test.as file associated with the lists03.fla file into the new folder.

2. Open the copy of the test.as file that is in the current document's folder and replace the ActionScript lines there with the following:

```
import mx.controls.gridclasses.DataGridColumn;

function createItem(p1:String, p2:String):Object {
    return {A: p1, B: p2};
}


var colors = [
    createItem("White", "Paper"),
    createItem("Black", "Carbon"),
    createItem("Red", "Rose"),
    createItem("Green", "Field"),
    createItem("Blue", "Sky")
];

function customLabelFunction(item:Object):String {
    if (item -- undefined) return undefined;
    return "The " + item.B + " is " + item.A;
}

combobox1.dataProvider = colors;
list1.dataProvider = colors;
datagrid1.dataProvider = colors;

list1.labelFunction = customLabelFunction;
combobox1.labelFunction = customLabelFunction;

var column = new DataGridColumn("C");
column.headerText = "Calculated";
column.labelFunction = customLabelFunction;
datagrid1.addColumn(column);
```

3. Save both the Flash document and the test.as file.

Figure 13-4 shows the result of testing our last example.

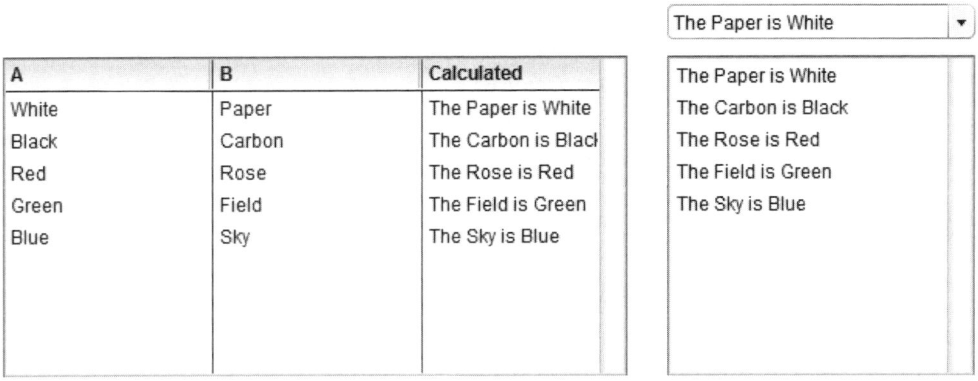

Figure 13-4. Customizing the text values displayed in the component instances

Similarly to the previous example, we still have a createItem function used to populate the colors array, but this time, each item as only two properties: A, associated to a color name, and B, associated to a real-world example of that color (such as "Sky" for "Blue"). We used this logic for producing a custom label function that returns a String combining the values of both properties of an item:

```
function customLabelFunction(item:Object):String {
    if (item == undefined) return undefined;
    return "The " + item.B + " is " + item.A;
}
```

It will be the component architecture that invokes such a function and passes the proper data item to it. All we have to do is to programmatically specify when this function, which we name customLabelFunction, must be used instead of the actual value of a data item's property.

In the case of the list1 and combobox1 instances, we do this by assigning the function to their labelFunction properties:

```
list1.labelFunction = customLabelFunction;
combobox1.labelFunction = customLabelFunction;
```

In the case of a DataGrid instance, the work to be done is just slightly more complicated, since we must specify which column will use the labelFunction. We exploit this necessity to also add columns dynamically while defining their calculated values:

```
var column = new DataGridColumn("C");
column.headerText = "Calculated";
column.labelFunction = customLabelFunction;
datagrid1.addColumn(column);
```

The datagrid1 instance starts with two columns only, one for each property in the data items (A and B). In the previous lines, we create a DataGridColumn object named C, utilized to add a third column to the datagrid1 instance via the addColumn method.

The DataGridColumn instance is also used to define the text that must appear in the column's header ("Calculated") and to specify the use of the previously implemented customLabelFunction to display content in the column's cells.

Of course, you could easily implement three different custom label functions, one for each component instance, once you have learned this technique. The overuse of the same function in our context aims to point out, once again, how highly compatible the functionality provided by the DataGrid, List, and ComboBox components is while emphasizing their differences.

The DataGridColumn class is used by the DataGrid class to implement columns on top of the List class implementation. Its location within the source of the component architecture is revealed by the import statement required to use it:

```
import mx.controls.gridclasses.DataGridColumn;
```

The getColumnAt method of the DataGrid component returns a DataGridColumn object associated to the specific column in the DataGrid instance. For instance, you may add the following lines in the context of our current example to modify the headers of the first two columns:

```
datagrid1.getColumnAt(0).headerText = "Column 1";
datagrid1.getColumnAt(1).headerText = "Column 2";
```

In the next section, you will learn how to define scroll policies to get rid of the scrollbar tracks that appear in our example even when they are not needed, since all the content is visible and there is nothing to scroll.

Scrolling

Looking back at the figures associated with our previous examples (Figures 13-1, 13-3, and 13-4), you may notice the unpleasant presence of an inactive vertical bar in the case of the list1 and datagrid1 instances.

Let us build an example that gets rid of those unnecessary vertical bars and at the same time illustrates how to handle the scroll policies of those components:

1. Open the Flash document created earlier, named lists04.fla, and save it as lists05.fla in a new folder. Also copy the test.as file associated with the lists04.fla file into the new folder.

2. Open the copy of the test.as file that is in the current document's folder and replace the ActionScript lines there with the following:

```
function createItem(p1:String, p2:String):Object {
    return {label: p1, data: p2};
}

var colors = [
    createItem("White", "Paper"),
    createItem("Black", "Carbon"),
    createItem("Red", "Rose"),
```

```
        createItem("Green", "Field"),
        createItem("Blue", "Sky")
];

combobox1.dataProvider = colors;
list1.dataProvider = colors;
datagrid1.dataProvider = colors;

datagrid1.hScrollPolicy = "off";
datagrid1.vScrollPolicy = "auto";
list1.vScrollPolicy = "auto";

combobox1.rowCount = colors.length;
list1.rowCount = colors.length;
datagrid1.rowCount = colors.length;
```

3. Save both the Flash document and the `test.as` file.

Figure 13-5 shows the result of testing our last example.

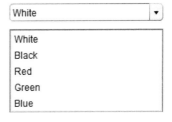

label	data
White	Paper
Black	Carbon
Red	Rose
Green	Field
Blue	Sky

Figure 13-5. Controlling the scrollbars in the component instances

You will notice that not only have the unnecessary vertical bars disappeared, but also both the data-grid1 and the list1 instances have had their heights redefined to accommodate the number of items in the colors array, resulting in a much cleaner and better balanced view.

Very few lines of code were enough to produce such results. A scrolling policy defines whether a scrollbar should appear or not. The component architecture defines three values for a scrolling policy:

- "off": Indicates that the scrollbar should not appear in any case
- "on": Indicates that the scrollbar should appear in any case
- "auto": Indicates that the scrollbar should appear if the content does not fit inside the visible area of a component instance

Such String values can be assigned to hScrollPolicy and vScrollPolicy, which define the horizontal and vertical scrolling policies of a component instance.

However, there are a few exceptions:

- The hScrollPolicy and vScrollPolicy properties do not apply to the case of the ComboBox component.

- In the case of the List component, the hScrollPolicy property does not support the "auto" option. Furthermore, if you set it to "on", the horizontal scrollbar will work only if you also define a value for the maxHPosition property, indicating the virtual width of the content area (how far the horizontal scrolling action can go).

- In the case of the DataGrid component, setting the hScrollPolicy property to "off" results in all the columns' widths being redefined in order to fit within the visible area of the component instance.

Knowing that, it should be clear what the following lines in our example do:

```
datagrid1.hScrollPolicy = "off";
datagrid1.vScrollPolicy = "auto";
list1.vScrollPolicy = "auto";
```

The first line disables the horizontal scrollbar in the datagrid1 instance by setting its horizontal policy to "off". As a result, the two columns are equally resized to fit within the visible area.

The second line sets the vertical policy of the datagrid1 instance to "auto"; this is enough to make the vertical bar disappear, as the content fits within the visible area of the component. The third line sets the vertical policy of the list1 instance to "auto", obtaining the same effect.

The example also uses the rowCount property, which is available for all of the three component instances:

```
combobox1.rowCount = colors.length;
list1.rowCount = colors.length;
datagrid1.rowCount = colors.length;
```

The rowCount property is very useful because it automatically redefines the height of a component instance so that its visible area can display an exact number of rows. In our example, we decide to display as many rows as the items in the DataProvider object (colors). The combination of setting the vScrollPolicy property to "auto" and displaying as many rows as the items in the DataProvider object causes the disappearance of the vertical unnecessary scrollbars in both the list1 and datagrid1 instances.

In the case of the combobox1 instance, the rowCount property affects the drop-down list that appears when you click its down arrow. If you test it, you will notice that the drop-down list does indeed show all of the data items and, consequentially, does not show any vertical scrollbar.

Next we will examine what sorting options are offered by the component architecture to arrange the data items, and their visual counterparts, following a specific order.

Sorting

Not surprisingly, considering the strict relationship between items of a component instance and data items, whenever you need to sort the former, you eventually end up sorting, directly or indirectly, the latter in its associated DataProvider object.

You could experiment with sorting by adding a single line to the previous example:

```
datagrid1.sortItemsBy("data", "DESC");
```

The previous line invokes the sortItemsBy method to sort the items by arranging the values of the data column (and its related data item's property) in descending order. You could use ASC instead of DESC to sort them in ascending order.

Figure 13-6 shows the resulting view after adding this line to the previous example.

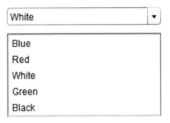

Figure 13-6. Items sorted via sortItemsBy

Notice that all three component instances now reflect the same sort order since they all share the same DataProvider object. Although the values of the data property are not visible in the combobox1 and list1 instances, the values of the label property are sorted accordingly to match the order defined for the data property.

Basically, the values of the label property are presented in the following order: "Blue", "Red", "White", "Green", and "Black" to reflect the descending order of the values of the data property: "**S**ky", "**R**ose", "**P**aper", "**F**ield", and "**C**arbon", set programmatically by executing the sortItemsBy method.

Note that the sortItemsBy method is also available for both the combobox1 and list1 instance; therefore, using one of the next two lines would have caused the same result as the line we saw previously:

```
list1.sortItemsBy("data", "DESC");
```

or

```
combobox1.sortItemsBy("data", "DESC");
```

In the case of the DataGrid component, you do not even need to invoke the sortItemsBy method to sort its items in ascending or descending order, since the component default behavior does it for you. Clicking a column header sorts the items by applying alternatively an ascending/descending order to the values in that column. A small iconic arrow on the right side of the column header indicates whether the current sort order is ascending (arrow up) or descending (arrow down). You can exclude such default behavior for all columns by setting the sortableColumns property of a DataGrid instance to false. Alternatively, you can disable that option for specific columns only by setting the sortOnHeaderRelease property of a DataGridColumn instance to false.

Things get more complicated if you want to implement a fully custom sort order that is defined from more than one property at the same time. The component architecture allows you to do it, but we need to build an example to properly examine how it can be achieved:

1. Open the Flash document created earlier, named lists05.fla, and save it as lists06.fla in a new folder. Also copy the test.as file associated with the lists05.fla file into the new folder.

2. Open the copy of the test.as file that is in the current document's folder and replace the ActionScript lines there with the following:

```
function createItem(p1:String, p2:String):Object {
    return {lastName: p1, firstName: p2};
}

function customSort(item1:Object, item2:Object):Number {
    if (item1.lastName < item2.lastName) {
        return -1;
    } else if (item1.lastName > item2.lastName) {
        return 1;
    } else {
        if (item1.firstName < item2.firstName) {
            return -1;
        } else if (item1.firstName > item2.firstName) {
            return 1;
        } else {
            return 0;
        }
    }
}

var characters = [
    createItem("Kavula", "Humma"),
    createItem("Beeblebrox", "Zaphod"),
    createItem("Beeblebrox", "Bob"),
    createItem("Beeblebrox", "Konrad")
];

combobox1.dataProvider = characters;
list1.dataProvider = characters;
datagrid1.dataProvider = characters;
```

```
combobox1.labelField = "firstName";
list1.labelField = "firstName";

datagrid1.hScrollPolicy = "off";
datagrid1.vScrollPolicy = "auto";
list1.vScrollPolicy = "auto";

combobox1.rowCount = characters.length;
list1.rowCount = characters.length;
datagrid1.rowCount = characters.length;

function headerRelease(eventObject:Object):Void {
    var sortOrder:String = eventObject.target.sortDirection;
    var sortOptions:Number = 0;

    if (sortOrder.toUpperCase() == 'DESC') {
        sortOptions |= Array.DESCENDING;
    }
    characters.sortItems(customSort, sortOptions);
}
datagrid1.addEventListener("headerRelease", this);

characters.sortItems(customSort, Array.ASCENDING);
```

3. Save both the Flash document and the `test.as` file.

The increased number of ActionScript lines underscores how defining a sorting order that depends on more than one property at the same time can raise the level of complexity of our implementation. However, you may well have to satisfy a similar requirement and, therefore, this technique is worth a thorough examination.

We replaced the colors `DataProvider` object in our previous example with a characters one:

```
var characters = [
    createItem("Kavula", "Humma"),
    createItem("Beeblebrox", "Zaphod"),
    createItem("Beeblebrox", "Bob"),
    createItem("Beeblebrox", "Konrad")
];
```

Each item now has two properties (`lastName` and `firstName`) that are intended to be the last and first name of a character. This scenario is required to build a custom sorting function that establishes a somewhat logical relationship in its custom sorting process: items will be sorted by the `lastName` values at first and then, when those values are identical, by the `firstName` values. That is what the `customSort` function does:

```
function customSort(item1:Object, item2:Object):Number {
    if (item1.lastName < item2.lastName) {
        return -1;
    } else if (item1.lastName > item2.lastName) {
```

```
                return 1;
        } else {
            if (item1.firstName < item2.firstName) {
                return -1;
            } else if (item1.firstName > item2.firstName) {
                return 1;
            } else {
                return 0;
            }
        }
    }
```

Note that it will be the component architecture to pass two items at a time to the customSort function for comparison. The customSort function will return a number indicating

- Whether the first item is smaller than the second item (by returning –1)
- Whether the first item is greater than the second item (by returning 1)
- Whether the two items are identical (by returning 0)

Installing the customSort function in the datagrid1 instance is a matter of its own. We want the DataGrid items to be ordered following our custom order whenever the user clicks a column header. To do this, the _level0 object listens to the headerRelease event of the DataGrid component.

```
        datagrid1.addEventListener("headerRelease", this);
```

When the user clicks a column header, an headerRelease event is triggered by the component instance and the following handler is executed:

```
        function headerRelease(eventObject:Object):Void {
            var sortOrder:String = eventObject.target.sortDirection;
            var sortOptions:Number = 0;

            if (sortOrder.toUpperCase() == 'DESC') {
                sortOptions |= Array.DESCENDING;
            }
            characters.sortItems(customSort, sortOptions);
        }
```

All the headerRelease handler does is to run a sortItems method on the characters DataProvider object using our custom sorting function (customSort) and the appropriate sort order option that is being alternated by the component architecture ("ASC" and "DESC").

Unlike the sortItemsBy method, the sortItems method allows us to specify a custom sorting function that can redefine the order of the data items following any sort of rule and, therefore, even establish a relationship among different properties, as in the case of our example.

Since the sortItems method expects the options to be defined in terms of the Array class constants, a minimal translation must be applied to the value returned by the component architecture to match the proper Array constant:

```
if (sortOrder.toUpperCase() == 'DESC') {
    sortOptions |= Array.DESCENDING;
}
```

The final touch in our script is to define the initial sort order of the data items as Ascending:

```
characters.sortItems(customSort, Array.ASCENDING);
```

That is why, initially, testing the movie will display something like what you see in Figure 13-7.

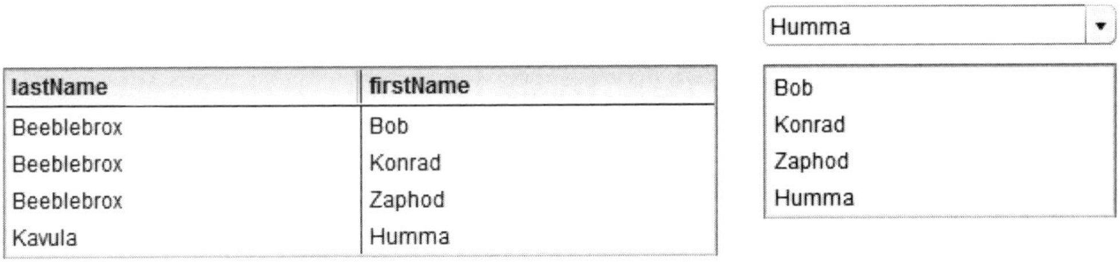

lastName	firstName
Beeblebrox	Bob
Beeblebrox	Konrad
Beeblebrox	Zaphod
Kavula	Humma

Humma

Bob
Konrad
Zaphod
Humma

Figure 13-7. Specifying a custom sort order that is defined from more than one field

Figure 13-7 shows that there are three Beeblebrox items before the fourth Kavula item since our custom function first looks at the values of the firstName property. However, the three Beeblebrox items are sorted accordingly to the values of the lastName property, as you can verify by looking at the order defined for Bob, Konrad, and Zaphod.

If you keep clicking a column header, you will apply the customSort function to the data items by alternating the ascending and descending options.

Whatever the data model associated with your application, you can now build any kind of custom sorting function and apply it to a component instance automatically or programmatically.

Let us now consider how the user can select items in the component instances and how you can retrieve or set a particular selection.

Selection management

The main choice when it comes to defining the selection options of a list-based component is between single and multiple selections. In the first case, only one item can be selected at any time: clicking one item will select it only after deselecting the previously selected one.

Setting the multipleSelection property to true enables multiple selections in the case of the DataGrid and List components. When multiple selections are enabled, the user can add further items to the currently selected ones by clicking them while keeping the *CTRL* key pressed.

Multiple selections are not supported by the ComboBox component, where only one item can be selected at any time and displayed in its TextInput subcomponent.

The following example will show how multiple selections can be set and retrieved programmatically and several other aspects related to the management of the selected item(s) of a component instance:

1. Open the Flash document created earlier, named `lists06.fla`, and save it as `lists07.fla` in a new folder. Also copy the `test.as` file associated with the `lists06.fla` file into the new folder.

2. Open the copy of the `test.as` file that is in the current document's folder and replace the ActionScript lines there with the following:

```
function createItem(p1:String, p2:String):Object {
    return {A: p1, data: p2};
}

function change(eventObject:Object):Void {
    var eventSource = eventObject.target;
    switch (eventSource._name) {
        case "datagrid1":
            trace(eventSource._name + " changed selection.");
            break;
        case "list1":
            trace(eventSource._name + " changed selection.");
            break;
        case "combobox1":
            trace(eventSource._name + " changed selection.");
            break;
    }
}

var colors = [
    createItem("White", "Paper"),
    createItem("Black", "Carbon"),
    createItem("Red", "Rose"),
    createItem("Green", "Field"),
    createItem("Blue", "Sky")
];

combobox1.dataProvider = colors;
list1.dataProvider = colors;
datagrid1.dataProvider = colors;

datagrid1.hScrollPolicy = "off";
datagrid1.vScrollPolicy = "auto";
list1.vScrollPolicy = "auto";
```

```
var selected = [0,2,4];

datagrid1.multipleSelection = true;
datagrid1.selectedIndices = selected;

list1.multipleSelection = true;
list1.selectedIndices = selected;

combobox1.selectedIndex = 2;

datagrid1.addEventListener("change", this);
list1.addEventListener("change", this);
combobox1.addEventListener("change", this);
```

3. Save both the Flash document and the test.as file.

Setting the multipleSelection property to true for both the datagrid1 and list1 instances enables multiple selections that you can also try manually by using the *CTRL*/*CMD* or *SHIFT* keys as usual, while the combobox1 instance shows how single selection is handled (and how it would be handled by the other two instances if their multipleSelection property was set to false).

In the case of single selection, the selectedIndex property can be used to set/retrieve the index of the currently selected item, like in the following:

```
combobox1.selectedIndex = 2;
```

In the case of multiple selections, the selectedIndices property is an array of numbers, each of which is the index of a selected item. The selectedIndices property can be both set and retrieved. In our example, we define a selected variable that later on we assign to the selectedIndices property of both the datagrid1 and list1 instances:

```
var selected = [0,2,4];

datagrid1.multipleSelection = true;
datagrid1.selectedIndices = selected;

list1.multipleSelection = true;
list1.selectedIndices = selected;
```

The selections that we define programmatically are displayed when you first run the example. Figure 13-8 shows that the same three items are selected in both the datagrid1 and list1 instances (indexes = 0, 2, and 4), while the combobox1 instance has the third item selected (index = 2).

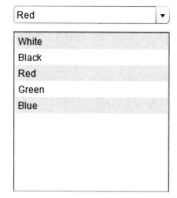

label	data
White	Paper
Black	Carbon
Red	Rose
Green	Field
Blue	Sky

Figure 13-8. Single and multiple selections

Our example also includes a change event handler function that is used to intercept a change in the selection of a component instance following the user interaction:

```
function change(eventObject:Object):Void {
    var eventSource = eventObject.target;
    switch (eventSource._name) {
        case "datagrid1":
            trace(eventSource._name + " changed selection.");
            break;
        case "list1":
            trace(eventSource._name + " changed selection.");
            break;
        case "combobox1":
            trace(eventSource._name + " changed selection.");
            break;
    }
}
```

Our change event handler does nothing more than publish the instance name of the object that triggered the even but, of course, in a real-world application you would look at its selected (or selectedIndices) property to know what is the newly selected item(s).

All of the three component instances support the change event and, in fact, we register the _level0 object as a listener of that event when triggered by any of them:

```
datagrid1.addEventListener("change", this);
list1.addEventListener("change", this);
combobox1.addEventListener("change", this);
```

We are close to completing the tour of the functionality provided by list-based components. The only aspect missing is how to make those instances interactively editable.

Making it editable

Rather oddly, List component instances do not support editing, while you can edit the contents of both of List's derivatives, the DataGrid and the ComboBox components, by setting their editable property to true.

Let us quickly build an example that shows not just how to make the datagrid1 and combobox1 instances editable, but also what the side effects are of this additional functionality:

1. Open the Flash document created earlier, named lists07.fla, and save it as lists08.fla in a new folder. Also copy the test.as file associated with the lists07.fla file into the new folder.

2. Open the copy of the test.as file that is in the current document's folder and replace the ActionScript lines there with the following:

```
function createItem(p1:String, p2:String):Object {
    return {label: p1, data: p2};
}

function enter(eventObject:Object):Void {
    var eventSource = eventObject.target;
    if (eventSource._name == "combobox1") {
            eventSource.addItem(eventSource.text, "A " +
                                eventSource.text + " Object");
            eventSource.text = "";
    }
}

var colors = [
    createItem("White", "Paper"),
    createItem("Black", "Carbon"),
    createItem("Red", "Rose"),
    createItem("Green", "Field"),
    createItem("Blue", "Sky")
];

combobox1.dataProvider = colors;
list1.dataProvider = colors;
datagrid1.dataProvider = colors;

datagrid1.hScrollPolicy = "off";
datagrid1.vScrollPolicy = "auto";
list1.vScrollPolicy = "auto";

datagrid1.editable = true;
combobox1.editable = true;

combobox1.addEventListener("enter", this);
```

3. Save both the Flash document and the test.as file.

To make the datagrid1 and combobox1 instances editable requires very little coding:

```
datagrid1.editable = true;
combobox1.editable = true;
```

The reason why our last example is still interesting lies in the possibility that it allows us to experiment with the new editable state of both component instances.

In the case of the combobox1 instance, becoming editable means that the TextInput subcomponent is initially empty, and you can actually add text to it, as in the case illustrated by Figure 13-9 that shows how the example would look if you select the combobox1 instance and start entering the Yellow text value in its TextInput subcomponent.

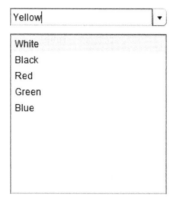

Figure 13-9. Adding text to a ComboBox instance

However, how do we store that "Yellow" text in the DataProvider object? It is your responsibility to implement what must be done with the text being edited in a ComboBox instance. In our example, we handle the enter event in order to add such text to the DataProvider object defined in our example. Once again, the _level0 object is registered as the event listener:

```
combobox1.addEventListener("enter", this);
```

And what its enter event handler does is to add an item to the DataProvider object via the addItem method and then clean the TextInput subcomponent of the combobox1 instance via its text property:

```
function enter(eventObject:Object):Void {
    var eventSource = eventObject.target;
    if (eventSource._name == "combobox1") {
        eventSource.addItem(eventSource.text, "A " +
                            eventSource.text + " Object");
        eventSource.text = "";
    }
}
```

Figure 13-10 shows how all of the three instances are updated if you press the *ENTER* key after adding the "Yellow" text to the combobox1 instance.

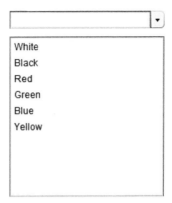

label	data
White	Paper
Black	Carbon
Red	Rose
Green	Field
Blue	Sky
Yellow	A Yellow Object

White
Black
Red
Green
Blue
Yellow

Figure 13-10. The "Yellow" item after being added interactively to the DataProvider object

Since the colors DataProvider object was shared by all of the three component instances, they have all been synchronously updated after the "Yellow" item was added to the DataProvider object.

That completes the analysis of the code in our last example. However, there is still a default behavior of the DataGrid component that you may find interesting to verify that does not require any additional lines of code; such behavior is a side effect of the following line:

```
datagrid1.editable = true;
```

DataGrid instances that can be edited allow you to select their cells and edit their content one by one. The DataProvider object will be automatically updated following your actions. Try it by selecting the cell containing the "Red" text and changing it into "Reds". As soon as you press the *ENTER* key, the DataProvider object will be updated with the new value and, once again, the "Reds" value will show in all of the three component instances since they share the same DataProvider object.

We have completed a tour of the functionality provided by the list-based components. By examining them together, you have quickly learned their many similarities and few differences, and this will certainly help you in using them proficiently in your projects.

We can now look at how to customize the appearance of those components via styles, skins, and more.

Supported styles

Our distinction between common and specific styles makes even more sense in this chapter since the common styles are jointly supported by the three components that we are examining, while the specific styles will usually be dealt with separately.

Let us build an example that customizes the appearance of our minimal example and then analyze what common and specific styles are redefined in it:

1. Open the Flash document created earlier, named `lists08.fla`, and save it as `lists09.fla` in a new folder. Also copy the `test.as` file associated with the `lists08.fla` file in the new folder.

2. Open the copy of the `test.as` file that is in the current document's folder and replace the ActionScript lines there with the following:

```
function createItem(p1:String, p2:String):Object {
    return {label: p1, data: p2};
}

function setCommonStyles(instance) {
    instance.setStyle("backgroundColor", 0xFFFFCC);
    instance.setStyle("color", 0x0000FF);
    instance.setStyle("rollOverColor", 0xAAFFFF);
    instance.setStyle("selectionColor", 0xAADDFF);
}

function setDataGridStyles(instance) {
    instance.getColumnAt(1).setStyle("backgroundColor", 0xFFCCFF);
    instance.setStyle("headerColor", 0xAAFFFF);
    instance.setStyle("vGridLines", true);
    instance.setStyle("hGridLines", true);
    instance.setStyle("vGridLineColor", "haloOrange");
    instance.setStyle("hGridLineColor", "haloOrange");
}

function setComboBoxStyles(instance) {
    instance.setStyle("defaultIcon", "Icon1");
}

function setListStyles(instance) {
    instance.setStyle("defaultIcon", "Icon1");
    instance.setStyle("alternatingRowColors", [0xFFFFCC, 0xFFCCFF]);
}

var colors = [
    createItem("White", "Paper"),
    createItem("Black", "Carbon"),
    createItem("Red", "Rose"),
    createItem("Green", "Field"),
    createItem("Blue", "Sky")
];

combobox1.dataProvider = colors;
list1.dataProvider = colors;
datagrid1.dataProvider = colors;
```

```
datagrid1.hScrollPolicy = "off";
datagrid1.vScrollPolicy = "auto";
list1.vScrollPolicy = "auto";

setCommonStyles(datagrid1);
setCommonStyles(list1);
setCommonStyles(combobox1);

setDataGridStyles(datagrid1);
setComboBoxStyles(combobox1);
setListStyles(list1);
```

3. Create a new movie clip symbol by selecting Insert ➤ New Symbol. Define both its name and its linkage identifier as Icon1.

4. Edit the Icon1 symbol and draw a rectangle shape in it. Note that the stroke should be set to 4 pixels in order to have a shape looking like the one shown in Figure 13-11. Define the size of the shape as (W: 8, H: 8) and its position as (X: 2, Y: 2). Alternatively, you can cut and paste the shape that you find in the lists09.fla source file associated with this section.

5. Save both the Flash document and the test.as file.

Figure 13-11 shows how this example looks after you test the movie.

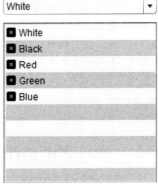

Figure 13-11. Stylized component instances

Our last example is essentially based on four functions:

- setCommonStyles: Applied to all of the three component instances, since it defines some of the styles that are common to all of them

- setListStyles: Applied to the list1 instance only, since it defines some of the styles that are specific to the List component

- setComboBoxStyles: Applied to the combobox1 instance only, since it defines some of the styles that are specific to the ComboBox component

- setDataGridStyles: Applied to the datagrid1 instance only, since it defines some of the styles that are specific to the DataGrid component

335

Each of these functions has a clear purpose, and you can easily modify any of them to try different styles once we have examined all the common and specific styles in the next sections of this chapter.

Common styles

The common styles include text and font styles (embedFonts, fontFamily, fontSize, fontStyle, fontWeight, textAlign, textIndent, and textDecoration) that will be discussed in Chapter 18.

Similarly, some of the color styles (color, backgroundColor, themeColor, and backgroundDisabled➡ Color) present the same consistent behavior that they have for every other component in the architecture.

However, in this section we are also going to consider a few other styles that are shared by the List, ComboBox, and DataGrid components (but not usually found in other components) as common styles:

- rollOverColor: This style defines the color of the highlighted bar that appears on an item when the mouse rolls over it.
- selectionColor: This style defines the color of the highlighted bar of a selected item.
- repeatDelay: Set to 500 by default, this is a number indicating how many milliseconds the component instance will wait while the user is pressing the button of the scrollbar subcomponent before repeating the scrolling action.
- repeatInterval: Set to 35 by default, this is a number indicating how many milliseconds separate a scrolling move when the component instance scroll is repeated automatically.

The setCommonStyles function in our previous example defines only four of the common styles, but you can, of course, add further setStyle calls to try any other style and/or change the values of the existing ones to experiment with different appearances.

The border styles are also among the common styles of the three components considered in this chapter. They are implemented via the RectBorder class that we examined in Chapter 11.

DataGrid-specific styles

In the case of the DataGrid component, you can also set the backgroundColor style of each DataGrid➡ Column instance as we do in the setDataGridStyles function in the following line:

```
instance.getColumnAt(1).setStyle("backgroundColor", 0xFFCCFF);
```

Apart from that, the DataGrid component also supports a few styles that are specific to its own instances:

- headerColor: Defines the background color of the column headers
- headerStyle: A style property that accepts a CCSStyleDeclaration object and applies its CSS definitions to the column headers

- vGridLines: A Boolean that, if true, displays vertical gridlines in the content area of the DataGrid instance
- hGridLines: A Boolean that, if true, displays horizontal gridlines in the content area of the DataGrid instance
- vGridLineColor: A color value defining the color of the vertical gridlines if displayed
- hGridLineColor: A color value defining the color of the vertical gridlines if displayed

The setDataGridStyles function in our examples set every specific style but the headerStyle.

List-specific styles

The List class supports only two specific styles that are both defined in the setListStyles function of our example:

- defaultIcon: The value is a linkage identifier of an exported symbol that can be used as an icon added to every row in the List instance.
- alternatingRowColors: The value is an array with at least two colors that replace the background color for the rows and are used cyclically for all the rows in the List instance.

The setListStyles function in our example defines both the defaultIcon and the alternating➥ RowColors styles as follows:

```
instance.setStyle("defaultIcon", "Icon1");
instance.setStyle("alternatingRowColors", [0xFFFFCC, 0xFFCCFF]);
```

ComboBox-specific styles

The ComboBox component supports the defaultIcon style similarly to the List component. The defaultIcon style is the only style set by the setComboBoxStyles function of our example, although the ComboBox component also supports two more specific styles for influencing speed and acceleration of its animation:

- openDuration: A number, 250 by default, defining the duration in milliseconds of the animation displayed when the List subcomponent of a ComboBox instance appears or disappears following the user action.
- openEasing: Influences the accelerations in the animation displayed when the List subcomponent of a ComboBox instance appears or disappears following the user action. See Appendix B for a list of the easing methods that can be assigned to this style property.

The setComboBoxStyles function in our example only defines the defaultIcon style, leaving the animation speed and accelerations to their default values.

Skinnability

This section, dedicated to skinning the List, ComboBox, and DataGrid components, is much shorter than you would expect for a variety of reasons:

- The components' infrastructures are mostly made of borders and scrollbars, the skinning techniques of which are described in other chapters.

- Borders depend on a purely coded skin implemented by the RectBorder class, which is examined in Chapter 11.

- The scrollbars subcomponent can be skinned, and the related technique is explained in Chapter 21.

- What you may really wish to "skin" is the items in the List and the ComboBox components or the cells of the DataGrid component. Those areas can be fully customized, but the process is dissimilar from skinning, and it is usually referred as **cell rendering**. Cell rendering is explained in the "Solved Mysteries" section of this chapter.

What is left in this section, then, is skinning the only bit of the ComboBox component that does not belong to any of the previously considered cases: its drop-down button. This is the goal of our next example:

1. Open the Flash document created earlier, named `lists09.fla`, and save it as `lists10.fla` in a new folder. Also copy the `test.as` file associated with the `lists09.fla` file into the new folder.

2. Open the copy of the `test.as` file that is in the current document's folder and replace the ActionScript lines there with the following:

```
function createItem(p1:String, p2:String):Object {
    return {label: p1, data: p2};
}

var colors = [
    createItem("White", "Paper"),
    createItem("Black", "Carbon"),
    createItem("Red", "Rose"),
    createItem("Green", "Field"),
    createItem("Blue", "Sky")
];

combobox1.dataProvider = colors;
list1.dataProvider = colors;
datagrid1.dataProvider = colors;

datagrid1.hScrollPolicy = "off";
datagrid1.vScrollPolicy = "auto";
list1.vScrollPolicy = "auto";
```

3. Create a new movie clip symbol by selecting Insert ➤ New Symbol. Define both its name and its linkage identifier as `ComboDownArrowUp`.

4. Edit the `ComboDownArrowUp` symbol and draw a shape in it. The shape's dimension should be approximately 14✕22 pixels, and its position should be set as (X: 0, Y: 0). Alternatively, you can reuse the graphics of the symbol included in the `lists10.fla` source file associated with this section.

5. Repeat steps 3 and 4 three times in order to create three more symbols: `ComboDownArrowOver`, `ComboDownArrowDown`, and `ComboDownArrowDisabled`. The purpose of the four symbols that you create is to visually represent the four states of the drop-down button of a ComboBox instance (up, over, down, and disabled). Therefore, each of its skins should have a different but consistent look to visually represent each state in a proper way. Once again, you can reuse the graphic assets included in the `lists10.fla` source file associated with this section.

6. Save both the Flash document and the `test.as` file.

Figure 13-12 shows the detail of the appearance of the ComboBox instance in this example, after you test the movie.

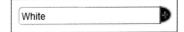

Figure 13-12. Skinning the drop-down button of a ComboBox instance

Skinning the ComboBox instance in our example only requires adding four exported symbols to its library with the proper linkage identifiers (ComboDownArrowUp, ComboDownArrowOver, ComboDown➡ ArrowDown, and ComboDownArrowDisabled). Figure 13-13 shows the skins in the library of the Flash document created for our example.

Name	Kind	Use Count	Linkage
ComboBox	Compiled Clip	-	Export: ComboBox
ComboBox Skins	Folder		
ComboDownArrowDisabled	Movie Clip	-	Export: ComboDownArrowDisabled
ComboDownArrowDown	Movie Clip	-	Export: ComboDownArrowDown
ComboDownArrowOver	Movie Clip	-	Export: ComboDownArrowOver
ComboDownArrowUp	Movie Clip	-	Export: ComboDownArrowUp
Graphic	Folder		

Figure 13-13. The ComboBox skins in the document's library

The next section will thoroughly examine the cell-rendering process that gives you much more control when it comes to customizing the appearance and behavior of the components examined in this chapter.

Solved mysteries

List-based components have a major "mystery" to solve: the cell-rendering process.

Cell rendering

Cell rendering is a term associated with the visual representation of a data item inside a partial area of a visual component, referred to as a **cell** due to the replicated presence of its structure within the visual component. Every cell has a data item associated with it and, since all of the data items are supposed to have the same properties, all you need to implement is a specific **cell renderer** for that kind of data item. Such a cell renderer is typically reused to render several cells inside a component instance.

In the case of the List and the ComboBox component, a cell is represented by a whole row, while in the case of the DataGrid component, a cell is identified as the content area lying in the intersection between a column and a row.

Figure 13-14 visually clarifies the role of cells in the cases of the List and the DataGrid components. The cells of the ComboBox component are identical to the List case, since they are implemented by its List subcomponent.

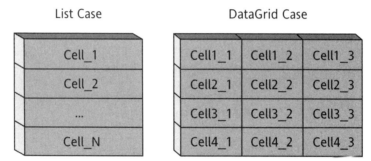

Figure 13-14. Cells in the List and the DataGrid cases

The component architecture implements a so-called Cell Renderer API that all cell renderers should be compliant with. However, at the moment of writing, putting such an API to work in your projects is a matter of interpretation and involves several undocumented issues. That is the main reason why the cell rendering process is included in this section of the chapter.

Here you will find a complete example that deals with every essential aspect of the cell rendering process and that you can customize to build your specific cell renderers.

Once again, we follow our concrete approach and build the example before looking into the functional requirements of a cell renderer and how it works:

1. Create a new Flash document and save it as `lists11.fla`.

2. Open the Document Properties dialog box by selecting Modify ➤ Document and set its dimensions as 700×300 pixels.

3. Drag the List component on stage to create one of its instances and name it list1. Using the Info panel, define its position as (X: 462, Y: 66) and its dimensions as (W: 200, H: 200).

4. Drag the DataGrid component on stage to create one of its instances and name it datagrid1. Using the Info panel, define its position as (X: 37, Y: 66) and its dimensions as (W: 400, H: 124).

5. Create an ActionScript file and save it as `test.as`. Add the following lines to it:

```
var colors = [
    {symbolBaseName: "White", colorValue: 0xFFFFFF},
    {symbolBaseName: "Black", colorValue: 0x000000},
    {symbolBaseName: "Red", colorValue: 0xFF0000},
    {symbolBaseName: "Green", colorValue: 0x00FF00},
    {symbolBaseName: "Blue", colorValue: 0x0000FF}
];

list1.dataProvider = colors;
datagrid1.dataProvider = colors;

datagrid1.vScrollPolicy = "auto";
list1.vScrollPolicy = "auto";

list1.rowCount = list1.length;
list1.cellRenderer = "CustomCellRenderer";

datagrid1.getColumnAt(1).width = 196;
datagrid1.getColumnAt(1).resizable = false;
datagrid1.getColumnAt(1).cellRenderer = "CustomCellRenderer";
```

6. Select the first frame in the document and add the following ActionScript line to it:

```
#include "test.as"
```

7. Create an ActionScript file and save it as `CustomCellRenderer.as`. Add the following lines to it:

```
import mx.core.UIComponent;
import mx.controls.List;

class CustomCellRenderer extends UIComponent {

    // unused by this cell renderer
    private var listOwner:List;
    private var owner:MovieClip;
    private var getCellIndex:Function;
    private var getDataLabel:Function;

    // specific to this cell renderer
    private var customSymbol_mc:MovieClip;

    function CustomCellRenderer() {}

    // it must do something if your cell can be resizable
    function size(): Void {}
```

```
    public function getPreferredWidth():Number {
        return 196;
    }

    public function getPreferredHeight():Number {
        return 20;
    }

    public function setValue(label:String, item:Object,
                            state:String):Void {
        switch (state) {
            case "normal":
                attachMovie(item.symbolBaseName,
➡ "customSymbol_mc", 1);
                break;
            case "highlighted":
                attachMovie(item.symbolBaseName + "Over",
                            "customSymbol_mc", 1);
                break;
            case "selected":
                attachMovie(item.symbolBaseName + "Selected",
                            "customSymbol_mc", 1);
                break;
        }
    }
}
```

8. Go back to the Flash document and create a new movie clip symbol by selecting Insert ➤ New Symbol. Define its name, its linkage identifier, and the name of its AS 2.0 Class as CustomCellRenderer.

9. You must now create 15 movie clips as exported symbols or import them from the completed source file associated with this chapter. The name of each symbol is the same as its linkage identifier. The linkage identifiers are Black, BlackOver, BlackSelected, Blue, BlueOver, BlueSelected, Green, GreenOver, GreenSelected, Red, RedOver, RedSelected, White, WhiteOver, and WhiteSelected. Each symbol must contain a bitmapped graphic (or a shape) of 196×20 pixels positioned at (X: 0, Y: 0). If you want to achieve the exact look shown in Figure 13-15, you must import the symbols from the completed source file associated with this chapter by opening it as an external library (File ➤ Import ➤ Open External Library) and dragging those symbols into the library of your Flash document.

10. Save the Flash document, the `test.as` file, and the `CustomCellRenderer.as` file.

Figure 13-15 shows the colorful result of testing our cell-rendering example. Rolling over the custom rendered cells or even selecting some will give you complete visual feedback of the implemented rendition.

symbolBaseName	colorValue
White	
Black	
Red	
Green	
Blue	

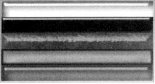

Figure 13-15. Outcome of a custom cell renderer

Of course, there is plenty to analyze in the last example. First of all, notice that we reused the same custom cell renderer for both the datagrid1 and list1 instances regardless of the different structures of a DataGrid and a List component. This shows the high flexibility of the cell rendering process whenever implemented properly.

The custom cell renderer was installed in both component instances via the cellRenderer property as in the following lines included in the test.as file:

```
list1.cellRenderer = "CustomCellRenderer";
.........
datagrid1.getColumnAt(1).cellRenderer = "CustomCellRenderer";
```

Note that, while the custom cell renderer is used to render every cell in the list1 instance, in the case of the datagrid1 instance we are using it to render the cells of the second column only. In fact, in the case of the DataGrid component, cell renderers can be installed on a per-column basis by accessing its DataGridColumn instances via the getColumnAt method as we did in the previous ActionScript line. These aspects are visually confirmed in Figure 13-14.

There is not much more to comment about the code in the test.as file, since it is similar to the implementation of our previous example with the exception of the following two lines:

```
datagrid1.getColumnAt(1).width = 196;
datagrid1.getColumnAt(1).resizable = false;
```

The previous two lines fix the width of the second column in the DataGrid instance to 196 pixels and make it not resizable to avoid having it resized by the user action. That is because we know that our custom cell renderer places a 196-pixels-wide bitmapped graphic in the cells of that column, and we do not want its look to be spoiled by the possibility of resizing that column interactively.

The main actor of this example is, undoubtedly, the custom cell renderer. Let us examine what it really is about.

Building a custom cell renderer

In the previous example, you built a custom cell renderer by associating an ActionScript class (CustomCellRenderer) with an exported symbol having the same name. This shows what a custom cell renderer actually is: a new component.

A cell renderer is the means provided by the component architecture to replace the default implementation of a cell with a custom component that, as such, can meet any requirement that you may have.

Instances of a cell renderer become, in effect, subcomponents in the context of the component that creates them.

Luckily, our custom cell renderer is a very simple component implemented by an empty exported symbol. The absence of skins or a component structure allows us to focus on the requirements of the Cell Renderer API.

However, you must not forget that a custom cell renderer is a component and can be implemented to exploit any other functionality provided by the component architecture.

After all, our custom cell renderer already creates the premises for this by inheriting from the UIComponent class:

```
class CustomCellRenderer extends UIComponent {
```

Such detail makes it clear, once again, of the component nature of a cell renderer.

Our CustomCellRenderer class defines two properties and two methods that are not used by its implementation but have been included because you could find a good use for them whenever implementing your own custom cell renderer:

- listOwner: Refers to the list instance that is the root object of the component
- owner: Refers to the cell instance that it is contained in the listOwner object and, in turn, contains the cell renderer instance
- getCellIndex: Method returning an object with two properties, columnIndex and itemIndex, numerically indicating the column and the row of the currently rendered cell
- getDataLabel: Method returning the name of the property in the data item that is playing the role of the label, as we saw earlier in this chapter

It is the component architecture that defines the implementation of these properties and methods. However, you must include their definition in your classes only if you are going to use them in your own code. You can strip their definitions from the CustomCellRenderer class and see that it still works fine since that functionality was not used in its implementation.

Our CustomCellRenderer class defines one property that is specific to its implementation: customSymbol_mc. The customSymbol_mc property refers to the specific color symbol that is dynamically attached to cell to represent its current value in the setValue method:

```
public function setValue(label:String, item:Object, state:String):Void {
    switch (state) {
        case "normal":
            attachMovie(item.symbolBaseName, "customSymbol_mc", 1);
            break;
        case "highlighted":
```

```
                attachMovie(item.symbolBaseName + "Over",
                            "customSymbol_mc", 1);
                break;
            case "selected":
                attachMovie(item.symbolBaseName + "Selected",
                            "customSymbol_mc", 1);
                break;
        }
    }
```

The setValue method is the most important method that you must provide when implementing a custom cell renderer: it basically defines how the cell will look depending on the values of the data item associated with it.

The setValue method receives three parameters from the component architecture that give you access to relevant information when writing the code that renders the cell's content:

- label: Provides the label value of the current cell. Not used in our example and basically a redundant parameter, since you find the same information (and more) in the next parameter.

- item: Provides access to the values of the data item associated with the current cell. Very useful to define the cell representation based on any combination of the related data item values.

- state: Very important, since it defines the current state of the cell: "normal", "highlighted", or "selected". Our example provides a separate implementation for each of these, states underlining their relevance in the appearance of a cell.

Finally, our custom cell renderer also implements a couple of methods (getPreferredWidth, getPreferredHeight) whose names are self-describing since they inform the component architecture about the dimensions preferred by our cell renderer. In our case, we know dimensions pretty well, since they are dictated by the bitmapped graphic assets dynamically created in the cell, which have dimensions of 196×20 pixels.

Note that the cell renderer in our example has fixed dimensions defined by the image contained in it. However, there may be cases when the size of a cell renderer is variable. In these cases, it is your responsibility to implement a size method that will rearrange the cell content according to its new dimensions. The size method has been included with an empty body in our CustomCellRenderer class to remind you to implement it if the content of your cells must be resizable. Of course, it is up to your requirements to specify how they should look once resized.

DataGrid column headers

Note that the DataGridColumn class allows you to specify a custom cell renderer for the column headers of a DataGrid component.

All you have to do is implement your own cell renderer, applying exactly the same technique discussed in this chapter, and then install it via the headerRenderer property of the DataGridColumn class as shown in the following example:

```
datagrid1.getColumnAt(1).headerRenderer = CustomHeaderRenderer;
```

The undefined item bug

Here we will look back at one of our previous examples that contained a workaround to a bug in the DataGrid component.

When implementing custom labels, we define a custom label function as follows:

```
function customLabelFunction(item:Object):String {
    if (item == undefined) return undefined;
    return "The " + item.B + " is " + item.A;
}
```

The following line is there just to cover for a bug in the current DataGrid implementation:

```
if (item == undefined) return undefined;
```

If you remove this line and run the example again, you will notice how the bug visually influences the DataGrid instance. Figure 13-16 shows the problem.

Figure 13-16. Note the partially empty lines in the DataGrid instance

Basically, while the List and ComboBox components check for the number of data items in the DataProvider object, the DataGrid component does not when it comes to custom label functions, and the outcome is clearly displayed in Figure 13-16.

The line we add resolves the problem by verifying the passed item is, in fact, undefined, in which case the customLabelFunction returns undefined as well, which is enough for the DataGrid component to behave as expected.

Reasons for subclassing the List, ComboBox, and DataGrid components

It is generally a good idea to subclass a component in any case when building a theme so as to have styles and skins encapsulated in its subclassed version.

However, the list-based component does not give many other motivations to be subclassed apart from very specific ones that may come from your own projects.

In fact, consider that the DataGrid component is, as a matter of fact, a subclassed version of the List component, since the `DataGrid` class inherits from the `List` class directly (and that is what subclassing is, after all).

Therefore, you may also subclass any of these components to create a component with a new and largely extended functionality.

Chapter 14

THE DATECHOOSER AND DATEFIELD COMPONENTS

DateChooser	DateField
mx.controls.DateChooser	mx.controls.DateField
Frequency: Common	Frequency: Rare
Complexity: Simple	Complexity: Simple
Stability: Robust	Stability: Quirky
Maturity: Pre-Exisitng	Maturity: Pre-Existing
Popularity: Widespread	Popularity: Widespread

Quite frequently your applications may request the user to input a date.

The two components examined in this chapter largely facilitate such interaction, since they both force the user to intuitively select an existing date via a calendar view, avoiding the need for any validation code that you should produce and handle if using a text input field for the same task.

The DateChooser component implements a calendar view that can be utilized to select a date, while the DateField component combines a read-only TextInput component with a DateChooser component that pops up whenever needed, in order to save space in the graphical user interface. In visual terms, the DateField component is a more compact version of the DateChooser component.

Building a minimal example will further clarify the role that these components can play in your applications.

> The completed source code introduced in this chapter is included in the file src14.zip, downloadable from this book's page at www.friendsofed.com.

Minimal example of the DataChooser and DataField components

Let us build a practical example that uses both components to compare their behavior:

1. Create a new Flash document and save it as dates01.fla.
2. Open the Document Properties dialog box by selecting Modify ➤ Document, and set its dimensions as 600×300 pixels.
3. Drag the DateChooser component on stage in order to create one instance. Define the newly created instance name as datechooser1. Set the datechooser1 position to (X: 50.0, Y: 40.0) via the Info panel.
4. Drag the DateField component on to the stage. Define the newly created instance name as datefield1. Set the datefield1 position at (X: 270.0, Y: 40.0) via the Info panel.
5. Save the Flash document.

Testing the movie will show one instance of the DateChooser component and one instance of the DateField component, as displayed in Figure 14-1.

Clicking the DateField component will reveal its DateChooser subcomponent, as illustrated in Figure 14-2.

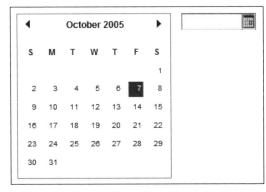

Figure 14-1. The minimal example

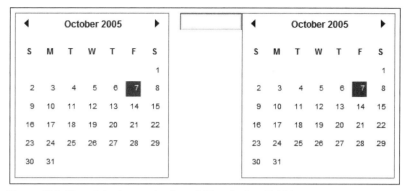

Figure 14-2. The minimal example after clicking the DateField instance

XLEFF version

The XLEFF version of our minimal example reflects the simplicity of including these components in a graphical user layout:

```
<datechooser
        name="datechooser1" x="50" y="40" width="205" height="214" />
<datefield name="datefield1"x="270" y="40" width="100" height="22" />
```

Note that you can find a preconfigured copy of the XLEFF sampler in the source files associated with this chapter to generate such a minimal example.

A richer example

While in the authoring environment, you can alternatively select the two instances in our minimal example to find out that they expose the same five parameters in the Parameters tab of the Properties panel:

- dayNames: An array of seven strings that are used to display the name of the days in the calendar view. The default value of this parameter is [S, M, T, W, T, F, S] where the first S stands for Sunday, the M stands for Monday, and so on.

- disabledDays: An array, initially empty, that can include up to seven numerical values ranging from 0 (Sunday) to 6 (Saturday). All the dates that fall on the days specified in this array are disabled and cannot be selected by the user.

- firstDayOfWeek: A numerical value indicating which day will be displayed first in the calendar view. Its default value is 0 (Sunday).

- monthNames: An array of twelve strings that are used to display the name of the months in the calendar view. The default value of this parameter is [January, February, March, April, May, June, July, August, September, October, November, December].

- showToday: A Boolean determining whether the current date is highlighted whenever visible in the calendar view. Its default value is true.

Although the use of these parameters is rather intuitive, building a richer example that uses all of them will make their functionality more evident:

1. Open the previously created dates01.fla Flash document and save it as dates02.fla.

2. Select the datechooser1 instance and click the Parameters tab of the Properties panel.

3. Redefine the seven values of the dayNames parameter as [D, L, Ma, Me, G, V, S].

4. Add two values to the disabledDays parameter: [0, 6].

5. Redefine the value of the firstDayOfWeek parameter as 1.

6. Redefine the twelve values of the monthNames parameter as [Gennaio, Febbraio, Marzo, Aprile, Maggio, Giugno, Luglio, Agosto, Settembre, Ottobre, Novembre, Dicembre].

7. Redefine the value of the showToday parameter as false.

8. Repeat the steps 3 to 7, after selecting the datefield1 instance on stage.

9. Save the Flash document.

Figure 14-3 shows the outcome of our last example after you click the datefield1 instance to display its DateChooser subcomponent.

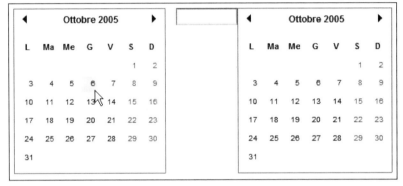

Figure 14-3. The minimal example when both of the calendar views are visible

The main purpose of the two parameters that allow us to change the names of days and months (dayNames and monthNames) is to implement localized versions of the calendar view. We use these two parameters to produce an Italian version of our minimal example, shown in Figure 14-3.

We also use the disabledDays parameter for making the weekend days not selectable: adding the values 0 (Sunday) and 6 (Saturday) to this parameter actually disables those days in every month view displayed in the components.

We change the default setting of the firstDayOfWeek from 0 (Sunday) to 1 (Monday), so that the calendar view displays the week starting from Monday instead of Sunday. Note that, since the names of the days have been redefined as [D = Domenica, L=Lunedi, Ma=Martedi, Me=Mercoledi, G=Giovedi, V=Venerdi, S=Sabato], the weeks start from L (Lunedi=Monday), as displayed in Figure 14-3.

Finally, we also change the default setting of the showToday parameter from true to false. As a result of this, the current date is not highlighted whenever visible in the calendar view.

Code version

Ensuring that all the dayNames and monthNames parameters have been defined consistently can become a very tedious, error-prone process, since you have to manually change lots of values in each of the instances in your application.

Luckily, each of the parameters examined in the previous section corresponds to a class property with the same name.

Setting those variables programmatically can be much more convenient, as illustrated by the following code:

```
var itaMonths =
        ["Gennaio","Febbraio","Marzo","Aprile","Maggio","Giugno",
         "Luglio","Agosto","Settembre","Ottobre","Novembre","Dicembre"];
var itaDays = ["D", "L", "Ma", "Me", "G", "V", "S"];

function setParameters(instance) {
    instance.monthNames = itaMonths;
    instance.dayNames = itaDays;
    instance.showToday = false;
    instance.firstDayOfTheWeek = 1;
    instance.disabledDays = [0, 6];
}

setParameters(datechooser1);
setParameters(datefield1);
```

The previous script defines two arrays (itaDays and itaMonths) containing the Italian names for months and days that can be assigned to the dayNames and monthNames properties of an instance whenever needed, allowing you to avoid rewriting those names again and again and reducing the chances of errors.

The outcome of the previous script is similar to that illustrated in Figure 14-3, and you can find a Flash document (dates02b.fla) using such code among the source files associated with this chapter.

How to retrieve and set a date

Implementing DateChooser and DateField components as you saw earlier has little practical value until you learn how to use those instances to retrieve user input or display a selected date.

Let us extend our minimal example to include the handling of the selected date:

1. Open the previously created dates01.fla Flash document and save it as dates03.fla in a new folder.

2. Select the first frame of the dates03.fla document and add the following ActionScript line to it:

```
#include "test.as"
```

3. Create a new ActionScript file and save it as test.as in the same folder as the dates03.fla file.

4. Add the following ActionScript code to the test.as file:

```
function change(eventObject:Object):Void {
    var eventSource = eventObject.target;
    if (eventSource._name == "datechooser1") {
        trace("datechooser1 new selection is: " +
            datechooser1.selectedDate);
    }
    if (eventSource._name == "datefield1") {
        trace("datefield1 new selection is: " +
            datefield1.selectedDate);
    }
}

datechooser1.addEventListener("change", this);
datefield1.addEventListener("change", this);

trace("datechooser1 new selection is: " + datechooser1.selectedDate);
trace("datefield1 new selection is: " + datefield1.selectedDate);

datechooser1.selectedDate =
        datefield1.selectedDate = new Date(2000,0,1);
```

5. Save both dates03.fla and test.as.

Testing our latest example will show that both instances display the same selected date (1 Jan 2000), as in Figure 14-4.

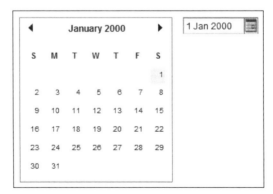

Figure 14-4. Setting and retrieving the selected date

The definition of the selectedDate property, available for both of the components, allows us to define which date was initially selected by both instances:

```
datechooser1.selectedDate =
        datefield1.selectedDate = new Date(2000,0,1);
```

Note that the value assigned to the selectedDate property is an object of the Date class.

The two lines that preceded the definition of the selectedDate property have been included to highlight that such a property is initially undefined:

```
trace("datechooser1 new selection is: " + datechooser1.selectedDate);
trace("datefield1 new selection is: " + datefield1.selectedDate);
```

These lines generate the following text in the output window just after testing the movie in the authoring environment, confirming that the selectedDate property is indeed undefined by default:

```
datechooser1 new selection is: undefined
datefield1 new selection is: undefined
```

Both the DateChooser and DateField components trigger a change event whenever the user selects a date. This is the reason for providing an implementation of the change event handler such as the following:

```
function change(eventObject:Object):Void {
    var eventSource = eventObject.target;
    if (eventSource._name == "datechooser1") {
        trace("datechooser1 new selection is: " +
            datechooser1.selectedDate);
    }
    if (eventSource._name == "datefield1") {
        trace("datefield1 new selection is: " +
            datefield1.selectedDate);
    }
}
```

Such an event handler verifies which instance (datechooser1 or datefield1) actually triggered the change event and shows a message in the Output window including the newly selected date.

Selecting a new date in one of the two instances would generate a message in the Output window similar to the following:

```
datechooser1 new selection is: Tue Jan 18 00:00:00 GMT+0000 2000
```

Conclusion: by using the selectedDate property and implementing an event handler for the change event, you can easily set and retrieve the date selected in both of the DateChooser and DateField components.

Both components also support the definition of selectable ranges that you can define to meet all sorts of requirements, as you are going to see in the next section.

Ranges definition

Both the DateChooser and DateField components introduce the concept of range to indicate a sequence of days that you may want to use to somewhat restrict the user selection.

Two different logic processes are available for defining what dates can be selected in a component instance:

- Disabling by providing a collection of ranges, each of them specifying a sequence of days that cannot be selected by the user
- Enabling by providing a single range of days and restricting the user selection to those days only

Let us first build an example of the disabling approach so that you can fully grasp how it works:

1. Open the previously created dates03.fla Flash document and save it as dates04.fla in a new folder.

2. Create a new ActionScript file and save it as test.as in the same folder where the dates04.fla file is.

3. Add the following ActionScript code to the test.as file:

```
var dRanges = [
    new Date(2000, 0, 2),
    { rangeEnd: new Date(1999, 11, 31) },
    { rangeStart: new Date(2000, 1, 1) },
    { rangeStart: new Date(2000, 0, 10),
      rangeEnd: new Date(2000, 0, 20) }
];

function commonSetup(instance) {
    instance.selectedDate = new Date(2000,0,1);
    instance.disabledRanges = dRanges;
}

commonSetup(datechooser1);
commonSetup(datefield1);
```

4. Save both dates04.fla and test.as.

Testing our latest example will produce an outcome similar to that displayed in Figure 14-4 with an important difference: you will not be able to select a date outside January 2000, although you can still navigate the calendar view via the navigation arrows, and you cannot select January 2 or any days between the 10th and 20th of January.

Such detailed configuration is implemented by using the disabledRanges property and by assigning the following dRanges array to it:

```
var dRanges = [
    new Date(2000, 0, 2),
    { rangeEnd: new Date(1999, 11, 31) },
    { rangeStart: new Date(2000, 1, 1) },
    { rangeStart: new Date(2000, 0, 10),
      rangeEnd: new Date(2000, 0, 20) }
];
```

The dRanges array in our example is carefully defined to include the four different kinds of range that you may include in an array that can be assigned to the disabledRanges property:

- **A Date object**: The first item in the dRanges array is a Date object. Including it in the dRanges array disables one single day: the one in the Date object.

- **A range object with a rangeEnd property only**: The presence of the rangeEnd property only indicates a range that starts from the beginning of time up to the day specified in such property. We used this option in our example to disable all the days up to 31 December 1999.

- **A range object with a rangeStart property only**: The presence of the rangeStart property only indicates a range that starts from the day specified and continues interminably into the future. We used this option in our example to disable all the days from 1 February 2000 onward.

- **A range object with both the rangeStart and the rangeEnd properties**: the presence of both properties defines a range that starts from a specific day specified in rangeStart and ends in the day specified in rangeEnd. We used this fourth and last option in our example to disable all the days ranging from the 10th to the 20th of January 2000.

The use of the disabling approach may sound overcomplicated, but it was provided to allow you to have the finest control over how to restrict the user selection.

The enabling approach is more intuitive and easier to implement, but it is less flexible, as demonstrated in the following example:

1. Open the previously created dates04.fla Flash document and save it as dates04b.fla in a new folder.

2. Create a new ActionScript file and save it as test.as in the same folder where the dates04b.fla file is.

3. Add the following ActionScript code to the test.as file:

```
var sRange = { rangeStart: new Date(2000, 0, 10),
➥ rangeEnd: new Date(2000, 0, 20) };

function commonSetup(instance) {
    instance.selectedDate = new Date(2000,0,12);
    instance.selectableRange = sRange;
}

commonSetup(datechooser1);
commonSetup(datefield1);
```

4. Save both dates04b.fla and test.as.

Once again, the test movie will have a look similar to our minimal example, with the difference that the selection options are restricted. In this case, you will be able to select only the days starting from the 10th of January 2000 up to the 20th of the same month.

Enabling a single range exclusively is achieved by assigning a range object with both the properties rangeStart and rangeEnd defined to the selectableRange property. In our example, this range object is defined as follows:

```
var sRange = { rangeStart: new Date(2000, 0, 10), rangeEnd: new
Date(2000, 0, 20) };
```

Before ending our study of the functionalities of both the DateChooser and the DateField components and learning how to customize them, you may find it interesting to know about a second event supported by these components: the scroll event.

The scroll event

In our example, both the DateChooser and the DateField components raise a scroll event whenever the user changes the month displayed in the calendar view by clicking one of the two arrow buttons.

The scroll event handler receives an event object including a detail property that can have one of four String values:

- nextMonth: Indicates the user clicked the next button arrow and the month being displayed belongs to the same year
- previousMonth: Indicates the user clicked the previous button arrow and the month being displayed belongs to the same year
- nextYear: Indicates the user clicked the next button arrow and the month being displayed belongs to the next year
- previousYear: Indicates the user clicked the previous button arrow and the month being displayed belongs to the previous year

The typical use of such an event is to keep different component instances synchronized on the same month and year, as illustrated in the following example:

1. Open the previously created dates04.fla Flash document and save it as dates05.fla in a new folder.

2. Create a new ActionScript file and save it as test.as in the same folder where the dates05.fla file is.

3. Add the following ActionScript code to the test.as file:

```
function scroll(eventObject:Object):Void {
    var eventSource = eventObject.target;
    var synchronized;

    if (eventSource._name == "datechooser1") {
        synchronized = datechooser2;
    } else {
        synchronized = datechooser1;
    }
```

```
        synchronized.displayedYear = eventSource.displayedYear;
        synchronized.displayedMonth = eventSource.displayedMonth;
}

datechooser1.addEventListener("scroll", this);
datechooser2.addEventListener("scroll", this);
```

4. Select the datefield1 instance on stage and delete it.

5. Drag the DateChooser component on stage in order to create a second instance. Define the newly created instance name as datechooser2. Set the datechooser2 position at (X: 330.0, Y: 40.0) via the Info panel.

6. Save both dates05.fla and test.as.

Testing the movie will now present two DateChooser instances on the stage, as displayed in Figure 14-5.

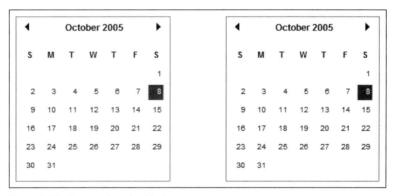

Figure 14-5. Two synchronized instances

To verify that the instances are indeed synchronized by exploiting the scroll event, you can click the arrow buttons of one of them and notice how the other one follows your action as well.

The code in the scroll event handler is rather intuitive: it verifies what instance raised the event (eventSource), stores the other instance in the synchronized variable, and then synchronizes the two instances via the displayedMonth and displayedYear properties.

In a real-world application, you would most probably use the scroll event to keep some other kind of view in synch with the user action.

Now that you have good knowledge of the functionality provided by the DateChooser and the DateField components, we can start looking into what you can do to customize their appearance.

Supported styles

Both the DateChooser and the DateField components support the same styles.

Among those styles are several common text and color styles that are handled similarly throughout the component architecture, allowing for the creation of a consistent look and feel when including different components in your applications.

Let us examine these component styles starting from the ones that are commonly shared with the other components in the architecture.

Common styles

The common text styles supported by both the DateChooser and the DateField components are embedFonts, fontFamily, fontSize, fontStyle, fontWeight, and textDecoration.

Text styles are intuitive to use and described in greater detail in Chapter 18, which is dedicated to the text-based components.

The common color styles supported by both the DateChooser and the DateField components are themeColor, backgroundColor, and color. They behave exactly as expected by allowing you to define a color scheme for the component appearance in a single step (themeColor) or setting the color of the component's background (backgroundColor) and the text color (color) separately.

We are going to use some of the common styles when building our next example, which also uses the specific styles in order to define a consistent, new appearance for both the DateChooser and the DateField components.

Specific styles

The specific styles of both the DateChooser and the DateField components have been provided to allow you to stylize some specific areas of their calendar view.

The common text styles that we saw before influence all the text content in the component instance. However, you can also apply those text styles to three component areas separately by using the specific style's objects:

- HeaderDateText: A global style that influences the appearance of text in the calendar view header (basically the text displaying the month's name). Such a header includes the text of the month's name being displayed and the arrow buttons.

- WeekDayStyle: A global style that influences the appearance of the text of the day names, just below the calendar header.

- TodayStyle: A global style that influences the appearance of the text of the current date when it is visible.

In addition to these three global style objects that allow the setting of the text styles of each particular area, the DateChooser and the DateField components also define a few color styles specific to their calendar view:

- borderColor: Defines the color of a 1-pixel border, which is around each instance of a DateChooser, and whose appearance cannot be influenced in any other way (styles or skins)
- headerColor: Defines the background color of the calendar view header, including the month's name and the two arrow buttons
- rollOverColor: Defines the background color of a date whenever the mouse is rolling over it
- selectionColor: Defines the background color of the selected date, if any
- todayColor: Defines the background color of the selected date, whenever visible

Common styles, specific global styles, and specific color styles should be combined to produce a consistent appearance of the component instances.

Our next example provides a demonstration of most of these styles working together to define a greenish version of the minimal example:

1. Open the previously created dates01.fla Flash document and save it as dates06.fla in a new folder.

2. Select the first frame of the dates06.fla document and add the following ActionScript line to it:

```
#include "test.as"
```

3. Create a new ActionScript file and save it as test.as in the same folder where the dates06.fla file is.

4. Add the following ActionScript code to the test.as file:

```
function setStyles(instance) {
    // COMMON TEXT STYLES
    instance.setStyle("fontFamily", "Courier New");
    instance.setStyle("fontSize", 12);

    // COMMON COLOR STYLES
    instance.setStyle("backgroundColor", 0xCCEECC);

    // SPECIFIC COLOR STYLES
    instance.setStyle("borderColor", 0x668866);
    instance.setStyle("headerColor", 0x668866);
    instance.setStyle("rollOverColor", 0x99FF33);
    instance.setStyle("selectionColor", 0x44FF11);
    instance.setStyle("todayColor", 0x668866);
}
```

```
if (_global.styles.TodayStyle == undefined) {
    _global.styles.TodayStyle = new CSSStyleDeclaration();
}
_global.styles.TodayStyle.setStyle("color", 0x99FF99);

if (_global.styles.WeekDayStyle == undefined) {
    _global.styles.WeekDayStyle = new CSSStyleDeclaration(0x006600);
}
_global.styles.WeekDayStyle.setStyle("color", c);

if (_global.styles.HeaderDateText == undefined) {
    _global.styles.HeaderDateText = new CSSStyleDeclaration();
}
_global.styles.HeaderDateText.setStyle("color", 0x99FF99);

setStyles(datechooser1);
setStyles(datefield1);
```

5. Save both dates06.fla and test.as.

Once you test the movie and click the datefield1 instance to make its DateChooser subcomponent appear, you will be able to appreciate the new, consistent look of both the calendar views, as displayed in Figure 14-6.

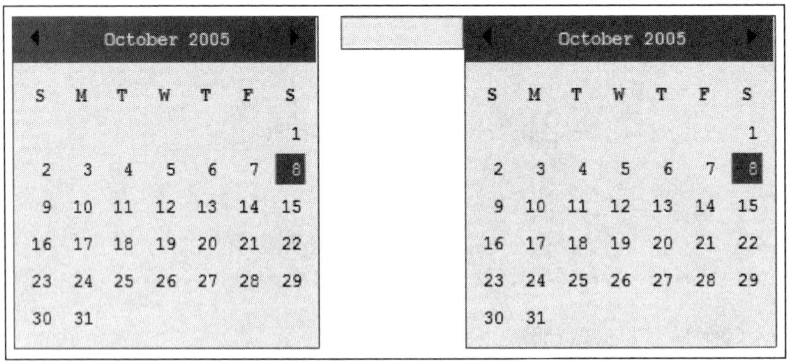

Figure 14-6. Stylized component instances

The new look was obtained by applying several variations of green to the color styles while also changing some text attributes.

In particular, most of the styles are set on a per-instance basis via the setStyles function, while the text color of three areas has been defined by creating their respective global styles and invoking the setStyle method on those global style instances as in the case of the header:

```
if (_global.styles.HeaderDateText == undefined) {
    _global.styles.HeaderDateText = new CSSStyleDeclaration();
}
_global.styles.HeaderDateText.setStyle("color", 0x99FF99);
```

As demonstrated by this example, styles can influence most of the appearance of the DateChooser and the DateField components. However, if you wish to refine their look even more, you can change the skins of the few component parts that we have not touched yet.

Skinnability

Skinning the DateChooser and the DateField components does not require a lot of work since very limited areas of both components can be skinned:

- The arrow buttons in the calendar view
- The icon on the right side of a DateField instance

Skinning the arrow buttons

The arrow buttons in the calendar view of both the DateChooser and the DateField components allow the user to navigate to the next or previous month. They are implemented by very simple black arrows that you may well wish to replace if you have defined a stylized version of your component like the one we produced in our last example.

Figure 14-7 shows the design of new arrows that we will use to skin the arrow buttons. You can find these graphic assets in the file dates07.fla in the source file associated with this chapter.

Figure 14-7. The design of the new arrow buttons

The DateChooser class defines six skin properties (three for each arrow button) to allow you to skin the arrow buttons:

- fwdMonthButtonUpSymbolName
- fwdMonthButtonDownSymbolName
- fwdMonthButtonDisabledSymbolName
- backMonthButtonUpSymbolName
- backMonthButtonDownSymbolName
- backMonthButtonDisabledSymbolName

The role of each skin name is quite intuitive if you consider that the two prefixes (back and fwd) indicate whether the skin is for the back button or the forward one, while the presence of Up, Down, or

Disabled clearly indicates which button state is associated with the skin. Quite weirdly, there are no skin properties for the Over state.

You may redefine those skin properties by subclassing the DateChooser component, but that would not affect the DateChooser subcomponent inside the DateField class.

Luckily, there is a quick way of applying the new skins to the arrow buttons that appear in the calendar views of both the DateChooser and the DateField components: create exported symbols with the linkage identifier defined as the value of those skin properties.

Those values are as follows:

- fwdMonthButtonUpSymbolName = "fwdMonthUp"

- fwdMonthButtonDownSymbolName = "fwdMonthDown"

- fwdMonthButtonDisabledSymbolName = "fwdMonthDisabled"

- backMonthButtonUpSymbolName = "backMonthUp"

- backMonthButtonDownSymbolName = "backMonthDown"

- backMonthButtonDisabledSymbolName = "backMonthDisabled"

The file dates07.fla that you find in the source files associated with this chapter was created starting from a copy of dates06.fla and then adding the exported symbols with the linkage identifiers defined following those values, also shown in Figure 14-8.

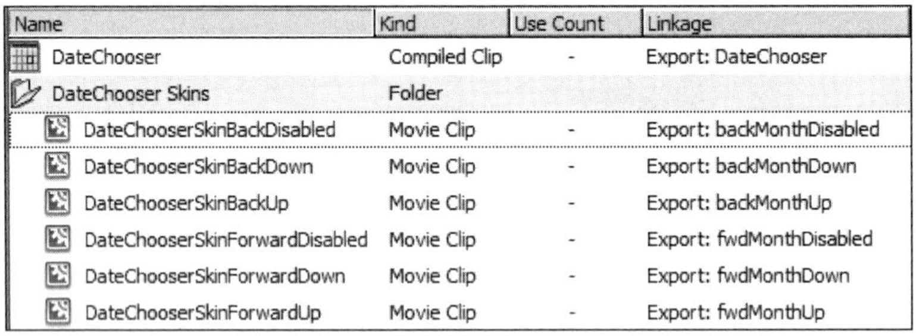

Name	Kind	Use Count	Linkage
DateChooser	Compiled Clip	-	Export: DateChooser
DateChooser Skins	Folder		
DateChooserSkinBackDisabled	Movie Clip	-	Export: backMonthDisabled
DateChooserSkinBackDown	Movie Clip	-	Export: backMonthDown
DateChooserSkinBackUp	Movie Clip	-	Export: backMonthUp
DateChooserSkinForwardDisabled	Movie Clip	-	Export: fwdMonthDisabled
DateChooserSkinForwardDown	Movie Clip	-	Export: fwdMonthDown
DateChooserSkinForwardUp	Movie Clip	-	Export: fwdMonthUp

Figure 14-8. The six exported symbols required to skin the arrow buttons in a calendar view

Figure 14-8 shows you what is relevant to skin the arrow buttons with your own graphic: to create six exported symbols with the proper linkage identifiers. Each of these symbols must contain the graphic that you provide for each particular button state.

This approach requires no programming, and it also influences the DateChooser subcomponent contained within a DateField instance as demonstrated by executing a test on the dates07.fla file and clicking the DateField instance, resulting in a layout like the one illustrated by Figure 14-9.

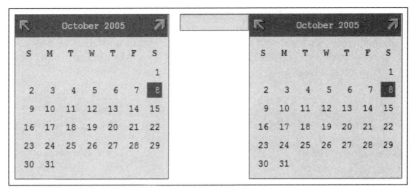

Figure 14-9. The new skins of the arrow buttons at work in both component instances

Skinning the DateField icon

A similar noncoding approach is used in the dates07.fla file to skin the icon of the DateField instance. Figure 14-10 shows a detail of the design adopted for the new icon.

Figure 14-10. The design of the new icon for the DateField instance

The DateField class defines four skin properties, and, reapplying the same technique discussed before, we are going to use their default values as the linkage identifiers of exported symbols to apply the new skins without coding. The four skin properties and their default values are as follows:

- downArrowUpName = "openDateUp"
- downArrowDownName = "openDateDown"
- downArrowOverName = "openDateOver"
- downArrowDisabledName = "openDateDisabled"

Since what we are actually skinning here is a single button instance, all you have to focus on by looking at those names (and their values) is the button state (Up, Down, Over, and Disabled) to understand when the related skin symbol is displayed.

A further look at the library in the dates07.fla file will confirm the presence of the four exported symbols and their related linkage identifier that you must define with your own graphic whenever customizing the DateField instances in your application. Figure 14-11 indicates the part of the library of the dates07.fla file related to those exported symbols that are contained in the DateField Skins folder of the document's library.

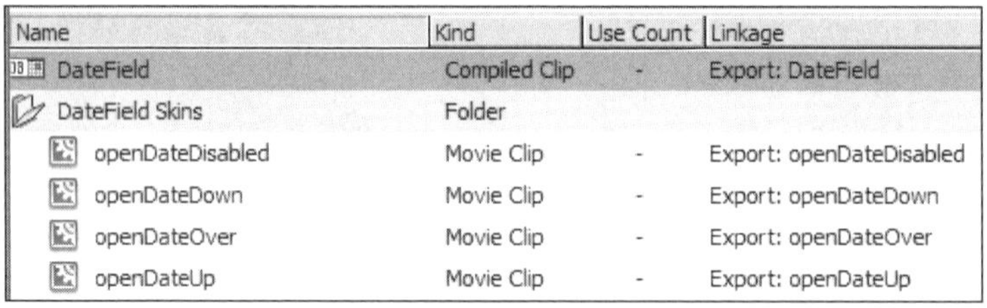

Name
Kind
Use Count
Linkage
DateField
Compiled Clip
-
Export: DateField
DateField Skins
Folder
openDateDisabled
Movie Clip
-
Export: openDateDisabled
openDateDown
Movie Clip
-
Export: openDateDown
openDateOver
Movie Clip
-
Export: openDateOver
openDateUp
Movie Clip
-
Export: openDateUp

Figure 14-11. The four exported symbols required to skin the icon of the DateField component

Figure 14-12 shows the new look of both the DateChooser and DateField components once you have applied the new styles and skins to them. This is how those components appear when you run a test on the dates07.fla file before clicking the DateField icon.

October 2005
S M T W T F S
1
2 3 4 5 6 7 8
9 10 11 12 13 14 15
16 17 18 19 20 21 22
23 24 25 26 27 28 29
30 31

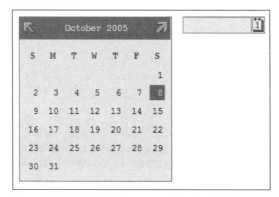

Figure 14-12. The DateChooser and the DateField components stylized and skinned (note the icon)

Solved mysteries

This section focuses on topics that are very specific to the current implementation of the components discussed in this chapter that could not be included in the previous sections.

While the DateChooser is a pretty stable component with no particular mystery to solve, the same cannot be said for the DateField component, as it presents an additional feature and a bug that fit in this section very well.

Let us start from the additional feature, which is useful to know and easy to implement.

Displaying the date in custom format

Adding the following ActionScript line at the end of the test.as script of the stylized example shown earlier (dates06.fla) will select a date in the datefield1 instance:

```
datefield1.selectedDate = new Date(2006,0,1);
```

Once a date is currently selected in a DateField instance, the component shows the date value in text format in its associated field, as illustrated in Figure 14-13.

Figure 14-13. The standard format of the date
displayed by the DateField component

What if you need to change the text format of the date's value? The DateField component implements a dateFormatter property that can be used to assign a function to the component instance that will display the date in a custom format. The following is an example of such a function:

```
datefield1.dateFormatter = function(d:Date):String {
    var months = ["Jan", "Feb", "Mar", "Apr", "May", "Jun", "Jul",
                  "Aug", "Sep", "Oct", "Nov", "Dec"];

    return  d.getFullYear() + ", "
            + d.getDate() + " " + months[d.getMonth()];
}
```

It is important to notice that such a function expects a Date object as a parameter and returns a String value. Adding the previous function at the top of the test.as script of the stylized example shown earlier will cause the datefield1 instance to format the value of its selected date, as displayed in Figure 14-14.

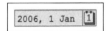

Figure 14-14. The DateField component displaying
its date value using our custom formatter

Providing a custom function for the dateFormatter property of a DateField instance is a very easy way to customize the representation of its Date value into any format that you may need to implement.

Our next topic is a bug in the component architecture, related to the DateField property, that cannot be solved so easily.

A DateField bug

In the example implemented in the dates05.fla file, we used the displayedMonth and displayedYear properties of the DateChooser component to keep two of its instances synchronized.

Those two properties provide a means to set or retrieve the current month (or year) displayed by a component instance and are officially implemented in the DateField component as well. However, they do not work properly in the DateField component, and you should not use them unless you can understand and fix the bug that causes their misbehavior.

The bug is clearly demonstrated by the following example:

1. Open the previously created dates01.fla Flash document and save it as dates08.fla in a new folder.

2. Select the first frame of the dates08.fla document and add the following ActionScript line to it:

   ```
   #include "test.as"
   ```

3. Create a new ActionScript file and save it as test.as in the same folder where the dates08.fla file is.

4. Add the following ActionScript code to the test.as file:

   ```
   function setYearAndMonth(instance):Void {
       instance.displayedMonth = 0;
       instance.displayedYear = 2000;
   }

   setYearAndMonth(datechooser1);
   setYearAndMonth(datefield1);
   ```

5. Save both dates08.fla and test.as.

The setYearAndMonth function sets both the displayedMonth and displayedYear properties of an instance, and it is applied to both of our instances: datechooser1 and datefield1.

Testing the movie and clicking the datefield1 instance to open its calendar view will reveal a display like the one illustrated in Figure 14-15.

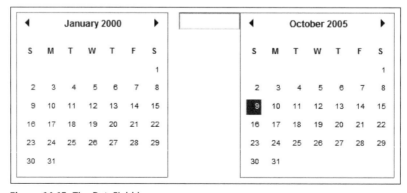

Figure 14-15. The DateField bug

Figure 14-15 shows that the displayedMonth and displayedYear defined via coding are displayed by the DateChooser instance, but not in the case of the DateField instance.

At the time of writing, this bug has not yet been fixed in the official version of the component architecture and, therefore, it is wise avoiding using the displayedMonth and displayedYear properties in the case of the DateField component.

Reasons for subclassing the DataChooser and DataField components

The approach chosen in this book is based on reusing, extending, and customizing the components, but does not include altering their source code in order to eliminate a bug like the one we just examined in the previous version.

The reason is pretty simple: altering the source code of the component architecture creates a different version from the official one, and this version may well be incompatible with future updates that will eventually fix that bug.

However, subclassing the component and fixing the bug in its subclassed version can resolve most problems, including the one mentioned in the previous section.

So far we have appreciated subclassing as the prime technique for customizing components. The presence of marginal misbehaviors in some of the existing components makes it an even more attractive option, since fixing a bug in a subclassed version of a component does not require altering the component architecture source code: you are just overriding it.

That is the theory.

The practice requires an in-depth analysis of the current internals of the component architecture, the use of the StandardComponents.fla containing the source (not compiled) version of each standard component, and very strong experience in programming.

The basic subclassing technique is exposed in Chapter 9, but its applications are limitless. Its use for fixing the component architecture bugs goes beyond the scope of this book. Hopefully, by the end of this book, you will have learned enough to be able to analyze the existing source code of the component architecture and make up your own mind about how to fix bugs within it.

Chapter 15

THE LOADER, SCROLLPANE, AND PROGRESSBAR COMPONENTS

Loader mx.controls.Loader		ScrollPane mx.containers.ScrollPane		ProgressBar mx.controls.ProgressBar
Frequency: Common		Frequency: Common		Frequency: Common
Complexity: Plug and Play		Complexity: Simple		Complexity: Simple
Stability: Robust		Stability: Robust		Stability: Quirky
Maturity: Pre-Existing		Maturity: Classic		Maturity: Pre-Existing
Popularity: Widespread		Popularity: Widespread		Popularity: Widespread

The Loader and ScrollPane components are two containers that share a similar purpose. Both can display internal content stored in an exported symbol resident in the library of the Flash document, or load and display external content stored in a JPEG file or in another SWF file.

The ProgressBar is a component designed to provide visual feedback of the loading process when either the Loader or ScrollPane component loads content from an external source over the Internet. In some cases, you may use an instance of the ProgressBar on its own; however, most of the time, you will use it in conjunction with either a Loader or ScrollPane instance.

This chapter will cover these three components, first demonstrating each separately, and then exploring how the ProgressBar component interacts with each of the two container components. By comparing the functionality of the Loader and ScrollPane components, you will better understand how they work and know which one to pick when you have a specific requirement.

> The completed source code introduced in this chapter can be found in the package `src15.zip`, downloadable from this book's page at www.friendsofed.com.

Minimal examples

In the following examples, we will build minimal implementations that expose the core functionality of each component separately. Later in the chapter, we will explore how these components interact with each other.

The Loader component is a simpler container than the ScrollPane component and, therefore, the most convenient starting point.

A minimal example of the Loader component

The objective of the minimal example is to capture the very basic purpose of a component by providing the simplest implementation possible. In the case of the Loader component, this concept is applied up to the point that no coding is required to implement our first example. Follow these steps to create it:

1. Create a new Flash document and save it as `lsp01a.fla`.
2. Open the Document Properties dialog box, via the Modify ➤ Document menu option, and set the stage dimensions as 800×600 pixels.
3. Drag the Loader component onto the stage in order to create one instance of the component. Name the newly created instance `loader1`.
4. Select the `loader1` instance and set its position at X: 0.0, Y: 0.0 and its dimensions as W: 600.0, H: 450.0.
5. Keeping the `loader1` instance selected, define its contentPath parameter, via the Parameters tab in the Properties panel, as `dragon.jpg`.
6. Save the Flash document.

Note that this example uses a JPG image 800 × 600 pixels in size, stored in a file named dragon.jpg, which you can find in the source files associated with this chapter. It must be copied into the same folder that contains the newly created Flash document.

Testing the example will result in the Loader instance being filled with the dragon.jpg file, as illustrated in Figure 15-1.

Figure 15-1. The minimal Loader example

Figure15-1 emphasizes the borders of the movie with a shadow to highlight that the loaded image occupies only a portion of it. That portion is defined by the size and position of loader1.

The original image of 800 × 600 pixels was scaled to fit within the area of the loader1 instance (600 × 450). This behavior is enabled by setting the scaleContent parameter to true, which is the default. Figure 15-2 shows both the stage and the parameters as they were defined in the authoring environment.

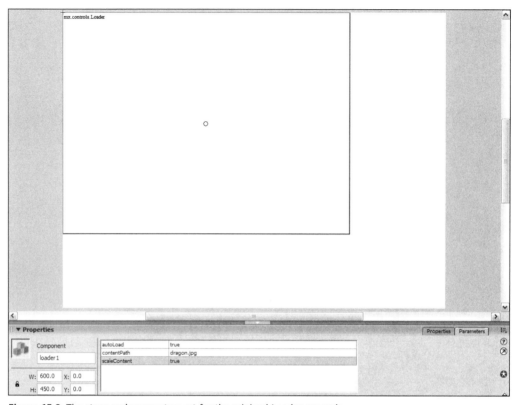

Figure 15-2. The stage and parameters set for the minimal Loader example

As you can see in Figure 15-2, you can set the following three parameters of the Loader component in the authoring environment:

- autoLoad: A Boolean that, whenever true (the default), indicates that the content is loaded automatically whenever the contentPath is defined. If this parameter is set to false, the content will not be loaded immediately after the contentPath is defined; it will be loaded only after you invoke the load method of the Loader class explicitly.

- contentPath: Accepts a string value specifying the location of the content that will be loaded into the component instance. The content can be either internal or external. Internal content is loaded if the string value refers to a linkage identifier of an exported symbol in the movie's library. External content is loaded when the string value refers to an absolute or relative URL pointing to a JPG file or an SWF file.

- scaleContent: A Boolean that allows you to choose how the content is handled by the loader. If this parameter is set to true (the default), the content is scaled to fit in the Loader dimensions. If it is set to false, the Loader instance is resized in order to display the whole content.

Note that each of those parameters corresponds to a property with the same name in the Loader class that you can access programmatically.

To better understand the Loader component's functionality (and, later on, fully grasp what makes the ScrollPane component a different option), select the loader1 instance in the previous example and set its scaleContent parameter to false. Then test the movie, and you will see the dragon.jpg image full scale (800 X 600), covering all of the movie's area. Figure 15-3 shows the two different results produced by the different settings of the scaleContent parameter. In the first case, when scaleContent is true, the image is resized to fit in the component instance. In the second case, when scaleContent is false, the component instance is resized to display the whole image.

Figure 15-3. Comparing the results of setting scaleContent to true (left) and setting it to false (right)

Basically, the Loader component behavior is characterized by resizing its contents. The ScrollPane component provides a different behavior, as you'll see in the next section.

A minimal example of the ScrollPane component

The procedure for implementing the minimal example of the ScrollPane component is almost identical to the one you used for the Loader component and, once again, no coding is required. Follow these steps:

1. Create a new Flash document and save it as lsp01b.fla.

2. Open the Document Properties dialog box, via the Modify ➤ Document menu option, and set the stage dimensions as 800 X 600 pixels. While the Document Properties dialog box is still open, you should also choose a different background color (such as dark gray: #666666) to emphasize the features of the component instance by visually isolating it.

3. Drag the ScrollPane component onto the stage in order to create one instance of the component. Name the newly created instance scrollpane1.

4. Select the scrollpane1 instance and set its position as X: 100.0, Y: 75.0 and its dimensions as W: 600.0, H: 450.0.

5. Keeping the scrollpane1 instance selected, define its contentPath parameter (via the Parameters tab in the Properties panel) as dragon.jpg.

6. Save the Flash document.

As in the previous example, a JPG image named dragon.jpg, 800 × 600 pixels in size, must be present in the same folder as the newly created Flash document.

When testing the movie, the scrollpane1 instance will load the dragon.jpg file, as illustrated in Figure 15-4.

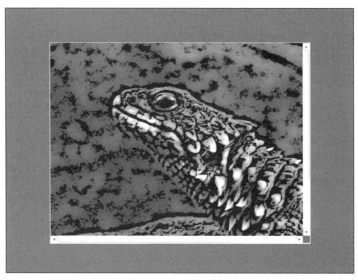

Figure 15-4. The minimal ScrollPane example

The main difference between the Loader component and the ScrollPane component is already apparent: in the case of the ScrollPane, neither the component instance nor the content (the image) is resized. Rather than resizing the component instance or its content, the ScrollPane component offers a different option for viewing all of the content: scrollbars. Because of this, you will not find a scaleContent parameter (or property) among the parameters of the ScrollPane component.

Actually, the contentPath parameter is the only parameter that the ScrollPane component has in common with the Loader component, and it is used to load the same types of internal and external content as the Loader, following the same rules, as described in the previous section. On the other hand, the ScrollPane component has seven parameters not implemented by the Loader component, as shown in Figure 15-5. Six of these parameters influence the way the scrollbars work, and they will be discussed in Chapter 21.

▼ Properties				Properties	Parameters
Component	contentPath	dragon.jpg			
scrollpane1	hLineScrollSize	5			
	hPageScrollSize	20			
	hScrollPolicy	auto			
W: 600.0 X: 100.0	scrollDrag	false			
	vLineScrollSize	5			
H: 450.0 Y: 75.0	vPageScrollSize	20			
	vScrollPolicy	auto			

Figure 15-5. The ScrollPane parameters

The only parameter that is truly specific to the ScrollPane component is scrollDrag, set to false by default. Setting the scrollDrag parameter (or the corresponding property) to true will allow the user to scroll the content by dragging over it. The scrollDrag option is usually used in conjunction with hiding the scrollbars, to offer the user an alternative scrolling navigation technique. You can see how this works by setting the following parameters in the previous example:

- scrollDrag: true
- hScrollPolicy: off
- vScrollPolicy: off

Now let's move on to an example of the third component included in this chapter.

A minimal example of the ProgressBar component

Let's build a codeless minimal example of the ProgressBar component. Follow these steps:

1. Create a new Flash document and save it as lsp01c.fla.

2. Open the Document Properties dialog box, via the Modify ➤ Document menu option, and set the stage dimensions as 600 × 450 pixels.

3. Drag the ProgressBar component on the stage in order to create one instance of the component. Name the newly created instance progressbar1.

4. Select the progressbar1 instance and set its position at X: 225.0, Y: 210.0.

5. Save the Flash document.

Testing this example will result in the display of a frozen bar like the one shown in Figure 15-6.

The ProgressBar instance in this example does not move, and it permanently shows the message "LOADING 0%." However, the minimal example does demonstrate the purpose of the ProgressBar component, which is to show the progress of an activity. In fact, without any activity going on in our example, the ProgressBar instance quite rightly doesn't move from its starting point. Now let's see the ProgressBar in action.

Figure 15-6. The frozen ProgressBar instance in the minimal example

The ProgressBar's animated behavior

Extending the previous minimal example by simulating an ongoing process will demonstrate the animated behavior of the ProgressBar component. Here are the steps:

1. Open the lsp01c.fla file you created in the previous example and save it as lsp02a.fla in a new folder.

2. Create an ActionScript file and save it as test.as in the same folder as the lsp02a.fla file.

3. Add the following code to the newly created test.as file:

```
function updateProgress() {
    switch (phase) {
        case 1:
            progressbar1.label = "Phase 1: Creating Characters";
```

```
                progressbar1.setProgress(1, 4);
                break;
            case 2:
                progressbar1.label = "Phase 2: Creating Cities";
                progressbar1.setProgress(2, 4);
                break;
            case 3:
                progressbar1.label = "Phase 3: Creating Trees";
                progressbar1.setProgress(3, 4);
                break;
            case 4:
                progressbar1.label = "Phase 4: Completing Generation";
                progressbar1.setProgress(4, 4);
                break;
            default:
                clearInterval(id);
                progressbar1.setVisible(false);
                break;
        }
        phase++;
    }

    progressbar1.label = "Initializing..";
    progressbar1.mode = "manual";

    progressbar1.setSize(200,30);
    progressbar1.move(200,210);

    var phase:Number = 1;
    var id:Number = setInterval(updateProgress, 2000);
```

4. Select the first frame in the lsp02a.fla document and add the following ActionScript line to it:

```
#include "test.as"
```

5. Save both the lsp02a.fla and test.as files.

When testing the movie, you will notice that the ProgressBar instance now moves every two seconds and disappears after reaching its full scale (100%). Also, the message in the component label changes depending on which phase is being simulated.

The sequence of phases and their associated messages simulate activities to generate several resources. The simulation is achieved by using the ActionScript function setInterval to define an interval that will call the updateProgress function, implemented every two seconds in the example:

```
    var id:Number = setInterval(updateProgress, 2000);
```

The updateProgress function moves the ProgressBar instance forward by invoking its setProgress method, as in this line:

```
progressbar1.setProgress(1, 4);
```

The setProgress method expects two parameters: a first number indicating the current step and a second number indicating the total number of steps. The previous line could basically be read as "set the progress of the bar as step 1 of 4."

Of course, when invoking the setProgress method, you can use the unit that best suits your requirements. For instance, in the most frequent case of a percentage, the following line would set the bar progress at 70%:

```
progressbar1.setProgress(70, 100);
```

updateProgress modifies the text associated with the ProgressBar at each new phase by assigning a description to the its label property, like so:

```
progressbar1.label = "Phase 1: Creating Characters";
```

When the numeric variable phase becomes greater than 4, the simulated activity is considered complete, the interval is canceled, and the ProgressBar instance is hidden via the setVisible method, inherited from the UIObject class:

```
clearInterval(id);
progressbar1.setVisible(false);
```

The other two methods inherited from the UIObject class, setSize and move, make the ProgressBar instance larger and reposition it at the center of the movie, respectively:

```
progressbar1.setSize(200,30);
progressbar1.move(200,210);
```

The mode property of the ProgressBar class influences the way a ProgressBar instance interacts with other components, as you will see later in this chapter. Since in our current example, there is no such interaction, we set the mode property as manual:

```
progressbar1.mode = "manual";
```

Apart from demonstrating the animation of the ProgressBar component, this example shows how you can use this component to externalize the progress of any activity in your application by programmatically controlling its progress.

Before moving on to the topic of component instance interaction, let's look at another use of the ProgressBar component that you might find worthwhile.

The indeterminate ProgressBar

In the previous example, you learned how to use the ProgressBar component to expose the progress of any activity. However, in some cases, you cannot quantify such progress. In those cases, you can still use the ProgressBar as a sort of visual placeholder that remains visible as long as a certain activity is going on. The following example shows how to use the ProgressBar component in this manner.

379

1. Open the lsp02a.fla file you created in the previous example and save it as lsp02b.fla in a new folder.

2. Create an ActionScript file and save it as test.as in the same folder as the lsp02b.fla file.

3. Add the following code to the newly created test.as file:

```
function doneIt() {
    clearInterval(id);
    progressbar1.setVisible(false);
}

progressbar1.label = "Initializing..";
progressbar1.mode = "manual";
progressbar1.indeterminate = true;

progressbar1.setSize(200,30);
progressbar1.move(200,210);

var id:Number = setInterval(doneIt, 3000);
```

4. Save both the lsp02b.fla and test.as files.

Testing the movie will display the ProgressBar instance with an animated striped fill, resembling the one shown in Figure 15-7.

The ProgressBar instance disappears after three seconds, indicating that the simulated initializing process has been completed. We used the setInterval function once again, this time to simulate an activity of unknown duration:

Figure 15-7. The indeterminate appearance of the ProgressBar component

```
var id:Number = setInterval(doneIt, 3000);
```

The doneIt function, invoked after three seconds, coincides with the end of the simulated activity and, in fact, cancels the interval and hides the ProgressBar instance:

```
function doneIt() {
    clearInterval(id);
    progressbar1.setVisible(false);
}
```

It is the indeterminate property of the ProgressBar class that allows you to change the appearance of the component instance so radically. The indeterminate property must be set to true programmatically (it's set to false by default) in order to apply the animated striped fill appearance to the ProgressBar instance, and in that case, the mode property must be set as manual as well:

```
progressbar1.mode = "manual";
progressbar1.indeterminate = true;
```

This example complements the previous one. By knowing both approaches, you can now implement visual feedback for processes, the duration of which can be either known or unknown at runtime.

XLEFF versions

The package associated with this chapter includes several configurations of the XLEFF sampler that generate layouts similar to the ones produced by the previous examples. The following XML line easily replicates the minimal example of the Loader component:

```
<loader x="145" y="50" width="600" height="450" name="loader1"
        contentPath="dragon.jpg" />
```

Once again, the nomenclature used by XLEFF closely resembles that of the component architecture. Because of that, you can modify the scaling behavior of the Loader component by defining the scaleContent attribute of the loader XML element, like so:

```
<loader x="50" y="0" width="600" height="450" name="loader1"
        contentPath="dragon.jpg" scaleContent="false" />
```

Similarly, it is possible to generate the XLEFF version of the ScrollPane minimal example via the following XML line:

```
<scrollpane x="145" y="50" width="600" height="450" name="scrollpane1"
            contentPath="dragon.jpg" />
```

In the case of the ProgressBar component, you must remember that XLEFF separates the graphical user interface of an application from its implementation and, therefore, the XML description will generate an unanimated ProgressBar instance. The objective of generating such a ProgressBar instance dynamically is to use it in an application:

```
<progressbar x="370" y="270" width="150" height="30"
             name="progressbar1" />
```

You can easily transform the previous XML description into one generating an indeterminate ProgressBar by setting the indeterminate and mode attributes, which mimic the component architecture properties with the same names:

```
<progressbar x="370" y="270" width="150" height="30"
             name="progressbar1" indeterminate="true" mode="manual" />
```

With the minimal examples completed, we are ready to move on to some enhanced versions.

Combined examples

Now that we have examined the behavior of the Loader, ScrollPane, and ProgressBar components separately, we are going to build a few richer examples to explore how the ProgressBar component interacts with the two container components. The ProgressBar supports a couple of communication modes that can be exploited by both the Loader and the ScrollPane components.

The ProgressBar communication modes

The mode property of the ProgressBar class defines how an instance of the ProgressBar component will communicate with an instance of another component, such as the Loader and the ScrollPane components. The source property of the ProgressBar class stores a reference to the component instance that will be communicate with the ProgressBar instance.

The ProgressBar class implements three different communication modes. You can select the communication mode that best suits your requirements by assigning one of the following string values to the mode property of a ProgressBar instance:

- manual: Specified when communication among component instances is not necessary (the source property is undefined). Earlier in this chapter, you saw a couple examples that use this option in order to define the progress displayed in the bar programmatically.

- polled: In this case, the ProgressBar instance will communicate with the component instance referred to in its source property. The communication will rely on the fact that the class of the source instance implements a couple of methods, getBytesLoaded and getBytesTotal, which are invoked by the ProgressBar instance to become aware of the progress made by the source instance. Since both the Loader and the ScrollPane components support those two methods, you can use the polled mode with both of them.

- event: In this case also, the ProgressBar instance will communicate with the component instance referred to in its source property. However, when selecting the event mode, the ProgressBar instance registers itself as a listener for two events (progress and complete) raised by the source instance. It follows that the class implementing the source instance must support these two events. Since both the ScrollPane and the Loader components support these events, you should be able to use this mode with both of them. However, it doesn't work with the ScrollPane component (see the "Solved mysteries" section later in this chapter for a solution to this bug).

Let's now build a couple of examples that will show you how to exploit the mode and source parameters of the ProgressBar component to monitor the progress of the Loader and ScrollPane components whenever they load external content.

Codeless interaction

Thanks to the communication modes supported by the ProgressBar component, you can easily associate a ProgressBar instance with another component instance, considered as the source, as long as the class implementing the source instance supports a couple of events (progress and complete) or methods (getBytesLoaded and getBytesTotal) that are compatible with the ProgressBar specification.

Both the Loader component and the ScrollPane component are capable of interacting with the ProgressBar component. Let's build a couple of examples that demonstrate this codeless interaction.

ProgressBar and Loader interaction

First, we will build an example using the same JPG file, dragon.jpg, that we used in the first two examples of this chapter.

1. Create a new Flash document and save it as `lsp04a.fla`. Save the `dragon.jpg` file into the same location as this file.

2. Open the Document Properties dialog box, via the Modify ➤ Document menu option, and set the stage dimensions as 600 × 450 pixels.

3. Drag the ProgressBar component onto the stage in order to create one instance of the component. Name the newly created instance `progressbar1`.

4. Select the `progressbar1` instance and set its position as X: 225.0, Y: 210.0.

5. Keeping the `progressbar1` instance selected, set its source parameter in the Parameters tab of the Properties panel as `this._parent.loader1`.

6. Create a new layer. Select the first frame of the new layer and drag the Loader component onto the stage. A Loader instance will be created in the new layer. Name the Loader instance `loader1`.

7. Select the `loader1` instance and set its position at X: 0.0, Y: 0.0 and its dimensions as W: 600.0, H: 450.0.

8. Keeping the `loader1` instance selected, define its contentPath parameter, via the Parameters tab in the Properties panel, as `dragon.jpg`.

9. Save the Flash document.

Testing the movie via the usual command (Control ➤ Test Movie) will not be sufficient to see the ProgressBar in action. The `dragon1.jpg` file is on your hard disk and, because of that, it will be loaded so quickly that you may only barely notice the presence of the ProgressBar instance before it disappears.

However, the Flash authoring environment is capable of simulating the download of a file over the Internet. The View ➤ Simulate Download menu command becomes available while you are testing the movie. Select it to make the ProgressBar instance visible by simulating the download of the `dragon.jpg` file from the Web. Figure 15-8 shows the progress of the ProgressBar instance, which you should see after simulating the download in the Flash authoring environment.

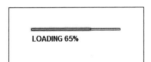

Figure 15-8. Simulating the download

In this example, we connected the `progressbar1` instance to the `loader1` instance via the source parameter of the ProgressBar instance defined as follows:

```
this._parent.loader1
```

The value of the source parameter will be evaluated in the scope of the ProgressBar instance. That is why we pointed at the `loader1` instance via a relative path (`this._parent`), based on the fact that, in our example, both the `progressbar1` and `loader1` instances are inside the same container (`_level0`). However, depending on the structure of your application, the `loader1` instance could be in a different container, and in that case, you should define a relative path that correctly points to it.

Note that we didn't define the mode parameter of the `progressbar1` instance since its default value (event) is compatible with the Loader component.

ProgressBar and ScrollPane interaction

Producing an example that uses a ScrollPane instance requires almost the exact same steps as you followed with the Loader (actually, the only difference is due to a bug in the ProgressBar). Once again, we will use the same dragon.jpg file that we have used in earlier examples.

1. Create a new Flash document and save it as lsp04b.fla. Save the dragon.jpg file into the same location as this file.

2. Open the Document Properties dialog box, via the Modify ➤ Document menu option, and set the stage dimensions as 600 × 450 pixels.

3. Drag the ProgressBar component on the stage to create one instance of the component. Name the newly created instance progressbar1.

4. Select the progressbar1 instance and set its position at X: 225.0, Y: 210.0.

5. Keeping the progressbar1 instance selected, set its source parameter in the Parameters tab of the Properties panel as this._parent.scrollpane1.

6. Keeping the progressbar1 instance still selected, change the settings of its mode parameter in the Parameters tab of the Properties panel from event to polled.

7. Create a new layer. Select the first frame of the new layer and drag the ScrollPane component onto the stage. A ScrollPane instance will be created in the new layer. Name the ScrollPane instance as scrollpane1.

8. Select the scrollpane1 instance and set its position at X: 0.0, Y: 0.0 and its dimensions as W: 600.0, H: 450.0.

9. Keeping the scrollpane1 instance selected, define its contentPath parameter, via the Parameters tab in the Properties panel, as dragon.jpg.

10. Save the Flash document.

Once again, you need to simulate the download to see the progress of the ProgressBar instance by first testing the movie via the usual command (Control ➤ Test Movie) and then selecting the View ➤ Simulate Download menu option, as you did in the previous example.

Building this example, which associates a ScrollPane instance with a ProgressBar, has required the same steps as the previous example plus one: changing the mode parameter of the progressbar1 instance from event into polled. This shouldn't be necessary, since the ScrollPane component supports the required events (progress and complete), just as the Loader component does. However, setting the mode parameter back to event will stop the progressbar1 instance from progressing (try it for yourself). That is due to a bug in the ProgressBar component that will be explained and solved in the "Solved mysteries" section later in this chapter. For the moment, you should remember to use the polled mode (instead of the event mode) whenever associating a ScrollPane instance with a ProgressBar via its source parameter, like so:

```
this._parent.scrollpane1
```

We walked through these two examples, associating a ProgressBar instance with a Loader and then a ScrollPane, without writing a single line of code. However, a bit of programming can make those examples more flexible, while demonstrating how to control the communication between those components programmatically. So, let's see how to take control of the communication process.

Mediated interaction

The interaction between component instances in the previous two examples was beyond our control as developers. We just used the source parameter of the ProgressBar instance to connect two instances, which then started communicating with each other in event (or polled) mode. Such a high level of automation empowers the authoring environment but has its limitations. For one, the progressbar1 instance is still visible in both examples, although you cannot see it because it is in the layer below the one hosting the Loader (or ScrollPane) instance.

If you swap the order of the two layers in those examples, you will notice that the progressbar1 instance is not hidden after the image is fully loaded. Apart from this detail, you may wish to take full control over what's happening for several other reasons. For example, you may need to synchronize other activities in your application.

To demonstrate, we will extend the previous examples by implementing an intermediate layer of logic that mediates between the progressbar1 instance and its associated source instance (either a Loader or a ScrollPane instance). This technique can be used to fully exploit the association between those component instances.

Let's start, once again, with the Loader component.

1. Create a new Flash document and save it as lsp05a.fla in a new folder. Copy the dragon.jpg file, used in the other examples, into the same folder.

2. Open the Document Properties dialog box, via the Modify ➤ Document menu option, and set the stage dimensions as 600 × 450 pixels.

3. Drag the Loader component onto the stage in order to create an instance of the component. Name the newly created instance loader1.

4. Select the loader1 instance and set its position at X: 0.0, Y: 0.0 and its dimensions as W: 600.0, H: 450.0.

5. Create a new layer. Select the first frame of the new layer and drag the ProgressBar component onto the stage. A ProgressBar instance will be created in the new layer. Name the ProgressBar instance progressbar1. This time, the ProgressBar instance is on top of the Loader instance, since it is hosted in the topmost layer.

6. Select the progressbar1 instance and set its position at X: 225.0, Y: 210.0.

7. Create a new layer and name it actions. Select its first frame and attach the following ActionScript line to it:

```
#include "test.as"
```

8. Create a new ActionScript file and save it as test.as in the same folder containing the other two files.

9. Insert the following code in the new ActionScript file:

```
function progress(eventObject:Object) {
        var alreadyLoaded =➥
eventObject.target.getBytesLoaded();
        var total = eventObject.target.getBytesTotal();
        progressbar1.setProgress(alreadyLoaded, total);
}
```

385

```
function complete() {
        progressbar1.setVisible(false);
}

loader1.addEventListener("progress", this);
loader1.addEventListener("complete", this);
progressbar1.mode = "manual";

loader1.contentPath = "dragon.jpg";
```

10. Save both lsp05a.fla and test.as.

Running the simulated test of the movie will show the same outcome as the earlier ProgressBar and Loader codeless examples. However, the approach used here is quite different and gives you control of several aspects. First, this time, the ProgressBar instance is on top of the Loader instance, and it becomes invisible when the following line is executed:

```
progressbar1.setVisible(false);
```

By setting the ProgressBar mode to manual, you have inserted an intermediate listener object (_level0 in our example) that intercepts both the progress and complete events when raised by the Loader instance.

Note that the progress event handler in our example redirects the progress information to the progressbar1 instance via its setProgress method.

```
function progress(eventObject:Object) {
        var alreadyLoaded =➡
eventObject.target.getBytesLoaded();
        var total = eventObject.target.getBytesTotal();
        progressbar1.setProgress(alreadyLoaded, total);
}
```

Redirecting the progress information is a necessary step once the progressbar1 instance is in manual mode. The progressbar1 instance would not be able to show any progress without receiving such information. However, intercepting both events (complete and progress) gives you full control over the interaction between the two component instances.

Intercepting these events allows you to do something when they are triggered. In our example, we exploited this control only by making the ProgressBar instance disappear once the loading process is completed. In a real-world application, you may use this technique to synchronize other objects. Also, by applying this same technique, you can easily build an extended version of the Loader component that encapsulates a ProgressBar.

In the source files associated with this chapter, you will also find an example (lsp05b.fla) that demonstrates the same technique applied to the ScrollPane case. To implement this, you simply need to replace the Loader instance with a ScrollPane instance. The fact that this technique works by just replacing instances of different components is a further demonstration of its value and of the benefits of a well-designed (and utilized) component architecture.

Supported styles

Since both the Loader and the ScrollPane components are containers, there isn't much that can be customized in terms of their appearance. In fact, the Loader component does not support any style, and the only style that has some effect on the ScrollPane component is the themeColor style, which influences its scrollbars. Therefore, the only styles that we will examine in this chapter are those of the ProgressBar component.

The ProgressBar component supports the following styles:

- **Text styles**: For customizing the appearance of its label, the ProgressBar supports embedFonts, fontFamily, fontSize, fontStyle, fontWeight, textDecoration, and textIndent. If you do not already know how these text styles behave, refer to Chapter 18.

- **Color styles**: You can colorize a ProgressBar instance consistently by using the themeColor style that, as you've already seen, is supported in conjunction with the Halo theme by default. Other common color styles supported by the ProgressBar component are color and disabledColor, which define the color of the text in the label and of the component instance when it is disabled, respectively.

Let's customize one of our previous examples to demonstrate how you can stylize a ProgressBar.

1. Open the lsp02a.fla file you created earlier and save it as lsp06.fla in a new folder.
2. Create an ActionScript file and save it as test.as in the same folder that contains the lsp06.fla file.
3. Add the following code to the newly created test.as file:

```
function updateProgress() {
    switch (phase) {
        case 1:
            progressbar1.label = "Phase 1: Creating Characters";
            progressbar1.setProgress(1, 4);
            break;
        case 2:
            progressbar1.label = "Phase 2: Creating Cities";
            progressbar1.setProgress(2, 4);
            break;
        case 3:
            progressbar1.label = "Phase 3: Creating Trees";
            progressbar1.setProgress(3, 4);
            break;
        case 4:
            progressbar1.label = "Phase 4: Completing Generation";
            progressbar1.setProgress(4, 4);
            break;
        default:
            clearInterval(id);
            progressbar1.setVisible(false);
            break;
```

```
        }
      phase++;
    }

    function setStyles(instance) {
        instance.setStyle("themeColor", "haloOrange");
        instance.setStyle("color", "haloOrange");
        instance.setStyle("fontFamily", "Courier New");
        instance.setStyle("fontSize", 12);
        instance.setStyle("fontStyle", "italic");
        instance.setStyle("fontWeight", "bold");
    }

    progressbar1.label = "Initializing..";
    progressbar1.mode = "manual";

    progressbar1.setSize(300,30);
    progressbar1.move(150,210);

    setStyles(progressbar1);

    var phase:Number = 1;
    var id:Number = setInterval(updateProgress, 2000);
```

4. Select the first frame in the `lsp02a.fla` document and add the following ActionScript line to it:

   ```
   #include "test.as"
   ```

5. Save both the `lsp02a.fla` and `test.as` files.

Most of the code in this example is identical to the code we created and analyzed earlier (when we first created the `lsp02a.fla` example in the "The ProgressBar's animated behavior" section). We reused that example and applied a few styles to the ProgressBar instance to achieve the customized look that you can see by testing the movie, as shown in Figure 15-9.

Figure 15-9. A stylized ProgressBar instance

Basically, by using the `themeColor` style, you can affect only the bar of the component instance. Therefore, we also used the `color`, `fontFamily`, `fontSize`, `fontStyle`, and `fontWeight` styles to customize the appearance of the ProgressBar instance's label in a way that is consistent with the new color set for the bar.

```
instance.setStyle("themeColor", "haloOrange");
instance.setStyle("color", "haloOrange");
instance.setStyle("fontFamily", "Courier New");
instance.setStyle("fontSize", 12);
instance.setStyle("fontStyle", "italic");
instance.setStyle("fontWeight", "bold");
```

Skinnability

Even in the case of skinning, there isn't much to do about components such as the Loader and the ScrollPane, since they are essentially containers. However, you may be tempted to redefine their borders, implemented by a RectBorder instance. See Chapter 11 for a detailed explanation of how to customize borders based on a RectBorder instance.

In the case of the ScrollPane component, you may also need to skin its subcomponents—the scrollbars. See Chapter 21 for details on how to skin scrollbars.

Once again, the ProgressBar is the only component covered in this chapter that has specific visual parts that you can customize. The ProgressBar is made up of two entities: the bar showing the progress of the monitored activity and the track. Figure 15-10 highlights these two parts of the component in their default skins.

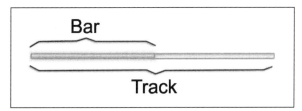

Figure 15-10. The bar and track of a ProgressBar component

The ProgressBar class defines three skin properties that are associated with the track:

- progTrackLeftName = "ProgTrackLeft"
- progTrackMiddleName = "ProgTrackMiddle"
- progTrackRightName = "ProgTrackRight"

Basically, the track is divided into three skins: two skins associated with the track's edges (ProgTrackLeft and ProgTrackRight) and a skin associated with the middle of the track, which is usually resized to cover the distance from one edge to the other.

The ProgressBar class also defines three skin properties that are associated with the bar, since it is divided in the same way as the track:

- progBarLeftName = "ProgBarLeft"
- progBarMiddleName = "ProgBarMiddle"
- progBarRightName = "ProgBarRight"

As with the track, two skins are dedicated to the edges of the bar (ProgBarLeft and ProgBarRight), while a third skin (ProgBarMiddle) is used for its middle part and usually stretches to join the edges.

If you are wondering how to skin the ProgressBar component when it appears in its indeterminate state, you should know that its class defines a further skin property:

- progIndBarName = "ProgIndBar"

The ProgIndBar skin replaces the ProgBarMiddle skin in the middle part when the indeterminate property is true, while the skins used for the edges of the bar (ProgBarLeft and ProgBarRight) remain the same.

In the source files associated with this chapter, you will find an example (lsp07.fla) that replaces those seven skins. Open it in the authoring environment while you read the rest of this section in order to examine the symbols included in the document's library to replace the standard skins of the ProgressBar, as shown in Figure 15-11.

Name	Kind	Use Count	Linkage
ProgressBar	Compiled Clip	-	Export: ProgressBar
ProgressBar Assets	Folder		
Elements	Folder		
ProgBarLeft	Movie Clip	-	Export: ProgBarLeft
ProgBarMiddle	Movie Clip	-	Export: ProgBarMiddle
ProgBarRight	Movie Clip	-	Export: ProgBarRight
ProgIndBar	Movie Clip	-	Export: ProgIndBar
ProgTrackLeft	Movie Clip	-	Export: ProgTrackLeft
ProgTrackMiddle	Movie Clip	-	Export: ProgTrackMiddle
ProgTrackRight	Movie Clip	-	Export: ProgTrackRight
Images	Folder		
ProgressBarAssets	Movie Clip	-	Export: ProgressBarAssets

Figure 15-11. The library of the skinning example

This example uses the simplest of the techniques for replacing the skins of a component: providing exported symbols that have the same names as the default values of the skin properties (ProgTrackLeft, ProgTrackMiddle, ProgTrackRight, ProgBarLeft, ProgBarMiddle, ProgBarRight, and ProgIndBar). Note that, when skinning the ProgressBar component, the library must contain an additional exported symbol: ProgressBarAssets (also shown in Figure 15-11).

Creating the ProgressBarAssets symbol is a straightforward process since it contains one instance of each of the seven skin symbols. Figure 15-12 illustrates the contents of the ProgressBarAssets symbol and further clarifies the role of each skin symbol included in it.

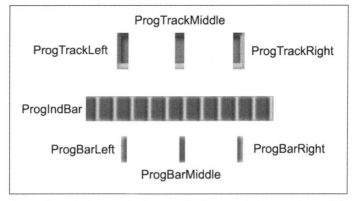

Figure 15-12. Contents of the ProgressBarAssets symbol (the custom skins)

The lsp07.fla file is basically the skinned version of the previous lsp02a.fla example. The new skins give the ProgressBar track a carved look, while the bar appears in a rust color. Figure 15-13 shows the skinned version of the ProgressBar displaying a message that is one of those defined in the lsp02a.fla example.

Figure 15-13. A skinned ProgressBar instance

In this example, I made a couple of adjustments to the ProgressBar instance to improve its appearance with the new skin. In particular, I placed the instance's label in the center by accessing the labelPlacement property, like so:

```
progressbar1.labelPlacement = "center";
```

The labelPlacement property of the ProgressBar class accepts five string values (left, right, top, bottom, and center). The default value of the labelPlacement property (bottom) would have not worked well in this example, since the new skin is taller than the default one and the ProgressBar component is quite rigid in defining the positioning of its label. Also, the use of the center option for the labelPlacement property would have not been sufficient to achieve the look you see in Figure 15-13, since the label text would have overlapped the left edge. I resolved that issue by setting the textIndent style of the component instance to 10, moving the text ten units on the right:

```
instance.setStyle("textIndent", 10);
```

391

For the rest, the example implements a startExample function that allows you to quickly switch the indeterminate state on and off:

```
function startExample(showIndeterminate:Boolean) {
    if (showIndeterminate) {
        phase = 6;
        id = setInterval(updateProgress, 12000);
        progressbar1.indeterminate = true;
        progressbar1.label = "";
    } else {
        phase = 1;
        id = setInterval(updateProgress, 2000);
        progressbar1.label = "Initializing    ";
    }
}
```

To experiment, open the test.as file associated with the lsp07.fla document, and change the line:

```
startExample(false);
```

to:

```
startExample(true);
```

Then test the movie again to see the appearance of the custom skin defined for the ProgressBar whenever is in the indeterminate state, as shown in Figure 15-14.

Figure 15-14. Custom skin for the indeterminate state of the ProgressBar component

Solved mysteries

The current implementation of the ProgressBar component has a subtle bug that you saw when implementing the lsp04b.fla example. In that case, we tried to use the event option of the ProgressBar mode property while referring a ScrollPane instance as the source object. However, we were instead forced to use the polled option, since event does not work with the ScrollPane component, regardless of the fact that this component supports both the progress and the complete events.

If you open the file ProgressBar.as, available in the source code of the component architecture (see Appendix A for instructions on how to locate this file), and look for the event handler of the progress event (function progress), you will find that its implementation does not use the parameters of the event object (current and total) but assumes that the source object implements two further properties: bytesLoaded and bytesTotal.

If you attach the following code to the first frame of the `lsp04b.fla` example, you will then be able to set the mode parameter of the `progressbar01` instance to event and, this time, it will work in the case of using a ScrollPane instance as the source object:

```
import mx.controls.ProgressBar;

ProgressBar.prototype.progress = function(eventObject:Object):Void {
    this.setProgress(eventObject.current, eventObject.total);
}
```

This solution overrides the progress event handler of the `ProgressBar` class to provide an implementation that, in a single line of code, does what such an event handler was expected to do: use the values associated with the event object to set the progress of the ProgressBar instance.

The fact that the solution to this bug is very simple is an opportunity to emphasize how event-driven communications must work among components belonging to the same architecture. The relevance of this patch goes beyond this single case because it reinforces a communication standard based on events throughout the architecture. Furthermore, it can be applied without altering the original source code of the component architecture.

This case also highlights the importance of having the source code of the component architecture available. This way, whenever something does not work as specified, you have the chance to analyze its code and possibly find your own solution to the problem.

Reasons for subclassing

The patch explained in the previous section is a good enough reason for creating a subclassed version of the ProgressBar component. Of course, you may also wish to subclass the ProgressBar component to create a distributable skinned version associated with a theme of your own creation.

The Loader and ScrollPane components usually don't require to skinning (the scrollbars in the ScrollPane component can be skinned separately, as you will see in Chapter 21). However, if you find the opportunity to subclass them, it would certainly pay off to add a ProgressBar instance to their subclassed versions. That way, you will not need to implement the interactions described in this chapter every time you want to use them.

Chapter 16

THE MENU AND MENUBAR COMPONENTS

Menu mx.controls.Menu	MenuBar mx.controls.MenuBar
Frequency: Common Complexity: Simple Stability: Robust Maturity: Classic Popularity: Widespread	Frequency: Common Complexity: Simple Stability: Robust Maturity: Classic Popularity: Widespread

The MenuBar and the Menu components replicate a couple of features that are very common in modern software applications: menu bars and pop-up menus.

The Menu component implements a pop-up window that the user utilizes to select from several menu items listed in a menu fashion. You can create Menu instances on the fly that react to a user event such as a mouse click.

Menu instances are also created dynamically on demand by the MenuBar component.

As usual, building a minimal example for both components will show you their core functionality better than any description.

> *The completed source code introduced in this chapter can be found in the package* `src16.zip`, *downloadable from this book's page on* `www.friendsofed.com`.

Minimal examples

In this section, you can find minimal examples of the Menu and MenuBar components that will show you the core features of these components while focusing on their most immediate and practical use.

Minimal example of the Menu component

Let us start from the Menu component, since it also is a subcomponent of the MenuBar component that we will examine just after.

1. Create a new Flash document and save it as `mnu01a.fla`.
2. Open the Document Properties dialog box by selecting Modify ➤ Document, and set its dimensions as 640✕480 pixels.
3. Drag the Menu component on the stage in order to create one instance of the component, but then delete it just after. We will create the Menu instance dynamically, and this step is to add the Menu component to the document's library.
4. Select the first frame in the document and attach the following ActionScript code to it:

   ```
   #include "test.as"
   ```

5. Create a new ActionScript file and save it as `test.as` in the same folder where you saved the `mnu01a.fla` file.
6. Add the following code to the ActionScript file you just created:

   ```
   import mx.controls.Menu;

   var popupMenu1:Menu = Menu.createMenu();
   popupMenu1.addMenuItem({label: "Command 1",
   ➥ instanceName:"menuItem1"});
   ```

```
popupMenu1.addMenuItem({label: "Command 2",
➡ instanceName:"menuItem2"});
popupMenu1.addMenuItem({label: "Command 3",
➡ instanceName:"menuItem3"});

this.onMouseUp = function(Void):Void {
    popupMenu1.show(this._xmouse, this._ymouse);
}
```

7. Save the mnu01a.fla and test.as files.

Testing the example will show an empty stage. However, a pop-up menu will appear whenever you click the stage close to the point where you clicked, as displayed in the Figure 16-1.

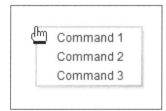

Figure 16-1. The minimal example after you click somewhere on the stage

Although very minimal, this example shows all of the most important features of the Menu component. First of all, it shows how they are created dynamically:

```
var popupMenu1:Menu = Menu.createMenu();
```

createMenu is a static method of the Menu class and, as such, you do not need an instance of this class to invoke it. All you need to access this method is the name of the class as specified in the previous line of code.

The createMenu method returns an instance of the Menu component that is not visible. This is why we implement the onMouseUp event handler of the _level0 object; every time you click the empty stage, the show method of the Menu class is invoked, and the popupMenu1 instance is displayed starting from the current mouse coordinates:

```
this.onMouseUp = function(Void):Void {
    popupMenu1.show(this._xmouse, this._ymouse);
}
```

Note that, just after creating the popupMenu1 instance, we add three menu items to it by invoking the addMenuItem method of the Menu class. The addMenuItem method requires one object with properties describing what kind of menu item must be added to the Menu instance. We will examine this method in greater detail later on in this chapter when we build a richer example that shows all sorts of menu items that can be created.

Minimal example of the MenuBar component

The MenuBar component is made of buttons that appear in its bar and Menu instances that are associated with those buttons, as displayed by the following example:

1. Create a new Flash document and save it as mnu01b.fla.

2. Open the Document Properties dialog box by selecting Modify ➤ Document, and set its dimensions as 640×480 pixels.

3. Drag the MenuBar component on the stage in order to create one instance. Define its instance name as menubar1.

4. Select the menubar1 instance and set its position at (X: 0.0, Y: 0.0) and its dimensions as (W: 640.0, H: 22.0).

5. Select the first frame in the document and attach the following ActionScript code to it:

   #include "test.as"

6. Create a new ActionScript file and save it as test.as in the same folder where you saved the mnu01b.fla file.

7. Add the following code to the ActionScript file just created:

```
var menu1 = menubar1.addMenu("Menu 1");
menu1.addMenuItem({label: "Command 1",
➥ instanceName:"menuItem1"});
menu1.addMenuItem({label: "Command 2",
➥ instanceName:"menuItem2"});
menu1.addMenuItem({label: "Command 3",
➥ instanceName:"menuItem3"});

var menu2 = menubar1.addMenu("Menu 2");
menu2.addMenuItem({label: "Command 4",
➥ instanceName:"menuItem4"});
menu2.addMenuItem({label: "Command 5",
➥ instanceName:"menuItem5"});
menu2.addMenuItem({label: "Command 6",
➥ instanceName:"menuItem6"});
```

8. Save the mnu01b.fla and test.as files.

The code in this example is very linear but repetitive. We invoke the createMenu method of the MenuBar class twice to create two Menu instances that, as in the previous example, are not visible immediately when you test this movie.

Although not visible, the Menu instances exist as subcomponents of the MenuBar instance and, in fact, we can use the object reference returned by the createMenu method to invoke the addMenuItem of the Menu class and add three menu items to each of the Menu instances in this example.

Testing this example, the MenuBar instance displays two buttons in its bar, one for each of the Menu instances created and associated with the MenuBar instance. Figure 16-2 shows how the MenuBar instance appears initially.

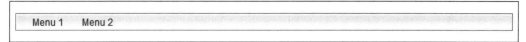

Figure 16-2. The MenuBar minimal example when it starts

Note that the two objects in the MenuBar are buttons and not Menu instances. A Menu instance is displayed only when you click one of those buttons, as illustrated by Figure 16-3.

Figure 16-3. A Menu instance displayed after you click a button in the MenuBar instance

The objective of this minimal example is to emphasize the core functionality of the MenuBar component and how it relates to its subobjects, which are, in fact, instances of the Menu component.

The following examples will exploit the fact that the MenuBar component creates instances of the Menu component to allow you to explore the features of both components at the same time.

Let us then explore the extra features of both the MenuBar and Menu components by building the next, richer, examples.

Richer examples

We are going to build a richer example in order to demonstrate several features that were not exposed by the minimal examples. The objectives of our next example are

- To showcase every menu item type
- To demonstrate creating nested menu instances
- To see how to handle the user input whenever a Menu item is selected

The MenuBar and Menu components provide two radically different ways to build the structure of Menu instances: programmatically, as we saw earlier, and via an XML description, following the same approach of XML layout engines that we discussed during Part 2 of the book.

The first of our richer examples will extend the programmatic approach utilized earlier in this chapter.

Generating richer menus by coding

Let us extend the MenuBar minimal example created earlier.

1. Open the document mnu01b.fla created earlier and save it in a new folder as mnu02a.fla.
2. Create a new symbol (behavior: movie clip) by selecting the Insert ➤ New Symbol menu options, and define both its name and its linkage identifier as icon1.

3. Draw a shape into the newly created symbol or reuse the graphics that you can find in the completed `mnu02a.fla` file associated with this chapter. Place the shape at (X: 0, Y:0) and define its size as (W: 14, H: 14).

4. Repeat the previous two steps a couple of times to create another two symbols with names and linkage identifiers of icon2 and icon3. Once again, you can define a simple shape for each of them or reuse the graphic that you find in the source file associated with this chapter.

5. Create a new ActionScript file and save it as `test.as` in the same folder where you saved the `mnu02a.fla` file.

6. Add the following code to the ActionScript file you just created:

```
var menu1 = menubar1.addMenu("Menu 1");
menu1.addMenuItem({label: "Item 1.1",
➥ instanceName:"menuItem1_1"});
menu1.addMenuItem({label: "Item 1.2",
➥ instanceName:"menuItem1_2"});
menu1.addMenuItem({label: "Item 1.3",
➥ instanceName:"menuItem1_3"});
menu1.addMenuItem({label: "Item 1.4",
➥ instanceName:"menuItem1_4", enabled: false});
menu1.addMenuItem({type: "separator"});
menu1.addMenuItem({label: "Item 1.5", instanceName:"menuItem1_5",
➥ icon: "icon1"});
menu1.addMenuItem({label: "Item 1.6",
➥ instanceName:"menuItem1_6", icon: "icon2"});
menu1.addMenuItem({label: "Item 1.7",
➥ instanceName:"menuItem1_7", icon: "icon3"});

var menu2 = menubar1.addMenu("Menu 2");
menu2.addMenuItem({label: "Item 2.1", instanceName:"menuItem2_1",
➥ type: "radio", groupName: "groupA", selected: true});
menu2.addMenuItem({label: "Item 2.2", instanceName:"menuItem2_2",
➥ type: "radio", groupName: "groupA"});
menu2.addMenuItem({label: "Item 2.3", instanceName:"menuItem2_3",
➥ type: "radio", groupName: "groupA"});
menu2.addMenuItem({type: "separator"});
var menuitem2_4 = menu2.addMenuItem({label: "Item 2.4",
➥ instanceName:"menuItem2_4"});
menuitem2_4.addMenuItem({label: "Item 2.4.1",
➥ instanceName:"menuItem2_4_1", type: "check", selected: true});
menuitem2_4.addMenuItem({label: "Item 2.4.2",
➥ instanceName:"menuItem2_4_2", type: "check", selected: true});
menuitem2_4.addMenuItem({label: "Item 2.4.3",
➥ instanceName:"menuItem2_4_3", type: "check", selected: true});
menu2.addMenuItem({type: "separator"});
menu2.addMenuItem({label: "Item 2.5", instanceName:"menuItem2_5",
➥ type: "radio", groupName: "groupB"});
```

```
menu2.addMenuItem({label: "Item 2.6", instanceName:"menuItem2_6",
➥ type: "radio", groupName: "groupB", selected: true});
menu2.addMenuItem({label: "Item 2.7", instanceName:"menuItem2_7",
➥ type: "radio", groupName: "groupB"});

menubar1.addEventListener("change", this);

function change(eventObject:Object):Void {
    var a:Object = eventObject.menuItem.attributes;

    trace("======= change event =======")
    trace("instanceName: " + a.instanceName);
    trace("label: " + a.label);
    trace("selected: " + a.selected);
    trace("===========================")
}
```

7. Save the mnu02a.fla and test.as files.

The structure of the Flash document in our last example is identical to that of the MenuBar minimal example, containing only a single instance of the MenuBar component. The ActionScript file, however, contains several lines for creating two Menu instances that are richer than those of the previous example.

In this example, menu items are still created via the addMenuItem method of the Menu class by passing an object that acts as menu item descriptor. The descriptor object of a menu item can have up to seven different properties:

- label: A String value storing the text to be displayed in the menu item.

- instanceName: A String value storing the name of the menu item instance that can be used to access the menu item individually but, most importantly, to distinguish it from other menu item instances.

- type: A String value storing the type of the menu item. When undefined, it coincides with the "normal" value. Other possible values are "separator", "radio", and "check".

- groupName: A String value that makes sense only if the type of the menu item is "radio". In that case, it allows grouping "radio" menu items that can be selected by mutual exclusion, as in the case of the RadioButton component. It stores the name of a radio group (of menu items).

- selected: A Boolean value that makes sense only if the type of the menu item is "radio" or "check", since those are the only two menu item types that can be selected/unselected. Its default value is false.

- enabled: A Boolean, true by default, that can be used to disable a specific menu item.

- icon: A String value storing a linkage identifier of a symbol in the document library that can be used as icon inside the menu item.

The type property is arguably the most important of the seven properties, since it influences the behavior of the menu item.

When the user selects a "normal" menu item, the component instance raises a change event, but the user selection is not stored in the state of the menu item.

The user cannot select a menu item of the "separator" type; these act as a sort of visual divider between two menu items, as suggested by their type name.

Selecting "radio" and "check" menu items also results in triggering a change event. In addition, the new state of the menu item is stored in its selected property.

Running our latest example will visually highlight the behaviors and the available appearances of menu items, once you start experimenting with the Menu instances that pop up after you click one of the two buttons in the MenuBar instance.

Figure 16-4 shows the Menu instance appearing after you click the Menu 1 button.

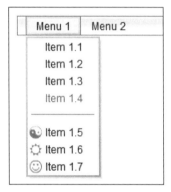

Figure 16-4. Normal menus, enabled or disabled, with or without an icon and one separator

With the exception of the fifth item, which is a "separator", the Menu instance displayed in Figure 16-4 contains all "normal" menu items, created without defining any type property, since "normal" is the default.

Setting enabled to false disables the fourth menu item:

```
menu1.addMenuItem({label: "Item 1.4",
➥ instanceName:"menuItem1_4", enabled: false});
```

The last three "normal" menu items include an icon in their representation. An icon can be implemented by a graphic stored inside an exported symbol. The following line assumes that an exported symbol with the linkage identifier of icon1 is present in the document's library:

```
menu1.addMenuItem({label: "Item 1.5", instanceName:"menuItem1_5",
➥ icon: "icon1"});
```

Clicking the Menu 2 button in the MenuBar instance will display the second menu implemented by our example, as illustrated by Figure 16-5.

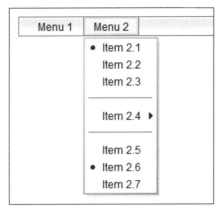

Figure 16-5. Two groups of radio menu items, two separators, and a nested menu

Apart from the two separators helping in visually arranging the other menu items, the first level of the Menu instance displayed in Figure 16-5 contains the following:

- A first set of three "radio" menu items (2.1, 2.2, 2.3)
- A "normal" menu item (2.4) that also links to a submenu
- Another set of three "radio" menu items (2.5, 2.6, 2.7)

We created two sets of "radio" menu items to demonstrate the use of the groupName property. Basically, the menu items in the first set (2.1, 2.2, 2.3) belong to the "groupA" radio group as specified in the following:

```
menu2.addMenuItem({label: "Item 2.1", instanceName:"menuItem2_1",
➡ type: "radio", groupName: "groupA", selected: true});
menu2.addMenuItem({label: "Item 2.2", instanceName:"menuItem2_2",
➡ type: "radio", groupName: "groupA"});
menu2.addMenuItem({label: "Item 2.3", instanceName:"menuItem2_3",
➡ type: "radio", groupName: "groupA"});
```

Similarly, we defined a "groupB" value for the groupName property of the remaining three "radio" menu items (2.5, 2.6, 2.7). The result of this grouping is that you can have two "radio" menu items selected in the same Menu instance, since they belong to two different radio groups. Selecting another "radio" menu item in "groupA" will deselect the menu item previously selected in that group, but will have no effect on the "radio" menu items in "groupB". Try it for yourself by experimenting with the example.

The only "normal" menu item (2.4) displayed in Figure 16-5 includes an arrow on its right side to indicate that, once selected, it will show its submenu, as illustrated in Figure 16-6.

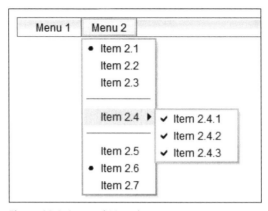

Figure 16-6. A nested Menu instance

The following lines of code created the nested Menu instance shown in Figure 16-6:

```
var menuitem2_4 = menu2.addMenuItem({label: "Item 2.4",
➥ instanceName:"menuItem2_4"}));
menuitem2_4.addMenuItem({label: "Item 2.4.1",
➥ instanceName:"menuItem2_4_1", type: "check", selected: true});
menuitem2_4.addMenuItem({label: "Item 2.4.2",
➥ instanceName:"menuItem2_4_2", type: "check", selected: true});
menuitem2_4.addMenuItem({label: "Item 2.4.3",
➥ instanceName:"menuItem2_4_3", type: "check", selected: true});
```

The most important detail to notice here is that we store the object reference returned by the first call to the addMenuItem method in a variable (menuitem2_4). In fact, the addMenuItem method returns a reference to the menu item instance that we usually do not store. However, such an object reference becomes precious when creating a nested menu, since it can be used to invoke its addMenuItem method to create a submenu associated with that specific menu item.

The nested menu example showcases the only type of menu item we have not displayed yet: the "check" menu item. In fact, the nested menu contains three "check" menu items, all of them initially checked by setting their selected property to true.

The fact that our richer example includes every menu item type will be useful later on when stylizing and skinning the component, since we will be able to preview every visual aspect of a menu item in the same example.

Our example also implements a handler for the change event triggered by the MenuBar instance whenever a menu item is selected:

```
menubar1.addEventListener("change", this);

function change(eventObject:Object):Void {
    var a:Object = eventObject.menuItem.attributes;

    trace("======= change event =======")
    trace("instanceName: " + a.instanceName);
    trace("label: " + a.label);
    trace("selected: " + a.selected);
    trace("============================")
}
```

The implementation of the change event handler shows that the event object has a menuItem property that provides a reference to the menu item instance that triggered the event, once selected by the user.

When handling a menu item instance, you must be aware that they are actually implemented as instances of the XMLNode class (a built-in ActionScript class). This is the reason why we have to go through the attributes property to eventually access the attributes of a menu item instance in the implementation of the change event handler.

The change event handler in our example reacts to the selection of a menu item by showing its instanceName, label, and selected attributes in the Output window.

If you test the movie in the authoring environment, you may notice a similar message added to the Output window every time that you select a menu item:

```
======= change event =======
instanceName: menuItem2_3
label: Item 2.3
selected: true
============================
```

Our example shows how to retrieve the information stored in the event object of the change event. Knowing which menu item was selected and how to access its attributes allows you to execute the proper code specific to your applications.

Generating richer menus using XML

Our previous example revealed that menu items are stored as XMLNode instances, indicating that the whole structure of a Menu instance is translated into an XML-like structure whenever the menu is created.

Such a choice of implementation method was made to allow you to exploit XML when defining the structure of a Menu or even a MenuBar component instance. In the previous example, you had a chance to appreciate that repetitive calls to the addMenuItem method are not very readable, especially when it comes to nested menus, since the menu's structure is not immediately evident from ActionScript.

Due to the nature of its nested structure, XML represents the ideal choice for describing nested menus, and the component architecture provides you with a convenient alternative for creating menu items: you can define the structure of menus by passing an instance of the XML class to the dataProvider property of both the Menu and MenuBar classes.

Let us reimplement the previous richer example by exploiting this alternative so that you can learn the technique while at the same time comparing the two approaches.

1. Open the document mnu02a.fla created earlier and save it in a new folder as mnu02b.fla.

2. Create a new ActionScript file and save it as test.as in the same folder where you saved the mnu02b.fla file.

3. Add the following code to the ActionScript file just created:

```
var dp = new XML();
dp.ignoreWhite = true;

dp.onLoad = function(success:Boolean):Void {
    if (success) {
        menubar1.dataProvider = dp.firstChild;
    }
}

dp.load("menus.xml");

menubar1.addEventListener("change", this);

function change(eventObject:Object):Void {
    var a:Object = eventObject.menuItem.attributes;

    trace("======= change event =======")
    trace("instanceName: " + a.instanceName);
    trace("label: " + a.label);
    trace("selected: " + a.selected);
    trace("===========================")
}
```

4. Create a new text file using a text editor such as Notepad and save it as menus.xml in the same folder where you saved the mnu02b.fla file.

5. Add the following XML data to the menus.xml text file just created:

```
<menubar>
  <menu label="Menu 1">
    <menuitem label="Item 1.1" instanceName="menuItem1_1" />
    <menuitem label="Item 1.2" instanceName="menuItem1_2" />
    <menuitem label="Item 1.3" instanceName="menuItem1_3" />
    <menuitem label="Item 1.4" instanceName="menuItem1_4"
➥ enabled="false" />
    <menuitem type="separator" />
```

```
        <menuitem label="Item 1.5" instanceName="menuItem1_5"
➥ icon="icon1" />
        <menuitem label="Item 1.6" instanceName="menuItem1_6"
➥ icon="icon2" />
        <menuitem label="Item 1.7" instanceName="menuItem1_7"
➥ icon="icon3" />
      </menu>
      <menu label="Menu 2">
        <menuitem label="Item 2.1" instanceName="menuItem2_1"
➥ type="radio" groupName="groupA" selected="true" />
        <menuitem label="Item 2.2" instanceName="menuItem2_2"
➥ type="radio" groupName="groupA" />
        <menuitem label="Item 2.3" instanceName="menuItem2_3"
➥ type="radio" groupName="groupA" />
        <menuitem type="separator" />
        <menuitem label="Item 2.4" instanceName="menuItem2_4">
          <menuitem label="Item 2.4.1"
➥ instanceName="menuItem2_4_1" type="check" selected="true" />
          <menuitem label="Item 2.4.2"
➥ instanceName="menuItem2_4_2" type="check" selected="true" />
          <menuitem label="Item 2.4.3"
➥ instanceName="menuItem2_4_3" type="check" selected="true" />
        </menuitem>
        <menuitem type="separator" />
        <menuitem label="Item 2.5" instanceName="menuItem2_5"
➥ type="radio" groupName="groupB" />
        <menuitem label="Item 2.6" instanceName="menuItem2_6"
➥ type="radio" groupName="groupB" selected="true" />
        <menuitem label="Item 2.7" instanceName="menuItem2_7"
➥ type="radio" groupName="groupB" />
      </menu>
    </menubar>
```

6. Save the `mnu02a.fla`, `test.as`, and `menus.xml` files.

The most significant aspect of our latest example is that we are using XML data to specify the whole structure of the MenuBar instance following an approach that is very similar to that of the XML layout engines we discussed in Part 2 of the book.

The essential structure of the XML data included in the `menus.xml` file is as follows:

```
<menubar>
  <menu label="Menu 1">
  ..................................
  </menu>
  <menu label="Menu 2">
  ..................................
  </menu>
</menubar>
```

407

The menubar element is used to group menu elements that, in turn, will include their own menuitem elements. Each of the menuitem elements can have up to seven attributes that are named and work exactly as discussed earlier in this chapter. The following line is an example of a menuitem element also including an icon attribute:

```
<menuitem label="Item 1.5" instanceName="menuItem1_5" icon="icon1" />
```

The XML description stored in the menus.xml file reproduces the same menu structure as the previous example, as shown in Figures 16-4, 16-5, and 16-6.

The following XML snippet is yet another example of how convenient its use is when it comes to describing component-based user interfaces. In fact, a nested menu associated with a specific menu item can be easily and intuitively described by nesting the <menuitem> elements as done here:

```
<menuitem label="Item 2.4" instanceName="menuItem2_4">
  <menuitem label="Item 2.4.1"
➡ instanceName="menuItem2_4_1" type="check" selected="true" />
  <menuitem label="Item 2.4.2"
➡ instanceName="menuItem2_4_2" type="check" selected="true" />
  <menuitem label="Item 2.4.3"
➡ instanceName="menuItem2_4_3" type="check" selected="true" />
</menuitem>
```

Another advantage of the XML approach is that the resulting ActionScript code is much simpler and, therefore, more readable.

The few lines of ActionScript in our latest example create an XML instance to load the content of the menus.xml file and, once that content is loaded, the code assigns it to the dataProvider property of the MenuBar instance:

```
menubar1.dataProvider = dp.firstChild;
```

In a very similar way, you could use the dataProvider property of the Menu class to create XML-driven Menu component instances. Of course, the root element of the XML file should be a menu element instead of a menubar element.

XLEFF version

Part 2 introduced the concept of XML layout engines, describing the many benefits that they can offer. We also explored the use of XLEFF as a concrete example of an XML layout engine based on the Flash component architecture.

The Menu and MenuBar components are not the only ones to support XML as a description language when it comes to generate their instances: the Tree component uses XML for the same purpose in a very similar way (see Chapter 19).

The implementation of those components demonstrates the convenience of XML, and XLEFF extends that convenient approach to all the components in the architecture by allowing the use of XML for describing the structure of every standard component.

In the case of the Menu and MenuBar components, XLEFF supports the same syntax of the component architecture with very few extensions to the menubar element to allow you to place the component on stage and define the name of its instance, like so:

```
<menubar x="0" y="0" width="890" name="menubar1">
   ............................................
</menubar>
```

If you wish to replicate our richer example by using XLEFF, the structure inside the menubar element should be exactly the same as that defined in the menus.xml file used by the mnu02b.fla example.

The source files associated with this chapter include a preconfigured version of the XLEFF sampler, which generates a menu bar instance similar to that created in the richer examples. Check this out to verify the similarities mentioned in this section.

Supported styles

The MenuBar component is capable of propagating style definitions to the Menu instances created as subcomponents.

Applying the following style to the menubar1 instance in our latest example would affect not only the text in the buttons of the bar, but also the text of each menu item in the Menu instances associated with those buttons:

```
menubar1.setStyle("fontFamily", "Courier New");
```

As a developer, you can exploit the fact that the MenuBar is capable of propagating styles to its Menu instances to define a consistent appearance throughout your application.

In this section, we are also going to exploit the style propagation mechanism by using our previous richer example based on the MenuBar as the vehicle for exploring the influence of styles on both MenuBar and Menu components at the same time.

Stylizing the MenuBar (and its Menu instances)

Both the MenuBar and the Menu components support several styles that behave consistently when applied to the standard components in the architecture. We usually refer to these styles as **common styles**.

Common styles

The common styles supported by the MenuBar and Menu components can be conveniently grouped into two categories, text styles and color styles:

- The common text styles supported by the Menu and MenuBar components are embedFonts, fontFamily, fontSize, fontStyle, fontWeight, textDecoration, and textIndent. Text styles are examined in greater detail in Chapter 18, which is dedicated to text-based components.
- The common color styles supported by the Menu and MenuBar components are themeColor (only supported by the default theme, Halo), color, backgroundColor, and disabledColor.

We will use most of these common styles in our next example, when we stylize the richer example built earlier in this chapter.

Apart from the common styles, there are several specific styles that apply to Menu instances that you can also set in a MenuBar instance to affect the menu items of its subcomponent instances (menus).

Specific styles

The following styles affect the Menu instances specifically:

- rollOverColor: Overrides the color of the background when the mouse cursor rolls over a menu item. However, it is better to use themeColor for this purpose, not only because it enforces consistency in the color scheme, but also because this style has a bug at the time of writing: it does not work for menu items associated with a nested menu.

- selectionColor: Overrides the color of the background when a menu item is selected by clicking it. It works, but it overrides the themeColor settings that can be used for the same scope and to enforce color scheme consistency. The use of this color style is not recommended.

- alternatingRowColors: Works the same as in the case of the List and Grid components (see Chapter 13). However, setting alternating background colors for menu items generally results in a confusing design. The use of this color style is not recommended.

- textRollOverColor: Defines the color of the text in a menu item whenever the mouse cursor rolls over it.

- textSelectedColor: Defines the color of the text in a menu item whenever clicked.

- useRollOver: true by default, if set to false, disables the rollover background effect. Not working as expected at the time of writing. The use of this style is not recommended.

- popupDuration: Defines the time spent to display a Menu instance when it pops out. Set to 50 (milliseconds) by default, it can be used to easily achieve interesting effects (try it with a setting of 1000).

- selectionDuration: Defines the duration of the animation started when you click over a menu item. Set to 200 (milliseconds) by default.

- selectionEasing: Influences accelerations and decelerations of the animation starting when a menu item is clicked. See Appendix B for a list of easing methods that can be assigned to this style property.

- defaultIcon: Defines an icon to be used as the default icon of all the menu items of type "normal" that do not have an icon attribute specified.

In the next section, we are going to apply several styles to the MenuBar instance implemented in our richer example so that we can appreciate their effect not only on the bar, but also on every kind of menu item.

Exploring the styles

The richer example that we built earlier represents the ideal starting point for exploring the influence of styles on both the MenuBar and the Menu components at the same time:

1. Open the document mnu02b.fla created earlier and save it in a new folder as mnu03.fla.

2. Edit the icon1 symbol that you find in the document's library and change the fill color of its shape to #CF9200 to match the color scheme implemented by the styles defined in this example. Apply the same fill color to the shapes in the other two symbols: icon2 and icon3.

3. Copy the file menus.xml from the folder containing mnu02b.fla to the folder containing the new mnu03.fla document since we will reuse the same XML description for populating the MenuBar instance in this example.

4. Create a new ActionScript file and save it as test.as in the same folder where you saved the new mnu03.fla file.

5. Add the following code to the ActionScript file just created:

```
var dp = new XML();
dp.ignoreWhite = true;

dp.onLoad = function(success:Boolean):Void {
    if (success) {
      menubar1.dataProvider = dp.firstChild;
    }
}

dp.load("menus.xml");

function setStyles(instance:Object):Void {
    instance.setStyle("themeColor", "haloOrange");

    instance.setStyle("color", 0xCF9200);
    instance.setStyle("backgroundColor", 0xFFFEE3);
    instance.setStyle("textRollOverColor", 0xCF9200);
    instance.setStyle("textSelectedColor", "yellow");
    instance.setStyle("disabledColor", 0xDFCE93);

    instance.setStyle("fontFamily", "Courier New");
    instance.setStyle("fontSize", 14);
}

setStyles(menubar1);
```

6. Save the mnu03.fla and test.as files.

Our latest example reuses the XML data created earlier (menus.xml), allowing us to study the influence of styles on the appearance of various menu items (menus.xml describes a MenuBar instance showcasing each existing menu item type).

The purpose of this example is to stylize the previous example by applying several styles to the menubar1 instance via the setStyles function. Setting the style properties is the first step in creating a fully customized appearance of the MenuBar instance and its Menu subcomponents.

The setStyles function implements a color scheme mainly based on the themeColor style, capable of colorizing several features of a component instance at the same time.

The example implements an orange-based color scheme by first defining the themeColor style properties as haloOrange:

```
instance.setStyle("themeColor", "haloOrange");
```

The remaining color style properties, themeColor, color, backgroundColor, textRollOverColor, textSelectedColor, and disabledColor, are defined using color values that relate to the chosen color scheme:

```
instance.setStyle("color", 0xCF9200);
instance.setStyle("backgroundColor", 0xFFFEE3);
instance.setStyle("textRollOverColor", 0xCF9200);
instance.setStyle("textSelectedColor", "yellow");
instance.setStyle("disabledColor", 0xDFCE93);
```

The implementation of setStyles ends by defining a couple of font style properties:

```
instance.setStyle("fontFamily", "Courier New");
instance.setStyle("fontSize", 14);
```

The final outcome demonstrates how far the styles can go in customizing the appearance of the MenuBar and the Menu components. The result is analyzed in the Figures 16-7 to 16-10. You should use these figures as indications of the areas of the MenuBar to be examined in the authoring environment while testing the movie, since some of the color details discussed here may not be evident in the printed images.

Figure 16-7 shows the detail of the bar in the menubar1 instance. The text and color styles influence the labels of the button bars but leave the bar background untouched: the background will need to be skinned, and we will do so in the next section of this chapter.

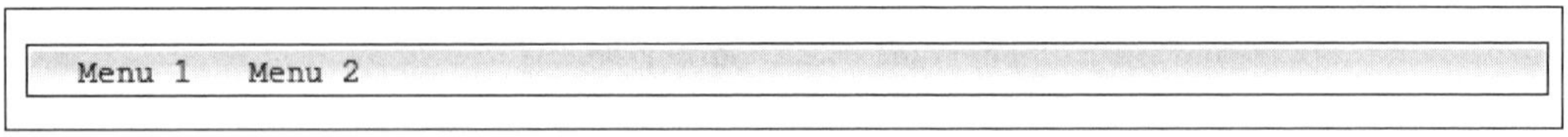

Figure 16-7. Stylized MenuBar instance, bar detail

Figure 16-8 shows the Menu 1 instance, which is largely influenced by the color scheme implemented in our latest example. Note that you have to colorize the icons manually, but this is a reasonable requirement, since you would provide your own icons when implementing your application. Figure 16-8 contains two subtle features that are not influenced by the color styles: the "separator" menu item and, more subtly, the outer border of the selected button in the menu bar. We will align these features to the color scheme being implemented in the next two sections of this chapter.

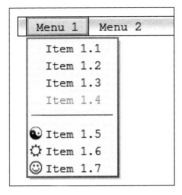

Figure 16-8. Stylized MenuBar instance, Menu 1 detail

Figure 16-9 shows the detail of the Menu 2 instance, highlighting that the icon associated with the "radio" menu items is not affected by the color styles; neither is the arrow of a menu item associated with a submenu. Both features will be aligned to the color scheme when skinning the component instance in the next section of this chapter.

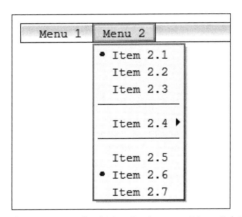

Figure 16-9. Stylized MenuBar instance, Menu 2 detail

413

Figure 16-10 shows the nested menu in our example. This demonstrates that the themeColor influences the background color of the selected menu item, while the textSelectedColor style influences the color of its text. However, the icon of the "check" menu items is still black and will need to be skinned in order to match our custom color scheme.

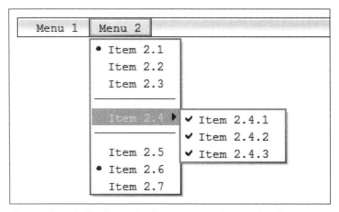

Figure 16-10. Stylized MenuBar instance, nested menu detail

The conclusion is that several visual aspects cannot be influenced by styles:

- The background of the menu bar
- The custom icons of the menu items
- The "separator" menu item
- Part of the background of the buttons in the menu bar
- The icon of menu items associated with a nested menu
- The icons of "radio" and "check" menu items

Apart from the custom icons of the menu items, you have still to learn how to customize all the remaining visual aspects in the previous list. Skinning our current example will show you how to fully customize the appearance of the MenuBar and the Menu components.

Skinnability

The previous section left us with a number of tasks to accomplish in order to fully customize the appearance of a MenuBar instance (and its Menu subcomponents).

Customizing the visual aspects that do not yet adhere to the orange-based color scheme implemented in our example has now become mostly a matter of providing a modified version of the existing skins.

No changes will be required to the code or the XML data of the previous example in order to skin the component instance. The following procedure describes the steps for adding the skin symbols to our previous example that must be modified in order to complete the implementation of a custom version of the MenuBar and Menu components.

The mnu04.fla file found in the source files associated with this chapter contains a completed version of the skinned component; examine this to verify how the skin symbols must look in the finalized version of the example that you are going to build now:

1. Open the document mnu03.fla created earlier and save it in a new folder as mnu04.fla.

2. Copy the menus.xml and test.as files from the folder containing mnu03.fla to the folder containing the new mnu04.fla document—we will reuse the ActionScript code and the XML data from the previous example.

3. Open the file HaloTheme.fla as an external library by selecting the File ➤ Import ➤ Open External Library menu options. This file is part of the component architecture source that you can locate on your machine by following the instructions described in Appendix A.

4. Open the library of the mnu04.fla file (Window ➤ Library). You should now have both libraries (mnu04.fla and HaloTheme.fla) opened and accessible in the authoring environment.

5. The folders Menu Assets and MenuBar Assets can be found inside the HaloTheme.fla library by selecting Flash UI Components 2 ➤ Themes ➤ MMDefault. Drag both folders into the mnu04.fla library so you have a copy of the MenuBar and Menu assets in there. You can now close the HaloTheme.fla library. After this step, the contents of the mnu04.fla library should look like those shown in Figure 16-11.

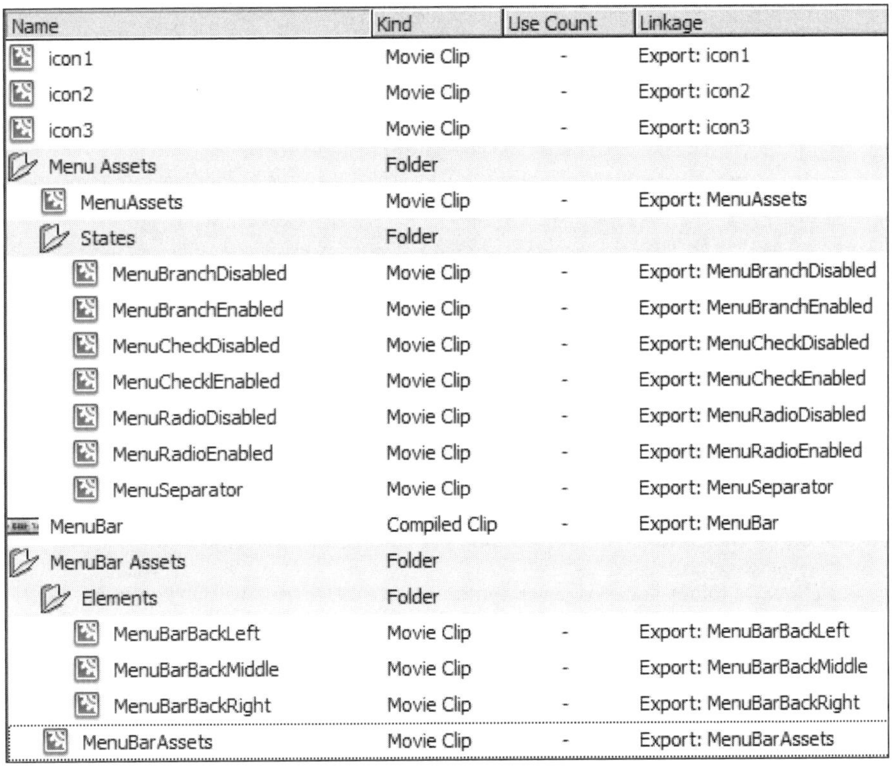

Name	Kind	Use Count	Linkage
icon1	Movie Clip	-	Export: icon1
icon2	Movie Clip	-	Export: icon2
icon3	Movie Clip	-	Export: icon3
Menu Assets	Folder		
MenuAssets	Movie Clip	-	Export: MenuAssets
States	Folder		
MenuBranchDisabled	Movie Clip	-	Export: MenuBranchDisabled
MenuBranchEnabled	Movie Clip	-	Export: MenuBranchEnabled
MenuCheckDisabled	Movie Clip	-	Export: MenuCheckDisabled
MenuCheckIEnabled	Movie Clip	-	Export: MenuCheckEnabled
MenuRadioDisabled	Movie Clip	-	Export: MenuRadioDisabled
MenuRadioEnabled	Movie Clip	-	Export: MenuRadioEnabled
MenuSeparator	Movie Clip	-	Export: MenuSeparator
MenuBar	Compiled Clip		Export: MenuBar
MenuBar Assets	Folder		
Elements	Folder		
MenuBarBackLeft	Movie Clip	-	Export: MenuBarBackLeft
MenuBarBackMiddle	Movie Clip	-	Export: MenuBarBackMiddle
MenuBarBackRight	Movie Clip	-	Export: MenuBarBackRight
MenuBarAssets	Movie Clip	-	Export: MenuBarAssets

Figure 16-11. The library's content after you added the MenuBar and Menu assets

6. Save the mnu04.fla file.

Our latest example is not yet complete since we must still modify the symbols in the `Menu Assets` and `MenuBar Assets` folders that we have copied.

However, it is important that you learn the role of each of those symbols before applying any change to them.

The MenuBar Assets folder contains three exported symbols that implement the skin of the menu bar background. Their linkage identifiers (MenuBarBackLeft, MenuBarBackMiddle, and MenuBarBackRight) are the values of three skin properties implemented by the MenuBar class:

- menuBarBackLeftName = "MenuBarBackLeft"

- menuBarBackMiddleName = "MenuBarBackMiddle"

- menuBarBackRightName = "MenuBarBackRight"

The background of the menu bar is divided into three sections: the two edges (left and right) and the area in between (middle). While the edge skins are not resized, the middle section of the skin is usually stretched to fill the gap between the two edges.

In order to define the background of the menu bar consistently with the color scheme in our example, you must edit the three symbols in the document library and modify their design and color. Figure 16-12 shows the design that you can find in the completed version of the `mnu04.fla` file included in this chapter's source files.

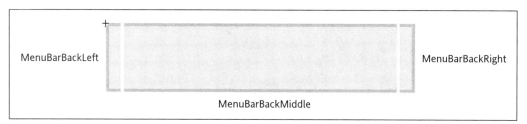

Figure 16-12. The three skins provided for the new background of the menu bar

The Menu class does not support any skin properties for the symbols that you find in the `Menu Assets` folder in the document's library. However, modifying those symbols will actually skin the menu items despite the absence of skin properties, which means that you cannot use exported symbols with different linkage identifiers and, therefore, your changes will affect every menu item instance in your application. This is not a major limitation, since it does not affect the consistency of the menu items' appearance; on the contrary, their consistency is enforced by this limitation.

The `Menu Assets` folder contains seven symbols that can be used to skin the menu items:

- MenuBranchEnabled and MenuBranchDisabled: Defines the arrow icon of a menu item associated with a nested menu whenever the menu item is enabled or disabled, respectively

- MenuCheckEnabled and MenuCheckDisabled: Defines the icon of a "check" menu item whenever it is enabled or disabled, respectively

- MenuRadioEnabled and MenuRadioDisabled: Defines the icon of a "radio" menu item whenever it is enabled or disabled, respectively

- MenuSeparator: Defines the skin of the "separator" menu item

Although it is easy to modify the graphic of those symbols, to change their colors is enough to provide them with an appearance that is consistent with the orange-based color scheme of our example.

Once again, you can change their colors as you like or examine the completed source file associated with this chapter (mnu04.fla) to check out a consistently colorized version of these skins.

Figure 16-13 shows the stylized and skinned MenuBar instance and its Menu 2 subcomponent, which you can appreciate in its true colors by running the completed source file (mnu04.fla) in the authoring environment.

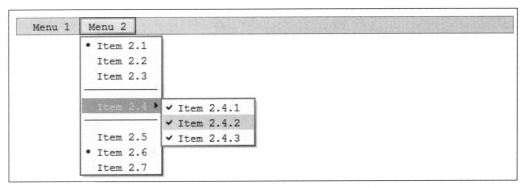

Figure 16-13. The stylized and skinned MenuBar instance in its orange-based color scheme

It may seem that we have customized every visual aspect of the MenuBar and the Menu components. While this is true for the Menu component, the menu bar still has a detail that is not touched by styles and skins.

The nature of this detail is close to the internals of the component architecture, which makes it a case for the "Solved mysteries" section up next.

Solved mysteries

Despite being fairly simple components, both the MenuBar and the Menu components have a mystery to be solved.

First let us complete the process of fully customizing the MenuBar instance of our richer example. The styles and skin implemented so far in our examples have customized every aspect of their appearance except one, related to the buttons in the menu bar.

Further customization of a MenuBar skin

A thorough examination of Figure16-13 reveals that the outer border of the selected button (Menu 2) is still black and, therefore, not influenced by the themeColor style nor by any of our other custom settings.

Furthermore, simply rolling over a button in the menu bar would reveal that its rollover state is not influenced by the style settings and the new skins, as shown in Figure 16-14.

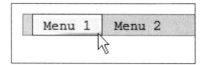

Figure 16-14. The background of the button in the menu bar when the mouse cursor rolls over it

We are now going to extend our last example to take full control of the appearance of the buttons in the menu bar:

1. Open the document mnu04.fla created earlier and save it in a new folder as mnu05.fla.

2. Copy the menus.xml and test.as files from the folder containing mnu04.fla to the folder containing the new mnu05.fla document. The XML data of the previous example will be reused as it is, while you will add a few lines of code to the test.as file.

3. Open the test.as file copied in the folder of this example and add the following lines of code at the beginning without replacing or changing any of the existing lines:

```
import mx.controls.menuclasses.MenuBarItem;

MenuBarItem.prototype.createChildren = function (Void):Void {
  this.super.createChildren();
  this.createLabel("cell",20);
  this.cell.setValue(this.__initText);
  this.createClassObject(CustomActivatorSkin, "border_mc", 0,
➥ {styleName:this.owner, borderStyle:"none"});
  this.useHandCursor = false;
  this.trackAsMenu = true;
}
```

4. Create a new ActionScript file and save it as CustomActivatorSkin.as in the same folder containing the other files of the current example.

5. Add the following lines of code to the newly created CustomActivatorSkin.as file:

```
import mx.skins.RectBorder;
import mx.skins.SkinElement;
import mx.core.ext.UIObjectExtensions;

class CustomActivatorSkin extends RectBorder {

  static var symbolName:String = "CustomActivatorSkin";
  static var symbolOwner:Object = CustomActivatorSkin;

  var className = "CustomActivatorSkin ";

  var drawRoundRect:Function;
```

```
    function CustomActivatorSkin() {}

    function init():Void {
      super.init();
    }

    function size():Void {
      drawHaloRect(width,height);
    }

    function drawHaloRect(w:Number,h:Number):Void {
      var borderStyle = getStyle("borderStyle");
      var themeCol = getStyle("themeColor");

      clear();

      switch (borderStyle) {

        case "none":
          drawRoundRect( x,y,w,h,0,0xffffff,0);
          break;

        case "falsedown":
          drawRoundRect( x,y,w,h,0,0xDFCE93,100);
          drawRoundRect( x+1,y+1,w-2,h-2,0,
➥ [0x333333,0xfcfcfc],100,-90,"radial");
          drawRoundRect( x+1,y+1,w-2,h-2,0,themeCol,50);
          drawRoundRect( x+3,y+3,w-6,h-6,0,0xffffff,100);
          drawRoundRect( x+3,y+4,w-6,h-7,0,0xFFDEA3,20);
          break;

        case "falserollover":
        drawRoundRect( x,y,w,h,0,themeCol,50);
        drawRoundRect( x+3,y+4,w-6,h-7,0,0xFFDEA3,100);
        break;
      }
    }

    static function classConstruct():Boolean {
      UIObjectExtensions.Extensions();
      _global.skinRegistry["CustomActivatorSkin"] = true;
      return true;
    }

    static var classConstructed:Boolean = classConstruct();
    static var UIObjectExtensionsDependency = UIObjectExtensions;
}
```

6. Go back to the mnu05.fla document and create a new movie clip symbol by selecting Insert ➤ New Symbol. Once the Create New Symbol dialog box is open, define the symbol name and its linkage identifier as CustomActivatorSkin. Before closing the dialog box, also define the ActionScript 2.0 class associated with the symbol as CustomActivatorSkin.

7. Save the mnu05.fla, test.as, and CustomActivatorSkin.as files.

In this example, we extended the component architecture in order to be able to replace the default purely coded skin of the buttons that appear in the menu bar. These buttons are implemented by the MenuBarItem class, utilizing the mx.skins.halo.ActivatorSkin to draw the background of the buttons in a MenuBar instance.

In order to use our own purely coded skin, we override the createChildren method of the MenuBarItem class by using the prototype-based technique:

```
MenuBarItem.prototype.createChildren = function (Void):Void {
    this.super.createChildren();
    this.createLabel("cell",20);
    this.cell.setValue(this.__initText);
    this.createClassObject(CustomActivatorSkin, "border_mc", 0,
➥ {styleName:this.owner, borderStyle:"none"});
    this.useHandCursor = false;
    this.trackAsMenu = true;
}
```

The new createChildren method executes almost the same code of the architecture with one exception: it creates an instance of the CustomActivatorSkin class instead of the default mx.skins.halo.ActivatorSkin class, giving control to our custom purely coded skin that is implemented by the CustomActivatorSkin exported symbol via its associated class.

Once again, the CustomActivatorSkin class implementation resembles that of the preexisting ActivatorSkin class of the Halo theme that you can find in the component architecture source code.

However, when it comes to drawing the border and the background of the buttons in the menu bar, in the drawHaloRect method, the class executes our custom code that draws borders and background by using colors consistent with the orangey color scheme implemented in this chapter's examples.

Now we can really affirm that there is not a single visual aspect of the MenuBar and the Menu components that has not been customized by the techniques exposed in this chapter.

However, this "Solved mysteries" section still has a couple of interesting topics worth your consideration. Let us get to these now.

Creating persistent Menu instances

The instances of the Menu component have a very short life on the stage by design, since they appear in response to an event such as clicking a menu bar button, and they disappear after the user selects a menu item.

However, the Menu component can be used in many more contexts if it is provided an option for keeping a Menu instance on the stage.

In the next example, we are going to extend the component architecture to implement a persistent property for Menu instances that, whenever set to true, stops the Menu instance from disappearing from the stage:

1. Create a new Flash document and save it as mnu06.fla.
2. Open the Document Properties dialog box by selecting Modify ➤ Document, and set its dimensions as 640×480 pixels.
3. Drag the Menu component onto the stage in order to create one instance of the component, but then delete it just after. We will create the Menu instance dynamically, and this step is to add the Menu component to the document's library.
4. Select the first frame in the document and attach the following ActionScript code to it:

```
#include "test.as"
```

5. Create a new ActionScript file and save it as test.as in the same folder as the mnu06.fla file.
6. Add the following code to the ActionScript file you just created:

```
import mx.controls.Menu;

Menu.prototype.hideAllMenus = function(Void):Void {
    if (this.getRootMenu().persistent) {
        return;
    }
    this.getRootMenu().hide();
}

var popupMenu1 = Menu.createMenu();
popupMenu1.persistent = true;

var dp = new XML();
dp.ignoreWhite = true;
dp.onLoad = function(success:Boolean):Void {
    if (success) {
        popupMenu1.dataProvider = dp.firstChild;
        popupMenu1.show(10, 10);
    }
}

dp.load("menu.xml");
```

7. Create a new text file using a text editor such as Notepad and save it as menu.xml in the same folder where you saved the mnu06.fla file.

421

8. Add the following XML data to the `menu.xml` text file just created:

```
<menu>
    <menuitem label="Item 1.1" instanceName="menuItem1_1"
➥ type="radio" groupName="groupA" selected="true" />
    <menuitem label="Item 1.2" instanceName="menuItem1_2"
➥ type="radio" groupName="groupA" />
    <menuitem label="Item 1.3" instanceName="menuItem1_3"
➥ type="radio" groupName="groupA" />
    <menuitem type="separator" />
    <menuitem label="Item 1.4" instanceName="menuItem1_4">
        <menuitem label="Item 1.4.1" instanceName="menuItem1_4_1"
➥ type="check" selected="true" />
        <menuitem label="Item 1.4.2" instanceName="menuItem1_4_2"
➥ type="check" selected="true" />
        <menuitem label="Item 1.4.3" instanceName="menuItem1_4_3"
➥ type="check" selected="true" />
    </menuitem>
    <menuitem type="separator" />
    <menuitem label="Item 1.5" instanceName="menuItem1_5"
➥ type="radio" groupName="groupB" />
    <menuitem label="Item 1.6" instanceName="menuItem1_6"
➥ type="radio" groupName="groupB" selected="true" />
    <menuitem label="Item 1.7" instanceName="menuItem1_7"
➥ type="radio" groupName="groupB" />
</menu>
```

9. Save the `mnu06.fla`, `test.as`, and `menu.xml` files.

This example also demonstrates that you can use the `dataProvider` property of the Menu class in the same way it was used before in the case of the MenuBar class: to define the structure of the component instance by using an XML description.

The XML data used in this example is identical to the data that created the Menu instance labeled Menu 2 in the MenuBar example. The only difference is that the <menu> element does not have a label attribute, because in this case it would be meaningless (that label is utilized by the button in the menu bar).

However, the main objective of this example is to extend the component architecture to allow a Menu instance to stay on the stage.

If you test the movie, you will find that the ActionScript code in the `test.as` file implements this functionality successfully, since the Menu instance displayed in Figure 16-15 does not go away after you select a menu item.

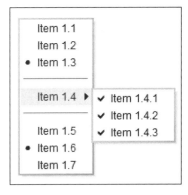

Figure 16-15. A Menu instance made persistent

The Menu instance is created by using the createMenu static method of the Menu class that was already used in the minimal example at the beginning of this chapter. Then, just after its creation, we exploit the relaxed type of the popupMenu1 declaration to add a persistent property to the Menu instance dynamically:

```
var popupMenu1 = Menu.createMenu();
popupMenu1.persistent = true;
```

This persistent property is put to good use by our own version of the hideAllMenus method of the Menu class that overrides its default implementation:

```
Menu.prototype.hideAllMenus = function(Void):Void {
    if (this.getRootMenu().persistent) {
        return;
    }
    this.getRootMenu().hide();
}
```

Our version of the hideAllMenus method behaves as expected by hiding the Menu instance only if the persistent property is false or undefined. In the case that the persistent property has been defined as true, our custom version of the hideAllMenus method returns, avoiding hiding the Menu instance.

This is yet another demonstration of how it is possible to extend a component architecture with small, accurate changes and add a new functionality that makes a component reusable in several other contexts: a persistent menu may well be used as an alternative form of navigation when designing the user interface of a component-based application.

423

Reasons for subclassing the Menu and the MenuBar components

This chapter gives you plenty of reasons for subclassing the Menu and MenuBar components—when you subclass a component, you are able to encapsulate any of the features that have been discussed here. For example, you may subclass the Menu component to provide an implementation of the persistent property compatible with strict typing.

But probably the best reason for subclassing the Menu and MenuBar components lies in providing a distributable version of them, customized by applying the styles, skins, and techniques examined in this chapter.

Chapter 17

THE NUMERICSTEPPER COMPONENT

NumericStepper
mx.controls.NumericStepper

Frequency: Rare
Complexity: Simple
Stability: Quirky
Maturity: Pre-Existing
Popularity: Specific

The NumericStepper component is an editable text field that can be used to ask the user to select a numeric value.

The component includes two small up and down arrow buttons on its right-hand side, allowing users to increment/decrement the current value of a numeric quantity specified programmatically or at authoring time (1 by default). This component can be utilized when the user must select a numeric value within a range of limited options such as when voting on an article or when selecting a loan over a fixed number of years.

The minimal example implemented in the next section will further illustrate the use of this rather small and peculiar component.

> The completed source code introduced in this chapter can be found in the package src17.zip, downloadable from this book's page at www.friendsofed.com.

Minimal example of the NumericStepper component

As you are going to find out now, building a minimal example of the NumericStepper component is mostly about setting the parameters of its instance in the authoring environment:

1. Create a new Flash document and save it as ns01.fla.

2. Open the Document Properties dialog box by selecting Modify ➤ Document, and set its dimensions as 200✕200 pixels.

3. Drag the NumericStepper component on the stage in order to create one instance of the component. Name the new instance numericstepper01 and define its position as (X: 60, Y: 89).

4. Select the numericstepper01 instance and access the Parameters section of the Properties panel in order to set the following parameters: (maximum = 100; minimum = 10; stepSize = 10; value = 50). Figure 17-1 shows the Properties panel after you completed the current step.

5. Save the ns01.fla file.

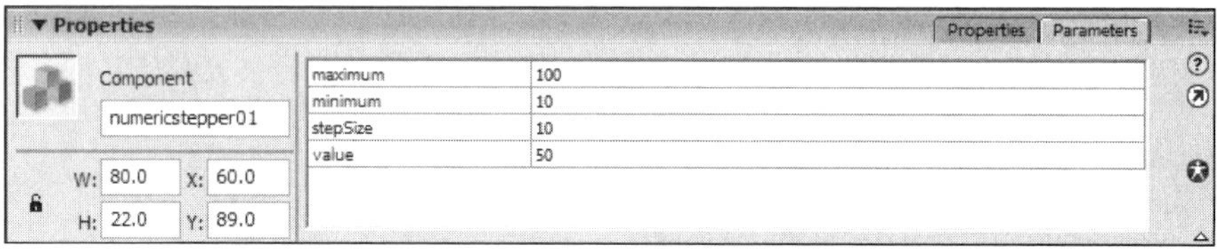

Figure 17-1. The parameters of NumericStepper instance defined in the minimal example

For each of the four parameters set in our first example, there is a corresponding property in the NumericStepper class with the same name. Those parameters and their respective properties (maximum, minimum, stepSize, and value) fully define the behavior of a NumericStepper instance, as you can verify by testing the example in the authoring environment.

Figure 17-2 shows the numericstepper01 instance with its initial numeric value (50) set via the value parameter.

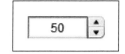

Figure 17-2. A NumericStepper instance

The value starts at 50. Every click on the up arrow button on the right side of the component instance will increase its value by the unit defined in the stepSize parameter (10 in this case). Clicking the up arrow will have no effect once the value has reached the level specified in the maximum parameter (100).

Very similarly, every click on the down arrow button will decrease the value by the unit defined in the stepSize parameter; the down arrow button will become ineffective once the value has reached the level set by the minimum parameter.

Note that the text field of a numeric stepper is editable, allowing you to specify a value not present in the ordered set. However, this value is not stored in the component instance, and the value you set by editing the field changes to the closest value in the ordered set as soon as the component instance loses the focus. You can experience this behavior by entering the value 92 in the numericstepper01 instance and then clicking somewhere on the stage so that it loses the focus: the value will be adjusted automatically to 90, which is the closest among the acceptable values defined by our previous settings.

Since the only purpose of the NumericStepper component is to retrieve a numeric value that satisfies the constraints defined by its settings, our next example will focus on the process of retrieving such a value.

XLEFF version

Generating a NumericStepper instance using the XML layout engine introduced in the second part of the book is very straightforward, as demonstrated by the following XML version of our minimal example:

```
<numericstepper x="400" y="260" value="50" stepSize="10" maximum="100"
➥ minimum="10" name="numericstepper01">
```

You can find a fully configured version of the XLEFFsampler, running the minimal example, among the files associated with this chapter and play with the attributes of the numericstepper element to generate different NumericStepper instances.

Retrieving the value

The NumericStepper class implements three properties that you can access programmatically at any time to retrieve the value currently stored in the component instance and the values that follow or precede it:

- value: Simply returns the current numeric value stored in the component instance
- previousValue: The value that precedes the current value in the set of acceptable values for the component instance
- nextValue: The value that follows the current value in the set of acceptable values for the component instance

429

The NumericStepper class also implements a change event that is broadcast to all the registered listeners whenever the value of the component instance changes.

In the next example, you are going to implement a change event handler to examine how the NumericStepper component actually works:

1. Open the document ns01.fla created earlier and save it in a new folder as ns02.fla.

2. Select the first frame in the document and attach the following ActionScript code to it:

```
#include "test.as"
```

3. Create a new ActionScript file and save it as test.as in the same folder where you saved the ns02.fla file.

4. Add the following code to the ActionScript file you just created:

```
function change(eventObject:Object):Void {
    var ns = eventObject.target;
    trace("EVENT change: " + ns.value);
}

numericstepper01.addEventListener("change", this);
```

5. Save the ns02.fla and test.as files.

The purpose of the event handler implemented in our example is to keep track of every occurrence of the change event by showing the value associated with the NumericStepper instance in our example whenever a change event is raised.

Testing the example in the authoring environment will result in the same stage previously shown in Figure 17-3. However, the following text will appear in the Output window if you click the up arrow button of the NumericStepper instance once:

```
EVENT change: 60
```

Simultaneously, the component instance will show the new value (60) in the text field.

By clicking another four times on the same up arrow button you can increment the component's value up to its maximum (100). After that, any further click of the up arrow button will not change the value associated with the component instance, and the change event will not be raised. No additional text lines will appear in the Output window after the following:

```
EVENT change: 60
EVENT change: 70
EVENT change: 80
EVENT change: 90
EVENT change: 100
```

Clicking the down arrow button will decrease the value to 90, and another text line will appear in the Output window:

```
EVENT  change:  60
EVENT  change:  70
EVENT  change:  80
EVENT  change:  90
EVENT  change:  100
EVENT  change:  90
```

The previous tests demonstrated that the component instance actually raises a change event every time its value changes as a result of a click of its arrow buttons.

Minor bug for Flash MX 2004 users

In case you are using a version of the component architecture released with the Flash MX 2004 authoring environment, you should be aware that the implementation of the change event is not consistent in a particular case, as demonstrated by the following test.

While still testing the movie in the authoring environment, change the component value to 24 by simply replacing the text in its field and then click on the stage, away from the component instance so that it loses the focus.

The value that you entered in the field (24) is adjusted to the nearest acceptable value (20) as soon as the component instance loses the focus.

The problem is that no message like the following one appears in the Output window:

```
EVENT  change:  20
```

The value of the component instance clearly has changed, but no change event was raised by the NumericStepper instance in this case.

We will come back on this issue later on, in the "Solved mysteries" section of this chapter, after completing the examination of the NumericStepper component.

Styles supported by the NumericStepper component

Almost every style supported by the NumericStepper component is a common style, shared with the other components in the architecture.

The NumericStepper component supports a few common color styles (themeColor, color, backgroundColor, and disabledColor) and several common text styles (embeddedFonts, fontFamily, fontSize, fontStyle, fontWeight, textAlign, and textDecoration) that are described in greater detail in Chapter 18.

The NumericStepper component supports three styles that are specific to this component:

- symbolColor: Influences the color of the arrow in the buttons on the right side of the component. Note that, while being supported by the Sample theme, this style is not supported by the default theme, Halo.

- repeatDelay: Indicates the delay, in milliseconds, that a component instance waits when the user first presses one arrow button before starting to repeat its associated action. Its default value is 500 milliseconds, and you may experiment with shorter values if you wish to increase the reactivity of a component instance.

- repeatInterval: Indicates the interval, in milliseconds, between two repeated actions once the component enters into repeat mode because of the user holding one of the arrow buttons. Its default value is 35.

The following example applies several styles to a NumericStepper instance to let you grasp how much can be achieved by using styles and what is left to skin in order to fully customize the appearance of this component:

1. Open the document ns02.fla created earlier and save it in a new folder as ns03.fla.

2. Create a new ActionScript file and save it as test.as in the same folder where you saved the ns03.fla file.

3. Add the following code to the ActionScript file you just created:

```
function setStyles(instance:Object):Void {
    instance.setStyle("themeColor", "blue");
    instance.setStyle("color", "blue");
    instance.setStyle("disabledColor", 0xDDDDDD);
    instance.setStyle("backgroundColor", 0xE0E0FF);
    instance.setStyle("fontFamily", "Courier New");
    instance.setStyle("fontSize", 12);
    instance.setStyle("fontStyle", "italic");
    instance.setStyle("fontWeight", "bold");
    instance.setStyle("textAlign", "right");
}

setStyles(numericstepper01);
```

4. Save the ns03.fla and test.as files.

In the case of the NumericStepper component, the influence of the themeColor style property is minimal: it only affects the arrow buttons when you roll over or click them.

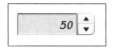

Figure 17-3. A stylized NumericStepper instance

The other styles utilized in the example help in conferring a bluish look to the component instance by defining the color of the background and the text. Also, they redefine the font and text alignment to achieve the appearance shown in Figure 17-3.

In the next section, you will skin the arrow buttons to align the color of their arrow symbols to the bluish color scheme implemented in this example and complete the customization of the appearance of a NumericStepper instance.

Skinning the NumericStepper component

The NumericStepper class defines eight skin properties, but as a matter of fact the component utilizes nine skins. The following is a complete list of the eight skin properties and their default values plus the linkage identifier of the skin that does not have a corresponding skin property:

- upArrowUp = "StepUpArrowUp"
- upArrowDown = "StepUpArrowDown"
- upArrowOver = "StepUpArrowOver"
- upArrowDisabled = "upArrowDisabled"
- downArrowUp = "StepDownArrowUp"
- downArrowDown = "StepDownArrowDown"
- downArrowOver = "StepDownArrowOver"
- downArrowDisabled = "StepDownArrowDisabled"
- {No Skin Property} = "StepTrack"

The first eight skins are divided in two groups of four, each defining the appearance of the up arrow and down arrow buttons, respectively. The four skins of each group match the typical four states of a button (Up, Down, Over, and Disabled).

The ninth skin is used for the appearance of the track between the arrow buttons. Such a track appears only when you define a NumericStepper taller than its default height (22 pixels) and therefore it is useless in the vast majority of applications.

However, the next example will be based on a component instance taller than 22 pixels so that you can visually appreciate the presence of this ninth skin and replace it with a custom one, whenever needed:

1. Open the document ns03.fla created earlier and save it in a new folder as ns04.fla.
2. Select the numericstepper01 instance and set its height via the Info panel to 50 pixels.
3. Create a new ActionScript file and save it as test.as in the same folder where you saved the ns04.fla file.
4. Add the following code to the ActionScript file you just created:

```
function setStyles(instance:Object):Void {
    instance.setStyle("color", 0x096BA0);
    instance.setStyle("disabledColor", 0xDDDDDD);
    instance.setStyle("backgroundColor", 0x29BBF0);
    instance.setStyle("fontFamily", "Courier New");
    instance.setStyle("fontSize", 40);
    instance.setStyle("fontStyle", "italic");
    instance.setStyle("fontWeight", "bold");
    instance.setStyle("textAlign", "center");
}

setStyles(numericstepper01);
```

433

5. At this point you should define nine exported symbols that will replace the component's original skins. You can either reuse the graphics that you will find in the completed file associated with this chapter or provide your own. The names of the nine exported symbols (with linkage identifiers to match) are StepDownArrowDisabled, StepDownArrowDown, StepDownArrowOver, StepDownArrowUp, StepTrack, StepUpArrowDisabled, StepUpArrowDown, StepUpArrowOver, StepUpArrowUp. Figure 17-4 shows the symbols that should appear in the document's library after you created them.

StepDownArrowDisabled	Movie Clip	-	Export: StepDownArrowDisabled
StepDownArrowDown	Movie Clip	-	Export: StepDownArrowDown
StepDownArrowOver	Movie Clip	-	Export: StepDownArrowOver
StepDownArrowUp	Movie Clip	-	Export: StepDownArrowUp
StepTrack	Movie Clip	-	Export: StepTrack
StepUpArrowDisabled	Movie Clip	-	Export: StepUpArrowDisabled
StepUpArrowDown	Movie Clip	-	Export: StepUpArrowDown
StepUpArrowOver	Movie Clip	-	Export: StepUpArrowOver
StepUpArrowUp	Movie Clip	-	Export: StepUpArrowUp

Figure 17-4. The nine exported symbols providing the new skins of the NumericStepper component

6. Defining the nine skin symbols in the library is not sufficient to activate them. An additional exported symbol, a movie clip with name of NumericStepperAssets and matching linkage identifier, must be created. This movie clip must contain one instance of each of the nine exported symbols created in the previous step. Figure 17-5 shows the content of this exported symbol with the skins that you can find in the completed file associated with this chapter.

Figure 17-5. The contents of the NumericStepperAssets symbol: the nine skins of the component

7. Save the ns04.fla and test.as files.

Testing the example in the authoring environment will show a NumericStepper instance that is significantly taller than the default one that you saw in the previous examples, as shown in Figure 17-6.

Figure 17-6. A stylized and skinned instance of the NumericStepper component

The bluish rectangle between the two arrow buttons is the track that was skinned by providing a StepTrack exported symbol, which is usually not visible when the component height defaults to 22 pixels or less.

If you play a bit with the example, you can appreciate the skins defined for the over and down states of the arrow buttons. You may also notice a disturbingly large text cursor flashing whenever the text field in the component has the focus.

In the next section, we will get rid of the flashing cursor while providing a fix for the hole in the implementation of the change event that we experimented with earlier.

Solved mysteries

After learning the main purpose of NumericStepper component, you will probably be aware that its main mystery concerns why it is editable.

If you use it to enforce the user to select a numeric value from a restricted set of options, defined by its four properties (maximum, minimum, stepSize, and value), why should the user be able to edit it like a text field and input invalid numeric values in it that are adjusted when the component instance loses the focus?

This section is dedicated to adding an editable property to NumericStepper instances so that you can disable the editing option and make the value modifiable by the arrow buttons only. By doing so, the value shown by the NumericStepper instance will be always valid.

Note that disabling the editing option is also a workaround for the minor bug mentioned earlier in this chapter affecting MX 2004 users only.

Let us examine how to implement an editable property that is capable of disabling the editing of the text field when set to false.

1. Open the document ns04.fla created earlier and save it in a new folder as ns05.fla.
2. Create a new ActionScript file and save it as test.as in the same folder where you saved the ns05.fla file.
3. Add the following code to the ActionScript file just created:

```
import mx.controls.NumericStepper;

NumericStepper.prototype.draw = function():Void {
  if (this.editable != undefined && this.editable == false) {
    this.inputField.label.type = "dynamic";
    this.inputField.label.selectable = false;
  } else {
    this.inputField.enabled = this.enabled;
  }

  this.prevButton_mc.enabled = this.enabled;
  this.nextButton_mc.enabled = this.enabled;

  this.size();
  this.initializing = false;
  this.visible = this.__visible;
}
```

```
function setStyles(instance:Object):Void {
    instance.setStyle("color", 0x096BA0);
    instance.setStyle("disabledColor", 0xDDDDDD);
    instance.setStyle("backgroundColor", 0x29BBF0);
    instance.setStyle("fontFamily", "Courier New");
    instance.setStyle("fontSize", 40);
    instance.setStyle("fontStyle", "italic");
    instance.setStyle("fontWeight", "bold");
    instance.setStyle("textAlign", "center");
}

setStyles(numericstepper01);

numericstepper01.editable = false;
```

4. Save the `ns05.fla` and `test.as` files.

This fix overrides the draw method of the NumericStepper component by using the prototype property. The custom draw method replicates the functionality of the original implementation with a couple of substantial differences. First, it verifies whether an editable property is defined for the component instance and whether its value is false:

```
if (this.editable != undefined && this.editable == false) {
```

Next, if the editable property is defined as false, the new draw method changes the type of the text field from its default "input" to "dynamic", which neatly makes it read-only:

```
this.inputField.label.type = "dynamic";
```

The following line that makes the text not selectable has been added for purely cosmetic reasons and can be deleted if you ever need to make the text selectable:

```
this.inputField.label.selectable = false;
```

Testing the movie will result in the same customized instance shown in Figure 7-7. However, any attempt to edit the text in the component instance's text field will fail, and you will be able to change the component's value only if you click the arrow buttons.

Reasons for subclassing the NumericStepper component

Apart from the usual motives that are true for almost every component (packaging styles and skins for distribution), the NumericStepper component offers a further reason to subclass it: encapsulating the implementation of the editable property so that you can forget to add it to your projects every time that you need it.

If you ever subclass the NumericStepper component, you may also enhance its behavior by disabling the proper button, up or down, when reaching the maximum or minimum value respectively, providing a visual feedback (button disabled) showing that one of the two ends of the range has been reached.

Chapter 18

THE TEXTAREA, TEXTINPUT, AND LABEL COMPONENTS

TextArea		
mx.controls.TextArea		
Frequency: Common		
Complexity: Heavy		
Stability: Robust		
Maturity: Classic		
Popularity: Widespread		

TextInput		
mx.controls.TextInput		
Frequency: Common		
Complexity: Simple		
Stability: Robust		
Maturity: Classic		
Popularity: Widespread		

Label		
mx.controls.Label		
Frequency: Common		
Complexity: Simple		
Stability: Robust		
Maturity: Classic		
Popularity: Widespread		

Although text content plays an important role in several components in the architecture, the three components examined in this chapter are undoubtedly those that depend on it the most. You can rely on the TextArea, TextInput, and Label components whenever you need to retrieve or display text content.

The main differences characterizing the text components are as follows:

- The Label component is read-only, while the TextInput and TextArea components can be edited, allowing users to modify their text content.
- The text content of the Label and TextInput components is implemented as a single line of text, while the TextArea component handles multiline text.

As usual, implementing a minimal example will help you focus on the core features of these components.

> *The completed source code introduced in this chapter can be found in the package* `src18.zip`, *downloadable from this book's page at* www.friendsofed.com.

Minimal example

The following minimal example roughly imitates a very familiar user interface: that of an e-mail message.

Figure 18-1 shows how an instance of the Label component appears alongside an instance of the TextInput component to highlight its purpose (the "Subject" of the message), while an instance of the TextArea component is exploited to retrieve the multiline content of the message itself.

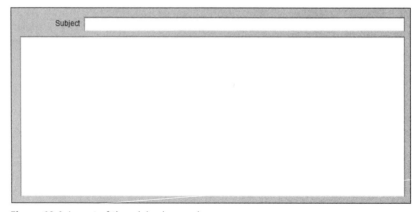

Figure 18-1. Layout of the minimal example

Let us build the minimal example so you can start appreciating the functionality of these text-based components:

1. Create a new Flash document and save it as `text01.fla`.

2. Open the Document Properties dialog box by selecting Modify ➤ Document, and set its dimensions as 640×480 pixels. Before closing the dialog box, define the Background color as #AACCFF.

3. Drag the TextArea component on the stage in order to create one instance of the component. Select the newly created component instance and define its name as textarea01 via the Properties panel.

4. While the textarea01 instance is still selected, use the Info panel to define its location and dimensions as (X: 10, Y: 40) and (W: 620, H: 250).

5. Drag the TextInput component on the stage in order to create one instance of the component. Select the newly created component instance and define its name as textinput01 via the Properties panel.

6. While the texinput01 instance is still selected, use the Info panel to define its location and dimensions as (X: 115, Y: 10) and (W: 515, H: 22).

7. Drag the Label component on the stage in order to create one instance of the component. Select the newly created component instance and define its name as label01 via the Properties panel. While in the Properties panel, select the Parameters tab and set the values of the autoSize and text parameters as right and Subject, respectively.

8. While the label01 instance is still selected, use the Info panel to define its location as (X: 10, Y: 10).

9. Save the `text01.fla` file.

Testing the example will display an interface similar to the one shown in Figure 18-1.

You can verify that the text of the Label instance cannot be changed or selected, while both the TextInput and the TextArea instances allow you to enter text whether it be a single line of text, as in the first case, or multiline text, as in the second case.

Checking out the parameters of the component instances in the authoring environment will highlight further similarities and differences among these components.

- The only parameter shared by all of the three components is text. The purpose of the text parameter is to allow you to enter some text that will become the initial content of the component instance. However, the use of the text parameter is very limiting in the case of the TextArea component, since it does not allow you to enter multiline content.

- Both the Label and the TextArea components share an html parameter, storing a Boolean value that is false by default. By setting this parameter to true, you will be able to use some of the most basic HTML tags to format the text in the component instance. Refer to the specification of the Flash Player that you are targeting for a complete list of the HTML tags that you can utilize.

- Both the TextInput and the TextArea components share an editable parameter that stores a Boolean value that is true by default. By setting this property to false, the user will not be able to edit the content of the component instance.

- The TextInput and the TextArea components also share a parameter named password, which stores a Boolean value that is false by default. Setting this parameter to true reveals its purpose: to hide the text content while being entered by the user.

- The Label component has a specific parameter, named autoSize, influencing the component's behavior when the text content is wider and/or taller than the component instance's initial dimensions. The autoSize parameter accepts a String value that can be one of the following four options: "none", "center", "left", and "right".

- Finally, the TextArea has one specific parameter also, wordWrap, which stores a Boolean value that is true by default. When this parameter is set to true, the text content wraps inside the visible area of the component instance.

Each of the parameters in the previous list corresponds to a property in the component class with the same name; these allow you to modify the behavior of a component instance dynamically via ActionScript.

XLEFF version of the minimal example

Describing the layout of the minimal example using XML and XLEFF is, as in many other cases, just a matter of creating a few elements whose names, attributes, and values reflect the name of the components and their properties:

```
<label x="135" y="135" text="Subject" autoSize="right"
➥ name="label01" />
<textinput x="240" y="135" width="515" name="textinput01" />
<textarea x="135" y="165" width="620" height="250"
➥ name="textarea01" />
```

The src18.zip package associated with this chapter includes the XLEFF sampler preconfigured using the previous XML snippet to generate the described layout.

How the Label component resizes automatically

Unless you fully grasp how it works, the functionality provided by the autoSize parameter (and property) of the Label component can deface the layout of a user interface at runtime by positioning the text content where you do not expect it.

When you test the movie, you will notice that the text of the label01 instance in the minimal example appears to have moved away from its authoring time location; the change of position is due to the setting specified for the autoSize parameter ("right").

The autoSize parameter (and its corresponding property of the Label class) can do more than just align the text content; it can also resize or even reposition the instance depending on the runtime dimensions of the text content.

The diagrams shown in Figure 18-2 and Figure 18-3 help in visualizing the actual behavior of the Label component depending on the settings available for the autoSize parameter: "none", "center", "left", and "right".

Figure 18-2 shows four Label instances as they have been placed in the authoring environment. There is a box behind each component instance to emphasize the original locations and dimensions of each instance.

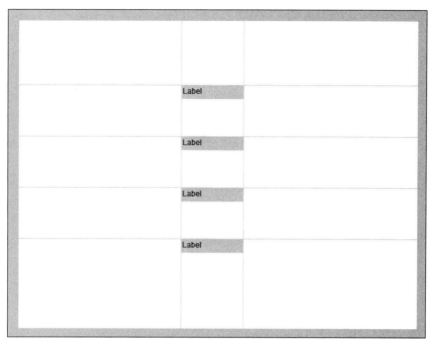

Figure 18-2. Four Label instances in the authoring environment

The following code can be utilized for trying the four different options:

```
function expand(instance) {
    instance.text = "Sampling the autoSize property";
    instance.setStyle("fontSize", 26);
}

label01.autoSize = "none";
label02.autoSize = "center";
label03.autoSize = "left";
label04.autoSize = "right";

expand(label01);
expand(label02);
expand(label03);
expand(label04);
```

Figure 18-3 highlights what really happens to the component instances after defining the autoSize parameter and then expanding their contents.

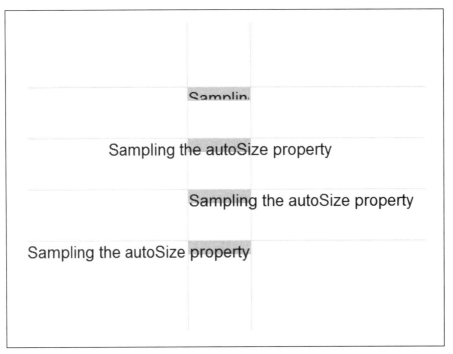

Figure 18-3. Impact of the autoSize property on four different Label instances

The custom grid placed underneath the four Label instances in Figure 18-3 helps you to appreciate what happens to each Label instance:

- autoSize = "none": This is seen in the topmost Label instance in Figure 18-3; the instance location and dimensions are not changed. As a result, only part of the text content is visible.

- autoSize = "center": This is seen in the second Label instance from the top in Figure 18-3; both the location and dimensions of the Label instance change. The instance is stretched in order to display the whole text content. Its y-coordinate remains the same, though it is repositioned horizontally, and its new position is centered on the original position displayed by the box behind the component instance.

- autoSize = "left": This is seen in the third Label instance from the top in Figure 18-3; the dimensions of the Label instance are modified in order to display the whole text content, while its position is still the same as it was defined in the authoring environment.

- autoSize = "right": This is seen in the fourth Label instance from the top in Figure 18-3; both the location and dimensions of the Label instance change. The instance is stretched in order to display the whole text content. Its y-coordinate remains the same, though it is repositioned horizontally so that the right edge of the instance coincides with the right edge as was defined in the authoring environment.

The presence of the custom grid in Figure 18-2 and Figure 18-3, designed behind the Label instances, plays a decisive role in visualizing the influence of the autoSize property, since it captures the position and dimensions of each instance before their content is expanded programmatically.

You can find such a grid inside the text01b.fla file in the src18.zip package associated with this chapter.

The text field inside

Being a Flash developer, you are probably familiar with text field objects. Each of the three components examined in this chapter relies on a text field object, which is implemented in the Flash Player and externalized by the TextField built-in class of ActionScript 2.

A text field object can be created dynamically via the TextField class or at authoring time via the Text Tool that you find in the Tools palette. Table 18-1 illustrates which properties of the TextField class are exposed by the Label, TextInput, and TextArea classes.

Table 18-1. TextField properties propagated by the component classes

TextField Property	Label	TextInput	TextArea
text	Yes	Yes	Yes
html	Yes	No	Yes
length	No	Yes	Yes
maxChars	No	Yes	Yes
password	No	Yes	Yes
restrict	No	Yes	Yes
styleSheet	No	No	Yes
wordWrap	No	No	Yes

You have already learned about the purpose of the text, html, password, and wordWrap properties earlier on when examining their associated parameters. The following list describes the functionality associated with the other properties appearing in Table 18-1, confirming that they reflect the corresponding properties of the TextField class:

- length: Exposed by both the TextInput and the TextArea components. As in the case of the TextField class, this property is read-only and returns the number of characters in the text field.
- maxChars: Exposed by both the TextInput and the TextArea components. As in the case of the TextField class, this property limits the number of characters that can be entered in the text field by the users.

- restrict: Exposed by both the TextInput and the TextArea components. As in the case of the TextField class, this property restricts the set of characters that can be entered in the text field by the users. See the ActionScript language reference for a description of the syntax of the String value assigned to this property. This property is undefined by default, indicating that the user can enter any character. In general, the user can enter a character only if it is included in the string value, so the easiest (and clearest) way to use this property is to plainly list all the accepted characters, as in this example:

```
textarea01.restrict = "0123";
// the user can now enter only the following characters:
// '0', '1', '2' and '3'
```

- styleSheet: Only exposed by the TextArea component, this property allows you to attach (or detach) a Cascading Style Sheet object to the text field object. The use of this property is detailed in the "Solved mysteries" section of this chapter, where CSS will be used to influence both HTML and XML data.

After analyzing the commonalities among the three components and the built-in TextField class, in the next section we will move our focus to component-specific functionality by creating a richer example.

Richer example of the TextInput and TextArea components

Both the TextInput and TextArea components also support a few specific events that we are going to examine in our next example in this section.

Handling the input process

The main purpose of the TextInput and the TextArea components is to retrieve and/or display text content. Basically, the only substantial difference between the two components is that the TextInput component limits the content to a single line, while the TextArea component can handle multiline content.

Both components implement a change event that you can use to track changes to the text content of a component instance and synchronize the rest of your application accordingly. The TextInput component also implements an enter event, notifying that the *ENTER* key has been pressed while a TextInput instance had the focus.

Building the following example will help you understand how these events work and when best to utilize them in your applications:

1. Open the document text01.fla created earlier and save it in a new folder as text02.fla.

2. Select the first frame in the document and attach the following ActionScript code to it:

```
#include "test.as"
```

3. Create a new ActionScript file and save it as `test.as` in the same folder where you saved the `text02.fla` file.

4. Add the following code to the ActionScript file just created:

```
textinput01.addEventListener("change", this);
textinput01.addEventListener("enter", this);
textarea01.addEventListener("change", this);

function change(eventObject:Object) {
    trace(eventObject.target._name + " : " +
➥ eventObject.target.text);
}

function enter(eventObject:Object) {
    trace("ENTER KEY PRESSED");
}
```

5. Save the `text02.fla` and `test.as` files.

During the test, the resulting movie will present the same layout of the minimal example shown in Figure 18-1. However, in this example, the _level0 object is listening to both the change and enter events.

Entering the characters a, b, and c in the textinput01 instance will result in the following messages appearing in the Output window:

```
textinput01 : a
textinput01 : ab
textinput01 : abc
```

Very similar lines will appear in the Output window if you enter the same characters in the textarea01 instance:

```
textarea01 : a
textarea01 : ab
textarea01 : abc
```

Considering that the change event handler implemented in our example is

```
function change(eventObject:Object) {
    trace(eventObject.target._name + " : " +
➥ eventObject.target.text);
}
```

the messages appearing in the Output window clearly demonstrate that the change event handler is invoked every time that the text content of a component instance changes following your user action.

While still testing, you can verify how the textinput01 and the textarea01 instances handle the *ENTER* key differently:

- Hitting the *ENTER* key while textarea01 has the focus results in adding a newline character at the cursor's position. Also, a change event is triggered since the text content of the component instance is indeed changed.

- Hitting the *ENTER* key while textinput01 has the focus has no effect on the text content of the component instance. However, an "ENTER KEY PRESSED" message appears in the Output window since an enter event was raised and the associated handler executed. In real-world applications, the enter event handler is usually exploited to validate the text content against some specific requirement.

Now that you can proficiently utilize the core features of the text-based components discussed in this chapter, we can move on to customizing their appearance starting from their supported styles.

Supported styles

The styles supported by the Label, TextInput, and TextArea components can be considered common in the broader sense adopted in the previous chapters, indicating that they are style properties also supported by other components in the architecture.

The following common color styles are supported by all of the three components examined in this chapter: themeColor, color, and disabledColor.

backgroundColor, also a common color style, is supported by the TextInput and TextArea components only, since the background of the Label component is transparent.

The following text styles are common to the three text-based components examined in this chapter plus several other components in the architecture:

- embedFonts: Accepts a Boolean value, which is false by default. This style must be set to true whenever the fontFamily style refers to a font that has been included (embedded) in the SWF movie.

- fontFamily: A String value storing the name of the font utilized for the text. The default value of this important style property is "_sans".

- fontSize: A Number value indicating the size of the font in points. Its default value is 10.

- fontStyle: A String value set to "normal" by default. The only alternative value for this style property is "italic".

- fontWeight: A String value set to "none" by default. The only alternative value for this style property is "bold". Assigning the value "normal" to this property resets it to the default value of "none".

- textAlign: A String value set to "left" by default. Other valid values for this style property are "center" and "right". Note that in the case of the Label component, the value assigned to this style property is effective only if the autoSize property of the Label instance is set to "none".

- textDecoration: A String value set to "none" by default. The only alternative value for this style property is "underline".

- `textIndent`: A Number value specifying the text indentation in pixels. Its default value is 0.
- `marginLeft`: A Number value specifying the text left margin in pixels. Its default value is 0.
- `marginRight`: A Number value specifying the text right margin in pixels. Its default value is 0.

Both the TextInput and the TextArea components also support the borderStyle style property, which is implemented by the RectBorder class and, therefore, shared among all the components in the architecture that use this class for drawing their borders.

The default value of the borderStyle style property is inset=. Alternative values are none, outset, and solid. When the component's theme is Halo, as in the default case, another four border styles options are available: default, alert, dropDown, and menuBorder.

The most convenient way of defining the color of the border is via the themeColor style property, which is capable of defining a consistent color scheme automatically.

Alternatively, you can define several color style properties that only affect borders: borderColor, buttonColor, borderCapColor, highlightColor, shadowCapColor, and shadowColor. Note that some of those border colors are effective only when the border type, chosen via the borderStyle style property, supports them.

The following example demonstrates how the appearance of the text-based component examined in this chapter can be almost fully customized by simply applying style definitions to them:

1. Open the document text02.fla created earlier and save it in a new folder as text03.fla.
2. Create a new ActionScript file and save it as test.as in the same folder where you saved the text03.fla file.
3. Add the following code to the ActionScript file just created:

```
function setStyles(instance) {
    instance.setStyle("themeColor", "blue");
    instance.setStyle("color", "blue");
    instance.setStyle("fontFamily", "Courier New");
    instance.setStyle("fontSize", 12);
    instance.setStyle("fontWeight", "bold");
    instance.setStyle("backgroundColor", 0xDDE0FF);
    instance.setStyle("borderStyle", "alert");
}

setStyles(label01);
setStyles(textinput01);
setStyles(textarea01);
```

4. Save the text03.fla and test.as files.

Testing the movie will show you how a few style settings are sufficient to radically alter the appearance of the layout previously defined in the minimal example.

Enter some text content in the textinput01 and textarea01 instances in order to fully appreciate the new look. Figure 18-4 shows the stylized layout after some sample text was entered in both the component instances.

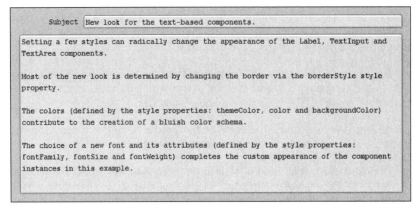

Figure 18-4. The stylized version of the minimal example

Note on the skins

As an exception from the other chapters dedicated to customizing components, this chapter does not include a section dedicated to the skins.

Apart from the fact that the appearance of the text-based components discussed here can be almost completely customized via style properties, as you saw earlier, the reasons I have not included a skin section in this chapter are as follows:

- The Label component does not use any skins.
- The TextInput and TextArea components use the RectBorder class to draw their borders, and the technique for customizing this class is included in Chapter 11.
- The TextArea component can have scrollbars that can be skinned, and these are described in Chapter 21.

Solved mysteries

Every component hides some secret and arguably simple components, and the text-based ones examined in this chapter are no exception.

This section will examine how to satisfy a couple of very frequent requirements that have been somewhat forgotten in the current version of the component architecture.

Hiding the background

Due to the highly graphical nature of the Flash technology, you may occasionally need to hide the background of the TextInput and TextArea components to show some design underneath the component instances.

This option was certainly considered when implementing the component architecture, but, unfortunately, this feature is only barely supported.

At the time of writing, you can make the background invisible by globally defining the backgroundColor style property as follows:

```
_global.styles.TextArea.setStyle("backgroundColor", "transparent");
```

The flexibility of such an option, however is very poor, since

- The transparent value works only if set globally as shown in the previous code, where it is applied to the TextArea global style. Applying the transparent value to an instance does not work. The fact that there is no way of setting this option individually forces all the TextArea instances in your application to have a transparent background.

- Quite weirdly, defining the transparent setting in the TextArea global style also affects TextInput instances. Therefore, executing the previous line of code will affect not only every TextArea instance in your application, but also every TextInput instance as well.

- The transparent setting of the backgroundColor style property doesn't affect the borders of component instances that remain visible, and most probably defaces the design underneath the component. This results in more work for you, even if this is a minor issue, since you can hide the border by invoking the method setStyle, as in the following example:

```
instance.setStyle("borderStyle", "none");
```

The following example will extend both the TextArea and the TextInput classes so that you will be able to hide the background and the borders of specific component instances in a single step:

1. Open the document text03.fla created earlier and save it in a new folder as text04a.fla.

2. Create a new ActionScript file and save it as test.as in the same folder where you saved the text04a.fla file.

3. Add the following code to the ActionScript file just created:

```
import mx.controls.TextInput;
import mx.controls.TextArea;

TextInput.prototype.setBackground =
➡ function(showIt:Boolean):Void {
    this.border_mc.setVisible(showIt);
}

TextArea.prototype.setBackground =
➡ function(showIt:Boolean):Void {
    this.border_mc.setVisible(showIt);
}
```

451

```
textinput01.setBackground(false);
textarea01.setBackground(false);

textinput01.text = "there still is TextInput instance here";
textarea01.text = "there still is TextArea instance here";
```

4. Save the text04a.fla and test.as files.

Testing the movie will result in the total absence of component backgrounds and borders from the layout of the minimal example, as shown in Figure 18-5.

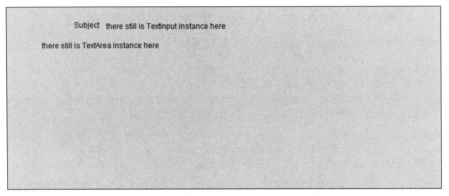

Figure 18-5. Hiding the background and border of the TextInput and TextArea instances

The disappearance of backgrounds and borders makes it really difficult to distinguish the text in the Label instance from the text in the TextInput and TextArea instances. However, both the TextArea and the TextInput instances are still there and are fully functional, and you can verify this by clicking their sample text and editing it.

The solution relies on implementing a setBackground method for both the TextInput and TextArea classes so that you can hide/unhide the background of an instance at will by invoking it with the proper Boolean parameter (false to hide, true to unhide) as in the calls that we make in the example:

```
textinput01.setBackground(false);
textarea01.setBackground(false);
```

The implementation of the setBackground method of both classes is identical, since it exploits a similarity in the internal structure of the TextArea and TextInput components: both create a child sub-component named border_mc that represents the background and the border of a component instance.

Since the border_mc instance inherits from the UIObject class, we can invoke the setVisible method on it and satisfy our requirement in a way that is compatible with the existing design of the component architecture:

```
this.border_mc.setVisible(showIt);
```

By implementing a specific feature, this example is yet another demonstration that extending the architecture is not only possible, but also easy, when reapplying the patterns included in its implementation.

The next section deals with a problem that you may have encountered when trying to load content into a TextArea instance from an external text file.

Handling the combination linefeed/CR

Loading content into a TextArea instance from an external text file is an option commonly used that can present an unpleasant issue depending on what platform you are running: text lines can appear separated by blank lines that were not included in the original text content. The problem only appears when utilizing ASCII text files created in the Windows platform, and it is due to the way newlines are stored in the file.

Even if you work on the Mac platform only, you should still be aware of this issue, since there may be cases when you must utilize text files produced by Windows users.

The following example aims to reproduce the problem so that you can appreciate its full extent:

1. Create a new Flash document and save it as text04b.fla.
2. Open the Document Properties dialog box by selecting Modify ➤ Document, and set its dimensions as 400✕400 pixels.
3. Drag the TextArea component on the stage in order to create one instance of the component. Select the newly created component instance and define its name as textarea01 via the Properties panel.
4. While the textarea01 instance is still selected, use the Info panel to define its location and dimensions as (X: 0, Y: 0) and (W: 400, H: 400).
5. Select the first frame in the document and attach the following ActionScript code to it:

   ```
   #include "test.as"
   ```

6. Create a new ActionScript file and save it as test.as in the same folder where you saved the text04b.fla file.
7. Add the following code to the ActionScript file just created:

   ```
   var contentLoader:LoadVars = new LoadVars();
   contentLoader.onData = function(content:String) {
       if (content != undefined) {
           textarea01.text = content;
       }
   }

   contentLoader.load("content.txt");
   ```

8. Create a new text file using a Windows text editor such as Notepad or copy the content.txt file included in the source code associated with this chapter in the same folder where you saved the text04b.fla file.

9. Unless you are using the `content.txt` file included in the source files associated with this chapter, you must fill the text file with sample text, ensuring that it contains several lines of it.

10. Save the `text04b.fla`, `test.as`, and `content.txt` files.

The outcome of our last example should be similar to the one shown in Figure 18-6 where the sample text in the `content.txt` file appears fragmented by numerous blank lines that were not present in the original content.

Figure 18-6. Loading a text file in a TextArea instance can produce an unexpected result.

This is yet another case where finding a solution is more an issue of knowing what is going on rather than writing plenty of code.

The Windows and Mac operating systems store text files in a different way. Table 18-2 presents what character(s) they utilize to represent a newline.

Table 18-2. Newlines as they are represented in text files by different operating systems

Operating System	ASCII Character(s)	Escape Sequence(s)
Microsoft Windows	0D 0A	\r\n
Apple Macintosh OS 9 and earlier	0D	\r
Apple Macintosh OS X and higher	0A	\n

Basically, Mac OS utilizes a single character (either the carriage return \r or the line-feed \n, depending on the operating system version) to represent a newline, while Windows uses two characters each time (\r followed by \n).

As you saw earlier, the TextArea component is implemented on top of a native text field object. At the time of writing, text field objects interpret the combination \r\n as a double newline, and that explains the presence of an additional, unnecessary, blank line every time there is a newline a Windows text file.

Fixing the problem, once its cause is identified, is a matter modifying a single line of ActionScript in our example. We previously used a LoadVars instance to load the text content stored in the external file:

```
var contentLoader:LoadVars = new LoadVars();
contentLoader.onData = function(content:String) {
    if (content != undefined) {
        textarea01.text = content;
    }
}
```

The LoadVars class allows us to easily retrieve the content of the text file in a String instance named content. Since the String class provides several powerful methods, we can replace the line

```
textarea01.text = content;
```

with

```
textarea01.text = content.split("\r\n").join("\r");
```

to properly get rid of the double newline characters in one step.

The fix proposed here breaks the String instance into individual lines, utilizing the couple of characters "\r\n" as separator for the split method, and then rejoins those lines, utilizing the "\r" character as separator by invoking the join method.

Note how this code will not alter text files produced using the Mac OS platform, since they do not contain any occurrence of "\r\n".

Figure 18-7 shows how the content in the TextArea instance of our example becomes faithful to the content in the external text file after you fixed the problem by modifying the source code as indicated.

```
Oh, the DataGrid, babe, has such cells, dear
And it shows them pearly white
Just a couple of scrollbars has old component, babe
And it keeps them, ah, out of sight
Ya know when that event triggers with its data, babe
Other events start to spread
Fancy skins, oh, wears that old component, babe
So there's never, never a trace of background

Now on the stage, huh, huh, whoo a new movie, un huh
Lies a new instance just oozin' life, eek
And a structure sneakin' around the window
Could that something be XML?

There's a style, huh, huh, down by the sheet dontcha know
Where a font's just a'drooppin' on down
Oh, that font is just, it's there for the weight, dear
Five'll get ya ten old pixels are back in town
Now d'ja hear about the new software? it disappeared, babe
After drawin' out all his hard-earned cash
And now the developer spends just like a sailor
Could it be our boy's done somethin' rash?
```

Figure 18-7. Content of the TextArea instance after fixing the "blank lines" problem

Reasons for subclassing the Label, TextInput, and TextArea components

Encapsulating skins, or even styles, is a typical reason for considering subclassing a component.

However, since the text-based components examined in this chapter do not support skins of their own (the skins of the scrollbars can be customized separately without touching the TextArea component, as you will see in Chapter 21), building a theme does not represent a strong reason for subclassing the Label, TextInput, and TextArea components.

As you learned earlier in this chapter, almost every aspect of the appearance of the text-based components can be influenced by proper style settings; so you may decide not to subclass these components whenever creating a theme, but just influence their appearance by defining a set of global styles associated with your theme.

Subclassing becomes a significantly more interesting option if you want to extend these components, in particular, the TextArea component. Subclassing the TextArea component allows you to encapsulate both the features discussed in the "Solved mysteries" section of this chapter into an extended version of the component so you can avoid having to reapply those techniques every time that you need them.

After learning the techniques exposed in this chapter and the previous ones, you can start making your own decisions in terms of design and implementation and, for instance, implement the visibility/invisibility of the background as a property instead of a method.

Chapter 19

THE TREE COMPONENT

| Tree |
| mx.controls.Tree |
| Frequency: Common |
| Complexity: Simple |
| Stability: Robust |
| Maturity: Classic |
| Popularity: Widespread |

The Tree component allows you to add hierarchical views to your application that the user can exploit to browse and select structured information.

The Tree component can play an important role in object-oriented applications due to its ability to provide an intuitive and yet faithful representation of the object model encapsulating the application-specific logic.

Although the Tree component is most frequently utilized to implement interactive "tables of contents" for help guides or other kinds of information systems, the actual extent of its use is limited only by your imagination.

This chapter is dedicated to dissecting the structure of the Tree component so that you will be able to customize both its appearance and behavior without limits.

> *The completed source code introduced in this chapter can be found in the package* `src19.zip`, *downloadable from this book's page at* www.friendsofed.com.

Minimal example of the Tree component

Building a minimal example exposing the basic features of the Tree component is the first step in the direction of taking full control over its functionality:

1. Create a new Flash document and save it as `tree01.fla`.

2. Open the Document Properties dialog box by selecting Modify ➤ Document, and set its dimensions as 240×336 pixels.

3. Drag the Tree component on the stage in order to create one instance of the component. Select the new component instance and define its name as tree01 via the Properties panel.

4. While the tree01 instance is still selected, use the Info panel to define its location and dimensions as (X: 0, Y: 0) and (W: 240, H: 336).

5. Select the first frame in the document and attach the following ActionScript code to it:

```
#include "test.as"
```

6. Create a new ActionScript file and save it as `test.as` in the same folder where you saved the `tree01.fla` file.

7. Add the following code to the ActionScript file you just created:

```
var xmlLoader:XML = new XML();
xmlLoader.ignoreWhite = true;
xmlLoader.load("tree.xml");
xmlLoader.onLoad = function(success:Boolean):Void {
  tree01.dataProvider = this;
  tree01.setIsOpen(tree01.getTreeNodeAt(0), true);
}

tree01.vScrollPolicy = "auto";
```

8. Create a new text file using a text editor such as Notepad in Windows and save it as `tree.xml` in the same folder where you saved the `tree01.fla` file.

9. Add the following XML snippet to the `tree.xml` file:

```
<node label="ROOT NODE (branch)">
  <node label="Child node 1 (leaf)" />
  <node label="Child node 2 (branch)">
    <node label="Child node 2.1 (leaf)" />
    <node label="Child node 2.2 (leaf)" />
    <node label="Child node 2.3 (branch)">
      <node label="Child node 2.3.1 (leaf)" />
      <node label="Child node 2.3.2 (leaf)" />
    </node>
    <node label="Child node 2.4 (leaf)" />
  </node>
  <node label="Child node 3 (branch)">
    <node label="Child node 3.1 (leaf)" />
    <node label="Child node 3.2 (leaf)" />
    <node label="Child node 3.3 (leaf)" />
  </node>
  <node label="Child node 4 (leaf)" />
  <node label="Child node 5 (leaf)" />
</node>
```

10. Save the `tree01.fla`, `test.as`, and `tree.xml` files.

The structure of a Tree instance is quite simply made of nodes. The Tree component distinguishes between two kinds of nodes:

- **Branch**: A branch node is a node that has one or more child nodes.
- **Leaf**: A leaf node is a node that has zero child nodes.

XML is used to describe the node-based structure of a Tree instance.

The XML syntax supported by the Tree component is very intuitive since it is made of a single XML element, the node element, which you can nest to describe the branches of the Tree instance. The following XML snippet describes a branch node with two leaves (nodes without children):

```
<node>
  <node />
  <node />
</node>
```

The XML snippet stored in the `tree.xml` file of our example describes a tree structure using node XML elements and their `label` attributes, which define the text being displayed when nodes appear in the tree view.

The `label` attribute of the node XML element is the only attribute supported by the Tree component, although some official sources mention a second attribute (`isBranch`).

461

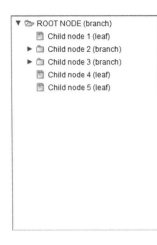

As a matter of fact, the isBranch attribute is not supported by the Tree component. Later on in the "Solved mysteries" section of this chapter, you will learn how to add support for additional attributes, including isBranch.

Testing the minimal example will result in the Tree component instance appearing as shown in Figure 19-1.

Figure 19-1. The Tree instance in the minimal example

The labels utilized in the minimal example expressly distinguish between branch nodes and leaves in the text. Such a distinction is visually supported by the Tree component by associating a folder icon with branch nodes and a document icon with leaves.

By default, branch nodes are closed, that is, they do not show their child nodes.

The root node, labeled ROOT NODE (branch), is open, since we included the following line in the example:

```
tree01.setIsOpen(tree01.getTreeNodeAt(0), true);
```

This line uses the getTreeNodeAt method to retrieve the first node of the tree using a zero-based index and the setIsOpen method to open it. Figure 19-2 shows a couple of branch nodes, labeled Child node 2 (branch) and Child node 3 (branch), that are still closed, since they were not opened programmatically.

Users can open/close a node by clicking the disclosure icon, represented by the arrow appearing just before the folder icon of a branch node.

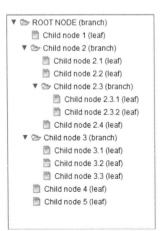

If you open all the branch notes in the minimal example by clicking their disclosure icons, you will eventually expose the whole node-based structure described in the tree.xml file and shown in Figure 19-2.

Figure 19-2. The whole node-based structure of the minimal example exposed

Looking at the whole structure of the Tree instance implemented in the minimal example, you can appreciate the following additional roles played by its nodes:

- **Root**: A root node is a node that does not have the parent node.
- **Parent**: A parent node is a node with one or more child nodes.
- **Child**: A child node is a node contained by another node, its parent node.
- **Sibling**: Sibling nodes are nodes that share the same parent node.
- **Ancestor node**: A node is an ancestor of another node if it contains it directly as a child or indirectly by containing its parent or one of its ancestors.
- **Descendant node**: A node is a descendant of another node if that node is one of its ancestors.

Terms such as leaf, branch, root, parent, child, sibling, ancestor, and even descendant will frequently be used in the remainder of the chapter to refer to the role played by a node in the context of a tree-like structure.

Although the internal structure of the Tree component closely resembles the tree-like nature of XML, you should consider the XML data produced for the Tree component more as an XML snippet rather than a complete and valid XML document.

While XML documents can only have one root element, it would not have made sense to introduce this limitation in the Tree component, since it would have reduced the number of its applications.

You can easily create an example of a Tree instance with several root nodes by replacing the XML snippet in the tree.xml file of the minimal example with the following:

```
<node label="Root node 1" />
<node label="Root node 2">
  <node label="Child node 2.1" />
  <node label="Child node 2.2" />
  <node label="Child node 2.3">
    <node label="Child node 2.3.1" />
    <node label="Child node 2.3.2" />
  </node>
  <node label="Child node 2.4" />
</node>
<node label="Root node 3">
  <node label="Child node 3.1" />
  <node label="Child node 3.2" />
  <node label="Child node 3.3" />
</node>
<node label="Root node 4" />
<node label="Root node 5" />
```

Testing the example with the new XML snippet will now show a Tree instance with five root nodes like the one in Figure 19-3.

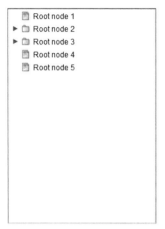

Figure 19-3. A Tree instance with five root nodes

The minimal example utilizes an instance of the built-in XML class to load the contents of tree.xml and assign it to the dataProvider property of the Tree class:

```
var xmlLoader:XML = new XML();
xmlLoader.ignoreWhite = true;
xmlLoader.load("tree.xml");
xmlLoader.onLoad = function(success:Boolean):Void {
    tree01.dataProvider = this;
    tree01.setIsOpen(tree01.getTreeNodeAt(0), true);
}
```

As I mentioned earlier, a valid XML document can have only one root element because of the W3C DOM Level1 recommendation. However, the last example successfully loaded an XML snippet containing five root elements, one for each root node shown in Figure 19-3, by exploiting the fact that the XML class does not check the validity of the loaded XML document and, therefore, is capable of loading and parsing XML snippets that contain more than one root element.

XLEFF version of the minimal example

The Tree component is one of the few components in the architecture that already uses XML for describing its internal structure.

XLEFF extends the benefits deriving from XML to all the components in the architecture by exposing and enhancing their functionality using a syntax very similar to the one already in use in the architecture.

The following XML snippet, which you can test by using the preconfigured XLEFF sampler included in the files associated with this chapter, shows how similar this syntax is:

```
<tree x="350" y="100" width="240" height="336"
➥ name="tree01" vScrollPolicy="auto">
  <node label="ROOT NODE (branch)" open="true">
    <node label="Child node 1 (leaf)" />
    <node label="Child node 2 (branch)">
      <node label="Child node 2.1 (leaf)" />
      <node label="Child node 2.2 (leaf)" />
      <node label="Child node 2.3 (branch)">
        <node label="Child node 2.3.1 (leaf)" />
        <node label="Child node 2.3.2 (leaf)" />
      </node>
      <node label="Child node 2.4 (leaf)" />
    </node>
    <node label="Child node 3 (branch)">
      <node label="Child node 3.1 (leaf)" />
      <node label="Child node 3.2 (leaf)" />
      <node label="Child node 3.3 (leaf)" />
    </node>
    <node label="Child node 4 (leaf)" />
    <node label="Child node 5 (leaf)" />
  </node>
</tree>
```

Basically, the tree XML element wraps the same XML snippet used in the minimal example, an aspect that is highlighted by the next few lines:

```
<tree x="350" y="100" width="240" height="336"
➥ name="tree01" vScrollPolicy="auto">

similar node-based syntax

</tree>
```

In addition to the node-based syntax describing the structure of a Tree instance that you saw earlier, XLEFF also supports two other attributes for the node element:

- open: When set to "true", this attribute allows you to specify that the branch node must show its children.
- isBranch: When set to "true", this attribute allows you to change a leaf note into a branch node, even if the node does not have children (yet).

Supported styles

The Tree component supports numerous common style properties and several specific, even peculiar, style properties that allow you to customize its entire appearance without resorting to any skinning technique.

Color styles

The common color style properties supported by the Tree component are as follows:

- themeColor: Supported by the default Halo theme only. It allows you to pick a color that will act as base color in a color scheme automatically generated by the Halo theme.
- color: Defines the text color.
- disabledColor: Defines the text color of a component instance when disabled.
- backgroundColor: Defines the background color.
- backgroundDisabledColor: Defines the background color of a component instance when disabled.

In addition, the Tree component also supports the following specific color style properties:

- depthColors: Defines an array of colors, one for each nesting level in the Tree instance. The first color in the array defines the background color of the nodes at level 0 (root nodes), the second color defines the background color of the nodes at level 1, and so on.
- selectionColor: The background color of a node when it is selected.
- selectionDisabledColor: The background color of a selected node when the component instance is disabled.
- textSelectedColor: The text color of the label in a selected node.
- rollOverColor: The background color of a node when the mouse cursor rolls over it.
- textRollOverColor: The text color of the label in a node when the mouse cursor rolls over it.

Text styles

The Tree component supports the following common text style properties: embedFonts, fontFamily, fontSize, fontWeight, fontStyle, textAlign, textDecoration, and textIndent. Text style properties are discussed in greater detail in Chapter 18.

Animation styles

The Tree component supports a few style properties that can modify the behavior of the animations triggered when the component's state changes:

- openDuration: The duration in milliseconds of the animation displayed when a branch node opens to show its children or closes to hide them. The default value of this style property is 250.
- openEasing: A style property controlling the accelerations of the open/close animations by accepting a function provided by the transitions package included in the component architecture (see Appendix B for more information about the easing methods that can be assigned to this style property).

- selectionDuration: The duration in milliseconds of the animation shown when a node changes state from unselected to selected and vice versa. The default value of this style property is 200.

- selectionEasing: A style property controlling the accelerations of the animation launched when a node is selected (see Appendix B for more information about the easing methods that can be assigned to this style property).

Icon styles

Thanks to the icon style properties of the Tree component, you can customize the most graphic bits of the component: the icons appearing in a node.

All the icon style properties accept String values, which are linkage identifiers of exported symbols that you include in the document's library of your application to replace the default icons of the Tree component.

The Tree component supports five icon style properties:

- defaultLeafIcon: Determines the icon associated with leaf nodes

- disclosureOpenIcon: Determines the icon that the user must click to close a branch node

- disclosureClosedIcon: Determines the icon that the user must click to open a branch node

- folderOpenIcon: Determines the icon of a branch node when open

- folderClosedIcon: Determines the icon of a branch node when closed

Other component-specific styles

The Tree component also supports another couple of styles that allow you to customize specific visual aspects:

- indentation: The nodes in a Tree component are indented to let the user visualize the levels of nesting. The numeric value assigned to this style property determines the depth in pixels of an indentation step, which is set to 17 by default.

- useRollOver: When set to false, rolling with the mouse cursor over a node will not change its text and background colors anymore. As a result of this, the node will not be highlighted.

A note on skins

The Tree component does not implement skins of its own. The only skins appearing in a Tree instance are those of the RectBorder class for the border, detailed in Chapter 11, and the skins of its scrollbar's subcomponents, the customization of which is described in Chapter 21.

In the following section, you are going to implement an example that will demonstrate how you can change the whole appearance of a Tree component by simply using style properties.

Stylizing the minimal example

The objective of the following example is to redefine any visual aspect in a Tree instance by utilizing style properties:

1. Open the document `tree01.fla` created earlier and save it in a new folder as `tree02.fla`.

2. Create a new movie clip symbol by selecting Insert ➤ New Symbol, and define both its name and its linkage identifier as CustomClosedIcon. You can either reuse the graphic that you find in the completed files associated with this chapter or draw your own icon. The icon dimensions should be approximately 20✕20 pixels.

3. Repeat the second step four times in order to add four more exported symbols to the document's library. The names (with corresponding linkage identifiers) of the four symbols are CustomCollapseIcon, CustomExpandIcon, CustomLeafIcon, CustomOpenIcon.

4. Create a new ActionScript file and save it as `test.as` in the same folder where you saved the `tree02.fla` file.

5. Add the following code to the ActionScript file you just created:

```
function setStyles(instance):Void {
  instance.setStyle("backgroundColor", 0xffbb66);
  instance.setStyle("depthColors",
➥ [0xffbb66, 0xffcc99, 0xffddaa]);
  instance.setStyle("borderStyle", "default");
  instance.setStyle("color", 0x886644);
  instance.setStyle("textSelectedColor", "yellow");
  instance.setStyle("selectionColor", 0x99ccff);
  instance.setStyle("fontFamily", "Courier New");
  instance.setStyle("fontSize", 14);
  instance.setStyle("fontWeight", "bold");
  instance.setStyle("defaultLeafIcon", "CustomLeafIcon");
  instance.setStyle("disclosureClosedIcon", "CustomExpandIcon");
  instance.setStyle("disclosureOpenIcon", "CustomCollapseIcon");
  instance.setStyle("folderClosedIcon", "CustomClosedIcon");
  instance.setStyle("folderOpenIcon", "CustomOpenIcon");
  instance.setStyle("indentation", 17);
  instance.setStyle("useRollOver", false);
}

var xmlLoader:XML = new XML();
xmlLoader.ignoreWhite = true;
xmlLoader.load("tree.xml");
xmlLoader.onLoad = function(success:Boolean):Void {
  tree01.dataProvider = this;
  tree01.setIsOpen(tree01.getTreeNodeAt(1), true);
  tree01.setIsOpen(tree01.getTreeNodeAt(2), true);
}
```

```
tree01.vScrollPolicy = "auto";
tree01.rowHeight = 30;
tree01.multipleSelection = true;

setStyles(tree01);
```

6. Create a new text file using a text editor such as Notepad in Windows and save it as `tree.xml` in the same folder where you saved the `tree02.fla` file.

7. Add the following XML snippet to the `tree.xml` file:

```xml
<node label="Root node 1" />
<node label="Root node 2">
  <node label="Child node 2.1" />
  <node label="Child node 2.2" />
  <node label="Child node 2.3" />
</node>
<node label="Root node 3">
  <node label="Child node 3.1" />
  <node label="Child node 3.2" />
  <node label="Child node 3.3" />
</node>
<node label="Root node 4" />
<node label="Root node 5" />
```

8. Save the `tree02.fla`, `test.as`, and `tree.xml` files.

With the exception of the icons, which could look different if you did not use the images included in the source files associated with this chapter, testing our last example will result in the customized appearance shown in Figure 19-4.

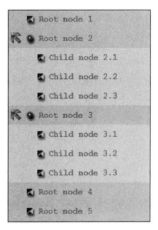

Figure 19-4. A stylized instance of the Tree component

As well as applying several style properties listed earlier in this chapter, our last example uses an additional style property:

```
instance.setStyle("borderStyle", "default");
```

The borderStyle style property and its default value depend on the implementation of the RectBorder class provided by the default Halo theme. The following line also contributes to the look shown in Figure 19-4 by making the row containing each node taller (the default value of the rowHeight property of the Tree class is 20 pixels):

```
tree01.rowHeight = 30;
```

The influence of a few style properties on the tree01 instance can be appreciated only after selecting one or more nodes. The multipleSelection property was set to true to highlight those aspects:

```
tree01.multipleSelection = true;
```

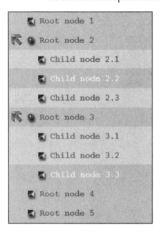

With multiple selection enabled, you can also select more than one node at a time by using the *Ctrl*/*Cmd* or *Shift* keys as usual. Selecting a couple of nodes while testing the last example will result in an appearance similar to the one shown in Figure 19-5.

Figure 19-5. The stylized Tree instance after you select a couple of nodes

You can retrieve the user selection, or define a selection programmatically, via two properties:

- selectedNode: Retrieves (or sets) the currently selected node in the case of a single selection.
- selectedNodes: Returns (or sets) the currently selected nodes in the case of multiple selections. Its value is an array of node instances.

So far you have learned the basic functionality of the Tree component and how to customize its appearance. In the next section, you will complete the exploration of its features while customizing its behavior.

Solved mysteries

The Tree component is based on a pretty robust implementation that also shows a peculiar approach to stylizing/skinning by allowing you to customize its appearance, including the inner graphics, by using styles only.

The fact that you can redefine its icons by using style properties gives you maximum flexibility in terms of its use: you can use a different icon set for each Tree instance in your application whenever needed.

The next example will exploit the robustness and the flexibility of the Tree component to extend it by adding further behaviors.

Taking full control

In some occasions, depending on the requirements that you are working on, you may find that clicking the disclosure icon to open/close branch nodes is not the most suitable option. In those cases, you may prefer to design and implement an interface where branch nodes can be opened or closed by clicking any part of a node's area.

In the next example, you will learn how to modify the behavior of the Tree component to achieve this and add further behaviors that can be very useful in a variety of circumstances:

1. Open the document `tree01.fla` created earlier and save it in a new folder as `tree03.fla`.

2. Set the background color of the new Flash document as #66cccc by accessing the Document Properties dialog box via Modify ➤ Document.

3. Create a new movie clip symbol by selecting Insert ➤ New Symbol, defining both its name and its linkage identifier as EmptyIcon. This symbol will remain empty.

4. Create a new movie clip symbol by selecting Insert ➤ New Symbol, defining both its name and its linkage identifier as CustomClosedIcon. You can either reuse the graphic that you find in the completed files associated with this chapter or draw your own icon, which should resemble a plus sign of at most 20✕20 pixels.

5. Create a new movie clip symbol by selecting Insert ➤ New Symbol, defining both its name and its linkage identifier as CustomOpenIcon. You can either reuse the graphic that you find in the completed files associated with this chapter or draw your own icon, which should resemble a minus sign of at most 20✕20 pixels.

6. Create a new ActionScript file and save it as `test.as` in the same folder where you saved the `tree03.fla` file.

7. Add the following code to the ActionScript file you just created:

```
import mx.controls.Tree;

Tree.prototype.setBackground = function(showIt:Boolean):Void {
  this.border_mc.setVisible(showIt);
}

function setStyles(instance):Void {
  instance.setStyle("themeColor", "haloOrange");
  instance.setStyle("backgroundColor", 0xffc070);
  instance.setStyle("depthColors", [0xffc070, 0xffc878, 0xffd080]);
  instance.setStyle("borderStyle", "default");
  instance.setStyle("color", 0x664422);
  instance.setStyle("selectionColor", 0xdddddd);
  instance.setStyle("rollOverColor", 0xcccccc);
  instance.setStyle("textRollOverColor", 0x664422);
  instance.setStyle("textSelectedColor", 0x664422);
  instance.setStyle("fontFamily", "Courier New");
  instance.setStyle("fontSize", 14);
  instance.setStyle("fontWeight", "bold");
  instance.setStyle("indentation", 10);
  instance.setStyle("defaultLeafIcon", "EmptyIcon");
```

```
    instance.setStyle("folderOpenIcon", "CustomOpenIcon");
    instance.setStyle("folderClosedIcon", "CustomClosedIcon");
    instance.setStyle("disclosureClosedIcon", "EmptyIcon");
    instance.setStyle("disclosureOpenIcon", "EmptyIcon");
}

var treeController:TreeController = new TreeController(true, true);
treeController.controlTree(tree01);

setStyles(tree01);

tree01.vScrollPolicy = 'auto';

tree01.setBackground(false);

var xmlLoader:XML = new XML();
xmlLoader.ignoreWhite = true;
xmlLoader.load("tree.xml");
xmlLoader.onLoad = function(success:Boolean):Void {
    tree01.dataProvider = this;
}
```

8. Create a new ActionScript file and save it as `TreeController.as` in the same folder where you saved the `tree03.fla` file.

9. Add the following code to the ActionScript file you just created:

```
import mx.controls.Tree;

class TreeController {
    public var autoCollapse:Boolean;
    public var persistent:Boolean;
    private var pendingNode:XMLNode;

    function TreeController(ac:Boolean, p:Boolean) {
        autoCollapse = (ac == undefined) ? true : ac;
        persistent = (p == undefined) ? false : p;
        pendingNode = null;
    }

    function change(eventObject:Object):Void {
        var t:Tree = eventObject.target;
        var selNode:XMLNode = t.selectedNode;
        var closingSibling = this.getOpenSibling(selNode, t);
        if ( (closingSibling != null) && this.autoCollapse) {
            if (t.getIsBranch(selNode)) {
                t.setIsOpen(closingSibling, false, true, true);
                this.pendingNode = selNode;
            }
        } else if (t.getIsBranch(selNode)) {
```

```
            var open:Boolean = t.getIsOpen(selNode);
            t.setIsOpen(selNode, !open, true, true);
        }
    }

    function nodeClose(eventObject:Object):Void {
        var t:Tree = eventObject.target;
        var node:XMLNode = eventObject.node;
        this.closeChildren(node, t);
        if ( (this.pendingNode != null) &&
➥ (t.getIsBranch(this.pendingNode)) ) {
            t.setIsOpen(this.pendingNode,
➥ node != t.selectedNode, true, true);
            this.pendingNode = null;
        }
    }

    function controlTree(t:Tree):Void {
        t.addEventListener('change', this);
        t.addEventListener('nodeClose', this);
    }

    private function getOpenSibling
➥ (node:XMLNode, t:Tree):XMLNode {
        var parent:XMLNode = node.parentNode;
        var n:XMLNode;
        for (var index = 0; index < parent.childNodes.length;
➥ index++) {
            n = parent.childNodes[index];
            if ( t.getIsOpen(n) ) return n;
        }
        return null;
    }

    private function closeChildren(node:XMLNode, t:Tree):Void {
        if (persistent) return;
        for (var index in node.childNodes) {
            if (t.getIsOpen(node.childNodes[index])) {
                closeChildren(node.childNodes[index], t);
            }
        }
        t.setIsOpen(node, false, false);
    }
}
```

10. Copy the `tree.xml` file utilized in the `tree02.fla` example in the folder where the `tree03.fla` file is. The XML snippet in the `tree.xml` file is the one with the five roots that we already used several times in this chapter.

11. Save the `tree03.fla`, `test.as`, and `TreeController.as` files.

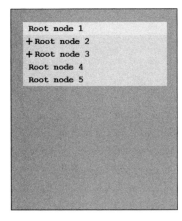

Testing the current example will display a customized version of the tree01 instance looking like the one shown in Figure 19-6.

Figure 19-6. Changing behavior and appearance of the Tree component

Both the branch nodes at the root level (Root node 2 and Root node 3) are initially collapsed, since their default initial state was not modified in the current example.

The main functionality implemented in this example is stored in the TreeController class. This class adds three new behaviors to the Tree component:

- Branch nodes can now be opened and closed by clicking anywhere inside the node area, removing the restriction of the disclosure icons.

- Only one branch node can be open at a specific level at any time. Clicking a sibling branch node to open it will result in a two-step transition: (1) the already opened sibling branch node is closed and (2) the clicked branch node is opened. This feature is optional and controlled by a Boolean property named autoCollapse. You can define the autoCollapse value via the constructor of the TreeController class or by directly assigning a value to the property. The default value of autoCollapse is true.

- When a parent branch node is closed, all of its descendants are closed or, alternatively, you can choose to leave them open although not visible until the parent node is open again. This feature is optional and controlled by a Boolean property named persistent. You can define the persistent value via the constructor of the TreeController class or by directly assigning a value to the property. The default value of persistent is false, meaning that when a parent node is closed, all of its descendants are closed as well.

In our example, we create a TreeController instance by setting both the autoCollapse and persistent properties to true via the class constructor:

```
var treeController:TreeController = new TreeController(true, true);
```

Since all of the three new behaviors are enabled from the start, you can interactively experience how they work by playing with the customized tree01 instance before further analyzing the code implementing these behaviors.

The TreeController instance (treeController) is literally "attached" to the Tree component instance (tree01) just after its creation via the controlTree method:

```
treeController.controlTree(tree01);
```

Looking at the source code of the controlTree method will clarify what this means:

```
function controlTree(t:Tree):Void {
  t.addEventListener('change', this);
  t.addEventListener('nodeClose', this);
}
```

Basically, treeController registers itself as a listener of two events of the Tree component instance: change and nodeClose.

The Tree class inherits the change event from its base class, List, and implements two additional events:

- nodeClose: Broadcasts whenever a branch node is closed. This event adds an additional property, called node, to the event object. The node property is a reference to the node that caused the event.

- nodeOpen: Broadcasts whenever a branch node is open. This event adds an additional property, called node, to the event object. The node property is a reference to the node that caused the event.

The implementation of the TreeController class does not need to listen to the nodeOpen event. Listening to the change and nodeClose events raised by the Tree component instance is sufficient to implement the new behaviors.

The change event handler of the TreeController class is invoked whenever you click a node of the Tree instance:

```
function change(eventObject:Object):Void {
  var t:Tree = eventObject.target;
  var selNode:XMLNode = t.selectedNode;
  var closingSibling = this.getOpenSibling(selNode, t);
  if ( (closingSibling != null) && this.autoCollapse) {
    if (t.getIsBranch(selNode)) {
      t.setIsOpen(closingSibling, false, true, true);
      this.pendingNode = selNode;
    }
  } else if (t.getIsBranch(selNode)) {
      var open:Boolean = t.getIsOpen(selNode);
      t.setIsOpen(selNode, !open, true, true);
  }
}
```

The change event handler main options are as follows:

- To close a sibling open node, if such open node exists and the autoCollapse property is set to true

- To open/close the clicked node, if it is a branch node, depending on its current state (closed/open, respectively)

475

While the second option has no further consequences, the first option only implements the first part of the two-step transition requested by autoCollapse. That's why the change event handler stores a reference to the clicked node in the pendingNode private property: that reference will be reused by the implementation of the second step of the transition.

Closing a sibling node will trigger a nodeClose event. This side effect makes the nodeClose event handler the ideal method for implementing the second step of the transition:

```
function nodeClose(eventObject:Object):Void {
  var t:Tree = eventObject.target;
  var node:XMLNode = eventObject.node;
  this.closeChildren(node, t);
  if ( (this.pendingNode != null) &&
➥ (t.getIsBranch(this.pendingNode)) ) {
    t.setIsOpen(this.pendingNode,
➥ node != t.selectedNode, true, true);
    this.pendingNode = null;
  }
}
```

The implementation of the nodeClose event invokes the closeChildren method, whose purpose is pretty much self-descriptive and will be analyzed in a short while. After closing the children of the node, the nodeClose event handler checks whether there is a pendingNode reference to a node that is waiting to be open and, if so, opens it, implementing the second step in the two-step transition requested by autoCollapse.

The closeChildren method invoked in the nodeClose event handler actually closes the children only if persistent is set to true. In fact, its first line is

```
if (persistent) return;
```

The TreeController class implements a second "utility" method, getOpenSibling, whose name is self-descriptive.

You have already learned about the algorithm implemented by the TreeController class. Apart from the functionality provided, the TreeController class also represents a real-world example of how to use several features of the Tree class:

- It exploits the fact that the nodes of a Tree component instance are implemented as instances of the XMLNode class.
- It shows how to check whether a node is actually a branch via the getIsBranch method.
- It demonstrates how to open/close methods via the setIsOpen method.
- It shows how to exploit the change and nodeClose events triggered by a Tree instance.

The next section introduces a simpler but possibly more important technique: how to add support for custom attributes added to the XML snippet describing the structure of a Tree instance.

Implementing isBranch and other XML attributes

As mentioned earlier in the book, several official sources show examples of XML snippets including an isBranch attribute that is not implemented nor used in any way by the Tree component.

The purpose of this "ghost" XML attribute may well be to allow the creation of empty branch nodes. Branch nodes must have children by definition. However, you may need to implement leaf nodes that look like, and in fact are, empty branch nodes that can be populated with children dynamically. The example in this section illustrates a convenient way of implementing custom XML attributes by supporting two of them:

- isBranch: If true, forces a leaf node to be a branch
- isOpen: If true, changes the default initial state of a branch node from closed to open

The combination of the isBranch and isOpen attributes gives you much greater flexibility in defining the initial configuration of a Tree instance via XML, as demonstrated by the following example:

1. Open the document tree01.fla created earlier and save it in a new folder as tree04.fla.

2. Create a new ActionScript file and save it as test.as in the same folder where you saved the tree04.fla file.

3. Add the following code to the ActionScript file just created:

```
import mx.controls.Tree;

Tree.prototype.initBranches = function(node:XMLNode):Void {
  if (node == undefined) {
    for (var i = 0; i <
➥ this.dataProvider.childNodes.length; i++) {
      this.initBranches(this.dataProvider.childNodes[i]);
    }
  } else {
    if ( (node.attributes.isBranch == "true") &&
➥ !(this.getIsBranch(node)) ) {
      this.setIsBranch(node, true);
    }
    if ( (node.attributes.isOpen == "true") &&
➥ !(this.getIsOpen(node)) ) {
      this.setIsOpen(node, true);
    }
    for (var i = 0; i < node.childNodes.length; i++) {
      this.initBranches(node.childNodes[i]);
    }
  }
}
```

```
var xmlLoader:XML = new XML();
xmlLoader.ignoreWhite = true;
xmlLoader.load("tree.xml");
xmlLoader.onLoad = function(success:Boolean):Void {
  tree01.dataProvider = this;
  tree01.initBranches();
}

tree01.vScrollPolicy = "auto";
```

4. Create a new text file using a text editor such as Notepad in Windows and save it as `tree.xml` in the same folder where you saved the `tree04.fla` file.

5. Add the following XML snippet to the `tree.xml` file:

```xml
<node label="ROOT NODE" isOpen="true">
  <node label="Child node 1" isBranch="true" isOpen="true" />
  <node label="Child node 2" isOpen="true">
    <node label="Child node 2.1" isBranch="true" />
    <node label="Child node 2.2" />
    <node label="Child node 2.3" isOpen="true">
      <node label="Child node 2.3.1" />
      <node label="Child node 2.3.2" />
    </node>
    <node label="Child node 2.4" />
  </node>
  <node label="Child node 3" isOpen="true">
    <node label="Child node 3.1" />
    <node label="Child node 3.2" />
    <node label="Child node 3.3" />
  </node>
  <node label="Child node 4" />
  <node label="Child node 5" isBranch="true" isOpen="true" />
</node>
```

6. Save the `tree04.fla`, `test.as`, and `tree.xml` files.

Figure 19-7 shows the fully expanded instance of the Tree component as it appears after testing the last example.

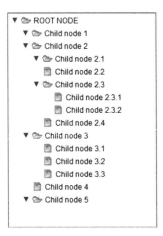

Figure 19-7. Open and empty branch nodes defined via XML

All the branch nodes in the tree structure are initially open because of the isOpen attributes defined in the XML snippet, as in the following:

```
<node label="ROOT NODE" isOpen="true">
```

Since every branch node is open, you can also notice that there are three empty branch nodes in the structure: Child node 1, Child node 2.1, and Child node 5.

Leaf nodes have been changed into empty branch nodes by defining the isBranch attribute as in the following:

```
<node label="Child node 5" isBranch="true" isOpen="true" />
```

Both the isOpen and isBranch attributes are implemented by the initBranches method, added to the Tree class via its prototype property:

```
Tree.prototype.initBranches = function(node:XMLNode):Void {
  if (node == undefined) {
    for (var i = 0; i <
➥ this.dataProvider.childNodes.length; i++) {
      this.initBranches(this.dataProvider.childNodes[i]);
    }
  } else {
    if ( (node.attributes.isBranch == "true") &&
➥ !(this.getIsBranch(node)) ) {
      this.setIsBranch(node, true);
    }
    if ( (node.attributes.isOpen == "true") &&
➥ !(this.getIsOpen(node)) ) {
      this.setIsOpen(node, true);
    }
    for (var i = 0; i < node.childNodes.length; i++) {
      this.initBranches(node.childNodes[i]);
    }
  }
}
```

The initBranches method is implemented using recursion:

- If initBranches is invoked without the node parameter (node == undefined), then initBranches applies itself recursively to each root node in the dataProvider property.

- When a node parameter is provided, initBranches performs three actions:

  1. Verifies whether the isBranch attribute is set and invokes the setIsBranch method of the Tree class to change a leaf node into a branch node, if that is the case

  2. Verifies whether the isOpen attribute is set and invokes the setIsOpen method of the Tree class to open the branch node, if that is the case

  3. Applies itself recursively to each child of the current node

You typically invoke `initBranches` without a parameter in order to apply it to the whole tree structure, as in the following:

```
xmlLoader.onLoad = function(success:Boolean):Void {
  tree01.dataProvider = this;
  tree01.initBranches();
}
```

The recursive implementation of `initBranches` makes it very easy to extend: all that you have to do is to test for another custom attribute and execute its associated code depending on the value assigned to the attribute.

The recursive algorithm used in `initBranches` stems from the implementation of XLEFF, the XML layout engine introduced earlier in the book. Its source code, available as open source at `www.xleff.org`, contains several other examples of recursion that you may find interesting.

Reasons for subclassing the Tree component

In this chapter, you learned about the power and flexibility of the Tree component. You also learned how to customize its appearance and behavior.

While the high flexibility offered by its styles weakens the motives for subclassing this component, the number of new behaviors that can be encapsulated in a subclassed version of this component makes this more costly option still attractive.

For instance, encapsulating the functionality implemented by the `TreeController` class presented in this chapter in an extended, subclassed, version of the Tree component would allow you to forget the existence of the `TreeController` class and utilize its functionality straightaway via a couple of new properties.

Chapter 20

THE WINDOW AND ALERT COMPONENTS

Window mx.containers.Window	Alert mx.controls.Alert
Frequency: Common	Frequency: Common
Complexity: Simple	Complexity: Simple
Stability: Robust	Stability: Robust
Maturity: Classic	Maturity: Classic
Popularity: Widespread	Popularity: Widespread

Both the components discussed in this chapter are containers that can be dragged around on the stage by the user.

The Window component is a general-purpose container with an empty area whose contents must be specifically implemented by you. The Alert component is a specialized version of the Window component; its contents are predefined and typically include a message for the user and a few optional buttons to retrieve the user's choice.

While the Alert component can be used in almost any kind of application, the Window component somewhat dictates a specific, window-based, model of the user interface.

The minimal example in the following section will show you the basics for implementing a window-based system, including interactions controlled with the help of the Alert component.

> *The completed source code introduced in this chapter can be found in the package* src20.zip, *downloadable from this book's page at* www.friendsofed.com.

Minimal example of the Window and Alert components

You have already learned how to implement a very minimal window-based system by completing the last example in Chapter 4.

In this section, you will extend that example by requesting the user confirmation before closing an opened window and, in doing so, you will also learn similarities and differences between the Window and the Alert components:

1. Create a new Flash document and save it as windows01.fla.

2. Open the Document Properties dialog box by selecting Modify ➤ Document, and set the stage dimensions as 800×600 pixels.

3. Drag the Window, the Alert, and the Button components on stage in order to create one instance of each component, and then delete the three resulting instances. By doing so, you ensure that the components have been added to the document's library so that they can be created dynamically via ActionScript at runtime.

4. Select the first frame in the document and attach the following ActionScript code to it:

   ```
   #include "test.as"
   ```

5. Create a new ActionScript file and save it as test.as in the same folder where you saved the windows01.fla file.

6. Add the following code to the ActionScript file you just created:

```
import mx.managers.PopUpManager;
import mx.containers.Window;
import mx.controls.Button;
import mx.controls.Alert;

var windowId:Number = 0;
var coords:Array = [50, 70, 90, 110, 130, 150, 170, 190, 210, 230];
var currentWindow:Window;

function onUserChoice(eventObject:Object):Void {
    if (eventObject.detail == Alert.YES) {
        currentWindow.deletePopUp();
    }
}

function getWindowInitObject(Void):Object {
    return {_x:coords[windowId % coords.length],
        _y:coords[windowId % coords.length],
        _width: 400,
        _height: 400,
        closeButton:true,
        title: "Window [" + (++windowId) + "]"
    }
}

function click(eventObject:Object):Void {
    var win:Window;
    var target:Object = eventObject.target;
    switch (target._name) {
        case "btnCreateWindow":
            win = Window(PopUpManager.createPopUp(this,
 ➥ Window, false, getWindowInitObject()));
            win.addEventListener("click", this);
            break;
        default:
            currentWindow = Window(target);
            Alert.show("Delete " + target.title + " ?",
 ➥ "Confirmation Request", Alert.YES | Alert.NO, null,
 ➥ onUserChoice, null, Alert.NO);
    }
}


var btn:Button = createClassObject(Button, "btnCreateWindow", 1,
 ➥ {_x:10, _y:10, label:'Create Window'});
btn.addEventListener("click", this);
```

7. Save the windows01.fla and test.as files.

A button labeled Create Window will appear on stage when you test the movie.

A new Window instance will be added to the stage every time that you click it. If you click the Create Window button five times, the stage will be populated with five window instances, as shown in Figure 20-1.

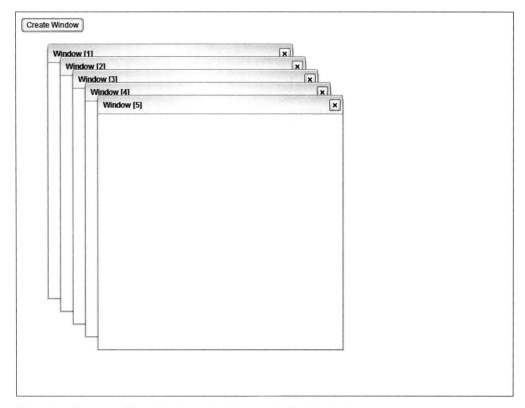

Figure 20-1. The stage of the minimal example after creating five Window instances

Differently from the example you saw in Chapter 4, clicking the close buttons of a dynamically created window does not immediately remove it from the stage. An Alert instance, like the one shown in Figure 20-2, will pop up, asking for user confirmation. After clicking one of the Alert instance's buttons, the Alert instance disappears, and the Window instance may also be removed from the stage, depending on whether you chose Yes or No.

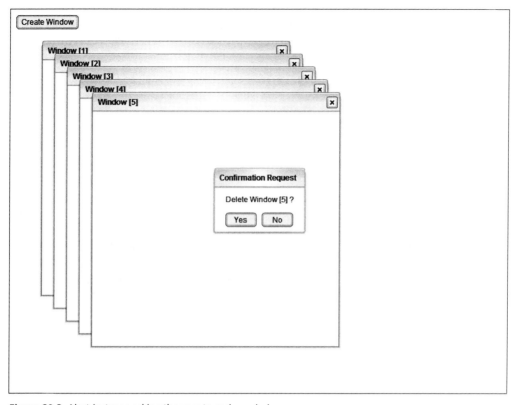

Figure 20-2. Alert instance asking the user to make a choice

In the following sections, we examine the significant aspects in the code of our minimal example.

Dynamically creating windows

In the previous chapters, you have learned that component instances can be created statically by dropping them on the stage at authoring time or dynamically by invoking the createClassObject method of the UIObject class, as explained in Chapter 2.

However, in the case of the Window component, the best option you have is to create a Window instance dynamically by using the PopUpManager class, as we did in the minimal example.

Because of the component's intended use and because of its implementation, Window instances behave quite erratically if created without the intermediation of the PopUpManager class, which has been included in the architecture for the exact purpose of creating pop-up windows dynamically.

The component architecture helps you manage the depth and focus of each component, which is particularly important when it comes to creating instances of components that can be dragged around on the stage. Basically, if you do not use the PopUpManager class, your application is doomed to show some inconsistent behavior related to focus or even depth management.

On the other hand, as our minimal example demonstrates, using the PopUpManager class for creating Windows is an easy task, accomplished with a single line of code:

```
win = Window(PopUpManager.createPopUp(this, Window, false,
➥ getWindowInitObject()));
```

The createPopUp method returns a MovieClip instance that, in our case, is a Window instance. This is why we could safely typecast it as a Window before assigning it to the win variable.

The createPopUp method takes five parameters:

- The first parameter is a reference to the parent object containing the Window instance. In the case of the minimal example, the parent object is defined by using the this identifier that, being evaluated in the context of the main timeline, refers to the root movie clip.

- The second parameter is a reference to the class used to dynamically create the instance. In the case of the minimal example, we utilized the Window class in order to create Window instances.

- The third parameter is a Boolean value indicating whether the instance will be modal or not. In the case of the minimal example, the Window instance is created as nonmodal to allow the user to interact with the other instances on stage, simulating a typical window-based system.

- The fourth parameter is very important, since it allows you to provide an object whose properties will be used to initialize the dynamically created instance. In our example, we implemented a getWindowInitObject function to create an initialization object dynamically so that we could provide different values for the Window instance's title and location.

- The fifth parameter was not used in the minimal example since it is an optional Boolean value that, if true, allows the component to broadcast mouse events even when they happen outside of the component's area. It is unlikely that you may ever need to use this parameter. It was included in the method's signature to support some of the component architecture internal features.

The createPopUp method returns a reference to the instance being created that we used in our minimal example to register the root movie clip as a listener of the Window's click event:

```
win.addEventListener("click", this);
```

The click event is raised by a Window instance whenever the user clicks the window's close button.

Since the root movie clip is also listening to the click event of the Button instance labeled Create Window, its click event handler examines the instance name of the object that triggered the event before deciding what to do:

```
var target:Object = eventObject.target;
switch (target._name) {
            . . . . . . . . . .
```

When the user clicks the btnCreateWindow instance, the click event handler creates a new Window instance by invoking the createPopUp method of the PopUpManager class.

The only alternative is that the user clicked the close button of a Window instance. In that case the click event handler creates an Alert instance to ask for a confirmation.

Dynamically creating alerts

Alert instances are supposed to be created dynamically only. An Alert instance appears when the user must make a choice and disappears once that the user makes it.

Alert instances can be easily created via the static show method of the Alert class, as in the case of our minimal example:

```
Alert.show("Delete " + target.title + " ?", "Confirmation Request",
➥ Alert.YES | Alert.NO, null, onUserChoice, null,  Alert.NO);
```

The show method accepts seven parameters:

- The first parameter accepts a String value containing the message to be displayed in the content area of the Alert instance.

- The second parameter accepts a String value that will be displayed in the title bar of the Alert instance.

- The third parameter accepts a Number value that determines which of four buttons will be displayed in the content area of the Alert instance (Alert.OK, Alert.CANCEL, Alert.YES, Alert.NO) and whether the Alert instance must be created as a nonmodal window (Alert.NONMODAL). You can specify more than one option at the same time by joining them via the | operator.

- The fourth parameter is an Object reference to the container of the Alert instance. The Alert instance is typically shown at the center of its container's area. In our minimal example, we passed the null value for this parameter to specify that the Alert instance should be contained in the _root object so that it would appear at the center of the stage as shown in Figure 20-2.

- The fifth parameter is a callback function that will be invoked by the component architecture when the user clicks one of the buttons in the Alert instance. This function will receive the click event object enriched with a further property, named detail, containing the value of the button that has been clicked by the user. In our minimal example, we implement a function named onUserChoice for this purpose. The onUserChoice function checks the value of the detail property to decide whether to close the current window by invoking the deletePopUp method of the Window class:

```
if (eventObject.detail == Alert.YES) {
    currentWindow.deletePopUp();
}
```

■ The sixth parameter is optional and not utilized in our minimal example. This `String` parameter allows you to specify the linkage identifier of an exported symbol that will be used as an icon inside the content area of the Alert instance. You can find an additional file among those in the package associated with this chapter named `windows01b.fla` that includes a sample icon; Figure 20-3 shows how the Alert instance looks when an icon is specified.

Figure 20-3. Alert instance using an exported symbol as icon

■ The seventh parameter is also optional. It accepts a numeric value that specifies which button in the Alert instance will act as the default button, if any. Any of the four button constants (`Alert.OK`, `Alert.CANCEL`, `Alert.YES`, `Alert.NO`) is a valid value for this parameter. In our minimal example, the `Alert.NO` button was designated as the default button.

Our minimal example clearly shows the typical life cycles of Window and Alert instances and every aspect of their core features. However, the minimal example does not define any content inside the Window instances that are created and remain empty.

Our next example will show you how to manage content inside a Window instance.

Managing the content of a Window instance

The content area of a Window instance is empty by default. It is your responsibility to implement the content of your Window instance.

In the next example, you will extend the minimal example implemented earlier to create Window instances hosting an image in their content areas:

1. Open the document `windows01.fla` created earlier and save it in a new folder as `windows02.fla`.

2. Create a new ActionScript file and save it as `test.as` in the same folder as the `windows02.fla` file.

3. Add the following code to the ActionScript file you just created:

```
import mx.managers.PopUpManager;
import mx.containers.Window;
import mx.controls.Button;
import mx.controls.Alert;
```

```
var windowId:Number = 0;
var coords:Array = [50, 70, 90, 110, 130, 150, 170, 190, 210, 230];
var images:Array = ["image01.jpg", "image02.jpg", "image03.jpg"];
var currentWindow:Window;

function onUserChoice(eventObject:Object):Void {
    if (eventObject.detail == Alert.YES) {
        currentWindow.deletePopUp();
    }
}

function getWindowInitObject(Void):Object {
    return {_x:coords[windowId % coords.length],
        _y:coords[windowId % coords.length],
        _width: 400,
        _height: 400,
        closeButton:true,
        visible: false,
        title: "Window [" + (++windowId) + "]"
    }
}

function click(eventObject:Object):Void {
    var win:Window;
    var target:Object = eventObject.target;
    switch (target._name) {
        case "btnCreateWindow":
            win = Window(PopUpManager.createPopUp(this, Window,
➥ false, getWindowInitObject()));
            win.addEventListener("click", this);
            win.addEventListener("complete", this);
            win.contentPath = images[(windowId-1) % images.length];
            break;
        default:
            currentWindow = Window(target);
            Alert.show("Delete " + target.title + " ?",
➥ "Confirmation Request", Alert.YES | Alert.NO,
➥ null, onUserChoice);
    }
}

function complete(eventObject:Object):Void {
    var window:Window = Window(eventObject.target._parent);
    var m:Object = window.getViewMetrics();
    window.setSize(window.content._width + m.left + m.right,
➥ window.content._height + m.top + m.bottom);
    window.setVisible(true);
}
```

```
        var btn:Button = createClassObject(Button, "btnCreateWindow", 1,
        ➡ {_x:10, _y:10, label:'Create Window'});
        btn.addEventListener("click", this);
```

4. Save the `windows02.fla` and `test.as` files.

The previous example uses three JPG files located in the same folder as the `windows02.fla` file.

You can find those JPG files in the package associated with this chapter. In case you want to replace them with your own graphics, their specifications are as follows:

- `image01.jpg`: 300×100 pixels
- `image02.jpg`: 300×225 pixels
- `image03.jpg`: 150×250 pixels

The names of the JPG files are stored in the following ActionScript array:

```
        var images:Array = ["image01.jpg", "image02.jpg", "image03.jpg"];
```

The image is assigned to the content area of a Window instance via its contentPath property, as in the following:

```
        win.contentPath = images[(windowId-1) % images.length];
```

The formula used to access a specific image, (windowId-1) % images.length, generates rotating indexes as in 0, 1, 2, 0, 1, 2, 0, 1, 2, 0, 1, 2, and so on, ensuring that one of the three images is used whenever you create a new window by clicking the Create Window button.

Testing the movie and clicking the Create Window button five times will result in a stage populated as shown in Figure 20-4. Note that the Window instances in Figure 20-4 have been moved from their original position by dragging their respective title bars to show a bit more of their contents.

Thanks to the contentPath property of the Window class, you can load three different kinds of content objects in the content area of a Window instance:

- An external JPG file, by providing its URL
- An external SWF file, by providing its URL
- An exported symbol, by providing its linkage identifier

The first option is arguably the simplest to achieve, and it was used in our example to allow you to focus on the relevant aspects of managing content in the case of the Window component.

Creating an external SWF file or even an exported symbol in the context of our example would be an unnecessary distraction, since the core technique contained in it works in the exact same way, whatever type of content object you choose to load in the content area of a Window instance.

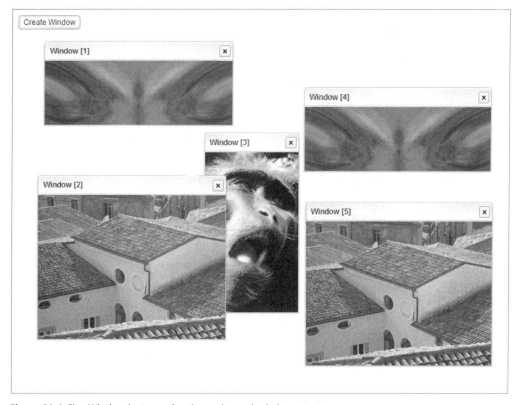

Figure 20-4. Five Window instances hosting an image in their content areas

The technique is based on the `complete` event triggered by a Window instance and can be summarized by the following steps:

1. Create an invisible Window instance.

2. Listen to the `complete` event of the created Window instance.

3. Load a content object in the Window instance via its `contentPath` property. Once the `complete` event has been raised by the Window instance, execute the following two steps:

4. Adjust the size of Window instance to fit its loaded contents.

5. Turn the Window instance visible.

In our example, the Window instance was created by invoking the `createPopUp` method of the PopUpManager in a line of code that is identical to that of the previous minimal example:

```
win = Window(PopUpManager.createPopUp(this, Window, false,
➥ getWindowInitObject()));
```

However, something is changed in the implementation of the getWindowInitObject that provides the initialization object for the Window instance. The object now contains an additional property:

```
visible: false,
```

The visible property set to false ensures that the Window instance is initially not visible. If you turn it to true, the example will still work, but you may notice some unpleasant, although temporary, rubbish on the stage when the Window instance is being created.

Once the createPopUp method returns a reference to the Window instance being created, the example registers the root movie clip as a listener of its complete event:

```
win.addEventListener("complete", this);
```

Only then is the contentPath property of the Window instance assigned the URL of a JPG file (this technique would work in the exact same way if, at this point, you would specify the URL of an SWF file or the linkage identifier of an exported symbol):

```
win.contentPath = images[(windowId-1) % images.length];
```

The first part of the technique is now completed, and the root movie clip listens for a complete event, communicating that the Window instance has been created and initialized properly. Once the complete event is raised by the component architecture, its associated event handler gets executed:

```
function complete(eventObject:Object):Void {
    var window:Window = Window(eventObject.target._parent);
    var m:Object = window.getViewMetrics();
    window.setSize(window.content._width + m.left + m.right,
➥   window.content._height + m.top + m.bottom);
    window.setVisible(true);
}
```

It is the complete event handler that executes the remaining two steps of the process described earlier. First, it resizes the Window instance using its setSize method, and then it turns the Window instance visible by invoking its setVisible method.

One important detail that should not pass unnoticed is the use of the content property of the Window class for accessing its content object and retrieving its dimensions.

The numeric values used in the setSize method, when defining the size of the Window instance, take into account the vertical space occupied by the title bar and the bottom border (m.top + m.bottom) and the horizontal space occupied by the left and right borders of the window instance (m.left + m.right). We retrieved the size of each edge by invoking the getViewMetrics method:

```
var m:Object = window.getViewMetrics();
```

The getViewMetrics method returns an object with four properties (left, right, top, and bottom), each of which stores a number indicating the space occupied by the respective edge of the component instance.

The result has already been shown in Figure 20-4: the Window instances are resized to accommodate the images accurately, regardless their different dimensions.

Looking back at the implementation of the complete event handler, there is an additional detail worthy of your attention: the way we retrieved a reference to the Window instance that raised the complete event:

```
var window:Window = Window(eventObject.target._parent);
```

The previous line shows an insight into the implementation of the Window component that is required to actually retrieve the reference to the Window instance. This reference is not eventObject.target as it should be, but eventObject.target._parent.

This intriguing detail is a consequence of the undocumented fact that it is the content subobject of a Window instance that actually raises the complete event. Accessing a reference to the Window instance becomes then a matter of accessing the _parent object of the target (content) object as in eventObject.target._parent.

The exploration of the core features of both the Window and Alert components is now complete, and we can start considering how to customize the appearance of these components.

Supported styles

The fact that the Alert class inherits from the Window class makes the Alert component a specialized version of the Window component.

Because of this, the Alert and Window component share several common styles:

- Common color styles such as color, disabledColor, backgroundColor, and themeColor (only supported by the default Halo theme).
- Common text styles such as embedFonts, fontFamily, fontSize, fontWeight, textAlign, textDecoration, and textIndent. Text styles are explored in greater detail in Chapter 18.
- The border styles, definable via the borderStyle property, and implemented by the RectBorder class examined in Chapter 11.

When it comes to text styles, however, the Alert component allows you to define them separately by implementing three static properties, each of which accepts an instance of the CSSStyleDeclaration class:

- titleStyleDeclaration: Affects the text in the title bar of an Alert instance
- messageStyleDeclaration: Affects the text of the message appearing in the content area of an Alert instance
- buttonStyleDeclaration: Affects the text in the buttons that appear in an Alert instance

The Window component has a peculiar style object too: the global style windowStyles. The Window component is a container and, as such, can propagate the style definitions set for a Window instance to its content object. The style properties that you set in the global style windowStyles will only affect the Window instances (and not their content objects).

If these peculiarities sound a little bit tricky, the next example will show you how to use them for producing a consistent, stylized look for Window and Alert instances:

1. Open the document `windows01.fla` created earlier and save it in a new folder as `windows03.fla`.

2. Create a new ActionScript file and save it as `test.as` in the same folder as the `windows03.fla` file.

3. Add the following code to the ActionScript file you just created:

```actionscript
import mx.managers.PopUpManager;
import mx.containers.Window;
import mx.controls.Button;
import mx.controls.Alert;
import mx.styles.CSSStyleDeclaration;

var windowId:Number = 0;
var coords:Array = [50, 70, 90, 110, 130, 150, 170, 190, 210, 230];
var currentWindow:Window;

function onUserChoice(eventObject:Object):Void {
    if (eventObject.detail == Alert.YES) {
        currentWindow.deletePopUp();
    }
}

function getWindowInitObject(Void):Object {
    return {_x:coords[windowId % coords.length],
        _y:coords[windowId % coords.length],
        _width: 400,
        _height: 400,
        closeButton:true,
        title: "Window [" + (++windowId) + "]"
    }
}

function click(eventObject:Object):Void {
    var win:Window;
    var alert:Alert;
    var target:Object = eventObject.target;
    switch (target._name) {
        case "btnCreateWindow":
            win = Window(PopUpManager.createPopUp(this, Window,
➥ false, getWindowInitObject()));
            setWindowStyles(win);
            win.addEventListener("click", this);
            break;
        default:
```

```
            currentWindow = Window(target);
            alert = Alert.show("Delete " + target.title + " ?",
➥ "Confirmation Request", Alert.YES | Alert.NO,
➥ null, onUserChoice, null, Alert.NO);
            setAlertStyles(alert);
    }
}

function setGlobalStyles(Void):Void {
    var winStyles:Object = _global.styles.windowStyles;
    winStyles.setStyle("color", 0x0000aa);
    winStyles.setStyle("fontFamily", "Courier New");
    winStyles.setStyle("fontSize", 14);
    winStyles.setStyle("fontWeight", "bold");
    winStyles.setStyle("textAlign", "center");

    var cssTitle = new CSSStyleDeclaration();
    var cssMessage = new CSSStyleDeclaration();
    var cssButton = new CSSStyleDeclaration();
    cssTitle.setStyle("color", 0x0000aa);
    cssMessage.setStyle("color", 0x000080);
    cssButton.setStyle("color", 0x0000ff);
    Alert.titleStyleDeclaration = cssTitle;
    Alert.messageStyleDeclaration = cssMessage;
    Alert.buttonStyleDeclaration = cssButton;
}

function setWindowStyles(win:Window):Void {
    win.setStyle("themeColor", 0x0000ff);
    win.setStyle("backgroundColor", 0xddddff);
}

function setAlertStyles(alert:Alert):Void {
    alert.setStyle("themeColor", 0x0000aa);
    alert.setStyle("backgroundColor", 0xaaaaff);
    alert.setStyle("fontFamily", "Courier New");
    alert.setStyle("fontSize", 14);
    alert.setStyle("fontWeight", "bold");
    alert.setStyle("textAlign", "center");
}

var btn:Button = createClassObject(Button, "btnCreateWindow", 1,
➥ {_x:10, _y:10, label:'Create Window'});
btn.addEventListener("click", this);

setGlobalStyles();
```

4. Save the windows03.fla and test.as files.

Testing our last example will demonstrate to what extent you can influence the appearance of the Window and Alert components. Figure 20-5 shows the stylized version of the same configuration previously captured in Figure 20-2.

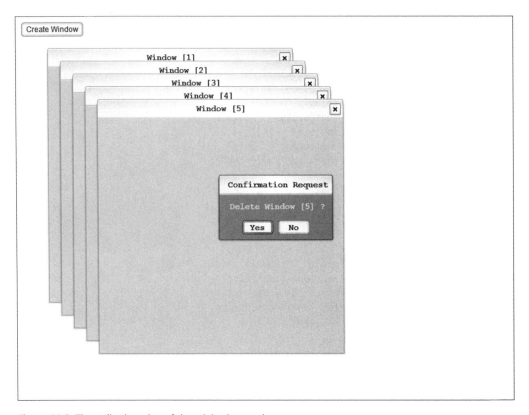

Figure 20-5. The stylized version of the minimal example

Several visual aspects have changed from the minimal example:

- Both Window and Alert instances have a new background color.
- Both Window and Alert instances utilize a different font.
- The text in the title bars of both Window and Alert instances appears in the middle of the bar now.
- The color of the text in the title bars (and in the Alert message and buttons) is changed to match the bluish theme implemented by our example.

The peculiarities in the implementation of styles in the cases of the Window and Alert components have been exploited in our example by arranging the code in three major functions:

- setWindowStyles: Sets the styles of Window instances on a per-instance basis. It is invoked just after creating a new Window instance and utilizes the instance setStyle method to define both its themeColor and backgroundColor style properties.

- setAlertStyles: Sets the styles of Alert instances on a per-instance basis. It is invoked just after creating a new Alert instance and utilizes the instance setStyle method to define its themeColor and backgroundColor style properties, in addition to some of its text-related style properties (fontFamily, fontSize, fontWeight, and textAlign).

- setGlobalStyles: The previous two functions define style properties on a per-instance basis in the same way adopted in many other examples in this book. It is this function that takes care of the peculiar global styles implemented by the Window and Alert components. It sets several text-related style properties using the windowStyles global style object of the Window component to avoid such style definitions being inherited by the content object of Window instance. It also creates three CSSStyleDeclaration instances, used to define a different text color for each of the three global styles specifically implemented by the Alert component: titleStyleDeclaration, messageStyleDeclaration, and buttonStyleDeclaration.

By following the approach illustrated here, you can implement a custom consistent look for both the Window and Alert component. However, you may have noticed that there are two parts of both components that are not affected by styles: the title bar background and, in the case of the Window component, the close button located on its right side.

Customizing those visual aspects requires the use of skins, as you are going to see in the next section.

Skinning the Window and Alert components

Completing the customization of the Window and Alert components involves providing new skins for the title bar and, in the case of the Window component, the close button.

Skin properties of the Window component

The Window component implements five skin properties, allowing you to skin its instances separately, if needed.

One of the Window's skin properties, skinTitleBackground, is dedicated to the title bar and used when drawing the title bar's background. Its default definition is

```
var skinTitleBackground:String = "TitleBackground";
```

The remaining four skin properties (skinCloseUp, skinCloseOver, skinCloseDown, and skinCloseDisabled) are utilized to skin the four states (up, over, down, and disabled) of the close button that can appear on the right side of the title bar. Their default definitions are

```
var skinCloseUp:String = "CloseButtonUp";
var skinCloseOver:String = "CloseButtonOver";
var skinCloseDown:String = "CloseButtonDown";
var skinCloseDisabled:String = "CloseButtonDisabled";
```

499

Skin properties of the Alert component

The Alert component implements its own style properties, and their implementation is quite different from the style properties of the Window component.

The greatest difference is in the fact that the Alert component implements its style properties as static properties. As a result, you can assign a custom skin to a style property of the Alert component by using a reference to its class name, as in

```
Alert.titleBackground = "CustomAlertTitleBackground";
```

Since the linkage identifier of the new skin is assigned to a static style property, the new skin will be applied to all the Alert instances. This is not really a limitation, since the intended use of Alert component makes it impossible to have more than one Alert instance on stage at the same time.

The titleBackground style property referred to in the previous line of code is the equivalent of the skinTitleBackground style property of the Window component: it defines the background of the title bar.

The Alert component also defines six skin properties that are used to skin the buttons that appear in its content area:

- buttonUp
- buttonUpEmphasized
- buttonDown
- buttonDownEmphasized
- buttonOver
- buttonOverEmphasized

The peculiarity of these skins is that they allow you to influence not only three of the typical states of a button (up, over, and down), but also the way a button looks when **emphasized**. A button is emphasized by the component architecture when it has been assigned the role of default button.

The skin properties of the Alert buttons are undefined by default, meaning that the default appearance of those buttons will be similar to that of instances of the Button component.

Adding skins to our previous stylized example

The following example completes the look defined by the stylized example in the previous section by adding a few custom skins to the Window and Alert instances:

1. Open the document windows03.fla created earlier and save it in a new folder as windows04.fla.

2. Create a new movie clip symbol by selecting Insert ➤ New Symbol. Define the symbol name as CustomAlertTitleBackground and click the Advanced button, if visible, to show Linkage properties. Click the Export for ActionScript checkbox and specify the following AS 2.0 Class: mx.skins.SkinElement. This symbol will be used to skin the background of the title bar of Alert instances.

3. Use the Rectangle tool to draw a borderless shape inside the newly created symbol. The shape should have the following attributes: (color: #9999FF, X:0, Y:0, W:400, H:20).

4. Create a new movie clip symbol by selecting Insert ➤ New Symbol. Define the symbol name as CustomWindowTitleBackground and click the Advanced button, if visible, to show Linkage properties. Click the Export for ActionScript checkbox and specify the following AS 2.0 Class: mx.skins.SkinElement. This symbol will be used to skin the background of the title bar of Window instances.

5. Use the Rectangle tool to draw a borderless shape inside the newly created symbol. The shape should have the following attributes: (color: #CCCCFF, X:0, Y:0, W:400, H:16).

6. Create a new movie clip symbol by selecting Insert ➤ New Symbol. Define the symbol name as CustomCloseButtonUp and click the Advanced button, if visible, to show Linkage properties. Click the Export for ActionScript checkbox to ensure that the symbol gets the default linkage identifier and is exported. This symbol will be used to skin the up state of the close button in the title bar of Window instances.

7. Draw a sort of "X" graphic in the new symbol or reuse the graphic that you can find in the source file associated with this chapter. Alternatively, experiment with your own icon, which should be located at (X:5, Y:4) and have an approximate dimension of 7✕7 pixels.

8. Following a similar process to the one illustrated in the previous two steps, create another three movie clip symbols to skin the remaining states of the close button. The names (with corresponding linkage identifiers) of the new symbols must be CustomCloseButtonDisabled, CustomCloseButtonDown, and CustomCloseButtonOver.

9. Create a new ActionScript file and save it as test.as in the same folder as the windows04.fla file.

10. Add the following code to the ActionScript file you just created:

```
import mx.managers.PopUpManager;
import mx.containers.Window;
import mx.controls.Button;
import mx.controls.Alert;
import mx.styles.CSSStyleDeclaration;

var windowId:Number = 0;
var coords:Array = [50, 70, 90, 110, 130, 150, 170, 190, 210, 230];
var currentWindow:Window;

function onUserChoice(eventObject:Object):Void {
    if (eventObject.detail == Alert.YES) {
        currentWindow.deletePopUp();
    }
}
```

```
function getWindowInitObject(Void):Object {
    return {_x:coords[windowId % coords.length],
        _y:coords[windowId % coords.length],
        _width: 400,
        _height: 400,
        closeButton:true,
        title: "Window [" + (++windowId) + "]",
        skinCloseUp: "CustomCloseButtonUp",
        skinCloseOver: "CustomCloseButtonOver",
        skinCloseDown: "CustomCloseButtonDown",
        skinCloseDisabled: "CustomCloseButtonDisabled",
        skinTitleBackground: "CustomWindowTitleBackground"
    }
}

function click(eventObject:Object):Void {
    var win:Window;
    var alert:Alert;
    var target:Object = eventObject.target;
    switch (target._name) {
        case "btnCreateWindow":
            win = Window(PopUpManager.createPopUp(this, Window,
➥ false, getWindowInitObject()));
            setWindowStyles(win);
            win.addEventListener("click", this);
            break;
        default:
            currentWindow = Window(target);
            alert = Alert.show("Delete " + target.title +
➥ " ?", "Confirmation Request", Alert.YES | Alert.NO,
➥ null, onUserChoice, null, Alert.NO);
            setAlertStyles(alert);
    }
}

function setGlobalStyles(Void):Void {
    var winStyles:Object = _global.styles.windowStyles;
    winStyles.setStyle("color", 0x0000aa);
    winStyles.setStyle("fontFamily", "Courier New");
    winStyles.setStyle("fontSize", 14);
    winStyles.setStyle("fontWeight", "bold");
    winStyles.setStyle("textAlign", "center");
```

```
        var cssTitle = new CSSStyleDeclaration();
        var cssMessage = new CSSStyleDeclaration();
        var cssButton = new CSSStyleDeclaration();
        cssTitle.setStyle("color", 0x0000aa);
        cssMessage.setStyle("color", 0x000080);
        cssButton.setStyle("color", 0x0000ff);
        Alert.titleStyleDeclaration = cssTitle;
        Alert.messageStyleDeclaration = cssMessage;
        Alert.buttonStyleDeclaration = cssButton;
    }

    function setWindowStyles(win:Window):Void {
        win.setStyle("themeColor", 0x0000ff);
        win.setStyle("backgroundColor", 0xddddff);
    }

    function setAlertStyles(alert:Alert):Void {
        alert.setStyle("themeColor", 0x0000aa);
        alert.setStyle("backgroundColor", 0xaaaaff);
        alert.setStyle("fontFamily", "Courier New");
        alert.setStyle("fontSize", 14);
        alert.setStyle("fontWeight", "bold");
        alert.setStyle("textAlign", "center");
    }

    var btn:Button = createClassObject(Button, "btnCreateWindow", 1,
    ➥ {_x:10, _y:10, label:'Create Window'});
    btn.addEventListener("click", this);

    setGlobalStyles();

    Alert.titleBackground = "CustomAlertTitleBackground";
```

11. Save the windows04.fla and test.as files.

When you test this last example (create five Window instances by clicking the Create Window button and then try to close the last one by clicking its close button), you will end up with a configuration of the stage similar to the ones resulting from the previous examples in this chapter.

You will also notice that the new custom skins have replaced the default one, producing a look like the one shown in Figure 20-6.

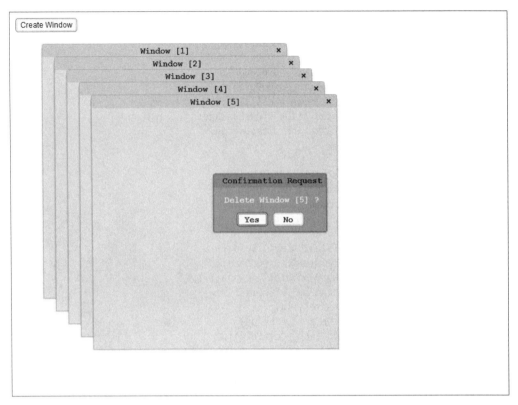

Figure 20-6. The stylized and skinned version of the minimal example

The five custom skins where applied to each Window instance during their creation process by extending the definition of the initialization object returned by the getWindowInitObject function as follows:

```
function getWindowInitObject(Void):Object {
    return {_x:coords[windowId % coords.length],
        _y:coords[windowId % coords.length],
        _width: 400,
        _height: 400,
        closeButton:true,
        title: "Window [" + (++windowId) + "]",
        skinCloseUp: "CustomCloseButtonUp",
        skinCloseOver: "CustomCloseButtonOver",
        skinCloseDown: "CustomCloseButtonDown",
        skinCloseDisabled: "CustomCloseButtonDisabled",
        skinTitleBackground: "CustomWindowTitleBackground"
    }
}
```

In our example, Alert instances now have a slightly different title bar from Window instances, since a separate skin was provided for it and set globally in the example's last line:

```
Alert.titleBackground = "CustomAlertTitleBackground";
```

There are a couple of details in the last example related to the title bar skins of both the Window and Alert components that should not pass unnoticed:

- The symbol used to skin a title bar defines the height of the title bar. Both the Window and Alert instances now show a thinner title bar since their custom skins are 16 and 20 pixels tall respectively, while the original, default skin used by both components is implemented by a symbol that is significantly taller (30 pixels).

- Simply providing a graphic is not sufficient in the case of the symbol used to skin the title bar. You also have to associate an ActionScript class (mx.skins.SkinElement) in order to implement the skin resizing behavior. You don't have to implement this class, though, since it is included in the component architecture.

Reasons for subclassing the Window and Alert components

The most typical reason for subclassing a component is to encapsulate styles and skins into its subclassed version so that it can be reused both quickly and uniformly inside your own projects.

In addition, the Window component gives you another strong reason that makes subclassing it a particularly attractive option: as you have learned from this chapter, the content area of the Window component is empty by default, and it is your responsibility to implement its content, reusing some or all of the techniques illustrated earlier.

Because of this, the Window class is typically subclassed to create document-oriented views, each of them specialized in the representation of a specific document type.

Chapter 21

HANDLING THE SCROLLBARS

UIScrollBar
mx.controls.UIScrollBar

Frequency: Rare
Complexity: Plug and Play
Stability: Quirky
Maturity: Pre-Existing
Popularity: Specific

The structure of this chapter slightly differs from the other chapters in Part 3 of the book because its most important topic is not a specific component but the use of the scrollbars in the design of the component architecture.

Scrollbars play an important role as subcomponents in the implementation of several important components: the ComboBox, DataGrid, List, ScrollPane, TextArea, and Tree components all utilize the same subcomponent to scroll their content.

In addition to those scrollbars, the architecture also provides the UIScrollBar, which is a rather odd component sharing the same functionality of the other scrollbars, although its range of application is rather limited.

The next section shows you the peculiar purpose of the UIScrollBar, while the second part of the chapter shows you how to customize the scrollbars when they appear as subcomponents inside larger components.

> *The completed source code introduced in this chapter can be found in the package* `src21.zip`, *downloadable from this book's page at* www.friendsofed.com.

Minimal example of the UIScrollBar component

The UIScrollBar component is probably the legacy of some functionality that has not yet reached a proper level of maturity. Still, it is something of a curiosity because it is the only true example of a plug-and-play component in the component architecture.

Its practical use, however, is almost pointless, since a similar, better, and more component-oriented functionality is provided by the TextArea component that is described in Chapter 18.

The current limitation of the UIScrollBar component is that it only works with native text fields and, because of that, its functionality strictly resembles that of the TextArea component, although it does not achieve the same level of encapsulation and flexibility.

However, you may find it useful if you are designing an interface where the scrollbar must not be visually attached to the text field, in which case you can also make it smaller or bigger than its associated text field.

The minimal example that follows will show you the sole purpose of the UIScrollBar component: to scroll the content of a text field.

1. Create a new Flash document and save it as `scrollbars01.fla`.
2. Open the Document Properties dialog box by selecting Modify ➤ Document, set its dimensions as 400 × 200 pixels, and select a background color of #3399CC.

3. Use the Text tool to create an input text field on stage. Figure 21-1 shows the Properties panel that you can use as reference for creating a text field with similar properties. While you can experiment with a slightly different size and location for the text field, do not forget to define its instance name as text01, define its type as Input Text, and turn on its border option to make it visible on the stage.

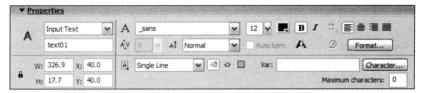

Figure 21-1. Properties of the text field in the minimal example

4. Turn on the object snapping by selecting View ➤ Snapping ➤ Snap to Objects.

5. Drag the UIScrollBar component on stage, paying particular attention to dropping it inside the bottom half of the text field area. By doing so, the newly created instance will automatically reposition and resize itself to fit underneath the text field. If this does not happen at your first attempt, drag the newly created instance inside the text field area until you are successful. Figure 21-2 shows how the combination text field and UIScrollBar instance should appear on stage.

Figure 21-2. The stage of the minimal example after snapping the UIScrollbar instance

6. Save the scrollbars01.fla file.

Testing the example will result in a runtime stage that looks very similar to the one shown in Figure 21-3. However, if you start writing inside the text field on stage and keep writing, you will notice that the UIScrollBar instance will become alive once the text field contains enough content to be scrolled. Figure 21-3 shows the lively appearance of the UIScrollBar instance after you reached that point.

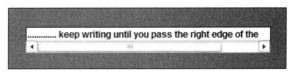

Figure 21-3. The UIScrollBar appearance after you have added enough content to the text field

Once alive, the UIScrollBar instance resembles the same scrollbars that you have found inside several standard components of the architecture and can be used to scroll the text field's content.

As mentioned earlier, it does not make sense to use the combination native text field plus UIScrollBar component when developing component-based applications, since the TextArea component can achieve the same functionality and much more by encapsulating the native text field.

As a matter of fact, the UIScrollBar component is much more interesting as a subcomponent of several standard components. In the next section, you will learn how to customize its appearance and behavior when included inside very important components that support the scrolling of their contents.

Customizing the scrollbars inside a component

Scrollbars play a relevant, functional role in the context of many important standard components.

The following standard components include one or two instances of the UIScrollBar component in order to implement content that can be scrolled horizontally and/or vertically:

- ComboBox (examined in Chapter 13)
- DataGrid (examined in Chapter 13)
- List (examined in Chapter 13)
- ScrollPane (examined in Chapter 15)
- TextArea (examined in Chapter 18)
- Tree (examined in Chapter 19)

The UIScrollBar instances within those components are not accessible directly. However, you can redefine the skins of the scrollbar globally, defining a new, consistent look for the scrollbars inside each of the components in the previous list.

This is the purpose of our next example, divided into two phases:

1. Create a stylized version of a DataGrid instance.
2. Redefine the appearance of both the horizontal and vertical scrollbars to match the new look of the DataGrid instance.

Step 1: Building a stylized version of the DataGrid component

In this section, you are going to quickly implement a stylized version of the DataGrid component in order to customize the look of the scrollbars in the next step. (Note that Chapter 13 already contains a stylized version of the DataGrid component, demonstrating in greater detail how the style properties influence that component.)

1. Create a new Flash document and save it as `scrollbars02a.fla`.
2. Open the Document Properties dialog box by selecting Modify ➤ Document, and set its dimensions as 440×340 pixels.

3. Drag the DataGrid component on stage to create one of its instances and name it datagrid01. Using the Info panel, define its position as (X: 20, Y: 20) and its dimensions as (W: 400, H: 300).

4. Select the first frame in the document and add the following ActionScript line to it:

```
#include "test.as"
```

5. Create an ActionScript file and save it as test.as. Add the following lines to it:

```
import mx.controls.DataGrid;

function setDataGridStyles(instance:DataGrid):Void {
    instance.setStyle("themeColor", 0xcccccff);
    instance.setStyle("borderStyle", "default");
    instance.setStyle("backgroundColor", 0xddddff);
    instance.setStyle("color", 0x003399);
    instance.setStyle("rollOverColor", 0x77CCCC);
    instance.setStyle("textRollOverColor", 0xFFFFFF);
    instance.setStyle("textSelectedColor", 0xFFFFFF);
    instance.setStyle("selectionColor", 0x55AAAA);
    instance.setStyle("headerColor", 0xcccccff);
    instance.setStyle("vGridLines", true);
    instance.setStyle("vGridLineColor", 0x2255BB);
    instance.setStyle("alternatingRowColors",
➥ [0xddddff, 0xd9d9f9]);
    instance.setStyle("fontFamily", "Tahoma");
    instance.setStyle("fontSize", 12);
    instance.hScrollPolicy = "auto";
    instance.vScrollPolicy = "auto";
}

function populate(instance:DataGrid):Void {
    var dp:Array = new Array();

    for (var i=0; i < 20; i++) {
        var element:Object = new Object();
        for (var j=9; j >=0; j--) {
            element["column" + j] = "item(" + j + "," + i +")";
        }
        dp.push(element);
    }

    instance.dataProvider = dp;
}

function initColumns(instance:DataGrid):Void {
    for (var i=0; i < instance.columnCount; i++) {
        instance.getColumnAt(i).width = 100;
    }
}
```

```
    setDataGridStyles(datagrid01);
    populate(datagrid01);
    initColumns(datagrid01);
```

6. Save the `scrollbars02a.fla` and `test.as` files.

Apart from setting style properties that are described in Chapter 13, our example implements a couple of functions:

- populate: Creates 200 elements in the DataGrid instance, distributed over 20 rows and 10 columns. Such fictious content will make the scrollbars active and provide content that can be scrolled both horizontally and vertically.

- initColumns: Invoked **AFTER** the DataGrid instance has been populated to set the width of each column to 100 pixels.

Testing the movie will produce an almost completely stylized version of the DataGrid instance, as shown in Figure 21-4.

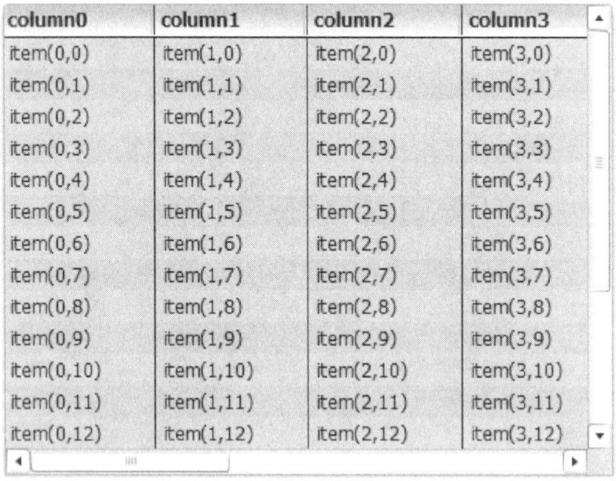

Figure 21-4. An almost completely customized DataGrid instance

The example shows both the horizontal and vertical scrollbars in their default look. In the following step, you are going to completely redefine their appearance.

Step 2: Skinning the scrollbars

The implementation of the UIScrollBar component relies on 31 exported symbols that can be found inside the `StandardComponents.fla` file provided with the component architecture source code (see Appendix A for locating this file and the rest of the component architecture source code in your system).

The very high number of exported symbols required by this component can make the process of skinning the scrollbars globally a daunting task if not approached methodically.

However, note that no further code must be added to our previous example in order to skin the scrollbars inside the DataGrid component: it is just a matter of including your own version of those symbols in the FLA document's library:

1. Open the file `scrollbars02a.fla` and save it in the SAME folder with the new name `scrollbars02b.fla`. By saving it in the same folder as the previous example, you will allow the new document to reuse the `test.as` file previously created.

2. Open the `StandardComponents.fla` file as an external library by selecting File ➤ Import ➤ Open External Library.

3. Locate the folder called `Scrollbar Assets` inside the `StandardComponents.fla` library. This folder can be found inside `Flash UI Components 2` ➤ `Themes` ➤ `MMDefault`.

4. Drag the `Scrollbar Assets` folder from the `StandardComponents.fla` library into the library of the `scrollbars02b.fla` document. With this step you ensure that the library of the FLA file implementing our example contains all of the symbols required to properly customize the appearance of the scrollbars.

5. Close the `StandardComponents.fla` library and leave the library of the `scrollbars02b.fla` document. You are now going to take a break to explore the contents of the `Scrollbar Assets` folder just copied inside the `scrollbars02b.fla` library.

Figure 21-5 shows the contents of the `scrollbars02b.fla` library at this point. Note that the `ScrollBar Assets` folder contains two subfolders that have been closed to show you its main structure:

- The `States` folder, containing 26 exported symbols that implement parts of the scrollbar skins. All of these symbols are required to implement a customized version of the scrollbars.

- The `Elements` folder, containing 27 symbols. Only two of these symbols are required to implement a customized version of the scrollbars.

- Three exported symbols: HScrollBar Assets, ScrollBar Assets, and VScrollBar Assets. All of these symbols are required to implement a customized version of the scrollbars.

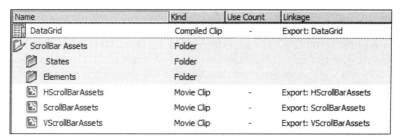

Figure 21-5. Main structure of the example's library

Making a manageable custom version of the scrollbars is also a matter of doing some cleanup:

6. Open the `Element` folder in the `scrollbars02b.fla` library and delete 25 symbols in it, leaving only the following two symbols: BtnDownArrow and BtnUpArrow.

The previous step removes all the predefined graphics that must be replaced in order to customize the scrollbars' skin. As a result, all of the symbols under the States folder are now made of several empty layers. Filling up those symbols with the appropriate graphic is what you still have to do to complete the customization process.

Your next task is to create seven graphic symbols that will be reused as skin parts inside the 26 exported symbols included in the States folder. Once created, you can store these seven graphic symbols in a new folder called Graphics, inside the ScrollBar Assets folder.

Figure 21-6 shows the contents of the Graphics folder once you have created these new graphic symbols. Note that the package associated with this chapter includes a completed version of the scrollbars02b.fla file that you can use as reference while working through the current example.

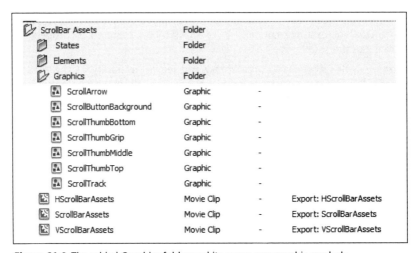

Figure 21-6. The added Graphics folder and its seven new graphic symbols

7. Create a new symbol with the type Graphic. Define the symbol name as ScrollArrow.

The purpose of the ScrollArrow symbol is to provide the skin of the arrow used in the arrow buttons of the scrollbar. This symbol must contain some kind of arrow of 6×4 pixels positioned at (X: 0, Y: 0). You can either draw your own arrow or cut and paste the graphic included in the completed version of the scrollbars02b.fla file, shown in Figure 21-7.

Figure 21-7. The graphic in the ScrollArrow symbol

8. Create a new symbol with the type Graphic. Define the symbol name as ScrollButtonBackground.

The purpose of the ScrollButtonBackground symbol is to provide the skin of the background in the arrow buttons of the scrollbar. This symbol should contain a shape of 16X16 pixels positioned at (X: 0, Y: 0). You can either draw your own shape or cut and paste the graphic included in the completed version of the `scrollbars02b.fla` file, shown in Figure 21-8.

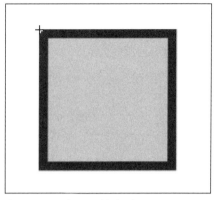

Figure 21-8. The graphic in the ScrollButtonBackground symbol

9. Create a new symbol with the type Graphic. Define the symbol name as ScrollThumbBottom.

The purpose of the ScrollThumbBottom symbol is to provide the skin of the bottom section of the thumb in the scrollbar. This symbol should contain a shape of 14X5 pixels positioned at (X: 0, Y: 0). You can either draw your own shape or cut and paste the graphic included in the completed version of the `scrollbars02b.fla` file, shown in Figure 21-9.

Figure 21-9. The graphic in the ScrollThumbBottom symbol

10. Create a new symbol with the type Graphic. Define the symbol name as ScrollThumbGrip.

The purpose of the ScrollThumbGrip symbol is to provide the skin of the grip icon that appears in the middle of the thumb in the scrollbar. This symbol should contain a shape of 5X8 pixels positioned at (X: 0, Y: 0). You can either draw your own shape or cut and paste the graphic included in the completed version of the `scrollbars02b.fla` file, shown in Figure 21-10.

Figure 21-10. The graphic in the ScrollThumbGrip symbol

11. Create a new symbol with the type Graphic. Define the symbol name as ScrollThumbMiddle.

The purpose of the ScrollThumbMiddle symbol is to provide the skin for the middle section of the thumb in the scrollbar. Note that this section appears behind the grip icon and should work as a sort of background for it. This symbol should contain a shape of 14X1 pixels positioned at (X: 0, Y: 0). You can either draw your own shape or cut and paste the graphic included in the completed version of the `scrollbars02b.fla` file, shown in Figure 21-11.

Figure 21-11. The graphic in the ScrollThumbMiddle symbol

515

12. Create a new symbol with the type Graphic. Define the symbol name as ScrollThumbTop.

The purpose of the ScrollThumbTop symbol is to provide the skin of the top section of the thumb in the scrollbar. This symbol should contain a shape of 14X5 pixels positioned at (X: 0, Y: 0). You can either draw your own shape or cut and paste the graphic included in the completed version of the scrollbars02b.fla file, shown in Figure 21-12.

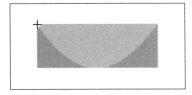

Figure 21-12. The graphic in the ScrollThumbTop symbol

13. Create a new symbol with the type Graphic. Define the symbol name as ScrollTrack.

The purpose of the ScrollTrack symbol is to provide the skin for the scrollbar track. This symbol should contain a shape of 16X4 pixels positioned at (X: 0, Y: 0). You can either draw your own shape or cut and paste the graphic included in the completed version of the scrollbars02b.fla file, shown in Figure 21-13.

Figure 21-13. The graphic in the ScrollBar symbol

The whole skin of the UIScrollBar component has been deconstructed into seven logical parts by the seven graphic symbols that you have just created. Figure 21-14 shows how those graphic symbols are combined to produce the custom appearance of the scrollbars in our example.

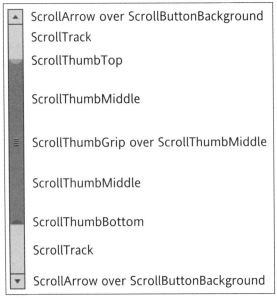

Figure 21-14. Roles of the graphic symbols in the scrollbar customized appearance

The seven graphic symbols are reused in different combinations by the 26 exported symbols requested to skin all of the states in a scrollbar instance. Table 21-1 shows which graphic symbols are reused by each exported symbol.

Table 21-1. Graphic symbols included in each exported symbol

Exported Symbol	Included Graphic Symbols
ScrollDownArrowDisabled	ScrollArrow and ScrollButtonBackground
ScrollDownArrowDown	ScrollArrow and ScrollButtonBackground
ScrollDownArrowOver	ScrollArrow and ScrollButtonBackground
ScrollDownArrowUp	ScrollArrow and ScrollButtonBackground
ScrollThumbBottomDisabled	ScrollThumbBottom
ScrollThumbBottomDown	ScrollThumbBottom
ScrollThumbBottomOver	ScrollThumbBottom
ScrollThumbBottomUp	ScrollThumbBottom
ScrollThumbGripDisabled	ScrollThumbGrip
ScrollThumbGripDown	ScrollThumbGrip
ScrollThumbGripOver	ScrollThumbGrip
ScrollThumbGripUp	ScrollThumbGrip
ScrollThumbMiddleDisabled	ScrollThumbMiddle
ScrollThumbMiddleDown	ScrollThumbMiddle
ScrollThumbMiddleOver	ScrollThumbMiddle
ScrollThumbMiddleUp	ScrollThumbMiddle
ScrollThumbTopDisabled	ScrollThumbTop
ScrollThumbTopDown	ScrollThumbTop
ScrollThumbTopOver	ScrollThumbTop
ScrollTrack	ScrollTrack
ScrollTrackDisabled	ScrollTrack
ScrollUpArrowDisabled	ScrollArrow and ScrollButtonBackground
ScrollUpArrowDown	ScrollArrow and ScrollButtonBackground
ScrollUpArrowOver	ScrollArrow and ScrollButtonBackground
ScrollUpArrowUp	ScrollArrow and ScrollButtonBackground

Completing our example is now a matter of including the proper graphic symbol instances inside the exported symbols, as shown in Table 21-1. The ScrollThumbGripDown exported symbol, for example, must include an instance of the ScrollThumbGrip graphic symbol, and so on.

The majority of the exported symbols listed in Table 21-1 contain only one graphic symbol instance positioned at (X: 0, Y: 0), with a few exceptions:

- In the cases of the eight exported symbols that include both the ScrollArrow and ScrollButtonBackground graphic symbols, you must create two layers and place the ScrollArrow instance on the top layer and the ScrollButtonBackground instance on the bottom layer. The ScrollArrow instance should also be moved to appear in the center of the ScrollButtonBackground instance.

- In the case of the four exported symbols whose names begin with ScrollDown, you must also flip the ScrollArrow instance vertically to make the arrow point down.

- Each graphic symbol instance in all the exported symbols associated with the scrollbar's thumb (whose names include "Thumb") should be placed at (X: 1, Y: 0) instead of at (X: 0, Y: 0).

When editing one of the exported symbols, you must create one new layer (or two depending on how many graphic symbol instances you are going to add following the specifications in Table 21-1) and delete all the preexisting layers. Those layers have been hosting the default design that you are replacing with the new custom one.

If you have any doubt, open the completed version of the scrollbars02b.fla file in the package associated with this chapter and check out its library.

Once the library of your last example is completed, you can test it and verify that the appearance of the scrollbars inside the DataGrid instance has been completely redefined, as shown in Figure 21-15.

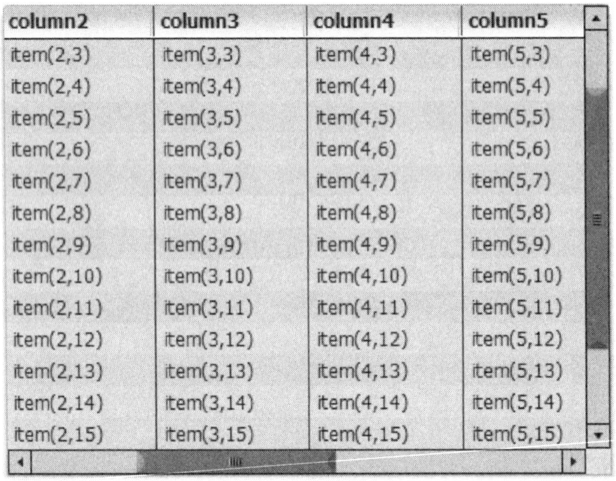

Figure 21-15. The completed customized version of the DataGrid instance, scrollbars included

The significance of the name of the exported symbols listed in the first column of Table 21-1 is almost self-descriptive. They contain a reference to the parts of a scrollbar instance (the buttons "DownArrow" and "UpArrow," the "Thumb" and its "ThumbGrip," the "Track") and also contain references to a specific state of a particular part ("Up," "Down," "Over," and "Disabled").

Starting from our last example, you can play with the existing simplified graphic and end up with your own custom version of the scrollbars to be used in your component-based applications.

As you can see, the process of skinning a scrollbar can be really lengthy, mostly because of the many exported symbols that are required to produce a new skin.

However, once you have created a new skin following this approach, it will apply consistently and seamlessly to all of the scrollbar instances in the component architecture, subcomponents included, without requiring any further work.

Conclusion

This chapter concludes the third and last part of the book.

After reading the book from cover to cover, you can now enjoy a high degree of control over the component architecture and its standard components and start implementing your own component-based applications in Flash.

Hopefully, this book has shown you that components can be used conveniently to produce powerful applications in a fraction of the time that would be required to develop the same applications without using them.

A software developer knows that there always is a lot of work to do, but also knows how to have fun doing it.

Enjoy your experiments and your next projects.

Part Four

APPENDIXES

Appendix A

LOCATING THE SOURCE CODE OF THE COMPONENT ARCHITECTURE

When looking for the source code of the component architecture, you will find two different file types:

- The ActionScript files implementing the classes and components of the architecture
- The FLA documents containing the components themselves and/or their collection of skins

Their location, however, can vary from one machine to the next, depending on several parameters:

- The **operating system** that is running on your machine, Windows or Mac OS X
- The **application folder** containing the installation of the Flash authoring environment
- The **user folder** that the operating system creates to host the data of your account
- The **application folder at user level**, which is a folder that you can find somewhere inside your user folder and that is dedicated to storing installation and user-specific data of the Flash authoring environment
- The **version** of your Flash authoring environment, which must be either Flash MX 2004 or Flash 8
- The **language** used by your Flash authoring environment, most frequently English (en), although it could be one of several other languages supported by the product

At installation time, Flash stores two identical copies of ActionScript source code in your system:

- A **Master Copy**, which can be found in the application folder. This source code should never be altered since it would not get recompiled. It is included to allow you to restore the User Copy, if needed, or to simply read it.

- A **User Copy**, which can be found in the application folder at user level. This source code will be recompiled, if modified. Although it is not a recommended practice, you may use this copy to create a customized, user-based version of the component architecture. Note that the examples in this book reuse the functionality of the component architecture, extending or even overriding part of it without ever modifying the original source code.

When looking for the ActionScript source code of the component architecture, you can use either the files in the Master Copy or those in the User Copy as long as you do not change them.

The next two sections will tell you where those copies are on your machine depending on what operating system you work with.

If you are a Windows user

The Master Copy is located in the following folder:

```
{application folder}\{Flash version}\{language}\First Run\Classes\mx
```

Typical examples are

```
C:\Program Files\Macromedia\Flash MX 2004\en\First Run\Classes\mx
```

and

```
C:\Program Files\Macromedia\Flash 8\en\First Run\Classes\mx
```

The User Copy is located in the following folder:

```
{application folder at user level}\{Flash version}\{language}\Configuration\Classes\mx
```

Typical examples are

```
C:\Documents and Settings\{username}\Local Settings\Application Data\Macromedia
\Flash MX 2004\en\Configuration\Classes\mx
```

and

```
C:\Documents and Settings\{username}\Local Settings\Application Data\Macromedia
\Flash 8\en\Configuration\Classes\mx
```

Note that in both of the typical examples, you should replace {username} with your own account name.

If you are a Mac user

The Master Copy is located in the following folder:

`{application folder}/{Flash version}/{language}/First Run/Classes/mx`

Typical examples are

`HD/Applications/Macromedia/Flash MX 2004/en/First Run/Classes/mx`

and

`HD/Applications/Macromedia/Flash 8/en/First Run/Classes/mx`

The User Copy is located in the following folder:

`{application folder at user level}/{Flash version}/{language}/Configuration/Classes/mx`

Typical examples are

`HD/Drive/Users/{username}/Library/Application Support/Macromedia`
`/Flash MX 2004/en/Configuration/Classes/mx`

and

`HD/Drive/Users/{username}/Library/Application Support/Macromedia`
`/Flash 8/en/Configuration/Classes/mx`

Note that in both of the typical examples, you should replace `{username}` with your own account name.

FLA source files

The component architecture source code includes three important FLA documents:

- `StandardComponents.fla`, containing the movie clips of each standard component in the architecture
- `HaloTheme.fla`, containing the assets of the default theme (Halo)
- `SampleTheme.fla`, containing the assets of a simpler theme (Sample)

Windows users will find these files in the following folder:

`{application folder}\{Flash version}\{language}\Configuration\ComponentFLA`

Typical examples are

`C:\Program Files\Macromedia\Flash MX 2004\en\Configuration\ComponentFLA` and

`C:\Program Files\Macromedia\Flash 8\en\Configuration\ComponentFLA`

Mac users will find such files in the following folder:

`{application folder}/{Flash version}/{language}/Configuration/ComponentFLA`

Typical examples are

`HD/Applications/Macromedia Flash MX 2004/en/Configuration/ComponentFLA/`

and

`HD/Applications/Macromedia Flash 8/en/Configuration/ComponentFLA/`

Link them

To avoid looking for this information again and again, it may be a good idea to create a couple of shortcuts to the folders containing the ActionScript and FLA source files respectively and place them on your desktop or wherever you can easily access them.

Appendix B

TRANSITIONS AND EASING CLASSES

The component architecture implements several transitions that can be applied indifferently to movie clips or component instances. When used in this section, the term **movie clip** refers to both movie clips and component instances.

A transition produces an animation that reveals or hides the content of a movie clip. Two terms are commonly used to indicate whether the transition reveals or hides content:

- **In**: Indicates that the content will be revealed by the transition
- **Out**: Indicates that the content will be hidden by the transition

If you want to use the transition classes by referring to their names in your code, you must import the following packages:

```
import mx.transitions.*;
import mx.transitions.easing.*;
```

Transitions are applied to a movie clip via the TransitionManager class by invoking the static method start, as in the following example:

```
TransitionManager.start(instance, transitionParams);
```

The start method is capable of stopping a transition that is already occurring in order to start a new one. The two parameters accepted by the start method are as follows:

- instance: A reference to a movie clip instance
- transitionParams: A reference to an object whose properties specify what type of transition must be started plus several parameters that influence the transition's behavior

Each transition type is named after the ActionScript class that implements it. The component architecture provides ten different types of transitions:

- Blinds: Reveals or hides the content of a movie clip by utilizing animated stripes in a blinds fashion
- Fade: Reveals or hides the content of a movie clip by fading it in or out
- Fly: Reveals or hides the content of a movie clip by sliding it in or out from a specified direction
- Iris: Reveals or hides the content of a movie clip by using a circle-shaped or square-shaped mask
- Photo: Reveals or hides the content of a movie clip by fading it in and out with the addition of a flashing effect, emulating the use of a photographic flash
- PixelDissolve: Reveals or hides the content of a movie clip simulating a pixel-based screen by hiding or showing a specified number of squares in a random sequence
- Rotate: Reveals or hides the content of a movie clip by spinning it around an amount specified in degrees
- Squeeze: Reveals or hides the content of a movie clip by expanding or squeezing it in a specified dimension (horizontal or vertical)
- Wipe: Reveals or hides the content of a movie clip by simulating the action of restoring or erasing it in a specific direction
- Zoom: Reveals or hides the content of a movie clip by enlarging or reducing its size in a zoom-like motion

Parameters common to all of the transition types

Four parameters are common to all of the transition types:

- type: This parameter specifies what type of transition should be started and accepts a reference to the transition class, as in the following:

  type: Blinds;

- direction: This parameter accepts a Number value specifying whether the transition will reveal (0) or hide (1) the content of a movie clip, like so:

  direction: 0; // revealing content, "in" transition
  direction: 1; // hiding content, "out" transition

- duration: This parameter accepts a Number value indicating the number of seconds of a transition's duration, as in the following:

duration: 4;

- easing: This parameter accepts the reference to a method or function. Such a function must define the accelerations in the transition's animation, if any. The following section is dedicated to the easing classes that provide several methods that you can use as values for the easing parameter.

Easing classes

The component architecture provides six easing classes:

- None: The methods of this class specify that the animation of a transition will have no accelerations.
- Back: The methods of this class specify that the animation of a transition will have accelerations that will temporarily extend the animation itself beyond its intended range.
- Bounce: The methods of this class specify that the animation of a transition will have accelerations that will simulate a bouncing motion at one or both ends of the animation.
- Elastic: The methods of this class specify that the animation of a transition will have accelerations that will simulate an elastic effect at one or both ends of the animation.
- Regular: The methods of this class specify that the animation of a transition will have a steady acceleration at the beginning or a steady deceleration at the end, or both.
- Strong: The methods of this class specify accelerations that are similar to those of the Regular class, although more pronounced.

Each easing class provides three different methods that can be assigned to the easing parameter of a transition:

- easeIn: Applies an acceleration at the beginning of the animation
- easeOut: Applies an acceleration at the end of the animation
- easeInOut: Applies accelerations to both ends of the animation

The None easing class also provides a fourth method, easeNone, which is typically used as the default value assigned to the easing parameter of a transition. Note that the four methods of the None easing class (easeNone, easeIn, easeOut, and easeInOut) implement the same easing function.

The following lines provide four examples of values that can be assigned to the easing parameter of a transition:

```
easing: None.easeNone;
easing: Bounce.easeIn;
easing: Elastic.easeInOut;
easing: Strong.easeOut;
```

Transition-specific parameters

In addition to the four parameters listed earlier (type, direction, duration, and easing) that are common to all of the transitions, some transition types require specific parameters that affect the transition's behavior. The following sections are dedicated to those specific parameters.

The Blinds transition

The Blinds transition requires two specific parameters:

- dimension: Accepts a Number value defining whether the stripes are horizontal (0) or vertical (1)
- numStrips: Accepts a Number value determining how many stripes will be used to reveal or hide the content

The Fly transition

The Fly transition requires one additional parameter:

- startPoint: Accepts a Number value from 1 to 9 defining the starting point of the transition. The numeric values follow a positional rule similar to that of a phone keypad (1 = top left, 2 = top middle, 3 = top right, 4 = left, 5 = center, 6 = right, 7 = bottom left, 8 = bottom middle, 9 = bottom right).

The Iris transition

The Iris transition requires two specific parameters:

- shape: Accepts a String value that must be either SQUARE or CIRCLE and defines the shape of the mask that is revealing or hiding the content
- startPoint: Same as for the Fly transition

The PixelDissolve transition

The PixelDissolve transition requires two specific parameters:

- xSections: Accepts a Number value that defines the number of vertical sections that divide the content when revealed or hidden by the pixel blocks
- ySections: Accepts a Number value that defines the number of horizontal sections that divide the content when revealed or hidden by the pixel blocks

The Rotate transition

The Rotate transition requires two specific parameters:

- ccw: Accepts a Boolean value that, if true, defines the rotation as counterclockwise
- degrees: Accepts a Number value (0 through 360) defining the span of the rotation in degrees

The Squeeze transition

The Squeeze transition requires one additional parameter:

- dimension: Accepts a Number value defining the direction of the expansion or contraction: 0 (horizontal) or 1 (vertical)

The Wipe transition

The Wipe transition requires one additional parameter:

- startPoint: Same as for the Fly transition

Example of a transition parameters object

The following example shows how the TransitionManager class, the parameters of a transition class, and a method of an easing class work together to start a specific transition:

```
import mx.transitions.*;
import mx.transitions.easing.*;

var outBlinds = {
    type: Blinds,
    direction: 1,
    duration: 3,
    easing: Regular.easeInOut,
    numStrips: 20,
    dimension: 1
};

TransitionManager.start(myClip, outBlinds);
```

To try the previous example in a Flash document, you must create a movie clip symbol with some content in it and create one instance of that symbol on stage, giving it the name of myClip. Refer to Chapter 4 for a complete example utilizing this approach.

INDEX

A

accessibility, 51–52

accessing attributes of node, 214–215

Accordion component
  description of, 75, 254
  implementing, 255
  minimal example of
    code-based version, 255
    codeless version, 256
    purposes, 254–255
    XLEFF version, 257
  Properties panel and, 256
  richer example of
    code-based version, 261–262
    codeless version, 259–261
  skin properties
    borders, 265
    headers, 266–268
  solved mysteries
    header styles, creating on per-instance
      basis, 271–272
    inheriting styles, 268–271
  structure of
    overview of, 257
    segment content area, 258
    segment header, 258
  subclassing and, 273
  supported styles
    common, 263–264
    overview of, 262
    specific, 265

AccordionHeader class, 270

actions layer, 87

ActionScript class
  associating symbol with, 6
  Object class and, 29

ActionScript Settings dialog box, Export frame
  for classes option, 183

addEventListener method, 23

addMenuItem method (Menu class), 401, 404

Alert component
  description of, 76
  minimal example of
    dynamically creating alerts, 489–490
    dynamically creating windows, 487–488
    overview, 484–487
  overview of, 484
  skin properties, 500–505
  subclassing, 505
  supported styles, 495–499

alerts, creating dynamically, 489–490

altering architecture, 137

alternatingRowColors style, 337

analyzing size report, 181–182

ancestors, 95

animated behavior andProgressBar
  component, 377–379

animation styles and Tree component, 466

Apple Macintosh source code, looking
  for, 523

application framework, 34, 92

applications
  building using screens
    content hierarchy in nested
      screens, 95–96
    forms visibility, 98
    overview of, 93–95
    path to external screens, 101–102
    screen hierarchies with external
      subtrees, 99–101
    slide presentation, creating
      dynamically, 102–114
    slides and forms, 96–99

component-based, codeless version of,
    deploying, 256
event-driven, 21
multiplier, 64
apps subtree, 184
arrow buttons in calendar view, skinning, 363–364
assets layer, 87
assigning objects to variables, 15
associating symbol with ActionScript class, 6
attributes of node, accessing, 214–215
authoring environment
    properties in, 12–14
    testing movie within, 7
authoring parameters, comparing for CheckBox
        and RadioButton, 297–298
authoring time, changing skins at, 237–240
autoLoad parameter (Loader component), 374
autoSize parameter (Label component), 442–445

B

Back class, 529
background, hiding, 450–452
bar of ProgressBar component, 389
base classes, 14
behavior styles, 221
benefits of component architecture, 132
Blinds transition
    description of, 528
    parameters, 530
border styles and Button component
    Halo theme case, 281–282
    Sample theme case, 282–284
borderColor style, 361
borders
    Accordion component, 265
    View class and, 53
Bounce class, 529
bounding box layer, 88
branch nodes of Tree component, 461–462,
        471–476
browser, tab order in, 123–124
browsing structure of XML document, 215–216

building
    component instance
        children, creating, 45
        drawing step, 45–46
        initialization step, 44
    custom cell renderer, 343–345
    stylized version of DataGrid component, 510–512
building application
    content hierarchy in nested screens, 95–96
    forms visibility, 98
    path to external screens, 101–102
    screen hierarchies with external subtrees, 99–101
    screens, using, 93–95
    slide presentation, creating dynamically
        buttons-based navigation, implementing, 110
        example, building, 103–104
        forms, working with, 114
        Loader components in child screens,
            using, 111
        navigation in master screen, adding, 109–110
        overview of, 102
        screen events and transition sequencing, 113
        screen hierarchy, creating, 108
        transition classes, importing, 112
        transitions, introducing, 111
    slides and forms, 96–99
business logic tier, 64, 207
Button class and Accordion component headers
        and, 266–268. See also CheckBox component;
        RadioButton component
Button component
    complexity of, 290
    description of, 66, 276
    example using parameters of, 278–279
    minimalist example of, 276–277
    number of skins of
        emphasizing button instances and, 289
        iconic buttons and, 289–290
        implementing toggle buttons and, 289
    parameters of, 277
    purely coded skins and, 234–236
    Reusability Card and, 61
    skin properties
        overview of, 284
        purely coded skin, implementing, 290–293

purely coded skin, replacing with handcrafted, 285–288
subclassing, 293
supported styles
common, 280
specific, 281–284
types of, 279
button components, 65. *See also* Button component; CheckBox component; RadioButton component
Button instances
at authoring time, 287
emphasizing, 289
at runtime, 287
states of, 287
buttons
emphasized, 500
generating, 143–144
iconic, 289–290
pill, implementing, 290–293
toggle, implementing, 289
buttons-based navigation, implementing, 110
ButtonSkin symbol, 236

C

CDATA section, 197
cell, description of, 339
cell renderer
building custom, 343–345
description of, 340
cell rendering
building custom cell renderer, 343–345
ComboBox, DataGrid, and List components, 339–343
skinning compared to, 338
cell-structured components
ComboBox, 70
DataGrid, 71
description of, 65
List, 70
Tree, 72
types of, 69
chain of inheritance, 20

change event
NumericStepper class and component, 430
TextInput and TextArea components, 446–448
Tree component, 475
change event handler, 330
CheckBox component
altered skin, 239
assets of, 239
CheckFalseUp, skin 245
compiled, and custom skin, 238
description of, 66, 296, 305
Espresso skinning of, 238
falseUpIcon property, 241–243
handcrafted skins, 229–230
minimalist example of
comparing authoring parameters, 297–298
steps for, 296
XLEFF version, 297
mixed skins, 231
skin properties, 302–303
subclassing, 307
supported styles
common, 298–300
specific, 300–302
CheckFalseUp skin (CheckBox component), 245
child screen
description of, 94
Loader components, using in, 111
children
of Accordion component
overview, of 257
segment content area, 258
segment header, 258
in screen hierarchy, 95
children-based layout and View class, 53
class construct in component architecture, relevance of, 4
class constructors
definition of, 6
empty, 15
class styles, 152–153
class-level styles, 225–226

classes
  AccordionHeader, 270
  ActionScript
    associating symbol with, 6
    Object class and, 29
  Alert, 489
  associating symbol with, 6
  Back, 529
  base, 14
  Bounce, 529
  Button, 266–268, 296
  Colorable, 17–19
  CSSStyleDeclaration, 223–224
  custom, and XLEFF sampler, 167–168
  CustomCellRenderer, 344
  DataGridColumn, 345
  easing, 529
  Elastic, 529
  Form, 92–93
  importing transition, 112
  Loader, 93
  Main
    event handler naming convention, 194
    overview of, 187–188
    skeleton of, 189–190
    user interface events, handling, 190–193
    XLEFF and, 145
  manager
    DepthManager, 115–120
    FocusManager, 120–124
    overview of, 114–115
    PopUpManager, 124–128, 487, 493
  MovieClip
    depth, handling, 115
    UIObject class and, 36
  moving after first frame, 183
  mx.core.UIObject, 36
  None, 529
  Object, 29
  PopUpManager, 124–128, 487, 493
  RectBorder, 265, 292
  Screen, 92–93
  ScrollView, 35, 54
  Slide
    methods, 97
    overview of, 92–93
    parameters, 97
  Strong, 529
  StyleManager, 115, 226
  SystemManager, 115
  TextField, 445
  TransitionManager, 115, 527
  TreeController, 474–476
  UIComponent, 51–52
  UIEventDispatcher, triggering, 22
  UIObject
    className property, overriding, 38
    component architecture and, 36
    component instances, building, 44–46
    createClassObject method, 39, 487
    creating component instance dynamically, 37
    integrating Flash components in component
      architecture, 40–43
    legacy of, 36
    support for styles and, 220
    symbolName property, overriding, 38
    symbolOwner property, overriding, 38
  View, 53–54
  Vogoness, 46–50
  Window, 492
  XLEFF and, 144–146
  XML
    code written by using, 209–210
    properties, 206
    services of, 202
    tree-like structure and, 205
    XModel class compared to, 210–216
  XML manager, 145
  XMLNode, 205–206
  XMLStage, 145
  XModel, 145, 209–210, 217
classic feature, 63
className property, overriding, 38
classpath, role of, 185–186
click function and Button component, 277
codeless version of component-based applications,
  deploying, 256

coding, generating richer menus by, 399–405
Color Names section of XML data structure, 151
color of component instances, setting in single
      statement, 11
color styles
   description of, 221
   Tree component, 466
Colorable class and inheritance, 17–19
ComboBox component
   cell rendering
      building custom cell renderer, 343–345
      overview of, 339–343
   colors array and, 312
   dataProvider property and, 311
   description of, 70
   List component and, 310
   minimalist example of, 310–312
   richer examples of
      Custom Labels, 317–320
      Itemization, 315–317
      Making It Editable, 331–333
      overview, 314
      Scrolling, 320–322
      Selection Management, 327–330
      Sorting, 323–327
   rowCount property, 322
   skin properties, 338–339
   subclassing, 347
   supported styles
      common, 336
      overview of, 333–336
      specific, 337
   XLEFF version of, 313–314
common feature, 61
common styles
   Accordion component, 263–264
   Button component, 280
   CheckBox component, 298–300
   ComboBox, DataGrid, and List components, 336
   DateChooser and DateField components, 360
   description of, 279
   Menu and MenuBar components, 409
   RadioButton component, 298–300
communications, event-driven, 393

compatibility of versions of component
      architecture, 4
complete event and Window instance, 493–494
complexity
   of usage criteria for Reusability Card, 62
   of user interface, 132
complexity relationship in component
      architecture, 35
component architecture
   altering, 137
   application-oriented features of, 92
   assets of, 34
   benefits of, 132
   class construct in, 4
   core classes
      ScrollView, 54
      UIComponent, 51–52
      UIObject, 36–39
      View, 53–54
   default theme of, 282
   expanding, 136
   exploiting, 132–133
   extending, 134–135
   history of, 4
   inheritance and, 35–36
   integrating Flash components in, 40–43
   objective of, 133
   overriding features of, 43
   overview of, 34
   source code of, looking for
      FLA documents, 523
      Mac user, 523
      overview of, 521–522
      shortcuts, creating, 524
      Windows user, 522
   storing knowledge into
      from abstract to concrete, 137–138
      altering, 137
      expanding, 136
      extending, 134–135
component framework
   completing, 37
   description of, 34
   size of, 60

component instances
  See also Button instances; Menu instances
  building
    children, creating, 45
    drawing step, 45–46
    initialization step, 44
  color of, setting in single statement, 11
  constructors and, 6
  creating, 5, 82
  creating dynamically, 37, 82–84, 118–120
  deselecting or selecting CheckBox or
    RadioButton, 296
  editing, 85
  group name and RadioButton, 305
  header styles, creating on per-instance basis,
    271–272
  Menu, 420–423, 404
  RadioButtonGroup, 305–307
  text values displayed in, customizing 319
  window, 126–127, 493–494
  _x and _y properties of, 43
component-based template
  defining, 172–173
  licensing issue
    progressive update of template, 181
    standard components source code,
      including, 179–181
  scenes
    Dynamic Assets, 176–178
    Main, 178–179
    Preloader, 174–176
    using, 173
  size report, analyzing
    moving classes after first frame, 183
    moving symbols after first frame, 182
    overview of, 181–182
components
  See also component instances; *specific
    components*; UI components
  creating, 5–7
  events
    implementing custom, 21–25
    listening to custom, 23
    overview of, 20–21
    triggering custom, 21–22

Flash, integrating in component architecture,
    40–43
inheritance and
  benefits of, 17–19
  multiple inheritance, 19–20
  overview of, 14–17
methods, adding, 7–8
plug and play, 62
polymorphism
  benefits of, 30–31
  example of, 26–29
  signature of method and, 29–30
properties in authoring environment, 12–14
properties, implementing
  explicitly, 9–10
  implicitly, 11–12
  overview of, 8
quirky, 62
refining implementation of, 46–50
robust, 62
skins and, 228
styles as properties of, 222–223
template for new, 54, 57
typical structure of
  actions layer, 87
  assets layer, 87
  bounding box layer, 88
  overview of, 85–86
user interaction, creating, 82–84
concrete methods, 44
constructors
  definition of, 6
  empty, 15
container, inheriting styles from, 226
container components, 65, 72. *See also* Accordion
    component; Loader component; Scrollpane
    component; Window component
content area of Accordion segment, 258–259
content hierarchy in nested screens, 95–96
content, managing
  CDATA section, 197
  overview of, 194–195
  pushing separation paradigm further, 196–197
  Window instance, 490–495

contentPath parameter
   Loader component, 374
   ScrollPane component, 376
contentPath property (Window class), 492
Create Window button, 486
createChildren method, 45, 50
createClassObject method (UIObject class), 39, 487
createMenu method (Menu class), 397
createPopUp method (PopUpManager class), 488, 493
createSegment method (Accordion class), 255
CSSStyleDeclaration class, 223–224
custom events
   implementing, 21–25
   listening to, 23
   triggering, 21–22
Custom Labels example of ComboBox, DataGrid, and List components, 317–320
custom styles, 154–155
CustomCellRenderer class, 344
customization
   overview of, 220
   skin properties
      handcrafted, 228–231
      mixed, 231–234
      overview of, 228
      purely coded, 234–236
   styles
      class-level, 225–226
      global, 227
      inheriting from container, 226
      lookup process, 221
      overview of, 220
      parameters controlled by, 221
      as properties of component instance, 222–223
      styleName property, 223–225
   themes
      changing skins and, 236–243
      purpose of, 236
      skins that reflect styles, 243–245
      subclassing and, 245–249
customizing
   See also customization
   MenuBar skin, 417–420

scrollbars
   building stylized version of DataGrid component, 510–512
   skinning scrollbars, 512–519
customSort function, 326–327

D

data tier, 64
DataGrid component
   building stylized version of, 510–512
   cell rendering
      building custom cell renderer, 343–345
      overview of, 339–343
   colors array and, 312
   dataProvider property and, 311
   description of, 71
   List component and, 310
   minimalist example of, 310–312
   richer examples of
      Custom Labels, 317–320
      Itemization, 315–317
      Making It Editable, 331–333
      overview, 314
      Scrolling, 320–322
      Selection Management, 327–330
      Sorting, 323–327
   rowCount property, 322
   skin properties, 338–339
   subclassing, 347
   supported styles
      common, 336
      overview of, 333–336
      specific, 336
   workaround to bug in, 346
   XLEFF version of, 313–314
DataGridColumn class, 345
dataProvider property
   List, ComboBox, and DataGrid components, 311
   Menu and MenuBar classes, 406, 422
DateChooser component
   code version of, 353
   description of, 77, 350
   implementing, 353–355
   minimal example of, 350

range definition, 355–358
richer example of, 351–352
scroll event and, 358–359
skin properties, 363–364
solved mysteries
   DateField bug, 367–368
   displaying date in custom format, 367
   overview of, 366
subclassing, 369
supported styles
   common, 360
   specific, 360–363
XLEFF version of, 351
DateField bug, 367–368
DateField component
   code version of, 353
   description of, 78, 350
   implementing, 353–355
   minimal example of, 350
   range definition, 355–358
   richer example of, 351–352
   scroll event and, 358–359
   skin properties, 363–366
   solved mysteries
      DateField bug, 367–368
      displaying date in custom format, 367
      overview of, 366
   subclassing, 369
   supported styles
      common, 360
      specific, 360–363
   XLEFF version of, 351
DateField icon, skinning, 365–366
dateFormatter property (DateField
   component), 367
dayNames parameter, 351
default button, setting, 123
defaultIcon style, 337
defective component, 62
defining
   FLA template, 172–173
   focus schema, 121–122

folder structure
   classpath, role of, 185–186
   overview of, 183–185
range, 355–358
deploying component-based applications without
   coding, 256
DepthManager class
   overview, of 114–115
   stacking objects and, 116–117
   testing behavior of, 118–120
descendants, 95
deselecting CheckBox or RadioButton instance, 296
designing systems, 145
developer and XML, 207–209
direction parameter (transitions), 528
disabledColor style property (Button
   component), 280
disabledDays parameter, 351
disabledRanges property, 356
disabling approach to range definition, 356
disabling focus rect, 124
dispatchEvent method, 22
displaying date in custom format, 367
document library, adding symbols to, 83
doLayout method, 53
draw method, 49
drawing component instances, 45–46
drawRoundRect method and Halo theme, 293
duration parameter (transitions), 529
Dynamic Assets scene, 173, 176–178
dynamically creating
   alerts, 489–490
   component instances, 37, 82–84, 118–120
   slide presentation
      buttons-based navigation, implementing, 110
      example, building, 103–104
      forms, working with, 114
      Loader components in child screens, using, 111
      navigation in master screen, adding, 109–110
      overview of, 102
      screen events and transition sequencing, 113
      screen hierarchy, creating, 108

transition classes, importing, 112
transitions, introducing, 111
user interface, 157
windows, 487–488

E

easing classes, 529
easing methods, 111
easing parameter (transitions), 529
editable parameter (TextInput and TextArea
    components), 441
editable property
    adding to NumericStepper component, 435–436
    List, ComboBox, and DataGrid components,
        331–333
editing
    component instances, 85
    exported symbols, 518
Elastic class, 529
emphasized button, 500
emphasizing button instances, 289
enabling approach to range definition, 357
essential feature, 61
event communication mode of ProgressBar
    component, 382
event handlers
    definition of, 23
    naming convention, 194
event management and XLEFF, 144
event-driven applications, 21
event-driven communications, 393
event-driven programming, facilitating
    Main class
        event handler naming convention, 194
        overview of, 187–188
        skeleton of, 189–190
        user interface events, handling, 190–193
    overview of, 186–187
events
    See also specific events
    implementing custom, 21–25
    initialize, 243
    intracomponent, 187
    listening to custom, 23

overview of, 20–21
screen, 113
triggering custom, 21–22
XLEFF sampler and, 169
expanding architecture, 136
exploiting component architecture
    benefits of, 132
    objective of, 133
Export frame for classes option (ActionScript
        settings dialog box), 183
Export in first frame option (Linkage Properties
        dialog box), 182
extending
    architecture, 134–135
    XMLStage class, 146
extends keyword
    ActionScript class and, 29
    inheritance and, 14–17

F

Fade transition, 528
falseUpIcon property, 241–243
falseUpSkin symbol, 286
firstDayOfWeek parameter, 351
firstFrameExporter symbol, 177
FLA source files, 523
FLA template
    defining, 172–173
    licensing issue
        progressive update of template, 181
        standard components source code,
            including, 179–181
    scenes
        Dynamic Assets, 176–178
        Main, 178–179
        Preloader, 174–176
        using, 173
    size report, analyzing
        moving classes after first frame, 183
        moving symbols after first frame, 182
        overview of, 181–182
Flash
    document types, 93
    timeline, 92

Flash components, integrating in component architecture, 40–43
Flash movie, 92
Flash MX 2004 bug in NumericStepper component, 431
Flash player and XML layout engine, 140
Flash rendering system and updating movie, 46
FLEX,XLEFF compared to, 140
Fly transition
    description of, 528
    parameters, 530
focus management, 52
focus rect, disabling, 124
focus schema, defining, 121–122
FocusManager class
    default button, setting, 123
    disabling focus rect, 124
    focus schema, defining, 121–122
    keyboard focus, managing, 120
    overview of, 114
    tab order in browser, 123–124
folder structure, defining
    classpath, role of, 185–186
    overview of, 183–185
Form Application document type, 93–96
Form class, 92–93
form rendered by XLEFF, 142
forms
    purpose of, 96–98
    slides compared to, 99
    working with, 114
forms visibility, 98
frequency of use criteria for Reusability Card, 61
function libraries, exploiting, 132
functional containment relationship in component architecture, 35
Functional Distance, 133
functions
    customSort, 326–327
    getWindowInitObject, 504
    jumpToMain function, 176
    setAccordionStyles, 264, 270
    setAlertStyles, 499
    setComboBoxStyles, 337
    setCommonStyles, 336
    setDataGridStyles, 337
    setGlobalStyles, 300, 499
    setListStyles, 337
    setWindowStyles, 499

G

generating richer menus
    by coding, 399–405
    using XML, 405–408
get method, 11
getCellIndex method, 344
getDataLabel method, 344
getStyle method, 222
getWindowInitObject function, 504
global styles, 227
graphic styles, 221
graphic symbols for scrollbars, 516–519
Graphics folder, 514
grouping style properties
    class-level styles and, 225–226
    inheriting styles from container, 226
    styleName property and, 223–225
groupName property (RadioButton instance), 305
guide layers, creating, 82

H

Halo theme
    Button component and, 281–282
    drawRoundRect method and, 293
handcrafted skins, 228–231
handling
    combination linefeed/CR, 453–455
    input process, 446–448
header styles of Accordion component, creating on per-instance basis, 271–272
headerColor style, 336, 361
HeaderDateText style, 360
headerRelease event, 326
headers and Accordion component, 266–268
headerStyle style, 336
heavy component, 62
hGridLineColor style, 337
hGridLines style, 337

hiding background, 450–452
hierarchical relationship in component architecture, 35
history of component architecture, 4
hScrollPolicy property, 321
html parameter (Label and TextArea components), 441

I

icon, Button instance, 279
icon parameter (Button component), 277
icon styles (Tree component), 467
iconic buttons, 289–290
identifying
    node name, 211
    node type, 212–213
implementation of components, refining, 46–50
implementing
    Accordion component, 255
    custom events, 21–25
    properties
        explicitly, 9–10
        implicitly, 11–12
        overview of, 8
    purely coded skin, 290–293
    toggle buttons, 289
    XML attributes of Tree component, 477–480
importing transition classes, 112
incoming slide, 97
indeterminate appearance of ProgressBar component, 379–380
Info panel
    container discrepancy, 162
    container level, 164
    stage level, 162
inheritance
    benefits of, 17–19
    component architecture and, 35–36
    multiple inheritance, 19–20
    overview of, 14–17
    specializing existing components and, 26
inheriting styles
    Accordion component and, 268–271
    from container, 226

init method, 44
initBranches method (Tree component), 479–480
initialize event, 243
innovative feature, 64
input process, handling, 446–448
Inspectable metadata tag, syntax of, 13
instances
    See also Button instances; Menu instances
    building
        children, creating, 45
        drawing step, 45–46
        initialization step, 44
    color of, setting in single statement, 11
    constructors and, 6
    creating, 5, 82
    creating dynamically, 37, 82–84, 118–120
    deselecting or selecting CheckBox or RadioButton, 296
    editing, 85
    group name and RadioButton, 305
    header styles, creating on per-instance basis, 271–272
    Menu, 420–423, 404
    RadioButtonGroup, 305–307
    text values displayed in, customizing 319
    window, 126–127, 493–494
    _x and _y properties of, 43
intracomponent events, 187
invalidate method, 46
invalidation, 46
Iris transition
    description of, 528
    parameters, 530
isBranch attribute of Tree component, implementing, 477–480
isInheritingStyle method, 226
Itemization example of ComboBox, DataGrid, and List components, 315–317
iterative approach, 30

J

jumpToMain function, 176

K

key-based navigation among content areas, Accordion segment header, 258
keyboard access, 51–52
keyboard focus, managing, 120
keywords, extends
    ActionScript class and, 29
    inheritance and, 14–17

L

Label component
    autoSize parameter, 442–445
    description of, 68
    minimal example of, 440–441
    parameters of, 441–442
    as read-only, 440
    solved mysteries
        handling combination linefeed/CR, 453–455
        hiding background, 450–452
    subclassing, 456
    supported styles, 448–449
    text content of, 440
    XLEFF version of, 442
label parameter (Button component), 277
labelPlacement parameter (Button component), 277
labelPlacement property (ProgressBar class), 391
layers of movie clips
    actions, 87
    assets, 87
    bounding box, 88
    defining, 86
leaf, 95
leaf nodes of Tree component, 461
length property (TextField class), 445
licensing issue and component-based template
    progressive update of template, 181
    standard components source code, including, 179–181
linefeed/CR combination, handling, 453–455
linkage identifier, 37
Linkage Properties dialog box
    ButtonSkin symbol and, 235–236
    Export in first frame option, 182

List component
    cell rendering
        building custom cell renderer, 343–345
        overview of, 339–343
    colors array and, 312
    ComboBox and DataGrid components and, 310
    dataProvider property and, 311
    description of, 70
    minimalist example of, 310–312
    richer examples of
        Custom Labels, 317–320
        Itemization, 315–317
        Making It Editable, 331–333
        overview, 314
        Scrolling, 320–322
        Selection Management, 327–330
        Sorting, 323–327
    rowCount property, 322
    skin properties, 338–339
    subclassing, 347
    supported styles
        common, 336
        overview of, 333–336
        specific, 337
    XLEFF version of, 313–314
listeners, 21
listening to custom events, 23
listings, slideshow.as, 104–107
listOwner property, 344
Loader class, 93
Loader component
    in child screens, using, 111
    description of, 74, 372
    minimal example of, 372–375
    ProgressBar component
        communication modes, 382
        interaction, 382–383
        mediated interaction, 385–386
    ScrollPane component compared to, 376
    skin properties, 389
    subclassing, 393
    supported styles, 387
    XLEFF version of, 381
logic layer. See XML layout engine
logical tab, 120

M

Macintosh (Apple) source code, looking for, 523
Main class
  event handler naming convention, 194
  overview of, 187–188
  skeleton of, 189–190
  user interface events, handling, 190–193
  XLEFF and, 145
Main scene, 173, 178–179
maintenance features, evaluating, 133
Making It Editable example of ComboBox, DataGrid, and List components, 331–333
manager classes
  DepthManager, 115–120
  FocusManager, 120–124
  overview of, 114–115
  PopUpManager, 124–128
managers, 92
managing
  content
    CDATA section, 197
    overview of, 194–195
    pushing separation paradigm further, 196–197
    of Window instance, 490–495
  keyboard focus, 120
manual communication mode of ProgressBar component, 382
Master Copy of ActionScript source code, 522
master screen
  description of, 94
  navigation in, adding, 109–110
maturity criteria for Reusability Card, 63
maxChars property (TextField class), 445
mediated interaction
  ProgressBar and Loader components, 385–386
  ProgressBar and ScrollPane components, 386
Menu component
  description of, 78, 396
  minimal example of, 396–397
  subclassing, 424
  XLEFF version of, 408–409
Menu instances
  nested, 404
  persistent, creating, 420–423

MenuBar component
  description of, 79, 396
  minimal example of, 398–399
  richer example of
    coding, 399–405
    XML, 405–408
  skin properties, 414–417
  solved mysteries
    customizing skin, 417–420
    persistent Menu instances, creating, 420–423
  subclassing, 424
  supported styles
    common, 409
    examples of, 410–414
    specific, 410
  XLEFF version of, 408–409
metadata tags to expose properties, 12–14
methods
  addEventListener, 23
  adding to components, 7–8
  addMenuItem, 401, 404
  createChildren, 45, 50
  createClassObject, 39, 487
  createPopUp, 488, 493
  createSegment, 255
  dispatchEvent, 22
  doLayout, 53
  draw, 49
  drawRoundRect, 293
  easing, 111
  get, 11
  getCellIndex, 344
  getDataLabel, 344
  getStyle, 222
  init, 44
  initBranches, 479–480
  invalidate, 46
  isInheritingStyle, 226
  overriding, 43–44, 45, 52
  placeholder, 44
  registerInheritingStyle, 227
  removeEventListener, 23
  set, 11
  setEnabled, 52
  setStyle, 222, 224

show, 489
signature of, 29–30
size, 45–46, 52
sortItems, 326
sortItemsBy, 323
types of, 44
Microsoft Windows source code, looking for, 522
mixed skins, 231–234
modal windows, 127–128
modeless windows, 127
modifying XLEFF sampler, 161–164
monthNames parameter, 351
movie clips
    description of, 92
    layers of
        actions, 87
        assets, 87
        bounding box, 88
        defining, 86
MovieClip class
    depth, handling, 115
    UIObject class and, 36
movies, updating, 46
moving
    classes after first frame, 183
    symbols after first frame, 182
    window instances, 126
multiple inheritance, 19–20
multipleSelection property, 327, 329
multiplier applications, 64
multitiered model, 64
mx.core.UIObject class, 36
myColor property
    authoring environment and, 12
    implementing
        explicitly, 9–10
        implicitly, 11–12
        overview of, 8

N

naming convention for event handler, 194
navigation
    buttons-based, implementing, 110
    for forms, 96
    in master screen, adding, 109–110
    to screen in other subsystem, 101–102
    for slides, 97
nested Menu instances, 404
nested menus, describing, 406
nested screens, content hierarchy in, 95–96
nested structure of XML description, 139
nested styles, 153–154
node, accessing attributes of, 214–215
node name, identifying, 211
node type, identifying, 212–213
None class, 529
nonmodal windows, 127
novelty feature, 63
NumericStepper component
    description of, 80, 428
    minimal example of, 428–429
    parameters of, 428
    skin properties, 433–434
    solved mysteries, 435–436
    subclassing, 437
    supported styles, 431–432
    XLEFF version of
        bug for Flash MX 2004 users, 431
        change event and, 430
        properties of, 429

O

Object class and ActionScript class, 29
object model
    definition of, 204
    XML and XMLNode classes, 206
object-oriented programming (OOP)
    events and, 20
    inheritance and, 14, 19
    methods and, 7
    polymorphism and, 26
objective of component architecture, 133
objects
    assigning to variables, 15
    event, properties of, 22
    source,definition of, 21
    stacking, 116–117
onClipEvent statement, 243

one-to-one relationship between list and data
        items, 315
onModelledObject event, 210
onNewPoem event, 22–23
OOP. *See* object-oriented programming
openDuration style, 337
opening branch nodes of Tree
        component, 471–476
outgoing slide, 97
overriding
    default theme, 282
    features of component architecture, 43
    methods, 43–44, 45, 52
owner property, 344

P

packages, 185
parameters
    for all transitions, 528
    Blinds transition, 530
    Fly transition, 530
    Iris transition, 530
    PixelDissolve transition, 530
    Rotate transition, 530
    Squeeze transition, 531
    of text components, 441–442
    Wipe transition, 531
Parameters tab (Properties panel), 19, 351
parent screen, 95
parsing XML in ActionScript
    object models and trees, 204–206
    overview of, 202–203
    typical job of developer, 207–209
    XModel class and
        notes on use of, 217
        overview of, 209–210
        XML class compared to, 210–216
password parameter (TextInput and TextArea
        components), 442
path to external screens, 101–102
peculiar components
    Alert, 76
    DateChooser, 77
    DateField, 78

description of, 65
    Menu, 78
    MenuBar, 79
    NumericStepper, 80
    ProgressBar, 80
    types of, 76
    UIScrollBar, 81
persistent Menu instances, creating, 420–423
Photo transition, 528
pill buttons, implementing, 290–293
PixelDissolve transition
    description of, 528
    parameters, 530
placeholder methods, 44
placing XML layout engine, 139
plug and play component, 62
polled communication mode of ProgressBar
        component, 382
polymorphism
    benefits of, 30–31
    example of, 26–29
    signature of method and, 29–30
popularity criteria for Reusability Card, 64
PopUpManager class
    modal windows and, 127–128
    overview of, 114
    window instances, creating, 126–127, 487, 493
    window-based system, creating, 124–126
pre-existing feature, 63
predefined styles, 153
preloader, 173
Preloader scene, 173–176
programmatically, changing skins, 240–243
ProgressBar component
    animated behavior of, 377–379
    communication modes, 382
    description of, 80, 372
    Loader component
        interaction, 382–383
        mediated interaction, 385–386
    minimal example of, 377
    ScrollPane component
        interaction, 384
        mediated interaction, 386
    skin properties, 389–392

solved mysteries, 392–393
subclassing, 393
supported styles, 387–388
as visual placeholder, 379–380
XLEFF version of, 381
progressive update of template, 181
properties
in authoring environment, 12–14
of event objects, 22
falseUpIcon, 241–243
groupName and RadioButton instance, 305
implementing
explicitly, 9–10
implicitly, 11–12
overview of, 8
labelPlacement, 391
NumericStepper component, 429, 435–436
prototype, 249
RadioButtonGroup class, 306
styleName, 223–225
styles as, 222–223
Styles section of XML data structure, 152
TextField class, 445
Properties panel
Accordion component, 256
Button component, 277–278
Parameters tab, 19, 351
prototype property, 249
purely coded skins
Button component and
implementing, 290–293
overview of, 284
replacing with handcrafted, 285–288
overview of, 234–236

Q

quirky component, 62

R

RadioButton component
description of, 67, 296, 305
minimalist example of
comparing authoring parameters, 297–298

steps for, 296
XLEFF version, 297
RadioButtonGroup instance, 305–307
skin properties, 302–303
subclassing, 307
supported styles
common, 298–300
specific, 300–302
RadioButtonGroup instance, 305–307
range definition, 355–358
rare feature, 61
RectBorder class
purely coded skins and, 292
themes and, 265
refining implementation of components, 46–50
registerInheritingStyle method, 227
registration point of symbol, 164
Regular class, 529
Relative Space, 116
removeEventListener method, 23
repeatDelay style
List, ComboBox, and DataGrid components, 336
NumericStepper component, 432
repeatInterval style
List, ComboBox, and DataGrid components, 336
NumericStepper component, 432
replacing purely coded skin with
handcrafted, 285–288
requesting user confirmation before closing
window
dynamically creating alerts, 489–490
dynamically creating windows, 487–488
overview of, 484–487
Reserved Space, 116–117
restrict property (TextField class), 446
retrieving
date, 353–355
value with NumericStepper component, 429–431
Reusability Card
complexity of usage criteria, 62
frequency of use criteria, 61
maturity criteria, 63
overview of, 60
popularity criteria, 64
stability criteria, 62

robust component, 62
robustness, evaluating, 133
rollOverColor style, 336, 361
root element of XML document, 211
Rotate transition
    description of, 528
    parameters, 530
rowCount property, 322

S

Sample theme
    Button component and, 282–284
    styles supported by, 300–302
scalability
    evaluating, 133
    polymorphism and, 30–31
scaleContent parameter (Loader component), 374
scenes and component-based template
    Dynamic Assets, 176–178
    Main, 178–179
    overview of, 172–173
    Preloader, 174–176
Screen class, 92–93
screen events, 113
screen hierarchy
    creating dynamically, 108
    description of, 95
    with external subtrees, 99–101
    of subsystem, 102
screens
    building application using
        content hierarchy in nested screens, 95–96
        forms visibility, 98
        overview of, 93–95
        path to external screens, 101–102
        screen hierarchies with external
            subtrees, 99–101
        slide presentation, creating
            dynamically, 102–114
        slides and forms, 96–99
    Flash timeline and, 92
Screens window, 94
scroll event and DateChooser and DateField
    components, 358–359

ScrollArrow symbol, 514
scrollbars
    customizing
        building stylized version of DataGrid
            component, 510–512
        graphic symbols for, 516–519
        skinning scrollbars, 512–519
    description of, 508
    mixed skins and, 233
ScrollButtonBackground symbol, 515
scrollDrag parameter (ScrollPane component), 377
Scrolling example of ComboBox, DataGrid, and List
    components, 320–322
ScrollPane component
    description of, 73, 372
    minimal example of, 375–377
    ProgressBar component
        communication modes, 382
        interaction, 384
        mediated interaction, 386
    skin properties, 389
    subclassing, 393
    supported styles, 387
    XLEFF version of, 381
ScrollThumbBottom symbol, 515
ScrollThumbGrip symbol, 515
ScrollThumbMiddle symbol, 515
ScrollThumbTop symbol, 516
ScrollTrack symbol, 516
ScrollView class, 35, 54
segments of Accordion component
    content area, 258
    header, 258
    overview of, 257
selected parameter (Button component), 278
selectedData property (RadioButtonGroup
    class), 306
selectedDate property (Date class), 355
selectedIndex property, 329
selectedIndices property, 329
selecting CheckBox or RadioButton instance, 296
Selection Management example of ComboBox,
    DataGrid, and List components, 327–330
selection property (RadioButtonGroup class), 306
selectionColor style, 336, 361

separation paradigm, pushing further, 196–197

sequential approach, 31

set method, 11

setAccordionStyles function (Accordion
    component), 264, 270

setAlertStyles function, 499

setComboBoxStyles function, 337

setCommonStyles function, 336

setDataGridStyles function, 337

setEnabled method, 52

setGlobalStyles function, 300, 499

setListStyles function, 337

setStyle method, 222, 224

setting date, 353–355

setWindowStyles function, 499

show method (Alert class), 489

showToday parameter, 351

siblings, 95

signature of methods, 29–30

simple component, 62

size method, 45–46, 52

size report and component-based template
    moving classes after first frame, 183
    moving symbols after first frame, 182
    overview of, 181–182

skeleton of Main class, 189–190

skin properties
    See also skinning; skins
    Accordion component
        borders, 265
        headers, 266–268
    CheckBox component, 302–303
    ComboBox, DataGrid, and List
        components, 338–339
    DateChooser and DateField components
        arrow buttons in calendar view, 363–364
        DateField icon, 365–366
    Loader component, 389
    Menu and MenuBar components, 414–417
    ProgressBar component, 389–392
    RadioButton component, 302–303
    ScrollPane component, 389

skinning
    See also skin properties
    Alert component, 500–505
    Button component
        number of skins of, 289–290
        overview of, 284
        purely coded skin, implementing, 290–293
        purely coded skin, replacing with
            handcrafted, 285–288
    NumericStepper component and, 433–434
    scrollbars, 512–519
    Window component, 499–505

skins
    See also skin properties; skinning
    changing
        at authoring time, 237–240
        mirage of code separation and, 236–237
        programmatically, 240–243
    handcrafted, 228–231
    mixed, 231–234
    overview of, 228
    purely coded, 234–236
    specific context of, 220
    that reflect styles, 243–245

Slide class
    methods, 97
    overview of, 92–93
    parameters, 97

slide presentation, creating dynamically
    buttons-based navigation, implementing, 110
    example, building, 103–104
    forms, working with, 114
    Loader components in child screens, using, 111
    navigation in master screen, adding, 109–110
    overview of, 102
    screen events and transition sequencing, 113
    screen hierarchy, creating, 108
    transition classes, importing, 112
    transitions, introducing, 111

Slide Presentation document type, 93–96

slides
    forms compared to, 99
    purpose of, 96–98

slideshow.as listing, 104–107

software internationalization, 194

solved mysteries

    Accordion component

        header styles, creating on per-instance
basis, 271–272

        inheriting styles, 268–271

    DateChooser and DateField components

        DateField bug, 367–368

        displaying date in custom format, 367

        overview of, 366

    Menu and MenuBar components

        customizing skin, 417–420

        persistent Menu instances, creating, 420–423

    NumericStepper component, 435–436

    ProgressBar component, 392–393

    text components

        handling combination linefeed/CR, 453–455

        hiding background, 450–452

    Tree component

        implementing XML attributes, 477–480

        overview of, 470

        taking full control, 471–476

Sorting example of ComboBox, DataGrid, and List
components, 323–327

sortItems method, 326

sortItemsBy method, 323

source code

    of architecture

        from abstract to concrete, 137–138

        altering, 137

        expanding, 136

        extending, 134–135

        overview of, 134

    looking for

        FLA documents, 523

        Mac user, 523

        overview of, 521–522

        shortcuts, creating, 524

        Windows user, 522

source objects, 21

specific feature, 64

specific styles

    Accordion component, 265

    Button component and

        Halo theme case, 281–282

        Sample theme case, 282–284

    CheckBox component, 300–302

    ComboBox component, 337

    DataGrid component, 336

    DateChooser and DateField
components, 360–363

    description of, 279

    List component, 337

    Menu and MenuBar components, 410

    RadioButton component, 300–302

Squeeze transition

    description of, 528

    parameters, 531

stability criteria for Reusability Card, 62

stacking objects, 116–117

Stage section of XML data structure, 155–158

standard components source code, including,
179–181

stateless application framework, 97

storing knowledge into component architecture

    from abstract to concrete, 137–138

    altering, 137

    expanding, 136

    extending, 134–135

Strong class, 529

structure

    of components

        actions layer, 87

        assets layer, 87

        bounding box layer, 88

        overview of, 85–86

    of XML document, browsing, 215–216

style inheritance and Accordion component,
268–271

StyleManager class, 115, 226

styleName property, 223–225

styles
 See also common styles; specific styles
 Button component
  common, 280
  specific, 281–284
  types, of 279
 class-level, 225–226
 ComboBox component, 337
 ComboBox, DataGrid, and List
  components, 333–336
 DataGrid component, 336
 global, 227
 global context of, 220
 inheriting
  Accordion component and, 268–271
  from container, 226
 List component, 337
 lookup process, 221
 NumericStepper component, 431–432
 overview of, 220
 parameters controlled by, 221
 as properties of component instance, 222–223
 skins that reflect, 243–245
 styleName property, 223–225
 XLEFF and, 144
Styles section of XML data structure
 class styles, 152–153
 custom styles, 154–155
 nested styles, 153–154
 overview of, 151–152
 predefined styles, 153
styleSheet property (TextField class), 446
stylized version of DataGrid component,
  building, 510–512
subclasses, 14
subclassing
 Accordion component, 273
 alternative to, 249
 Button component, 293
 CheckBox and RadioButton components, 307
 ComboBox, DataGrid, and List components, 347
 DateChooser and DateField components, 369
 Loader component, 393
 Menu and MenuBar components, 424

NumericStepper component, 437
 overview of, 168, 245–248
 ProgressBar component, 393
 ScrollPane component, 393
 text components, 456
 Tree component, 480
 Window and Alert components, 505
subsystem, 101
supported styles
 Accordion component
  common, 263–264
  overview of, 262
  specific, 265
 DateChooser and DateField components
  common, 360
  specific, 360–363
 Loader component, 387
 Menu and MenuBar components
  common, 409
  examples of, 410–414
  specific, 410
 ProgressBar component, 387–388
 ScrollPane component, 387
 text components, 448–449
 Tree component
  animation, 466
  color, 466
  icon, 467
  indentation, 467
  minimal example and, 468–470
  text, 466
  useRollOver, 467
 Window and Alert components, 495–499
symbolColor style of NumericStepper
  component, 432
symbolName property, overriding, 38
symbolOwner property, overriding, 38
symbols defined to skin
 CheckBox component, 304
 RadioButton component, 304
symbols, moving after first frame, 182
SystemManager class, 115
systems, designing, 145

T

Tab key and keyboard focus, 120
tab order in browser, 123–124
tab target, 121
templates
  for building application made of subsystems,
    creating, 99–100
  component-based
    defining, 172–173
    licensing issue and, 179–181
    screens and, 173–179
    size report and, 181–183
  for new components, 54, 57
testing
  DepthManager behavior, 118–120
  movie within authoring environment, 7
  tab order of movie, 120
  XML data, 159–161
text components
  comparison of, 440
  description of, 65
  Label, 68
  parameters of, 441–442
  solved mysteries
    handling combination linefeed/CR, 453–455
    hiding background, 450–452
  subclassing, 456
  supported styles, 448–449
  text field objects and, 445
  TextArea, 69
  TextInput, 68
  types of, 67
text field objects and text components, 445
text parameter (text components), 441
text styles
  Alert component, 495
  description of, 221
  Tree component, 466
text values displayed in component instances,
    customizing, 319
TextArea component
  description of, 69
  handling input process, 446–448
  minimal example of, 440–441

parameters of, 441–442
solved mysteries
  handling combination linefeed/CR, 453–455
  hiding background, 450–452
subclassing, 456
supported styles, 448–449
text content of, 440
UIScrollBar component compared to, 508
XLEFF version of, 442
textarea element and XML example, 215
textDecoration style property (Button
    component), 280
TextInput component
  description of, 68–69
  handling input process, 446–448
  minimal example of, 440–441
  parameters of, 441–442
  solved mysteries
    handling combination linefeed/CR, 453–455
    hiding background, 450–452
  subclassing, 456
  supported styles, 448–449
  text content of, 440
  XLEFF version of, 442
themeColor style property (Button
    component), 280
themes
  Button component and
    Halo, 281–282
    Sample, 282–284
  changing skins
    at authoring time, 237–240
    mirage of code separation and, 236–237
    programmatically, 240–243
  default, overriding, 282
  description of, 168, 185, 220
  purpose of, 236
  Sample, styles supported by, 300–302
  skins that reflect styles, 243–245
  subclassing
    alternative to, 249
    overview of, 245–248
todayColor style, 361
TodayStyle style, 360
toggle buttons, implementing, 289

toggle parameter (Button component), 278

track of ProgressBar component, 389

transition classes, importing, 112

transition sequencing, 113

TransitionManager class, 115, 527

transitions

    applying, 527

    example of, 531

    introducing, 111

    parameters common to all types of, 528–529

    types of, 528

transparent setting of backgroundColor style
        property, 451

Tree component

    description of, 72, 460

    minimal example of, 460–464

    nodes of, 463

    solved mysteries

        implementing XML attributes, 477–480

        overview of, 470

        taking full control, 471–476

    subclassing, 480

    supported styles

        animation, 466

        color, 466

        icon, 467

        indentation, 467

        minimal example and, 468–470

        text, 466

        useRollOver, 467

    XLEFF version of, 464–465

TreeController class, 474–476

triggering custom events, 21–22

type parameter (transitions), 528

type property of menu item, 401

U

UI components

    button, 65–67

    categories of, 65

    cell-structured, 69–72

    container, 72–75

    peculiar, 76–81

    text, 67–69

UIComponent class, 51–52

UIEventDispatcher class, triggering, 22

UIObject class

    className property, overriding, 38

    component architecture and, 36

    component instances, building, 44–46

    createClassObject method, 39, 487

    creating component instance dynamically, 37

    integrating Flash components in component
        architecture, 40–43

    legacy of, 36

    support for styles and, 220

    symbolName property, overriding, 38

    symbolOwner property, overriding, 38

UIScrollBar component

    description of, 81, 508

    minimal example of, 508–510

    mixed skins and, 232–233

updating movie, 46

user confirmation, requesting before closing
        window

    alerts, dynamically creating, 489–490

    overview of, 484–487

    windows, dynamically creating, 487–488

User Copy of ActionScript source code, 522

user interface

    complexity of, 132

    describing via XML, 139

    dynamically generated, 157

    XLEFF equivalent for generating, 297

    XLEFF sampler

        custom classes and, 167–168

        events and, 169

        overview of, 164–165

        patterns of, 165

        substructures of, 166–167

user interface events, handling, 190–193

user interface tier, 64

V

value, retrieving with NumericStepper
        component, 429–431

variables, assigning objects to, 15

verifying class style before creating object, 300

versions of component architecture, compatibility
of, 4
vGridLineColor style, 337
vGridLines style, 337
View class, 53–54
visual aspects and styles, 414
visual placeholder, ProgressBar component
as, 379–380
Vogon component
custom event, implementing, 23–25
inheritance and, 14, 17–19
methods, adding, 7–8
minimal version of, creating, 5–7
onNewPoem event, 23
polymorphism
example of, 26–29
signature of method and, 29–30
properties in authoring environment, 12–14
properties, implementing
explicitly, 9–10
implicitly, 11–12
overview of, 8
UIEventDispatcher class, triggering, 22
Vogoness class, refining implementation of
components, 46–50
vScrollPolicy property, 321

W

W3C DOM Level1 recommendation, 205
WeekDayStyle style, 360
widespread feature, 64
Window component
description of, 74
managing content of, 490–495
minimal example of
alerts, dynamically creating, 489–490
overview, 484–487
windows, dynamically creating, 487–488
overview of, 484
skin properties, 499–505
subclassing, 505
supported styles, 495–499
window instances, 126–127, 493–494
window-based system, creating, 124–126

windows, creating dynamically, 487–488
Windows (Microsoft) source code, looking for, 522
Wipe transition
description of, 528
parameters, 531
wordWrap parameter (TextArea component), 442

X

XLEFF
See also XML layout engine
Accordion component, 257
benefits of, 194
buttons, generating, 143–144
classes and, 144–146
ComboBox, DataGrid, and List
components, 313–314
DateChooser and DateField components, 351
description of, 140–141
as example of subsystem, 185
features of, 144
form rendered by, 142
internal architecture of, 145–146
Loader component and, 381
Menu and MenuBar components, 408–409
NumericStepper component
bug for Flash MX 2004 users, 431
change event and, 430
properties of, 429
object model and, 192
ProgressBar component, 381
ScrollPane component, 381
text components, 442
Tree component, 464–465
user interface generated dynamically by, 190–193
Web site for, 146
XLEFF equivalent for generating user interface, 297
XLEFF sampler
complex user interface, examining
custom classes and, 167–168
events and, 169
overview of, 164–165
patterns of, 165
substructures of, 166–167
description of, 158

modifying and reloading, 161–164
using, 159–161
XML
benefits of, 202
data structure
Color Names section, 151
overview of, 150
Stage section, 155–158
Styles section, 151–155
description of, 150
generating richer menus using, 405–408
parsing in ActionScript
object models and trees, 204–206
overview of, 202–203
typical job of developer, 207–209
XModel class and, 209–210, 217
XModel class compared to XML class, 210–216
Tree component and, 461–464
W3C DOM Level1 recommendation, 205
XML attributes of Tree component,
implementing, 477–480
XML class
code written by using, 209–210
properties, 206
services of, 202
tree-like structure and, 205
XModel class compared to
accessing attributes of node, 214–215
browsing structure of XML document, 215–216
document root and other nodes, 211
identifying node name, 211
identifying node type, 212–213
overview of, 210–211

XML layout engine
See also XLEFF
benefits of, 138–140
description of, 138
in Flash context, 140
XML Layout parameter, 189
XML manager classes and XLEFF, 145
xmlDefFileName variable, 159
XMLNode class
childNodes property, 205
properties, 206
xmlObj
description of, 203
tree-like structure, 204–205
XMLStage class and XLEFF, 145
XModel class
notes on use of, 217
overview of, 209–210
XLEFF and, 145
XML class compared to
accessing attributes of node, 214–215
browsing structure of XML document, 215–216
document root and other nodes, 211
identifying node name, 211
identifying node type, 212–213
overview of, 210–211

Z

z-order, 115
Zoom transition, 528

XML for Flash

1-59059-543-2 $39.99 [US]

Actionscript Animation
Making Things Move!

1-59059-518-1 $49.99 [US]

Flash 8

1-59059-542-4 $36.99 [US]

ASP.NET 2.0
for Flash

1-59059-517-3 $39.99 [US]

DOM Scripting
Web Design with JavaScript and the Document Object Model

Jeremy Keith

1-59059-533-5 $34.99 [US]

EXPERIENCE THE
DESIGNER TO DESIGNER™
DIFFERENCE

Fireworks MX 2004
ZERO TO HERO

Joyce J. Evans
Charles E. Brown

1-59059-306-5 $34.99 [US]

Paint Shop Pro 8
ZERO TO HERO

1-59059-238-7 $24.99 [US]

Windows
Movie Maker 2
ZERO TO HERO

1-59059-149-6 $24.99 [US]

PHOTOSHOP
MOST WANTED
MORE EFFECTS AND DESIGN TIPS

colin smith
al ward

1-59059-262-X $49.99 [US]

FLASH MX
MOST WANTED
EFFECTS & MOVIES

1-59059-224-7 $39.99 [US]

FLASH 3D CHEATS
MOST WANTED

1-59059-221-2 $39.99 [US]

FLASH MX 2004
GAMES MOST WANTED

1-59059-236-0 $39.99 [US]

ILLUSTRATOR CS
MOST WANTED
TECHNIQUES AND EFFECTS

MATT KLOSKOWSKI

1-59059-372-3 $39.99 [US]

Extending
Flash MX 2004
Complete Guide and Reference to JavaScript Flash

1-59059-304-9 $49.99 [US]

Apache Essentials
Install, Configure, Maintain

1-59059-355-3 $39.99 [US]

Macromedia
Dreamweaver MX 2004
Design Projects

1-59059-409-6 $39.99 [US]

New Masters of Flash
Volume 3

1-59059-314-6 $59.99 [US]

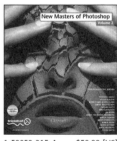

New Masters of Photoshop
Volume 2

1-59059-315-4 $59.99 [US]

Cascading
Style Sheets
SEPARATING CONTENT FROM PRESENTATION

Second Edition

Owen Briggs, Steven Champeon, Eric Costello, and Matt Patterson

1-59059-231-X $39.99 [US]

Constructing
Usable Shopping Carts
DESIGNING AND BUILDING GREAT E-COMMERCE APPLICATIONS

Clifton Evans, Jody Kerr, and Jon Stephens

1-59059-408-8 $34.99 [US]

EXTREME
PHOTOSHOP CS
PROFESSIONAL DESIGN AND ADVANCED ILLUSTRATION TECHNIQUES

By Matt Kloskowski

1-59059-428-2 $39.99 [US]

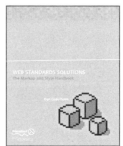

WEB STANDARDS SOLUTIONS
The Markup and Style Handbook

1-59059-381-2 $29.99 [US]

PODCAST
SOLUTIONS
The Complete Guide to Podcasting

by MICHAEL W. GEOGHEGAN
and DAN KLASS

1-59059-554-8 $xx.99 [US]